NIGEL MANSELL

MY AUTOBIOGRAPHY

NIGEL
MANSELL
MY AUTOBIOGRAPHY

NIGEL MANSELL OBE
with JAMES ALLEN

CollinsWillow
An Imprint of HarperCollins*Publishers*

First published in 1995
by CollinsWillow
an imprint of HarperCollins*Publishers*
London

© Nigel Mansell 1995

A CIP catalogue record for this book is
available from the British Library

ISBN 0 00 218497 4

Origination by Saxon
Printed in Great Britain by The Bath Press

*To Rosanne, Chloe, Leo and Greg
for giving me the love, understanding and support
which is so necessary to achieve so much.
Without you, none of this would have been possible.*

CONTENTS

This is a story about beating the odds through sheer determination and self-belief. It is a story about starting with nothing, taking risks and defeating the best racing drivers in the world to rewrite the record books of this most dangerous and glamorous sport.

It is about overcoming the dejection of being injured, having no money and no immediate prospects for the future. And it is about the sheer exhilaration of standing on top of the world and knowing that whatever happens next, no-one can take away from you what you have just achieved.

Nigel Mansell
Woodbury Park, Devon

NIGEL'S THANKS

To the late, great Colin Chapman and his wife Hazel for giving me the first opportunity, and to Enzo Ferrari for giving me the most historic drive in motor racing and two years of wonderful memories. To Ginny and Frank Williams and to Patrick Head for the twenty-eight Grand Prix wins and the World Championship in 1992; for six years and four races it was an awful lot of fun. To Paul Newman and Carl Haas for the 1993 Indycar World Series; and to Honda, Renault and Ford for giving me the power to win...

Without all these people and without the manufacturers and associated sponsors, none of the racing achievements in this book would have been possible. Rosanne and I and our family would like to thank you all for your support. A very big thank you.

PREFACE

Nigel Mansell's life is a wonderful example of the triumph of the human spirit over adversity. He has overcome enormous hurdles throughout his career thanks to an indomitable will, total self-belief and a burning desire to succeed.

All top Grand Prix drivers are heroes, you just have to stand by the side of the track during a race weekend to see that. But Nigel stands out from the crowd for his commitment, his determination and his natural showmanship. His force of will is apparent in everything he does. I once played against him in a soccer match for journalists, photographers and drivers on the eve of the Spanish Grand Prix in 1991, a week after the pit stop fiasco in Portugal, where Nigel's hopes of beating the great Ayrton Senna to the World Championship had followed his errant rear wheel down the pit lane.

Most of the players were there for fun, either a bit long in the tooth or too fond of their beer to be fully competitive, but Nigel played as if his life depended on it, crashing into every tackle and chasing every ball. His day ended in a twisted ankle, which swelled up like a grapefruit. He won the race that weekend of course. His injury was not play-acting, but a perfect illustration of how accident-prone the man is.

The chronicling of Nigel Mansell's career has always been uneven. A mismatch of personalities between him and many of my colleagues in the world of journalism has led him in for some heavy criticism, some of it justified, some of it no more than blind insults. I have always been sceptical about the criticism that Nigel has come in for and fascinated to know what really makes him tick. It struck me that, although a huge public feels it can identify with him, there are very few people in the sport who actually understand what he is all about.

Nigel and I spent over 16 months devising, developing and refining this book in order to make it the definitive text on his life and racing career. In these pages Nigel explains for the first time what lies behind his philosophy of life and his psychological approach to the sport he loves. A great deal of archive research was undertaken and over 30 hours of interviews carried out with people close to Nigel. Time after time fascinating revelations from them prompted equally fascinating reflections from Nigel. We have included some of the more revealing comments, where appropriate, as notes at the end of each chapter.

Sifting through all the evidence, I believe that the starting point for understanding Nigel Mansell lies in two comments made by Williams' director Patrick Head and Formula 1 promoter Bernie Ecclestone, when interviewed for this book. Bernie, who knows and understands Nigel better than most in the Formula 1 pit lane, said that he is 'a very simple, complex person' while Patrick described Nigel as 'not a driver who takes well to not-winning'. The veracity of these two statements is there for all to see in Nigel's own words in this book.

He is a great champion who has not been fully appreciated in his own time and perhaps it will only be in history, provided it is objectively written, that the full achievement of Nigel Mansell will come to be recognised.

I am greatly indebted to Nigel's many friends and colleagues who gave me information and insights and who pointed me towards the right areas to probe.

I would like to thank Murray Walker, Bernie Ecclestone, Gerald Donaldson, David Price, John Thornburn, Chris Hampshire, Sue Membery, Grant Bovey, Sally Blower, Anthony Marsh, Creighton Brown, Patrick Mackie, Mike Blanchet, Nigel Stroud, Frank Williams, Patrick Head, David Brown, Cesare Fiorio, Carl Haas, Paul Newman, Peter Gibbons, Bill Yeager, Derek Daly, Gerhard Berger, Keke Rosberg and Niki Lauda.

Special thanks to Peter Collins, Peter Windsor and Jim McGee for devoting a lot of time and help with my research, and to Rosanne Mansell for the stories, help with the editing and copious cups of tea. I am also greatly indebted to my father, Bill, and Sheridan Thynne for laboriously studying the draft manuscripts and making helpful suggestions.

Thanks also to the folks at CollinsWillow: Michael, Rachel and Monica and especially to Tom Whiting for an excellent piece of editing; Alberta Testanero at Soho Reprographic in New York; Bruce

Jones at *Autosport* magazine for use of the archive; Andrew Benson for archive material and Rosalind Richards and the Springhead Trust; Ann Bradshaw, Paul Kelly and Andrew Marriott for their support; Pip for keeping me sane; and to my parents Bill and Mary and my sister Sue.

Most of all, I would like to thank Nigel for giving me the opportunity to write this book with him and for opening the door and allowing me in.

James Allen
Holland Park, London

WHY RACE?

My interest in speed came from my mother. She loved to drive fast. In the days before speed limits were introduced on British roads, she would frequently drive us at well over one hundred miles an hour without batting an eyelid. She was a very skilful driver, not at all reckless, although I do recall one time, when I was quite young, she lost control of her car on some snow. She was going too fast and caught a rut, which sent the car spinning down the middle of the road. Although it was a potentially dangerous situation I was not at all scared. I took in what was happening to the car, felt the way it lost grip on the slippery surface and watched my mother fighting the wheel to try to regain control. I was always very close to my mother and I loved riding with her in the car. I was hooked by her passion for speed.

Racing has been my life for almost as long as I can remember. I told myself at a young age that I was going to be a professional racing driver and win the World Championship and nothing ever made me deviate from that belief. There must have been millions of people over the years who thought that they would be Grand Prix drivers and win the World Championship, fewer who even made it into Formula 1 and made people believe that they might do it and fewer still who actually pulled it off.

A lot of things went wrong in the early stages of my career. I quit my job, sold my house and lived off my wife Rosanne's wages in order to devote myself to racing; but this is a cruel sport with a voracious appetite for money and in 1978, possibly the most disastrous year of my life, Rosanne and I were left destitute, having blown five years worth of savings on a handful of Formula 3 races.

Not having any backing, I often had to make do with old, uncompetitive machinery. I had some massive accidents and was even given the last rites once by a priest whom I told, not unreasonably, to sod off. But we never gave in.

Along the way Rosanne and I were helped by a few people who believed in us and tripped up by many more who didn't. But I came through to win 31 Grands Prix, the Formula 1 World Championship and the PPG IndyCar World Series and scooped up a few records which might not be beaten for many years. For one magical week in September 1993, after I won the IndyCar series, I held both the Formula 1 and IndyCar titles at the same time.

Looking back now, it amazes me how we won through. I didn't have a great deal going for me, beyond the love and support of my wife and the certainty that I had the natural ability necessary to win and the determination not to lose sight of my goal. I did many crazy things that I wouldn't dream of doing now, because I felt so strongly that I was going to be the World Champion.

I have no doubt that without Rosanne I would not be where I am today. She has given me strength when I've been down, love when I've been desolate and she has shared in all of my successes. She has also given me three lovely children. None of this would have been possible without her.

Over the years there have been many critics. Hopefully they have been silenced. Even if they haven't found it in their hearts to admit that they were wrong when they said I would never make it, perhaps now they know it deep down.

I have always been competitive. I think that it is something you are born with. At around the age of seven I realised that I could take people on, whether it was at cards, Monopoly or competitive sports and win. At the time, it wasn't that I wanted to excel, I just wanted myself, or whatever team I was on, to win. I have always risen to a challenge, whether it be to win a bet with a golfing partner or to come through from behind to win a race. I thrive on the excitement of accepting a challenge; understanding exactly what is expected of me, focusing my mind on my objective, and then just going for it. I have won many Grands Prix like this and quite a few golf bets too.

As a child at school I played all the usual sports, like cricket, soccer and athletics and I always enjoyed competing against teams from other schools. But then another, more thrilling, pursuit began to clamour for my attention.

My introduction to motor sport came from my father. He was involved in the local kart racing scene and when he took me along for the first time at the age of nine, a whole new world of possibilities opened up. It was fast and exhilarating, it required bravery tempered by intelligence, aggression harnessed by strategy. Where before I had enjoyed the speeds my mother took me to as a passenger, now I could be in control. It was just me and the kart against the competition.

To a child, the karts looked like real racing machines. The noise and the smell made a heady cocktail and when you pushed down the accelerator, the vibrations of the engine through the plastic seat made your back tingle and your teeth chatter. It was magical. It became my world. I wanted to know everything about the machines, how they worked and more important how to make them go faster. I wanted to test their limits, to see how far I could push them through a corner before they would slide. I wanted to find new techniques for balancing the brakes and the throttle to gain more speed into corners. I wanted to drive every day, to take on other children in their machines and fight my way past them. I wanted to win.

At first I drove on a dirt track around a local allotment, then I went onto proper kart tracks. The racing bug bit deep. I won hundreds of races and many championships, and as I got more and more embroiled in the international karting scene in the late sixties and early seventies I realised that this sport would be my life. Where before I had imagined choosing a career as a fireman or astronaut, as every young boy did in those days, or becoming an engineer like my father, now I had an almost crystal clear vision of what lay ahead. My competitiveness, determination and aggression had found a focus.

I also used to love going to watch motor races. The first Grand Prix I went to was in 1962 at Aintree when Jim Clark won for Lotus by a staggering 49 seconds ahead of John Surtees in a Lola. I saw Clark race several times before his tragic death in 1968 and I used to particularly enjoy his finesse at the wheel of the Lotus Cortina Saloon cars. He had a beautifully smooth style and was certainly the fastest driver of his time. I can also remember rooting for Jackie Stewart when he was flying the flag for Britain. We went to Silverstone for the 1973 British GP, when the race had to be stopped after one lap because of a pile up on the start line. I'll never forget watching Jackie in his Tyrrell as he went down the pit straight in the lead and then straight on at Copse Corner. I thought: 'That's not very good' but it turned out that his throttle had stuck open.

Throughout the sixties and seventies as I tried to hoist myself up the greasy pole and move into their world, I followed the fortunes of the

Grand Prix drivers. My favourites were James Hunt and Jody Scheckter, while I particularly liked watching Patrick Depailler and Ronnie Peterson, who were both very gutsy, aggressive drivers with a lot of style.

I never saw him race but I had a lot of respect for the legendary fifties star Juan-Manuel Fangio. To win the World Championship five times is a remarkable achievement. I have read about him and met him several times and I only wish I could have seen him race. I'm told it was a stirring sight.

As I turned from child to adolescent and into adulthood I absorbed myself totally in motor racing, becoming totally wrapped up both in my own karting career and in the wider field of the sport. I am very much aware of the history of Grand Prix racing and I think that nowadays it is a lot more competitive than it was in the days of Fangio or Clark, although I'm sure that the people competing in those days would dismiss that idea.

People like to compare drivers from different eras and discuss who was the greatest of all time, but the cars were so different that it makes it impossible to say who was the best; you just have to respect the records that each driver set and the history that they made. What I think you can say is that anyone who is capable of winning a World Championship in one sport could probably have done it in another discipline if they had put their minds to it, because they all have something special in them which gives them the will to win.

I had that will to win and I knew all along that, given half a chance, I could make it to the top. Against the wishes of my father, I switched from karts to single-seater racing cars in 1976 and thus began the almost impossible seventeen year journey which took me to the Formula 1 World Championship in 1992 and the IndyCar World Series in 1993. Along the way I suffered more knocks than a boxer, more rejections than an encyclopedia salesman.

In our sport it is often said that truth is stranger than fiction. The most unbelievable things can happen in motor racing, especially Formula 1, and in my case they frequently did. I can laugh now at my childhood vision of a racing driver's life, it seems hopelessly naive in comparison to the reality.

We began writing my autobiography at possibly the worst time I can remember for trying to explain why I am a racing driver. My rival in many thrilling Grands Prix and a driver whose ability I respected enormously, Ayrton Senna, had just been killed in the 1994 San

Marino Grand Prix. It was a crushing blow. The last driver to have perished in a Grand Prix car was my old team-mate Elio de Angelis in 1986, another death which hit me hard. I had seen many drivers get killed during my career, but for some of the younger ones it came as quite a shock to realise how close to death they could come on the track.

It had been twelve years since anyone had died during an actual Grand Prix. There have been huge advances made in safety since those days which certainly helped me to survive some horrific accidents, but when Senna and Roland Ratzenberger were both killed in the same weekend the whole sport was left reeling. There had been many terrible accidents in the preceding twelve years, but the drivers had got away mostly unharmed. Racing had been lucky many times, now its luck had run out.

Every time I thought about it, shivers ran down my spine. It was difficult to comprehend that Ayrton was dead; that he would never be seen again in a racing car. Ayrton was always so committed. Like me, he explored the limits and we had some thrilling no-holds barred battles where both of us drove at ten tenths the whole way. A mistake by either driver in any of those situations would have given the race to the other. It was pure competition.

He won half of his Grands Prix victories by beating me into second place and I won half of mine by beating him. We are in the *Guinness Book of Records* for sharing the closest finish in Grand Prix racing, at the 1986 Spanish Grand Prix, where he just pipped me by 0.014s as we crossed the finish line; a distance of just 93 centimetres after nearly 200 miles of racing. Some of the battles we had are part of the folklore of racing.

At Hungary in 1989, for example, I seized the opportunity, as we approached a back marker, to slingshot past him and grab a memorable victory. But perhaps the most enduring image of our rivalry was the duel down the long pit straight in the 1991 Spanish Grand Prix. His McLaren-Honda against my Williams-Renault; both of us flat-out on a wet track at over 180mph, with only the width of a cigarette-paper separating us, both totally committed to winning, neither prepared to give an inch. Like me, Ayrton wanted to win and was not a driver who took well to coming second.

Naturally everybody wanted to know what I thought about Ayrton's death and whether it would make me retire. I had achieved a great deal, I didn't need the money, I was a forty-year-old married man with three children, why continue to take the risk? The press had a field day, some writing that I was considering retirement, others saying that I was negotiating a return to Formula 1 for some unheard-of sum of money. I have never had such a hard time justifying what I do for a living as I did in the weeks following Ayrton's death. Every day I even questioned myself why I was doing it.

It didn't help that this period coincided with preparations for my second Indianapolis 500; a race which I remembered painfully from the year before, when I nearly won despite a severe back injury caused by hitting a wall at 180mph in Phoenix the previous month.

Every journalist and television reporter I spoke to during this period wanted me to articulate my fears about racing and my thoughts on Ayrton's death. They were just doing their job, of course, and it was my responsibility as a professional sportsman to talk to them, but it became thoroughly demotivating. If it were not for the fact that I am totally single-minded when it comes to racing, the barrage of questions about death could so easily have taken the edge off my competitive desire.

My passion for racing, undiminished by over thirty years of experience, was the only thing that made me put my helmet on, get into my car and drive flat out.

I am a great believer in fate, something else I inherited from my mother, and this has helped me to come to terms with some of the most difficult times in my life. If things had worked out differently and I had stayed at Williams for another couple of seasons after I won the 1992 World Championship, I would have had a great chance to win again in 1993...but then the tragedy that befell Ayrton at Imola could have happened to me.

There are three or four drivers in the world who could have been in that particular car that day, but it wasn't Prost, it wasn't Damon Hill and it wasn't me. It was Ayrton. Probably through no fault of his own, one of the greatest racing drivers of all time is dead and it could quite easily have been me. So when people ask me whether I have any regrets I tell them, 'You cannot control destiny and in our business there are occasional stark reminders of that.' As a racing driver you must believe in fate. You wouldn't get back into another car if you didn't.

Over the years I have hurt myself quite badly in racing cars and this will have prompted many a sane person to wonder why I race. Naturally pain is the farthest thing from your mind when you are in a racing car. You have to blank it out completely and focus on the job in hand. This is a quality only the very top racing drivers have. You must be able to forget an injury. Your mind must push your body beyond the pain barrier. I have often found that adrenalin is the best painkiller of all. In a hard race, even if you aren't carrying an injury, your mind pushes your body beyond the point of physical exhaustion to achieve the desired result, which is winning.

When the race is over your brain realises that your body is exhausted and can't move and then you are reminded of the pain. I have been so drained after some races that I have been unable to get out of the car. But my ability to blank out pain has been invaluable throughout my career; indeed I doubt whether I would ever have made it had I not had that ability. I won my first single-seater championship in my first full year despite suffering a broken neck mid-season. I got my big break into Formula 1 in 1979 with a test for Lotus on one of the world's fastest Grand Prix circuits, Paul Ricard in France, and managed to get the job despite having a broken back at the time.

I even won the 1992 World Championship with a broken foot, which I sustained in the last race of 1991. An operation over that winter would have meant it being in plaster for three months. However, I was determined to get into perfect physical shape and to put in a lot of testing miles in the car to be ready for the following season. So I delayed the operation. I couldn't tell anyone because if the governing body found out they might have stopped me from racing.

The orthopaedic surgeons thought I was crazy. The foot was badly deformed and after every race that year I could barely walk. Some journalists chose to interpret my limp as play-acting which, in retrospect, is pretty laughable. But then what do they know? None of them have ever driven a modern Grand Prix car flat out for two hours.

If they had they would know that the cockpit is a very hostile environment. The body receives a terrible pummelling during the course of a race from the thousands of shocks which travel up through the steering wheel, the footrest and the seat as you fly along the ground at 200mph. Through the corners the g-forces try to snap your head off. When you brake your insides are thrown forwards with violence, your body gripped by a six-point harness, which pins you into your seat. When you accelerate your head is thrown back violently against the carbon fibre wall at the back of the cockpit, which is the only thing separating you from a 200 litre bag of fuel. On top of that, the cockpit is hotter than a sauna and you are wearing thick fireproof overalls and underwear. The only thing which is in any way designed for comfort is the seat, which is moulded to the driver's body.

If you have a good car and everything is right, you become at one with the car and it allows you to express yourself. It responds to your commands, goes where you point it and allows you to explore the limits with confidence. You can get into a straight fight with another driver, both pushing your machines to the limits, both determined to win. On days like that, driving a Formula 1 car is magical, another world. The pure essence of competition.

Other days you have to fight the car all the way. You might realise early in a race that your car is not handling properly but you have to try to drive around the problem. The car might catch you out or do something you don't expect, and this destroys your confidence in it. Everything becomes a struggle, but you fight to stay in the race with your competitors. You must do everything you can to remain competitive. Driving a Grand Prix car hard is always exhausting, but you must not let up or give in to pain until you reach the end. As Ayrton once said, 'All top Grand Prix drivers are fast, but only a very few of us are always fast.'

I often wonder what life would have been like had I chosen a less dangerous sport. I play golf to quite a high amateur standard and I'm pretty sure that if I had poured the same dedication and focus into it thirty years ago that I poured into racing, I could have made my living from it. Whether I could have reached the same level and got the same rewards, I'm not sure and I will never know. But I think in many ways if I had my time again I would like to find out.

It may sound improbable, but I have had days on the golf course where I have scored back-to-back eagles, or had a round of 65 including half a dozen birdies, and these have been some of the biggest thrills I've ever experienced. I love the idea that it's just you and a set of clubs against the golf course and the elements. It's a true test and if you get it right the sense of gratification is quite overwhelming. And if, by chance, it all goes wrong and you slice your ball into the trees, you don't hurt yourself. You just swallow your pride, grab a club and march in after it.

Having said that, I'm glad that motor racing has been my life. It has satisfied my desire to compete and, above all, to win. It has tested my limits and my resolve many times. It has bankrupted me, hospitalised me and some of the disappointments it has inflicted on me have almost broken my heart. It has also robbed me of some good friends.

But all of that is far outweighed by what it has given me. I have had two lifetimes worth of incredible experiences and more memories than if I were a hundred years old. I set out on this long and treacherous journey with nothing, except the belief that I had the talent to beat the best racing drivers in the world.

After a lot of hard work I was able to prove it.

PART ONE

THE SECRET OF SUCCESS

'I am interested only in success and winning races and if my brain and body did not allow me to be completely committed, I would know that I was wasting my time. The moment I feel that, I will retire on the spot.'

1

MY PHILOSOPHY
OF RACING

There are very few people who have any idea what it takes to be successful in this business.

Much of my life has been devoted to the pursuit of the Formula 1 World Championship. I was runner-up three times before I finished the job off in 1992. Yet if circumstances had been different and politics hadn't intervened, I might also have won a further two World Championships, in 1988 with Williams and in 1990 with Ferrari.

In both cases the essentials were there. The hard work developing the car had been done, but politics dictated that the pendulum should swing away from me. In 1988 Honda quit Williams and dominated the championship with McLaren, while in 1990 Alain Prost joined Ferrari, where we had developed a winning car, and proceeded to work behind the scenes to shift all the team's support, which I had worked for in 1989, to himself.

Although I consider myself strong in most sporting areas of motor racing, I am a poor politician and there is no doubt that this has accounted for me not winning more races and more championships.

Moreover, these experiences provide an object lesson in just how difficult it is to win a lot of Grands Prix and a World Championship; there is far more to it than simply beating people on the race-track. They also serve as a reminder that nothing in motor racing is ever certain. You might have all the right ingredients in place, the full support of the team, an excellent car, and yet some minor component can let you down or some freak accident, like a wheel nut coming off, can rob you of the prize after you've done most of the hard work.

There are no shortcuts to winning the World Championship, but in my fifteen years as a Grand Prix driver I have learned a lot about what it takes to win consistently.

My philosophy of driving a racing car is part and parcel of my philosophy of life. Achievement, success and getting the job done in every area of life, not just in the cockpit, are fundamental to my way of thinking. Everything has to be right. Whether it's getting to the golf club on time or having the right pasta to eat before a race, the demand for perfection everywhere is critical.

MOTIVATION IS THE KEY

Winning at the highest level of motor sport is not like winning in athletics or tennis or golf. In those sports you have just yourself to motivate. In motor sport, you require a huge team and huge resources and it is incredibly difficult to get it all to gel at the same time, to hit the sweet spot. Everything has to come together in unison.

When people think of Nigel Mansell the World Champion, they think that all my winning is done behind the steering wheel. Although important, the actual driving aspect is the final link in the chain. A lot of what it takes to be a champion takes place out of the car, unseen by the public. Winning World Championships as opposed to winning the odd Grand Prix is about always demanding more from your team and never being satisfied. This was a very important aspect of the 1992 World Championship and it is perhaps an area that the public understand least.

At Paul Ricard in September 1990 I tested the fairly unloved Williams-Renault FW13B. I changed everything on the car and got it going quicker than either Riccardo Patrese or Thierry Boutsen had managed that year, but it was clear to me that although Renault and the fuel company Elf had been doing a reasonable job, they had not been pushed hard enough to deliver the best. I immediately began demanding more from them, especially Elf. Having been at Ferrari for the past two years, I understood the progress which their fuel company Agip had made. Agip was producing a special fuel which gave Ferrari a significant horsepower advantage. I am a plain speaking man and I told them straight. The demands I made on them didn't endear me to them initially; in fact I pushed so hard that I was told at one point to back off. But I knew that if Williams-Renault and I were going to win the World Championship, we had to begin immediately raising the standards in key areas like fuel.

As I said, it didn't endear me to them to start with. No-one likes to be told that they can do a lot better, even less that they are well behind their rivals. Perhaps they thought that I was complaining for the sake of it, or 'whingeing'. I think whingeing is a rather naive term to use for trying to raise everybody up to World Championship level!

Eventually they came around to my way of thinking. In the case of Elf, it took them three or four months to realise that I meant business and another three to deliver the fuel that I wanted, but the performance benefits that began to emerge in the late spring of 1991 were the result of the pressure that I had put on both Renault and Elf in late 1990.

Ayrton Senna opened up a points cushion in the World Championship by winning the first four races of 1991 in the McLaren-Honda, but after that we were able to compete on more equal terms and as the year wore on and the developments came through onto the cars, the wins started to come thick and fast. From then on everybody kept the momentum going, always striving to do a better job than they thought was possible and the result was the total domination of the 1992 Championship. It took a year and a half to get the team into championship winning mode but together we did it.

Motivation is a vital area of a driver's skill. Towards the end of 1990 I visited the Williams factory in Didcot to meet the staff. Since I had left at the end of the 1988 season, the team had grown and new staff had been taken on. Consequently there were quite a few people there who didn't know me and who did not know how I work. I asked for everybody to come to the Williams museum where I did a presentation on what I thought it would take to win the World Championship. I needed them all to know that it isn't just a driver and a team owner who win World Championships, but the 200 or so people back at base, some of whom only give up the odd Saturday or Sunday to come in to work and do what is required to win, but who are all very important.

Similarly, in February 1992, around a month before the start of the season, I went to Paris with the then Williams commercial director, Sheridan Thynne to visit the Renault factory at Viry Chatillon. We went around the whole place, not just the workshops where they prepare the engines, but every office and every drawing office in the building. We shook hands with every single person from the managing director down to the secretaries and the cleaners and signed posters for each of them.

It was a good visit from a motivational point of view. It got everybody focused on what we were about to do and it helped all the

Renault people to understand me a bit better and to feel a part of the success. We were taken around and introduced to everybody by my engineer, Denis Chevrier. I subsequently found out that he had been on a skiing holiday that week and wasn't due back until the weekend. But so committed was he to the cause of winning the World title, that he had cut short his holiday to be there. That is the stuff of which championships are made.

We also visited Elf's headquarters and met with all of their people. I believe that this is a key part of building a successful team. You must push everybody involved with the team in every area and tell them that, although they are doing a good job, they can do better. A large part of it is demanding the best, better than people think they can achieve. From suppliers of components through to secretaries in the factory, everyone must be made to feel they can improve and to feel a part of the success when it comes. When I step from the car after winning a race or getting pole position, I shake hands with all my mechanics and congratulate them on the job that we have all done together.

Over the years, through sheer determination to succeed, I have learned all of the things that are required to win. I try to raise everybody's standards to a level that they don't always know they can achieve. I demand the highest standards from everyone around me and if everything is working right, then I just have to keep up my end of the deal on the track. If it's not going right and everybody is searching for answers it puts more pressure on the driver and makes it more difficult to get good race results.

I have also learned that you cannot please everybody and that no matter what you do or say and no matter how you carry yourself when you are in the spotlight, people are going to criticise you. Sadly that is a given element of my life and I have come in for a lot of criticism, some of it justified, most of it, I believe, not.

If pushing everybody to produce commitment at the highest level in order to win really is whingeing, then I'm a whinger – but I have the satisfaction of knowing that it leads directly to success.

There is a deplorable and negative characteristic of the British, which is to try to undermine success and to glorify the gallant loser. It is often called the 'tall poppy syndrome'. The media have a simplistic perception of a lot of stars; they like to stick a label on someone and work from there. Once the label is stuck on it is difficult to shake off. People are actually a lot more complicated than that and in most cases there is a great deal going on behind the scenes, which would explain a lot if only it were more widely known.

In 1992 I was criticised for implying that the victories we were accumulating were entirely due to me and not to the team and our fabulous car, FW14B. I always paid tribute to the team in post race press conferences, it's just that the media chose not to use those quotes in their articles. I did a long interview with the BBC at the end of the year, where I spent quite some time going into detail about how the team had done a great job, but they cut that part out when they aired the programme.

The way I work is that I am the captain of the ship and I work for the common good within a team. I don't like anyone telling me how to drive a racing car or what to do out on the track – that's my business and my record speaks for itself. Outside the car I listen to all of the technical advice and make use of all the expertise available. I am a team player and I know that unless some outside factor comes in to upset the balance, what's best for me is what's best for the team.

When you hire Nigel Mansell as your driver, the actual time spent in the car and what I can do with the car is far from all that you are buying. The ability to get the best out of the the car is well known, but also crucial is the ability to get the car into a shape to be used like that.

I need to be surrounded in a team by people who believe in me and who know that if I am given the right equipment, I'll get the results.

When I aligned myself to Williams in 1991/92, everybody worked my way and we delivered the goods: nine wins, fourteen pole positions and the title wrapped up in record time by August. If we hadn't delivered the goods then I could sympathise with the team's frustration and difficulty in continuing the relationship. But to change tack just because of pressure from the team's French partners to bring aboard one of their fellow countrymen, Alain Prost frustrated me enormously, although I could understand the reason behind it.

There is an old Groucho Marx joke which goes: 'I wouldn't want to be a member of a club which would have someone like me as a member.' I am the exact opposite of this. I only want to be in a team that wants me there and wants to work the best way both for the team and for me. If I feel that I do not have the team's full support, then I am quite prepared to leave.

I don't want to be in a situation where everyone is not pulling together.

BE FAST AND CONSISTENT

Patrick Head, Williams' technical director, has said that one of my major strengths as a racing driver is that I don't have on days and off days. I am consistently fast, which is a big help to a team when it comes to developing a car. They know that the speed at which I drive a car on any given day is the fastest that car will go, so they always have something consistent to measure against.

Of course, in reality, every human being has on days and off days, but if you are a real professional it shouldn't show in the car, because you are being paid to drive the car and to perform. Also your professional integrity should not allow you to take it easy on yourself when you feel like it. A champion needs to have that extra will and determination to get the job done so that, although you might not feel on top form out of the car, you perform to the highest levels in it. That takes a lot of energy but it is vital if you are going to be successful.

Sometimes you have to face the fact that even your best efforts are not going to yield the results. In my second year of Indycars in 1994, it just wasn't possible to do what we had done the year before and win races consistently with the car we had. I gave it a massive effort in bursts during qualifying and sometimes was able to get on pole or the front row, but the Penskes were so superior over a race distance that there was nothing I could do to beat them, even if I drove every lap of the race as if it were a qualifying lap. When it's not possible you can't make it happen. That's not to say that I gave up or resigned myself to making the numbers up. I was just being realistic.

I am often asked how I feel I have improved as a driver over the years. Obviously you cultivate your skills and talents in all areas, but if I had to be specific I would say that I have improved as a human being and that has matured my racing technique. I'm a little bit more patient now and I'm not as aggressive as I used to be, although there is still a lot of aggression there. I have much more knowledge of how to get the job done and I don't pressure myself into doing a certain lap time, which I used to do all the time.

I am a better thinker in a racing car nowadays, I don't feel that I have to lead every lap of a race. As long as I'm the one who crosses the line first that's the important thing.

I have also developed the courage to come into the pits when the car isn't working and to tell the crew that it's terrible, rather than feel that I have to tread on eggshells so as not to hurt their feelings. In the early days, when I complained about a car everybody would say, 'Oh, he's whingeing again, he's no good.' Now I have the self belief and I know what is right and what is wrong and stick to it. I don't just steam in and criticise, I make suggestions and pressurise people into accepting that something isn't good enough and needs to be changed. In other words I have become a little wiser about how to operate and do things.

MY UNUSUAL DRIVING STYLE

My driving style has changed little over the years that I have been racing. It is quite a distinctive style, because I tend to take a different line around corners from other drivers. The classic cornering technique, as taught by racing schools, is to brake and downshift smoothly while still travelling in a straight line and then to turn into the apex of the corner and apply the power. Thus you are slow into the corner and fast out of it.

I never consciously set out to ignore those rules, I just devised my own way of driving and stuck to it because I found it faster. It is a lot more physical and tiring than the classic style, but it's faster and that's what counts.

My style is to brake hard and late and to turn in very early to the apex of the corner, carrying a lot of speed with me. I then slow the car down again in the corner and drive out of it. Because I go for the early apex, I probably use less road than many other drivers. In fact if you put a dripping paint pot on the back of my car and on the back of another driver's car around a lap of a circuit like Monaco, you would probably find that my lap is 20 or 30 metres shorter than theirs!

To drive like this I need a car which has a very responsive front end and turns in immediately and doesn't slide at the front. I cannot drive on the limit in a car which understeers, for example. My cars tend to handle nervously because I need them to roll and be supple; a car which does this at high speed is an uncomfortable car to drive and is very demanding, but invariably it is faster. Because it's 'nervous' it will react quickly to the steering and will turn quicker into a corner. The back end feels like it wants to come around on you, but that's something you learn to live with. Although it's nervous it's got to be balanced properly, if it isn't then there's nothing you can do with it. A stable stiff car is reassuring to drive and won't do anything nasty to you, but it's not fast. If you want the ultimate then you've got to have something which is close to the limit. This makes demands on you physically, of course. It's much more tiring to drive a car this way and you need to have a particularly strong upper body and biceps in order to pick the car up by the scruff of the neck and hurl it around a corner.

The best car is not just a car which wins for you, but one which gives you the feedback that you need as a driver so you can have total confidence in it. The best car I ever drove was the active suspension Williams-Renault FW14B, in which we won the 1992 World Championship. It was a brilliant car because the only limiting factor was you, the driver. The car could do anything you wanted it to. For example, if you wanted to go into a particular corner faster than you had ever done before, all that was holding you back was the mental barrier of being able to keep your foot down. If you went for it, the car would see you through. I loved that.

SLOWING THINGS DOWN

Any top class racing driver must have the ability to suspend time by the coordination of eyes and brain. In other words, when you're doing 200mph you see everything as a normal person would at 50mph. Your eyes and brain slow everything down to give you more time to act, to make judgments and decisions. In real time you have a split second to make a decision, but to the racing driver it seems a lot longer. If you're really driving well and you feel at one with the car, you can sometimes even slow it down a bit more so it looks like 30mph would to the normal driver. This gives you all the time in the world to do what you have to do: read the dashboard instruments, check your mirrors, even radio your crew in the pits. That's why, when I say after I won the British Grand Prix, for example, that I could see the expressions on the faces of the crowd, it's because everything was slowed and I had time to see such things.

When you first drive a Grand Prix car, everything happens so quickly that you can sometimes frighten yourself. Once you've had some experience of racing at these speeds you can get into pretty much any racing car and go quickly, provided that you're comfortable with the car of course. The more time you spend in the car the more in tune you become with the speeds involved.

Sometimes unexpected things happen incredibly quickly and you just have to rely on instincts to see you through. A good example of this is the incident which occurred when I was with Ferrari at Imola in 1990, when Gerhard Berger in the McLaren pushed me onto the grass at the Villeneuve Curve. That was an incredible moment. It was a split second decision as I travelled backwards at nearly 200mph whether to put it into a spin or whether to try and catch it. I took the first option and managed to bring the nose around the right way and kept on going. Although I cannot say that I saw the direction I was pointing throughout the two full revolutions the car made, I was aware through instincts of exactly where I was going the whole time. The result was a spectacular looking double spin and I kept on going. I probably only lost about 40mph in the spin. Because the adrenalin was pumping so hard after it, I broke the lap record on the next lap.

At times like that you've got to be a bit careful. Your heartbeat gets up to 150-200 beats per minute. You don't think about it, but it is very important that you breathe properly, because you are on the verge of hyperventilating at that pulse level. It is vital that you understand your body and that you manage it as much as you do the car.

DRIVING ON THE LIMIT

Everybody has different limits, that's one of the things which differentiates good amateur drivers from great professional drivers. Most top Grand Prix drivers will go beyond their limits at some time in their career and a few really top ones are able to go beyond their limit, if the occasion demands, for a period of time. Ayrton Senna talked after qualifying at Monaco in 1988 of going into a sort of trance, where he was lapping beyond his limit, treading into unknown territory. He stopped after three laps because he frightened himself. While I would not describe the feeling as being like a trance, I have had a similar experience several times, most notably at Silverstone in 1987, when I caught and passed Nelson Piquet after 29 laps of totally committed driving. This experience of mesmerising speed is described in detail later in the book. More usually that feeling comes when you commit every ounce of your strength and determination on a qualifying lap.

When you go for the big one in qualifying, you give it everything you've got and on certain corners you over-commit. Now this is where the judgment comes in because if you over-commit too much then you won't come out of the corner the other side. You enter the corner at a higher speed than on previous occasions and if you are able to carry that speed through the corner you will exit quicker than before. You can't do it consistently because the car won't allow it and something will inevitably give. Of course you have to feel comfortable with the car. If it's bucking around all over the place and is unstable even at medium speed through a corner then you would be a fool to go in 20mph faster next time round.

Provided that the car is doing more or less what you want it to, you can hustle it around on one or two really quick laps. It then comes down to your own level of commitment and that depends on so many factors. Some drivers become less committed after they have children, others lose the edge after a major accident, others will become more committed when it's time to sign a new contract for next year!

Mental discipline plays a huge part in driving on the limit. A top athlete in any sport must be able to close his mind completely to extraneous thoughts and niggling doubts and concentrate 100%. If you want to be a champion, you need to be able to focus completely on the job in hand to the exclusion of everything else going on around you. Your brain must have a switch in it so that the minute you need to concentrate, your mind is right there and ready to go. I have been able throughout my career to give a consistently high level of commitment and even my harshest critics would admit that there are few more committed or focused drivers than me.

It's a personal thing. You have to be true to yourself and if I thought that I had lost my edge I would stop racing immediately. I am interested only in success and winning races and if my brain and body did not allow me to be completely committed I would know that I was wasting my time. The moment I feel that, I will retire on the spot.

You can only do what your brain and your body will allow you to do. For example, in qualifying for the British Grand Prix in 1992, the telemetry showed that I was taking Copse Corner 25mph faster than my team-mate Riccardo Patrese, using the same Williams-Renault FW14B. In fact over a whole lap I was almost two seconds faster than him. As we sat debriefing after the session, Riccardo looked at the printouts and said that he could see how I was taking Copse at that speed, but that he couldn't bring himself to do it. His brain was telling his body, 'If we go in that fast, we'll never come out the other side.'

Every really hot qualifying lap relies on the brain and body being in harmony and prepared, at certain key points, to push the envelope, to over-extend. That is the only way you are going to beat the Rosbergs, Piquets, Sennas and Schumachers of this world. It goes without saying that once you operate at that level, your self-belief must be absolute.

In all my career I have done maybe 10 perfect laps. One of the ones I savour the most was at Monaco in 1987. To do any kind of perfect lap is special, but when you do it at Monaco that's as good as it gets. When you run the film of the lap through your mind afterwards and you examine every gearchange, every braking point, every turn-in and how you took every corner and at the end of it you say 'I could not have done that faster', that's when you know you have done a perfect lap. You don't need to go out and try to do better. When you get a lap like that you don't even need to look at the stopwatch on your dashboard or read the pit boards. You know it's quick.

When I came back into the pits David Brown, my engineer and a man who would become one of my closest allies in racing, pointed out that the white Goodyear logos had been rubbed off the walls of the rear tyres where I had brushed the barriers! You have to skim the barriers at a couple of points when you're flying at Monaco, it's the only way to be really quick. It sounds frightening, but it's supremely exhilarating. I never feel more alive on any race track than I do on the streets of Monaco. Everything has to be synchronised and you need to have fantastic rhythm as well as aggression and a truckload of commitment to be fast there. I have always enjoyed the challenge, but I think also that the romantic in me responds to the idea of going well at this most celebrated of Grands Prix.

Generally speaking, although qualifying is important, merely lapping quickly, in other words driving fast, is not what turns me on the most. Competition is the most important thing and driving flat out against someone else with victory as the end result is my idea of heaven. Nevertheless, when you get a perfect lap in qualifying it feels absolutely marvellous. When I got out of the car at Monaco and looked at the white smears on the walls of the tyres where the manufacturer's logo had been wiped off, it even impressed me. There are no long straights at Monaco, it's all short chutes, but coming out of the tunnel I was clocked at 196mph, a full 17mph faster than Prost in the McLaren. I was six tenths faster than Senna and 1.7s faster than my team-mate Nelson Piquet and I had done not just one, but *three* laps which were good enough for pole!

From the point of view of a race, it's not a major psychological advantage over your rival to get pole position. Anybody can get pole position if they have an exceptional lap in the right equipment. The key is to prove that you have the ability to do it time and again. It's not one thing that gets you pole position, it's a package of things, but you do have to put together the perfect lap and to show that you can do it more than anyone else. I am very competitive and I approach qualifying and racing at the same level.

Some top drivers believe that the race is the most important thing and that their position on the grid does not matter too much. Double Indycar champion Al Unser Jr is like this, as to some extent was Alain Prost. They would concentrate on getting the set-up of the car absolutely perfect for the race and not over-extend themselves in qualifying. On one level you can see their point and I have done that a couple of times myself, notably at Hungary in 1989. It is the race after all which carries the points, but I have always believed that it is important to be quick and to show that you are strong throughout the weekend. Of course on certain tracks, like Monaco, there is a benefit to being at the front because it is hard to pass in the race.

Sometimes, as happened to me a great deal in the early part of my career, if your car is not up to scratch you are forced to make up the difference yourself. You do not want to be blown off in a bigger way than you have to be. So you delve deep into your reserves of commitment. You have to squeeze the maximum out of your car and out of yourself and whatever that yields is the absolute fastest that it is possible to go with the equipment. You can then go away satisfied in the knowledge that you've done the best job you can possibly do. Hopefully, if you are working your way up the ladder despite struggling with inferior equipment, the people who run the top teams will pay attention to you and maybe give you an opportunity in a good car.

It is also very important to be on the limit when testing a car because if you don't know what a car is going to do when you are on the limit, then you'll be in trouble when you race it. Anyone can drive at nine-tenths all day, but unless you understand what the car will do at ten-tenths and even occasionally eleven-tenths, then you are not being true to yourself, your car or your team.

When you are testing a car and you are not on the limit, you can make a change which might feel better to you, but which does not show on the stopwatch. If you then say, 'No, it feels better like that, it's only slow because I wasn't pushing it,' then you might subsequently find that the car won't work on the limit and in fact you've made it go slower by making the change. If you find that out during a race, you're in big trouble.

Sometimes making a car feel better doesn't make it quicker, and the name of the game in motor racing is to shave as many fractions of seconds off your lap time as possible and then to be able to lap consistently at your optimum speed. It's an uncomfortable truth for some, but the only thing that tells you that is the stopwatch.

Motor racing is in general, I think, the art of balancing risk against the instinct of self-preservation, while keeping everything under control. People can only aspire to great endeavours if they believe in their hearts that they can achieve their goals – and to my mind that's the difference between courage and stupidity.

Courage is calculating risks; when someone sets an objective, realises how dangerous it is, but then does it anyway, fully in control. They have to fight with their feelings and hopefully are honest with themselves when facing up to the dangers inherent in what they are doing. Then there are others who aren't really in control.

STARTING A RACE

The start of a Grand Prix is a very dramatic moment and there is a lot of chaos and confusion going on around you. But the most important thing you have to think about is your own start and making sure that you get away as well as you can. The first couple of corners in a Grand Prix can make a huge difference to the result. If you have pole position and you get a good clean start, you can open out a lead over the field, because they are jockeying for position behind you. Also it goes without saying that if it's wet and the cars are kicking up huge plumes of spray, there is only one place to be!

It's very important at the start to have mental profiles of each of the drivers around you, to know who's fired up that weekend and who's depressed, who's trying to be a hero and who is desperate for a result. If there's someone who has qualified way beyond expectations, then they will probably want to show that their position is justified so they are probably going to be dangerous. You need to know who is brainless, who is a cautious starter, and so on. You have to put all of this into your brain and let your instinct take you through. It's like reading the greens on a golf course, or knowing about the going on a race course. It's the finer points that matter.

Psychologically, the start is vital. In 1992 I had 14 pole positions and at the starts I went off like a rocket. I wasn't holding anything back. I would open out as big a gap as I could as fast as I could. Sometimes I was two or three seconds clear at the end of the first lap.

It was vital to dominate everybody, to intimidate everyone to the point where they knew who was going to win before the race even started. And it worked.

I was on a mission that year. No-one was going to beat me. I had psyched myself up throughout the winter and I was incensed when before the season started Patrick Head said when referring to the Williams drivers, 'We'll see who comes out better in 1992.'

That was an insult. My team-mate Riccardo Patrese was a great driver, but my credentials up to that point were a lot better and I had won three or four times as many races as him. What's more, having spent years as the number two driver, I was finally number one. I was determined to crush everybody. I had to dominate the Williams team and I wanted everybody to know that I was number one. I also wanted Ayrton Senna, the only person whom I perceived as being a threat, to know that I was going to win the World Championship at the earliest possible time. The relentless pressure I applied through qualifying and then at the start helped to cement that idea in people's minds.

Sometimes it can all go wrong at the start, as it did in Canada in 1982 when Didier Pironi stalled on the front row of the grid and Riccardo Paletti didn't see him, hit him and was killed. I was one of the cars who had to dodge Pironi and there was no time to think about it, you just had to act. It's the instinct of self-preservation. We all have this instinct because we don't want to die. You know when you race a car that if you don't do the right things at certain times, you could get killed or badly hurt. The start of a race is one of those times.

STRATEGY AND READING THE RACE

Peter Collins played a major role in helping me reach Formula 1 and he was my team manager for a few years at Lotus and Williams. I always used to laugh at him because he used to like to plan the race in minute detail beforehand and sometimes we would have ten different strategies in front of us. It was complete nonsense because usually something would happen that we hadn't even considered. Before the start we used to study the grid and he would say, 'What happens if he gets a good start and what if he gets a bad one?' But whatever you tried to plan, it all used to change.

Niki Lauda was always a great planner, but what he thought about never occurred either, so he gave up wasting his brain power, relaxed and was ready for anything that came up.

That's one of the strengths of my driving now. I don't think about things too much. I've had so much experience and so many things programmed into my brain that I'm prepared for anything. When something crops up, you don't have time to think about it anyway. If you try to think, you'll be too slow in reacting. A mixture of instinct and experience tells your hands and your feet to position the car so that if something does happen, you're in good shape. It takes years of experience to develop that ability. It just doesn't occur by chance.

Once you are in the race, you can read what's going on pretty well. You can control the race more in Formula 1 than you can in Indycar racing. In Indycar you rely on the team manager and the crew to call fuel strategies and the yellow flags can wreak havoc to your progress. You can win or lose a race because of yellow flags and that's according to the rules. It's a bit frustrating, but they are there for everybody, the fans and the television and the smaller teams. It can work for you and it can work against you. Does it level out? I'm not sure. I think I had a fair bit of luck in 1993, while in 1994 I had some bad breaks, but I'm happy that it worked out for me first time around.

Formula 1 is quite different. You win and lose a race out on the track. It's a pure sprint and it's very rare that a yellow flag or a pace car will intervene to deprive you of a win which you thought you had in the bag. You rely on pit signals and the radio link with the crew, but you can tell a lot from the cockpit about where the opposition is on the track.

OVERTAKING AND RACE CRAFT

The secret with overtaking is that you've got to be in total control of what you are doing before you set about passing other cars. If you are on the ragged edge just to keep your car at racing speed, then you are not going to be effective when trying to make up positions and compete with rivals. Some duels can last a long time and you need to be totally comfortable with your car before you can commit the mental and physical energy required to pass a Senna or a Prost on a race track.

When you come to pass someone, you first have to make sure that they know you're there. Sometimes they do, but will pretend that they don't and will try to block you or even put you off the track. It's up to you to decide when and where to engage them in psychological combat.

You first put the 'sucker move' on them, showing them your nose and setting them up with moves through certain corners to make them think that this is where you are going to attack. You are saying to them, 'This is the move which is going to come off,' when in reality you know that it isn't. You feint to one side and they think that this is your last-ditch attempt to come through, but it isn't. You've got something else in mind.

You save up your best move and don't give them any idea what it is or where it will come. Sometimes you only get one chance and winning a race depends on one proper effort. If it comes off you win, if it doesn't you lose. But to have many attempts and to fail all the time, merely weakens your position. You must show that you intend to come through and in many cases you can psyche your opponent out before the fight begins. Some will say, 'Oh God, it's Mansell, I can't possibly keep him behind me,' because they've had experience of being beaten in the past. This does not work on the real aces however. You've got to do something special to pass them and you'll probably only get one go.

This is one of the strongest areas of my driving and I haven't had too much trouble in my career passing people, with one exception. Ayrton Senna stood out during my career as the toughest opponent. Our careers coincided and between 1985 and 1992 we both wanted to win the same Grands Prix. When we both had competitive equipment we knew that to win we would have to beat the other.

We had some fantastic scraps, although in the early days he was quite dangerous to race against. He was so determined to win that he would sometimes put both you and himself into a very dangerous situation. It was a shame he did this. He was so good he didn't need to do it, but he so badly wanted to win.

Sometimes you over-estimate your opponent and this can have dire consequences. For example you might be lapping a back marker, thinking that he will react a certain way, the way you would react if you were in his shoes. If he reacts in a quite different way he might collide with you and then you've thrown away the race because you attributed a higher level of intelligence to a driver than he actually possesses. It is a far greater weakness, however, to under-estimate an opponent, for obvious reasons.

There is no doubt that at the pinnacle of the sport there are some very forceful competitors.

Mike Blanchet, a former competitor of Nigel's in Formula 3 and now a senior manager at Lola Cars: 'Nigel likes a car with a good turn-in. He likes a more nervous handling car, which would frighten most drivers. Most of them like a neutral car with a little understeer, which feels safer. Because of his reflexes and his physical upper body strength Nigel is able to carry a lot of speed into corners without losing control of the car. A lot of people would spin if they tried to take that much speed into a corner.'

Peter Windsor, a former Grand Prix editor of *Autocar* magazine and Nigel's team manager at Williams in 1991/92: 'Nigel drives a little like Stirling Moss used to. Moss always said, "Anyone can drive from the apex of a corner to the exit, it's how you get into the apex that matters." Nigel got a feel early on for turning in on the brakes, crushing the sidewall of the tyre and thereby getting more out of a tyre. From the outside he makes a car look superb and his technique is very exciting to watch. He gets on the power very early on the exit of the corner. If the track conditions change suddenly or unexpectedly then Nigel is more at risk than other drivers because he's more committed early on and more blind than others.'

Derek Daly, driver, turned TV commentator: 'Mansell's style is an aggressive style more than an efficient one, but it's very fast. He makes an early turn-in; he gets his business sorted out in the apex and gets out of the corner as soon as possible. The key to being quick is the time it takes from turning in to reaching the apex and then the momentum you carry through the apex and out the other side. That is an area of the track where a lot of people slow down too much. Mansell doesn't do that. He goes to the apex as soon possible, carrying lots of speed, lots of momentum and gets on his way. It is an unusual style – he often uses different lines through corners, but always the same cornering principle.'

2

THE BEST OF RIVALS

When I first started in Grand Prix racing there were many top names involved, each of which will always strike a particular chord in the hearts of Formula 1 fans around the world: Niki Lauda, Jody Scheckter, Gilles Villeneuve, Didier Pironi, Nelson Piquet, Patrick Tambay, Alan Jones, Carlos Reutemann, Alain Prost, Elio de Angelis, Jacques Laffite, Keke Rosberg, to name but a few. A lot of those drivers were either World Champions at the time or became champions in the next few years. Thirteen of them had won Grands Prix. I was lucky to enter Formula 1 at a time when there were far more significant names around than there are today.

In the late eighties there were only four 'aces' – Ayrton Senna, Alain Prost, Nelson Piquet and myself. Into the nineties and by the end of the 1994 season, Prost had joined Piquet in retirement and Senna had tragically died, so it was down to three: myself and the emerging talents of Damon Hill and Michael Schumacher. The new breed of drivers have not been able to establish themselves yet, either in the record books or the public's perception, and their reputations remain unproven.

The biggest thing for a driver is to gain worldwide recognition and respect and you only get that by doing the job for a number of years and getting the results. You need years of wins and strong placings to establish your name. No disrespect to any Grand Prix driver, but until you have won five and then ten and then fifteen and then twenty Grands Prix, you cannot be considered an ace.

Only three drivers have won more than thirty Grands Prix: Prost, Senna and myself. If you go down the list of prolific Grand Prix winners, many have either retired or died – Jackie Stewart, Niki Lauda, Jim Clark, Stirling Moss, Graham Hill, Juan Manuel Fangio, and so on. One reason for the gulf between the big names and the rest is that in the late eighties, when much more non-specialised media became interested in Formula 1, they could only focus on a limited number of drivers and so instead of looking at seven or eight drivers, they focused only on three and put them under the microscope. Because Prost, Senna and I were winning everything, the non-specialist media totally disregarded some other good up and coming drivers.

When I decided to commit myself to motor sport and to strive to be World Champion, I knew that I was an outsider. I was told at the beginning of my career that with a name like Nigel Mansell I would never make it to Formula 1 or make anything of myself in life. I guess I proved them wrong.

In the early stages of my racing career, as I struggled to scrape together the money to pursue my dream, I became aware of a group of drivers whom I nicknamed 'The Chosen Ones'. These are the people who are expected to make it, to go all the way to the top. The phrase 'future World Champion' is bandied about with reference to these people, some of whom do make it, many of whom don't. What unites them is that they have the backing and support of wealthy sponsors or corporations and their path to the top is marked out for them. Influential people in the industry back them and tip off the magazines and newspapers to 'keep an eye on this boy'. Consequently they get a lot of publicity and this pleases their sponsors, who put in more money. If you've got the money in this sport, you get the best equipment and on it goes. You can understand why these people are 'The Chosen Ones', because in this sport you need a lot of money and support to make it and people are unwilling to back outsiders, like me, who have no money.

But the unavoidable truth of the sport is that it takes talent to win races and championships. You cannot compete at the highest levels without having that talent. When I was coming through the ranks, 'The Chosen Ones' were drivers like Andrea de Cesaris and Chico Serra. They got huge backing and much ink was put on paper about how they would conquer the world. Yet neither of them won a single Grand Prix. Chico Serra was run in Formula 3 by Ron Dennis, now the boss of McLaren, and they used to have their own video cameras out on every corner so they could analyse what the car was doing. And yet Chico came up to me on the grid one day and said, 'Excuse me Nigel, could you tell me how many revs you're using at the start?'

The history of the sport is littered with examples like this and it's still going on today. Maybe there is a young outsider out there who is struggling to get the money together but has the self-belief and the determination never to give up. If there is, I hope he draws strength from this story and I wish him the best of luck. He's going to need it.

Others, like Ayrton Senna, Alain Prost and Michael Schumacher were more successful. None of them spent much time in poor equipment and all of them were well financed along the way. The main thing which united them, however, was their supreme talent. It annoys me when I read that I do not have the natural talent of a Senna or a Prost and that I 'made myself' a great driver. Firstly, you cannot run with, let alone consistently beat guys like that unless you have as much talent and, secondly, I have the satisfaction of knowing that two of the sport's greatest figures, Colin Chapman of Lotus and Enzo Ferrari, both considered me to be one of the most talented drivers they had ever hired. Their opinions speak for themselves.

Part of my problem was that I spent many years in number two driver roles and in terrible cars. It wasn't done deliberately, it was just a set of circumstances. Lotus gave me an opportunity to show a little of my flair as I led races, qualified well, and got on the podium a few times, but when I was given a real opportunity in 1985 at Williams I flourished, winning two races in my first season; and in my second year I won seven more and almost took the championship.

When the opportunity presented itself I grabbed it, but it took a little longer to come to me than it did to some of the better supported drivers.

Over the years I have driven against some of the legendary names of the sport and some of my favourite memories come from knowing and racing against these characters.

Driving as team-mate to Keke Rosberg with Williams in 1985 was a great experience. Whenever Keke did anything he did it at ten or eleven-tenths. He was always driving totally flat-out, and he had unbelievable commitment. I'll never forget his qualifying lap at Silverstone in 1985, when he set the first 160mph lap, the fastest ever lap in a Grand Prix weekend. If Keke wanted to go anywhere then he would do it by the most direct route. He was a real flair driver, instinctive and courageous. He didn't know much about the technicalities of a racing car and didn't spend too long working on the finer points of set-up. If his car was balanced, he would simply drive the wheels off it and that was always terrific to watch.

Before I joined Williams in 1985 Keke said that if Frank took me on he would leave. He had a very negative opinion of me, based on hearsay which at the time was coming from Peter Warr, who had taken over from Colin Chapman at Lotus and who was spreading all sorts of stories about me around the paddock. When Keke and I got together I could tell that he was working under duress, but to his credit his mind was not completely closed and as the months went on he clearly formed his own opinion of me which was much more favourable. From then on our relationship was terrific. He showed me a lot of things and I learned a lot from him about how to carry myself as a professional racing driver. He was fantastic with the sponsors and used to give really engaging and entertaining speeches to the corporate guests in the hospitality suites before a race. I watched him and learned from him.

We only spent one season together in the same team. The South African Grand Prix at Kyalami was the second to last race of that season. I'll never forget it and neither will he. I was on a real high because I had just won my first Grand Prix a few weeks before at Brands Hatch. I grabbed pole position and afterwards he came up to me and said, 'Now I know why you are so fast and why you have pole position here. It is because you are a complete bloody maniac. I watched you run right up alongside the concrete wall for fifty yards. You're mad.' He had a huge grin on his face and we both fell about laughing.

It was a hairy run, but it served its purpose and won me pole position. Keke could see that my confidence level was really up. The car was working well, the team was giving me full support and I had learned the secret formula for winning Grand Prix races. He could see that I was like a starving man who has just worked out how to get into the fridge. Nothing would stop me. The race was close. He and I were both under pressure from Senna and Prost. I won, making it two in a row. Keke has described it as one of the hardest races of his career and I would agree with that.

Gilles Villeneuve was a great driver, but more than that he was a great friend. We got on really well. When I first arrived in Formula 1, he took me under his wing and showed me a lot of things about how the Formula 1 game worked. We shared a lot of confidences. Like me, he was a plain speaking man and he always said what was on his mind. I understood where he was coming from and respected his judgements on people in the paddock. My arrival in Formula 1 coincided with the power struggle between the governing body and the constructors and Gilles encouraged me to go to the drivers meetings and take an interest in what was going on. He helped me a lot.

We had a lot of fun together, both on the track and off. The racing was pretty raw and competitive in those days and it was always cut-throat. The best man and the best car won on the day, but we had some massive scraps and then we would talk and have a laugh about it afterwards.

His road car driving was legendary and there are some great stories about him told by people who travelled with him at enormous speed on road journeys. I also travelled with him in his helicopter and because he was so fearless and such an accomplished person he could carry out the most extraordinary dives and manoeuvres as a pilot.

Gilles was a very special man, who lived his life to the full and who always drove at the limit. Looking back, the best race I had with him was at Zolder in Belgium in 1981. It was my first visit to the circuit and I managed to beat him for third place to claim my first podium in only my sixth Grand Prix start.

The following year we returned to Zolder for a rematch, but we never had the opportunity as Gilles was killed in an accident during qualifying. It was an awful incident in an awful year. Driving past the scene of the crash, I could see that it was serious as bits of his car were strewn all over the track and the surrounding area. I didn't stop because there were already a lot of people there and the emergency crews had arrived in force. I was practically in tears as I drove around the rest of the circuit, repeating over and over again to myself, 'Please, please let him be all right.' It was shattering blow when I found out later that he was dead.

Gilles has been sorely missed in Grand Prix racing ever since that terrible day. He brought a magic to it, a sparkle, which is what endeared him to Ferrari and the passionate Italian fans.

I was very happy when Gilles's son, Jacques landed a drive for Williams having moved over from Indycar, where I raced against him in 1994, straight into one of the two top Formula 1 teams. It's a real piece of history and I'm happy for Jacques. I was slightly amused when I heard he signed because I remembered Patrick Head, Williams technical director saying something about Indycar drivers being fat and slow ... then all of a sudden he's signed one up!

Another driver for whom I have great respect – and I believe the feeling is mutual – is Niki Lauda. He is a total professional, very analytical, with tremendous courage. He was a superb racing driver who won many races through his intelligent handling of the car.

Niki was very good at getting himself positioned within a team and he was one of the few drivers to get the best out of Ferrari. He told me that if I had used my head differently I would have won more championships and he's right. If I had been more political I would probably have won two or three more championships, but that's just not the way I am. I'm not the sort of political manoeuvrer that some of my rivals were. I'm more romantic than that. I like to think that I am what a racing driver should be. I like to win by having a fair race and a fair fight with someone. If there has been some skulduggery in the background which means that a fair fight isn't on the cards then that isn't my scene and I don't think it's worth as much. I've gained more satisfaction from what I have won and the things I have achieved. I do try to look after my interests a bit more these days. But when it comes to politics, I'll never be on the level of Alain Prost.

Alain Prost is the expert political manoeuvrer. He has won 51 Grands Prix, more than any other driver in the history of the sport, and he has four World titles, one less than Juan Manuel Fangio. You have to respect Prost's record, but at least one of his titles was won more by skilful manoeuvring away from the circuit than actually out on the track.

Prost almost always had the best equipment available at the time: he drove for Renault in the early turbo days, then switched to McLaren, who dominated the mid-eighties with their Porsche-engined cars and the late eighties with the support of the Honda engine.

He's a bit of a magpie. He uses his influence to pinch the most competitive drives. At Ferrari in 1990, Prost worked behind the scenes pulling strings and getting the management of Ferrari and its parent company FIAT on his side. At the end of 1989, Ferrari was my team and I was looking forward to a crack at the world title. Prost came along and tried to ease me out. The ironic thing is that Prost himself was fired by the management of Ferrari at the end of 1991.

When we did race on a level playing field he would rarely beat me. That's why he didn't want to compete with me on equal terms. Getting himself into a position where he doesn't have to compete on equal terms is part of his strength. That's part of the game, but it's more romantic and far more satisfying for everyone if you have equal equipment and say 'Let the best man win'. You have to be clever to get the car in shape, but to use political cleverness away from the circuit to get an advantage is not good for the sport.

It was disappointing not to be able to take him on in a fair fight either at Ferrari in 1990 or at Williams when he took my seat at the end of 1992. But it's not the end of the world because I know how good I am. I raced alongside him in 1990 and knew that the only way he could be quicker than me was when the equipment wasn't the same. I'm not interested in political manoeuvring or in working to disadvantage my team-mate. Naturally, I want success for myself and to win, this is positive, but I don't want to do it at the expense of the person with whom I am supposed to be collaborating. I am simply not motivated like that. It's so negative.

In my early Formula 1 days we got on reasonably well and played golf together occasionally, but as soon as I began to beat him on the track and to pose a serious threat to him, he didn't want anything to do with me, which was a shame.

Ayrton Senna was one of the best drivers in Grand Prix history. I was probably the only driver consistently to race wheel to wheel with him and there is no question that he was the hardest competitor in a straight fight; I wouldn't say the fairest, but certainly the hardest. You knew that if you beat Ayrton you had beaten the best.

He was often described as being the benchmark for all Formula 1 drivers. I believe that whoever is quickest on the day is the benchmark and it can move from race to race. Admittedly, because of his qualifying record Ayrton was more often the benchmark than I was. But it tended to move between Lauda, Prost, Piquet, Senna and me.

Ayrton tried many times to intimidate me both on and off the circuit. Once, at Spa in 1987 I told him to his face that if he was going to put me off he had better do it properly. We even had conversations where we started to respect each other's skill and competitiveness and agree not to have each other off. But he would then forget about the conversation or make a slip and have me off or hit me up the back. It must have been premeditated, because he was too good a driver to do it by accident.

It was unnecessary for Ayrton to act in this way, but I always took it that the fact he did it to me meant that I intimidated him. Nevertheless we did respect each other. We weren't bosom pals and we didn't run each other's fan clubs, but when both of us had anything like a decent car he knew that he would have to beat me if he was going to win and I knew that he was the one driver I would have to beat.

Ayrton was a natural racer and was willing to push the limits. Something terrible happened at Imola. There was no question that he was right on the limit when he went off. Perhaps something let him down on the car. He certainly pushed the limits and enjoyed it. We had that in common, we both enjoyed working on the ragged edge. That was where we would set our cars up and where we would drive when the need arose. If you are an honest professional racing driver that is what you have to do.

On my victory lap at Silverstone in 1991, I picked him up after his car had broken down at Stowe. I could see that he was getting a hard time from the crowd and I know what that's like from my own experiences in Brazil. So I thought I would help him get out of a tricky situation. It was amazing the criticism I received after that show of support. One magazine said that I was stupid to do it because I allowed him to see the Williams cockpit and to see what was on the dashboard display. It was so small-minded of them. There are some people who are going to criticise you no matter what you do.

When he won his third World Championship at Suzuka in 1991, I hung around after retiring from the race to congratulate him. Later we had a chat and it was probably the closest we ever got. There was a deep mutual respect between us and that's how I'd like to remember him.

Nelson Piquet was the other big name in Formula 1 during the late eighties. He was my team-mate at Williams in 1986/87, but it was an unhappy relationship. Nelson is a big practical joker with an annoying sense of humour; he also worked at splitting the team's loyalties and getting people to side with him.

When he joined Williams in 1986 he obviously thought that he was going to win everything, but I showed him up over the next two years and took a lot of wins away from him. Williams has the capability of running two cars close together because of the very high standard of their engineering and the way that Frank Williams and Patrick Head run things. You still have a number one and a number two driver in the sense that the team leader has priority on the spare car and so on, but the number two at Williams always has a good chance of winning races, as I did over those two years.

Nelson didn't like this and he tried to get Frank to give team orders, something which Frank refused to do. Nelson claimed that Williams was displaying favouritism towards its British driver, which wasn't true at all. To be fair, Nelson was a hard competitor when he wanted to be. He could be devastating on fast circuits. Although I beat him at Brands Hatch in 1986 and at Silverstone in 1987, he snatched pole position from me at both with some very committed laps. In a straight fight and when he felt like it, he was somewhere between Prost and Senna.

Michael Schumacher is obviously going to be the star of the future, but I know less about him. I remember when he arrived in Formula 1 he made a big impact, not least when he and Ayrton had a set-to during a test at Hockenheim. I always said that he was very talented, very quick and brave and perhaps now he is settling down to become a good, if not yet great driver. Winning his first World Championship has helped his cause, but only time will tell whether he's got what it takes to become a real ace. Unlike some champions he's not had to struggle as he made his way through the ranks. What's more, he has not had the opposition during his career that many of us had. But all credit to him, you've got to take your opportunities when you can and he certainly did that in 1994 with Benetton.

I am delighted for Damon Hill that he has been able to come on as strongly as he has. He's certainly grown in stature and is getting better all the time. When you drive for a top team with the best equipment and you have the opportunity to win consistently, you can improve a lot as a driver. When I did four races with him as his team-mate in 1994, I honestly believed I helped him and that gave me a lot of pleasure. To my mind, he has all the ingredients to win a World Championship, and I really think he's ready to win it. The pressure he is under is immense – only drivers at the front know what the pressure is like – and I think the way he and his wife Georgie have come through it is brilliant.

3

THE PEOPLE'S CHAMPION

Perhaps the biggest satisfaction I have derived from my success has been the relationship that I have developed and maintained with the people who follow motor racing on television and in the grandstands around the world – the fans.

After the Australian Grand Prix in 1986, where I lost the World Championship when my tyre blew out, I received hundreds of letters from all over the world. Many said, 'In our eyes, Nigel, you *are* the champion because you were the best this year. It doesn't matter that you didn't win it.' This was the biggest accolade I could have received, because it came from the people who really count. I was immensely proud of their recognition. To this day I have a special relationship with the fans. They let me know, by letters or in person at the race tracks, that I have touched their lives and I try whenever possible to show them that it works both ways. Perhaps more than any other driver in Formula 1, I relate to the fans and I go out of my way to be in touch with them.

I am a racer and an entertainer. When I race I create excitement. It's a trait which I sometimes wish I didn't have, because people always expect the impossible. The fans enjoy watching me race because they know that I always give 100% and never give up. As long as I'm in the race, there's a good chance that something exciting is going to happen. I make them laugh and cry and make them chew their finger nails with anxiety, but above all I try to make them feel that there is someone out there on the track with whom they can identify and who is giving it everything he's got.

In Formula 1 there is a rather snobbish tendency among the insiders, especially the press, to look down on the fans. Formula 1 is quite a closed world and the fans sit on the outside, fenced off from the paddock. But what links all of us, fans, drivers, journalists and insiders is a shared passion for the sport and we should never lose sight of the fact that without the support of the fans, we would all be out of work.

Being a professional sportsman, I feel a tremendous responsibility towards the public. If they are good enough to buy a ticket and support me, I feel I must try to deliver for them both on and off the track.

I was born in England so naturally I have an affinity with my home country. I have a large following there and I have been lucky to be able to share a great deal of success with them. The English fans are extremely loyal; many have supported me since my early days in Formula 1 and I see a host of familiar faces whenever I appear in England.

Much of my success in motor racing came at a time when the national teams in other sports were doing badly. I won my back-to-back Formula 1 and IndyCar world titles at the same time as the English soccer team failed to qualify for the World Cup and the cricket team was also going through a rough patch. Nobody likes to see their national team do badly in any sport. It lowers a country's self-esteem.

I became conscious during this period of being one of a few English sports stars out on a world stage who was actually delivering for the fans back home. Along with Nick Faldo, Linford Christie and Sally Gunnell, I felt responsible for carrying the torch. The public wanted someone to win for them and I was at the front of the line.

Having that kind of responsibility can be terrifying. Going into a Grand Prix weekend I would be aware that millions of people were looking to me to fly the flag and this would pile up on top of the expectations of the team, the sponsors and myself. But I have always maintained that pressure comes from within. You may be under pressure from all sides, but the secret is to control it, close your mind off to it and as you focus your mind on the job in hand, apply only as much pressure on yourself as you feel is required. A top sportsman must be able to control his emotions in this way and to keep all outside influences in perspective.

That said, I actually enjoy having a weight of expectation on me and it is something that I take very seriously. I rise to a big occasion and I thrive on the excitement of trying to win a major international race, whether it be the British Grand Prix or the Indianapolis 500. You can't have the satisfaction of winning an event of this kind without having experienced the terror which comes from the possibility that you might fail and let down the fans. I have had so many years of carrying the flag successfully that I am now less terrified of failure. Although I would never rest on my laurels, I feel I've been there long enough that I should be allowed some leeway to get it right again.

Nowhere have I ever felt a greater weight of expectation than in front of the home crowd at the British Grand Prix. When you perform before your home crowd the sense of excitement about the whole weekend is even more intense than usual. Right from your first laps of the track on a Friday you can feel the energy of the crowd. All the way around the circuit, it is as if they are in the cockpit with you or adding power to your engine. It lifts you and gives you strength to push harder to achieve your goal. When race day arrives the atmosphere is positively electric.

Perhaps the most amazing atmosphere I ever experienced was the British Grand Prix in 1992, when over 200,000 people packed into Silverstone. We had set some quick times in testing before the weekend, but nothing prepared me for the speed which we found during that weekend. At every corner of every lap during qualifying I could feel an energy and a passion, willing me on to take pole position. It all came together perfectly. The car felt right, I felt right and I had this extra force on my side which seemed to put extra power under my right foot on the straights and extra grip in my tyres around the corners. I managed a wonderful lap, which put me comfortably on pole, two seconds faster than anyone else was able to manage.

Afterwards I was in the transporter with Williams technical director Patrick Head and my engineer David Brown when Riccardo Patrese, my team-mate came in. He walked over to where we were talking and grabbed hold of my crotch.

'Hey, get off,' I yelled. 'What do you think you're doing?'

'Nigel,' he said laughing, 'I just wanted to feel how big those balls really are because that lap was unbelievable.'

That's quite a tribute coming from your team-mate because he is the only one who knows what the car is capable of.

The whole weekend had that magic about it. After I won the race, everyone went crazy and the crowd invaded the track. It was an incredible spontaneous outpouring of emotion. On the podium I almost cried I was so proud of what we had achieved. I felt completely at one with the crowd. They had willed me on to win and I had won for them. Now we could celebrate together.

I triumphed on home soil five times between 1985 and 1992, including my first ever Grand Prix win, the European GP in 1985. The crowd was amazing that day too. During the final laps of the race people in the crowd were counting me down the laps, holding up four fingers, then three, then two ... It had been two and a half seasons since a British driver had won a Grand Prix and they weren't going to let this one get away. I have special memories of all my home wins and of the support I had each time from the crowd.

The fans have given me a great deal of spiritual support, but I have also been lucky enough to receive several prestigious awards which reflect wider public recognition and which are very important to me because I am intensely patriotic. I was voted BBC Sports Personality of the Year twice, received the OBE from the Queen and I was sent a personal letter of congratulation by the Prime Minister when I won the World Championship. These are mementos that I treasure and they mean as much to me as any of my racing trophies. They symbolise something which goes beyond success in a sporting competition; they say that I have done something for my country, something of which I and the people of my country should be proud.

As I climbed up the ladder in Formula 1, I became increasingly aware of support for me in other countries, like Japan, Australia and Italy. I can't begin to describe what it feels like when you realise that people from different nations are getting behind you and giving you their support. It is a strange feeling, but also a deeply moving one. It heightens your determination to succeed, but moves everything onto a much wider playing field. Where before you identified with your home crowd because of shared origins and shared culture, now you realise that you have a much greater responsibility to a much larger number of people.

When I signed to drive for Ferrari in 1988 I was given the nickname *Il Leone* (The Lion) by the Italian fans. It was the biggest compliment that I could imagine. The Ferrari fans, or *tifosi* as they are called in Italy, are one of the most powerful groups of supporters in all of motor racing. They have had several British drivers to cheer on over the years: in the fifties Peter Collins and Mike Hawthorn were both Grand Prix winners and favourites with the *tifosi*, Hawthorn becoming Britain's first World Champion in 1958 while driving for Ferrari, and in 1964 former motorcycle racer John Surtees won the title for them.

Obviously when I joined Ferrari I was aware of all the history and

I had deep respect for the seriousness with which the *tifosi* follow the team. I was touched when they gave me that nickname. It was obviously significant to these passionate and committed people, so as the object of that passion I knew that it should be significant to me. It was certainly a flattering label. The lion is a symbol of power, strength and aggression. It has, of course, a strong historical association with England, which has a lion in its national emblem. It was also an appropriate nickname as, having been born in August, my star sign is Leo.

It was an honour to be able to develop a relationship with fans in Italy, Japan, Australia and many more far flung countries in which Formula 1 racing and its star drivers are celebrated. When I went to the States in 1993 to take on the top American stars, I received a warm welcome from the fans. As the season wore on and I won four oval races I became aware of a wider fan base all around the country. The American fans took to me and I took to them because I am a straightforward person, who is at heart what they would call a 'pedal-to-the-metal racer'.

I am also a family man and when my children were on holiday Rosanne and I would bring them to races. IndyCar is much more family oriented than Formula 1 and I really enjoyed that. There was a lovely moment on the podium after I won on the oval at New Hampshire. I invited my three children, Chloe, Leo and Greg to join me as I held aloft the winners trophy. Emerson Fittipaldi, who finished second, brought his two daughters Juliana and Tatiana up on the podium as well. The American public appreciates moments like that.

For a professional sportsman in the television age, fame is something which comes with the turf, and being at the very top in Formula 1 means being famous all over the world. In terms of the size of its global audience, the sixteen-race Formula 1 World Championship lies behind only the Summer Olympics and Soccer's World Cup and these events happen only every four years. In America, however, Formula 1 has only a cult following, while IndyCar and NASCAR racing rule the airwaves. Of course, when I moved to America I became more widely known, both through racing and through commercials and appearances on chat shows like David Letterman's.

But I remember one occasion not long after I moved my family to Clearwater in Florida which highlighted the differences in attitude to the sport across the Atlantic. I was at a children's party with my son Leo and during the course of the festivities I broke my toe. Naturally, I went to have it X-rayed at the local hospital, where the doctor on duty said that he needed to ask me a few questions for hospital records. He produced a clipboard and began scribbling.

'Name?'

'Nigel Mansell,' I replied.

'Occupation?'

When I told him that I was a race car driver there was not a glimmer of recognition. Because I had spent most of my time in the past few years in countries where Formula 1 has a huge following, I had forgotten what it was like not to be recognised. It was nice in those early days in Florida to be able to take the children out for a hamburger without someone approaching me for an autograph or to have their photograph taken. I could spend time with my family and enjoy being completely normal. Alas, this didn't continue for long.

In the summer of 1994, I came back to England to look at Woodbury Park, the golf course I had bought near Exeter. I took the family down to Exmouth and in the evening we sat on the beach eating fish and chips. Several people walked past and I heard one of them say, 'Blimey, that bloke looks just like Nigel Mansell,' thinking of course that it couldn't be me as I must be in America. I love moments like that.

Six months earlier, around Christmas time, I had come back to London to attend several awards dinners to celebrate my Indycar title. I went out for a meal with my friends Mark and Iona Griffiths after which, as it was a lovely night, we decided to have a stroll around the centre of London. It was about two o'clock in the morning and cars were pulling over and complete strangers rushing up to congratulate me on my Indycar Championship. Later, I came across four really drunk guys staggering down the street who, having obviously had a real Saturday night drinking session, didn't realise they were shouting rather than talking. They were pulling my leg and I was having a laugh with them – the cameraderie was just fantastic. I thought to myself: 'You couldn't do this at 2 am in America, Nigel.'

I am interested in people and I take the trouble to talk to them. Fame is something to be enjoyed at times and endured at others. As many young stars of sport and pop music have learned, fame can ruin your life and destroy your privacy. But it can also enhance your life, as I have found through my relationship with the fans. To get a feeling of warmth and respect from total strangers is a unique experience. But you must always be responsible and conduct yourself with dignity.

Being famous has its down sides too. If you make yourself accessible to the fans, there is always the threat of an attack, of the kind suffered by Monica Seles, the tennis star, who was stabbed in the back as she sat in her chair on court between games. Her fear of a repeat attack has kept her out of the game for a long time, but it's good to see her making a comeback. The incident sent shock waves reverberating throughout the professional sporting world. We realised that when we are surrounded by hundreds of people jostling to get closer, we are vulnerable. It worries any athlete in any sport. I don't know what motivates someone to make an attack on a sports star. The public must appreciate that sportsmen are not politically motivated, they are simply dedicated to being the supreme athlete at their discipline. There is absolutely no justification for attacking someone who seeks perfection in their sport.

What happened to Seles was distressing to every sportsman and woman in the world. 'If a star can be attacked in such a way...,' we all thought to ourselves, 'it could happen to me as well' and that was very worrying.

I always have people covering my back and I think that anyone who is reasonably famous takes precautions at times, because in this day and age it's wise to do so. But I'm privileged to say that over the years with all the fans I've met I've not once had any major problem. I wish I could say the same about the press.

My relationship with the press over the years has mostly been amicable and positive. I am an open person, I speak my mind and I take people as I find them. Consequently, with real professional journalists I have no problems. As I have already mentioned, I am a racer and I create excitement and this translates into good copy for the newspapers and magazines. Certainly over the years I have generated my fair share of dramatic headlines. But what never ceases to amaze me is the number of so-called experts in any sport who have never actually competed in that sport and who haven't got a clue as to what they are talking about. I have suffered at the hands of journalists who are unable to comprehend, much less swallow the scale of what I have achieved in motor racing. This is because years ago when I was working my way up to the top, the same people said that I would never make it and now their arrogance will not allow them to accept that they were wrong. There is a small group of journalists in the specialist press who pursue negative angles whenever they write about me and who have tried for many years to make me look bad.

When I got to the top, several of them actually came up to me to apologise for what they had written, because their editors were putting pressure on them to get an interview with me. I accepted their apologies and we sat down to talk. They fulfilled the wishes of their editors by publishing the required interviews and then the following week went back to rubbishing me. I have no respect for anyone who can behave like this.

Years ago, as I climbed the greasy pole, the things these people wrote in their magazines had an influence on my life. Now when they go to work on me, they make themselves look pathetic. You cannot argue with the history books, which reflect achievements whatever the sport. These people are annoyed because they are jealous of success.

I believe that sportsmen who have achieved a great deal and who have created history should be given the benefit of the doubt. They shouldn't have to put up with silly criticism. If it's objective or if they've done something wrong then there's no problem with that because they can learn from it. But to criticise for the sake of it is ridiculous.

Most famous people suffer to some degree at the hands of the press. I am relieved to say that I have not encountered the mauling or the total invasion of privacy suffered by some sportsmen, like Paul Gascoigne or Ian Botham. I have had my share of problems, but I have also had pleasure in working with some real pros.

As a professional sportsman I have a major responsibility towards the public and I think that the press have got to stand up and be as responsible because by reporting some of the things they do, they're not helping anyone. There's a lot of cheap journalism out there. The hacks forget how they earn their money and forget their obligations.

There are a few incredibly unethical people in journalism who are only interested in helping their bank balance and if motor racing gets undermined as a result, they'll move on to another sport or personality and start making things up about them. They'll concoct some sensational headline because they think it's clever and it will sell papers, regardless of how much trouble it causes everybody and how little evidence there is on which to base a story. They then go out and try to get a story to substantiate the headline. They're not interested in telling the news as it actually is. There is a great phrase among some newspaper editors: 'Don't let the truth get in the way of a great story.' I think that says it all.

A lot of people rubbish stars and then want to make money out of them. Over the years several scribblers have taken it upon themselves to write books about my life story. They claim to be my friends, to be close confidants of mine and to have unique insight into my character. They write poorly researched, hastily assembled potboilers with the simple aim of making money out of my name. How can people like this write a definitive book about my life without coming to me for the truth? What do they know of my past, my family life, my innermost thoughts? How can they have the barefaced cheek to rubbish me one minute and then become my 'biographer' the next? It's beyond belief, but is nevertheless true that some of my biggest critics have also made a lot of money out of me.

The sad truth is that they get paid good money to rubbish people. If you're in the spotlight then you've got to expect that this will happen. It comes with the territory. It doesn't matter whether you're in racing or soccer or an actor or a pop singer. For sure there are plenty of knockers out there, but you have to see the wider picture. Outside of the publicity you have to put up with, there are many levels of life and experience and although it's irritating, I don't ever let it put a large cloud over my life. In any case I have also had the pleasure of working with a great many professional journalists, who I am sure despair of the dross written by their low-life counterparts as much as we sportsmen and women do.

I saw the bigger picture long before I entered Formula 1. I paid close attention to what was written and said about the successful and the famous, especially in racing, so I would be prepared when I came in. But then even when I was in FF1600 I had journalists approach me saying that they could do a lot to further my career, raise my profile, or even proclaim me a 'future World Champion' if I would slip them some backhanders. So right there, in my formative days I got a good glimpse of the wider picture.

I later learned how to deal with the pressure of fame a lot better at Ferrari because the pressure is much greater there than at any other race team and the Italian press are very persistent.

I have always had my feet on the ground and have listened carefully to the advice of people I respect. I was lucky enough to meet the actor Sean Connery in the early eighties, just after I became a millionaire for the first time. He said to me that whenever you get money and success you will suddenly find lots of friends you never knew you had, all wanting you to finance some plan they have or lend them a few quid. The secret, he told me, was to keep your money, because you might never get another pay cheque like it.

Those words rang true to Rosanne and I and that's why we left England in the early eighties. We were paying 70% tax at the time. I said to Rosanne that my Formula 1 career could end at anytime. As hard as it had been to get in, we knew that it was the easiest thing in the world to be booted out. You only have to fall out of favour with someone or injure yourself and you'll be forgotten and your whole career is over.

Motor racing is a fickle business. I have worked hard for the success which I've achieved, but it could so easily not have happened.

4

FAMILY VALUES

I was born in a small room above my family's tea shop, in a quiet corner of a sleepy town called Upton-on-Severn, in the heart of England. The third of four children, I was christened Nigel Ernest James Mansell. It was August 1953.

It had been a momentous summer. Everest had been conquered for the first time by Sir Edmund Hillary and Sherpa Tensing; Queen Elizabeth II had been crowned at Westminster Abbey; and over in France, Mike Hawthorn, an Englishman driving for Ferrari, had beaten the great South American champion Juan Manuel Fangio in what was being hailed as the Formula 1 'Race of the Century'.

I remember my childhood at home being very happy. My brother Michael was a fair bit older than me and we were quite distant as we grew up. I was closer to my two sisters, Gail and Sandra and to my parents Eric and Joyce, whom I loved very much. Throughout my childhood and adolescent years before I left home, they were the model parents and I couldn't have wished for a better mother or father.

We weren't rich, but neither were we poor. My father was an engineer and had quite a senior job with Lucas Aerospace based in the Midlands. My mother, who had her hands full with a young family to look after, managed the day-to-day running of the family tea shop with help from my father.

When I was three, my father's job forced us to move closer to Birmingham and we ended up in an area called Hall Green, which is a southern suburb of the city and where we stayed a few years before moving on again. We seemed to move a great deal during my childhood. As soon as I settled into a new area and a new school we would up sticks and move again. It was pretty hard on me, especially

63

changing schools. When you go to a new school you don't know anybody and it takes time to settle in.

The second school I attended was a private preparatory school called Wellsbourne, which I liked a lot. I immediately took to sports and soon became the captain of the school soccer and cricket teams. I loved sport and it seemed to come naturally to me. I realised early on that I could derive tremendous satisfaction from competing against children in other school teams and winning. Even at the tender age of seven, winning was everything to me. I made quite a good sports captain because I so badly wanted to win that I always motivated the other players in my team to try harder.

Academically I was one of those children whose end of term report usually contained the phrase, 'He's bright and does well at the subjects he's interested in, but could try harder.' I didn't care too much about studying and I hated doing my homework. After school I preferred to kick a ball around with friends or to ride my bicycle rather than settle in for the evening with a few mathematical puzzles.

Although I got by in most subjects, I didn't like Latin at all and I really wanted to get out of it. Luckily the Latin professor headed up the school chess team and when I expressed my dislike for ancient languages he said to me, 'If you don't like Latin, I'll do a deal with you. If you get into the chess team, you can go to chess classes instead of coming to Latin.' At the time, chess was pretty big at Wellsbourne and we had regular competitions with other schools in which we used time clocks, large size boards and all the proper paraphernalia. It was all taken deadly seriously. I played intensively for two months, got into the chess team and never went to another Latin class.

Sadly the school closed down in the middle of a term and I was shunted into a school near my house called Hall Green Bilateral. It was a real culture shock. Whereas Wellsbourne had been an all-boys school with class sizes of around fifteen pupils, Hall Green was mixed and the classes were twice the size. To make matters worse, I started half way through the term, so I was out of step with everything.

It's a very difficult situation being the new boy. You stand out because you have a new uniform when everyone else's is worn in, and you don't know anybody. Before you get up to speed and settle in you get teased for being a 'dunce' and a 'thickie' because you don't know what's going on. At the age of between 7 and 14, other children don't care about you and they don't think for a moment about how you might feel. They only care about the things they are interested in, like sport, girls or being a bully. There were a lot of bullies at Hall Green Bilateral and predictably, soon after I arrived, they came to pick on the new kid.

I have never taken kindly to bullies and so I had a lot of problems. When they got rough with me I would always fight back and never give in. It was pretty nasty for a while. Although I was miserable at the time, I believe those formative years helped me a great deal in that they made me quite tough early on. Children can be unbelievably cruel to each other and if you can cope with that as a small child, very little in the adult world is likely to defeat you. As an adult I've been intimidated a great deal and I've been able to cope with and overcome all the hurdles.

I don't think a child usually forms a pattern of how he or she is until their middle teens, but I was forced to be my own person from a very early age because when you are thrown in at the deep end you learn to swim rather than sink. When you don't know anybody and nobody believes in you, you either shrink into nothing or you learn to believe in yourself and become more self-reliant.

My mother had a sixth sense when it came to people. She would be able to tell very soon after meeting them whether they were genuine or false, and I inherited that ability from her and put it to good use at school and later at college. It's an animal instinct, rather like dogs have, which tells you straight away whether someone is a friend or a foe. It has helped me to survive and to succeed in the business that I'm in. I have stopped a lot of people in their tracks when they have come over all gushing and insincere, or when they have tried to get me to do something I don't want to do. I hate falseness and deception.

Like my mother, I am very sensitive to what's going on around me. I am renowned for being an incredible fighter, yet I have a soft side to my character. Nothing gives me more pleasure than to do something for a friend or a family member. Throughout my life I have found that many people seem to regard kindness as a weakness and will prey on that perceived weakness. It's is a side of human nature that I will never understand. Kindness is fundamental to my nature. But if a tough decision has to be made, I can be as hard as nails. If I believe something is right I will go through a brick wall to make it happen.

I used to get up to quite a bit of mischief, as any young boy does, but I was always pretty responsible and early on I developed a clear set of beliefs and values. I learned to trust what I thought was right and wrong and to do what I thought was right for me. It became the code by which I have lived my life and according to which I have made every important decision.

Looking back, my formal education was totally inadequate at times, mainly because of the lack of continuity. But in another way it was marvellous, because I was constantly thrown in at the deep end with people and I learned more because I was up against it. I was always mechanically minded and when I went to technical college a lot of the work came as second nature to me. It was a question of applying myself and if I wanted to apply myself I did pretty well, whereas at school I did just enough to pass the exams.

After Hall Green Bilateral I moved again, to Hall Green College, where I stayed until I was 16. I got a couple of GCE O-levels and a few CSEs, then went to Solihull Technical College. I was 19 years old when I transferred to Matthew Bolton College in Birmingham to study engineering.

Although when I was young I had a lot of unpleasant problems to contend with in the playground and I struggled on the academic side, my athletic ability always kept me going. I became a good, disciplined athlete and my competitive spirit grew stronger and stronger throughout my school years. I loved to win and however steep the odds I never regarded any game as lost until the final whistle blew. I played hard at soccer, crunching into every tackle and chasing every ball. Even if we were playing a so-called 'friendly' match against another school, I felt it absolutely necessary to play to win. I was at my best when my team was a goal or two behind and we had to fight back. If we won after coming from behind the satisfaction was even greater than usual. I loved team sports. Although I also enjoyed solo sports like tennis, I was always a team player and I learned a lot of lessons from playing team sports which would stand me in good stead later in life.

I had a lot of fun playing sports. I remember one soccer match I had at college where I scored the winning goal completely by accident. I was running back from the goal, trying to slip away from the defender who was marking me. The ball was crossed into the middle, but I couldn't see it because my marker was standing in the way. Suddenly the ball came through, hit me right in the face and flew into the goal. My team-mates seemed pretty impressed with my header. I had no idea what had hit me and I fell to the ground, so everybody thought it was a diving header and were even more impressed. In reality it was a total fluke, but the result was marvellous!

Some people have suggested that my fighter's mentality was shaped by the fact that I come from Birmingham. They argue that because Birmingham is looked down upon by people in the more genteel South of England, its people have to fight harder for recognition. I think that's a bit of a myth. I don't believe that where you come from really matters. Although I am proud of my background, we have lived and travelled all over the world and my allegiance is to England rather than to any particular part of it.

My family and in particular my parents were very supportive of me as a child and my father backed my karting career. However, as will be explained in later chapters, they were not in favour of me pursuing a career as a professional racing driver. It caused a few problems for us initially, although they came around to my point of view in the end and we were reconciled. Their main objections to my chosen career were from the safety point of view as they didn't want me to get hurt or killed, but also my father saw a terrible struggle ahead for me and he just wanted me to be happy and settled. Our family did not have the money that many aspiring racing driver's families have and I think that my father felt frustrated at times that he was not in a position to do anything about it. He badly wanted to help, but he was inhibited financially. As a result I think he felt a bit out of place in the early days.

I persisted in my dogged pursuit of success in racing and when I made it into Formula 1 they were genuinely very happy for me. Unfortunately, my breakthrough into F1 with Lotus coincided with the awful news that my mother had terminal cancer.

She was a strong and marvellously brave lady through to the end, despite having to go through endless treatments of radiation therapy. I remember one time I took her to the hospital for her treatment and on the way home I had to stop three times for her to be sick. It was so upsetting. She was proud of me for getting into F1, but all she ever saw of my F1 career was the struggle. Neither did she get the chance to see her grandchildren.

My mother was terribly ill for a few years before eventually succumbing in 1984. Sadly, the illness had a bad effect on my father. As happens often when one partner has a terminal illness, it does odd things to the one who survives. My father had a hard time dealing with the situation and handling life. He went off at a tangent and nobody within my family, including myself, could understand him any more. He remarried two years later to a woman 26 years his junior. It put a strain on the family and upset me terribly.

Then he became very ill and he died too. In the space of three years I had lost both of my parents. It was very hard. Rosanne lost her mother five years before I lost mine, so we have one last surviving parent between us. When I see people today who are ten years older than me and who still have both their parents, I think that they should be very proud of them and very happy.

Losing both my parents in that way was upsetting, but you have to be strong and realise that you have your own life to lead and you must make the most of it. My life has shown me many times that virtually nothing is ever certain. The only thing which is certain is that one day you are going to die. The day you are born is the day you start to die. Everyone has their allotted time and that will be made up of good times and bad times. It doesn't matter who you are or how clever you are, you are going to age, gradually lose your health and fitness and eventually die. So when my parents were gone I said to myself, 'Right I've got to get on with my life and make my own decisions, because I'm only young once and there is a lot to be done.'

Rosanne and I turned to each other and worked through it. Our marriage has gone through many ups and downs but we have a solid family unit. We had no parental advice or guidance about bringing up our three children and in the business we're in that's not been easy. Hopefully, it is possible to bring up normal children in this kind of environment. You only really know when they grow up into adults, but I feel that our three children are just like anybody else's children. Certainly their father and mother think that they are exceptional. Rosanne and I are very close and the five of us are a tightly knit family. I wouldn't swap that for the world. Our children dearly love us and we dearly love them.

I became a father for the first time in August 1984, half way through my final year at Lotus, when Rosanne gave birth to our daughter Chloe. It was a magical experience. The births of all three of my children are some of the most special moments I have ever had.

Becoming a father changed me considerably. Life is very blinkered at times. Ignorance is blissful. Fatherhood opened up a whole new aspect of life which I don't think you can even begin to appreciate until you become a parent. You have a tremendous responsibility to this little child who can't feed itself or look after itself or do anything for itself until it reaches a certain age. Even then it has to have great counselling and schooling from its parents.

Rosanne and I waited seven years after we were married before we had children. We wanted to make sure that we had all the necessary security before we brought a child into this world. Parenthood is a huge responsibility. The financial burdens it places on you are great. To bring children into the world when you can't give them the basics and all the love they need, is totally irresponsible. All it does is create problems for everybody, not least yourself.

Without doubt my own experience of education has helped me to plan my children's schooling and to make sure that where my education fell short, theirs would not. Like any father I want them to have all the things which I did not have. Away from school, they are also getting an education on life from following Rosanne and me around the world. Having seen the inside of the Grand Prix scene, they are more worldly wise and have a better understanding of the wider picture than most children and certainly more than Rosanne and I had at their age. Chloe, Leo and Greg are learning certain disciplines which I would have found very useful at their age. For example, they will all be karate exponents to at least black belt level before they are eighteen and I am sure that they will grow up to be self-reliant and self-disciplined. Helping them to get the right start in life is the least I can do for them.

My family is the the most important thing in my life and I would go through a brick wall to give them the environment they need to flourish and grow.

After all, it's the way I was brought up.

PART TWO

THE GREASY POLE

*'I was told that with a name like Nigel Mansell
I would never make it or amount to anything in life ...'*

5

LEARNING THE BASICS

My father was quite a keen member of the local kart racing scene and he encouraged me to take an interest. We went down to watch a meeting at the local kart track and I remember being drawn in by the spectacle of these little machines buzzing around the twisty track. Some were being driven with more enthusiasm than skill, others looked more purposeful. Watching them exit the corners you could see the difference in speed between the ones who were really trying and those who were just out for fun. I felt I understood quite a lot about it straight away and I couldn't wait to get out there and see what I could do. I was hooked.

The great thing about kart racing in the late sixties and early seventies was that it was completely uncommercial. It was purely a family thing. The people involved were all very friendly and there was always a real community spirit about the local kart meetings. The whole family would turn out on a sunny Sunday afternoon, including mothers and sisters who would take turns to hold a spanner or cheer on their boy, when they weren't doling out lemonade and egg sandwiches.

Money didn't seem to make the difference between winning and losing back then. If your family was a bit better off than the next one you might have a few more engines or a couple more sets of tyres. But money wasn't a decisive factor. You could always go out in whatever kart you had and if you won, you had the satisfaction of knowing that it was more due to your efforts than anything else. I found that very satisfying.

Our first kart was a pretty crude piece of equipment, powered by a lawnmower engine. We bought it secondhand at a cost of £25. It wasn't up to much but I was terribly excited about it and spent as much of my spare time as possible driving it round dirt tracks in an allotment near where we lived. It wasn't very fast, but the important thing was that it needed no pedalling and it was thrilling to press down my foot and increase the speed.

A few other children had similar machines and we used to race them whenever we could escape from the house and our school homework. Before long I could beat everyone around the allotment and I was ready to go into properly organised local competitions, like the one I had visited a few months before.

Although the minimum age for a licence was 11 years and I was barely ten, we managed to get around the problem and I got my first licence. I was ready to go racing and based on my form around the allotment I felt confident that I would win my first race with ease.

Not surprisingly that first race was something of an eye opener. My primitive kart was hopelessly outclassed by the other machines and I watched in dismay as the field streamed away from me down the straight in the preliminary heats. I had my foot to the floor but I was going nowhere fast. To add insult to injury my engine stopped and I had to pull off the road. I sat there wondering what had happened. When I looked back I saw my engine lying in the middle of the track. The kart was so old that the bolts holding the engine in place had sheared. It was so humiliating. We got the engine welded on properly and went out to see what we could do, but it was a hopeless situation. The other children were so much faster that I felt I was standing still.

I had been naive in the extreme. There was far more to preparing a kart than I had imagined. That first race gave me a shocking lesson in the school of karting set-up. The other children's karts had both of the rear wheels driven, whereas ours only had drive to one wheel. Not only that but they had a box of different sized sprockets, so they always had the right gearing for each track, whether it was slow and twisty or fast and sweeping. Also I knew nothing at the time about minimum weights. The power to weight ratio of a kart is critical and so the trick was to get the kart down to the minimum weight permissable in the rules, while tuning the engine to give maximum power. Our poor underpowered kart was 40lbs overweight, so we really didn't have a prayer.

Most of the children were much older than me; some were as old as sixteen and I felt upset and humiliated by the sharp shock I had received. I went away at the end of that day a much wiser ten year old. I knew that I had a burning desire to race karts and my desire to beat everybody had been heightened by the experience. I was down, but I was determined to fight back.

I knew that we would never be competitive with the equipment we had so I put a lot of pressure on my father to get a newer and faster kart. Because karting was still uncommercialised, the cost of upgrading our equipment was not prohibitive. Looking back, I'm glad I was racing karts when I was. I shudder to think what it would cost today to buy competitive equipment.

My father was not rich and I had to justify the cost to him. I think he could see that I was very determined to race and that we needed better gear if we were to compete.

I knew even at that age that I was very competitive. No matter what field you compete in and no matter at what level, if you are born with the will to win then you know it from a very early age. At school you can see people around you who win and enjoy it, they really thrive on it. I was like that for me from the word go. By contrast you see other people who win or lose and it doesn't really matter much to them either way. That is an admirable quality to have, but if you are a racer and you want to be successful as a driver, then it is completely the wrong attitude.

Winning is pretty much everything. Once you've realised that, it dictates the whole way you look at competition. If your equipment isn't up to scratch, you do everything you can to upgrade it. No-one in our family was wealthy, but my grandparents used to give me equipment for my birthday and at Christmas. I remember putting pressure on them one year to give me a new engine.

Although winning is everything, that is not to say that you have to be a bad loser. I think you can be a good sportsman and be a gentleman and lose gracefully without losing your competitive edge. It's a subtle difference, but an important one. Psychologically you approach competition believing only that winning is everything and losing doesn't exist.

If you lose, there are always reasons why you have lost. This is where you've got to be honest with yourself and think, 'This is the reason why I lost today', rather than 'The car, or the engine, let me down.' It is important to be positive and to look for constructive reasons why you failed to win, but above all it is important to be honest with yourself. This is something I learned very early on in my competitive career. One of my strengths and probably at the same time one of my weaknesses is that I am very straightforward. I am honest with myself and with other people. I call things as I see them and sometimes that upsets a few people, as I would discover later in my career.

I won with my new kart and as the years progressed I moved up through the different junior karting categories. It was a thrilling time for me. The competition was fierce, but the atmosphere in the paddock was friendly. If you were short of a piece of equipment, you could always rely on someone in the paddock lending it to you.

All of my spare time and my school holidays were spent working on my kart and racing it. I can remember putting the kart in the boot of the car and going off to the little track at Chasewater testing. My father and I used to make dozens of trips like this. We would test engines and pistons and run bits in at Chasewater, then go back home and rub the pistons down and hone the barrels, then go back to the track to try it again. My father and I were extremely close in those days and I think in a way he was re-living his childhood through me, because he had a very bad time in the Second World War.

The karting became pretty serious as I began to race further and further afield. To start with it was the length and breadth of Britain, then when I was picked for the English team we began travelling to the continent and across the North Sea to Scandinavia. I was doing what I wanted to do, satisfying my competitive urge and loving every second of it.

Unfortunately, things were not quite so straightforward at school. Although the teachers did not object to me missing school to represent the country in international races, some of the other children at the school didn't like it at all. They were jealous and resented my success. One morning the headmaster announced in morning assembly that I would be going to Holland for two weeks to race for England. I was to be given a special two-week leave of absence from classes. The school hall buzzed with an uncomfortable mix of approval and resentment.

Although the trip sounded pretty exotic, in reality it meant that I would be well behind with my schoolwork when I got back and would have to put in many extra hours. Some of the other children didn't see it that way. They were jealous and they wanted me to know that I shouldn't consider myself special. There was an uneasy atmosphere in the playground later that morning and then suddenly I got hit on the back of the legs with a cricket bat. I went down and when several others joined in I was beaten up quite badly.

So I learned another important lesson: that no matter what you do you cannot please everybody and there will always be some who want to undermine your success. Their attacks, whether they be with a cricket bat in the school playground or, later on, with words in the press, always hurt. They are motivated by jealousy; people who said that you would never be any good and who are forced to eat their words when you go out and prove them wrong. It is a reaction against success achieved against the odds, a denial that somebody from within their midst could be successful and get the attention and the rewards that success brings. This is a negative side of human nature which I have run up against many times in my life, but which I don't believe I will ever understand. Sadly it is one of the prices you have to pay if you single-mindedly pursue your goal. It comes with the territory.

The karting trips abroad were great fun and often my father and I would be accompanied by my sisters Sandra and Gail. We would pack the car onto the ferry and set off on another adventure. I enjoyed meeting and racing against children from other countries, although it was always nice to come home once the job was done. The races were enjoyable and we had our fair share of successes. I had a few accidents too, but mostly these were harmless spills. Because the karts didn't travel terribly fast, parents were never too worried about their children getting hurt. I had one accident where I took off and flew into the branches of a tree. The chassis buckled under the impact, but I was perfectly alright. Not long afterwards I had my first serious accident.

It was an accident that shouldn't have happened, but in those days in kart racing there wasn't the quality control in the manufacture of components which there is today. Also the thoroughness of scrutineering and inspection was way behind today's standards. Unbeknown to me, the steering column on my kart was cracked when I started the race. I was coming down the hill on the fast kart track at Morecambe, travelling at probably 100mph and approaching a slight left-hander. I turned the wheel and the steering just snapped. I realised that I had no steering and at that speed there is no time to scrub off speed before you go off. I was in big trouble. I took off over a kerb and somersaulted. There was a huge impact and the back of my helmet struck something hard. I was knocked unconscious.

It must have looked like a serious crash. Whenever they take a driver's helmet off and his whole face is covered in blood you know that it's been a significant blow. I was taken to the Royal Lancaster

Hospital where I was found to be haemorrhaging from the ears and the nose. The scar tissue which is caused in the channels of the ears by an injury like that stays with you for life and I have actually lost some of my hearing as a result.

I remember drifting in and out of consciousness. It was rather like a dream. I also recall hearing a voice and as I came to, I caught a glimpse of a priest standing at the end of the bed. He was saying prayers and his last words were, 'And what else can I do for you my son?' I realised that he was giving me the last rites.

My head hurt and I was struggling to keep awake. I vividly recall coming to the realisation that the situation was very serious. I knew I had to fight. I was not about to let life slip away from me. I summoned up the strength to speak ... and promptly told the priest to sod off. Then I collapsed back into unconsciousness. I had a battle going on inside my head, but I have such a strong will to live that I came through that traumatic experience and before too long I was out of hospital and back at home with my family. It had been a frightening period but I knew that I had to go on and learn from it.

That accident taught me that I should always check four fundamental things before I race: the steering, the brakes, the suspension and the aerodynamic wings. I check them because if any one of them were to fail I would have no chance of controlling the car and could be killed. Pretty much anything else on the car can go wrong and you can stay in control. But if you lose any one of those four key things, it's curtains. If the suspension fails, you're on three wheels while if the brakes fail, you have no stopping power. If your front or rear wing fails or falls off then you have little or no control; and if the steering goes then you're a passenger on a high speed ride.

In the early days I had a lot of accidents I shouldn't have had. I've analysed every one of them because it is so important to learn. Accidents like the one I had at Morecambe weren't my fault, they were caused by failures on the machine. In large part this was because we never had the finance to get the best and safest equipment. In my early single-seater days many accidents were caused by component failures and even when I joined Lotus we had five suspension failures in one season.

Over the years I have been more down after accidents and retirements caused by mechanical failure than those where I was at fault. When something breaks and you crash, you've got to take it personally because you are the one who is sitting in the car and you realise that you are under threat from some major unknowns. It's far easier if you make a mistake to accept it and learn from it. For sure if it's a big error it might take a little longer to get over, but you can still rationalise it and put it out of your mind.

One of the worst mechanical failures I ever suffered was during the Canadian Grand Prix at Montreal in 1991. I was winning the race hands down, heading for my first win of the season, when the gearbox failed. It was a semi-automatic gearbox, which controls the gear selection electronically and was operated by pushing a lever on the back of the steering wheel. We had had a few problems with it at the start of the season, but we thought that those problems had now been solved. But coming through the hairpin on the last lap I couldn't find a gear to save my life. I had a box full of neutrals. The revs dropped and the engine cut out. That was it. To be leading the race by almost a minute and then to be forced to quit on the last lap was hard to take.

My engineer David Brown and I were trying to get over it as quickly as possible, when we read some truly idiotic suggestions in the press that I had switched the ignition off while waving to the crowd. It was a pathetic notion and it really hurt. Let's face it, you don't push as hard as you can for 68 laps and then switch your own engine off. It was bad enough losing the race through mechanical failure, but to have insult added to injury in that way was too painful to describe.

That accident at Morecambe had been a wake-up call, but I bounced back and carried on racing karts. As I reached the end of my teenage years, I had won seven Midlands Championships, one Northern Championship, one British Championship and many other races. It had been a lot of fun, but my attention was beginning to wander onto single-seater car racing and onto Formula Ford in particular. It was clearly time to move forward on the road towards Formula 1 and the World Championship.

Almost immediately I ran into problems.

Chris Hampshire, a karting colleague: 'There are probably a hundred people who raced against Nigel in karts, who look at where he's got to and say, "Now why couldn't I have done that?" Nigel had the determination to pull himself right up to the top. His will to win is enormous. He also had extraordinary reactions, much faster than most people's. By reacting so quickly, he seemed to make more time for himself.'

6

THE HUNGRY YEARS

My father didn't want me to go into single-seater racing. He had been right behind me all through my karting career and it had been his interest in karting that had got me started, but when it came to proper racing cars he decided to draw the line. Karting was fun, he said, but motor racing was serious. He had a good job and a comfortable, although by no means affluent lifestyle and he wanted the same for me. It was clear that he was hoping I would pursue a career in engineering as he had done. He was being realistic, trying to guard against what he saw as the likelihood that I wouldn't make it in motor racing. And knowing how competitive I was he thought that I would find it hard to bear the disappointment of failure.

After all, the odds against a lad from Birmingham going on to beat the world's best drivers and win the Formula 1 World Championship were huge. Every year thousands of young drivers start racing and join the ranks of the hopeful. Every season new teenage talents from Europe, as well as from countries further afield like Brazil, Colombia and Argentina, come pouring into England with pockets full of money to race in the most competitive starter championships in the world.

It was common knowledge in racing circles around the world that if you wanted to climb the ladder and get noticed by a Formula 1 team, you needed to race in the British Formula Ford and Formula 3 Championships. Britain has the most powerful motor racing industry and because most of the Formula 1 teams are based here, there is a huge network of information around the industry. A lot of the people who run teams in the junior formulae know people in Formula 1. Formula 3 team managers might tip off their friends in Formula 1 if they see a driver with special talent or someone who has reasonable talent and massive financial backing. For a young driver, being spotted by a Formula 1 team owner is what it's all about.

Unlike the local kart scene, in Formula Ford or Formula 3 money can make the difference between winning and losing. The cars and engines were all similar, so a few extra thousand pounds could buy you better engine tuning, which in turn would gain you a few precious horsepower over your rivals.

The British series had sent many of its champions on to Formula 1 and it was into this ultra-competitive environment that I wanted to throw myself. Considering that this was the goal of many other young drivers, most of whom had plenty of overseas sponsorship money, the chances of me being successful were less than my chances of winning the pools.

I don't hold it against my father that he was against me trying. What I was disappointed about was that he motivated me to stick with my engineering job with the promise that if I reached certain goals he would support me in my racing career. Out of the goodness of his heart, because he really did love me, he promised many things which never came to fruition.

I had joined my father at Lucas Aerospace at the age of 16 as an apprentice engineer. By this time I was all fired up to race cars and was desperate to get on with the next stage of my career. Given a fair chance I knew I would be able to make it. I realised that the jump to single-seater cars would be impossible without my father's help and eventually I persuaded him to make a deal with me. If I passed all my engineering exams, he would help to finance my racing.

It was a hard slog. I worked part of the time at Lucas and the rest of the time I attended classes at various technical colleges and polytechnics in and around Birmingham. It took several years and in the meantime I carried on karting. My father enjoyed my success and was proud of my competitiveness and determination, but I was longing for a chance to prove myself on a wider stage. I would arrive at a local kart meeting with the knowledge that, barring some mechanical disaster I was going to win fairly easily. It was still fun, but really I knew it was pointless. I had outgrown karts and could not wait to get into a proper racing car.

When I was twenty-one I passed the last exam and emerged with a Higher National Diploma in Engineering. By this time I had also made progress at Lucas and I now held the position of electronics instructor. Things looked rosy. I went to see my father to tell him that

I had qualified and to remind him of his promise. I was in for a nasty shock.

I found him in the laboratory at Lucas and cheerfully told him that I was going to be a racing driver. He asked me how I planned to finance my venture. When I reminded him of his promise he told me that my chances of making it were nil and that he would not be a part of it. I couldn't believe it. I tried to reason with him but he wouldn't budge. He would not help me race and that was that. I was furious. I had spent several years fulfilling my side of the bargain, going to endless engineering classes and now I was back to square one. My goal of moving into Formula Ford began to look distant. I felt bitter and disappointed. It was one of the worst days of my life.

I discussed it at great length with Rosanne, who by then had become my wife. I was determined to race. I knew that I had talent and refused to be beaten by the circumstances. Rosanne and I decided that, whatever the consequences, we were going to give it a go.

The cheapest and most sensible first move was to try out a Formula Ford car at a racing school. At least then I would know whether I could drive one or not. I might find that I didn't like it and return to karts, but I had to know what it was like.

We scraped together £15 which was enough for a one-day lesson in a Formula Ford car at the Mallory Park school. Most of the other students there on that day were signed up for a week-long course, but I couldn't afford such luxuries. I had one day to decide.

I went out in the car and immediately found it to my liking. It was fairly predictable and I felt quite comfortable with its behaviour. Because it was light and had narrow tyres it had a tendency to slide through corners. I quickly got a feel for what it would do next and felt that it was a car with which I would be able to express myself. That day at Mallory was enough to persuade me that my instinct was right. I should move on to Formula Ford racing.

But when he heard of my plan, my father was very angry and wouldn't speak to me. My mother was upset by the rift that the whole issue had caused and the situation was quite unpleasant for some time.

Rosanne and I went ahead and bought a second hand car which we saw advertised. It had obviously seen plenty of action and had passed through several owners, some not so caring. We scraped together our savings, sold a few items here and there and got the money together to buy the car and a trailer. Rosanne had a nice new road car, but it was too small to tow the race car, so we traded it in for an older but larger model. She was marvellous, always keeping me company in the garage late into the night when I was working either on the race car or on the road car. I remember the latter used to devour clutches in protest at having to tow the race car!

Most evenings I would come home from work at Lucas and go straight over to Rosanne's brother's workshop, where I used to make extra cash helping him out with his picture framing business. We used to work late into the evening mounting pictures in the frames, and then around eleven o'clock we would go out to the bars and clubs around Birmingham selling them. It was quite a good business, although the drawback was I often didn't get home until 3 am and I had to be at work again at 7.30. But the money came in useful – in fact, all money came in useful.

The racing car I had bought was in a bit of a state, but I was able to do something with it which I hadn't managed in karting – to win my first race. Fittingly it was at Mallory Park, a circuit which had played a big part in my decision to take the plunge. The field of drivers I beat was something of a mixed bag, but it didn't matter. I was on my way and very pleased about it too.

Although I could see many areas where the car needed improving, I felt comfortable with it and pushed it quite hard. I was not conscious of developing a style of driving at the time, it was more instinctive, but I was winning races and could already see the possibilities. I remember one particular race that first year when I was really charging through the field and came through strongly to win on the last lap. Rosanne told me later that the track commentator had been going crazy at the microphone, 'Mansell's coming up on the outside, he's not going to be able to do it there, he's on the wrong line. And he's done it!' I hope that same commentator was watching fifteen years later when I passed Gerhard Berger around the outside of the infamous Peraltada corner in the Mexican Grand Prix!

That first season went well for us. I won six races in all out of the nine that I entered and I went away feeling reasonably pleased with my progress. But my competitive instinct was gnawing at me. I wanted to win a lot of races and I knew that I needed a better car and a better budget if I was going to move forward.

As I had learned at school and in junior karting, there were a few people, like me, who loved winning and couldn't contemplate defeat, and plenty of others who were just racing for fun and didn't mind too much if they didn't win. It was never a game to me. I could see from that first season that my feelings about racing had been right. I had the ability to win and to make instinctive overtaking moves, which others wouldn't even dream possible.

Because of my engineering background I had a pretty good feel for the technical side of a racing car and was able to make adjustments to the car to make it faster on each circuit. Those Formula Ford cars were fairly basic technically, and a long way from the highly-sophisticated Formula 1 cars I would drive later. There weren't many things that you could adjust, but it still required clarity of thought and confidence in your own instincts to make the right changes to the car. From the early stages of my single-seater career I learned to trust what I felt was right and wrong on a car. That's not to say that occasionally even today I don't go down the odd blind alley while looking for an ideal chassis set-up, but for the most part I know which direction to head in as soon as I've done a couple of laps.

I felt confident that I had made the right choice in pursuing my racing career and was determined that I would become a professional racing driver as soon as possible.

The turning point came in 1977. I started the year with a slightly better car, although it was still pretty run-down compared to many of my competitors. The car was owned and run by a colourful Irishman called Patrick Mulleady and it was yet another case of trying to do the best I could in a dilapidated old car. At one race I qualified on pole position but, coming round to the grid on the parade lap, the driveshaft broke and fell through to the ground. I was beside myself with anger. I had given everything to put that old nail of a car on pole and here we were losing a race we could have won because of bad preparation. We did win a few races that season with the car, but when eventually one of the wheels fell off while I was leading by over ten seconds, it was clear that we needed help to move forward.

I had started to get noticed by this point and I decided to try my luck and approach a man called John Thornburn, a manager who had a reputation for running a good race team. One day I walked into his office and said, 'Hello, my name is Nigel Mansell and before you throw me out I don't want money, I want help.'

I had bought a slightly better car, but it was still pretty worn out and I was anxious to get it prepared as well as possible. John said he would have one of his mechanics take a look at it.

The following weekend I got pole position and a win with it. I rang

John up to thank him for his work and he was obviously stunned.

'What do you mean you won with it?' he gasped. 'When we looked at it, only three of the wheels were in line, the other was an inch and a half out of line because of all the shunts it's had. Either you've got a lot of talent or you were driving against a blind school, because that car is a load of crap.'

My next race was at Thruxton and without telling me, John came along as a spectator. He liked what he saw and told me that he would help. He said, 'You have a lot of natural talent, Nigel. There are plenty of quick drivers out there, but very few really talented racers. Remember that no-one can beat you except yourself.'

I knew he was right. I think it is true for anybody as long as they have equal equipment and total self-belief and have the capabilities or the talent to do the job. John told me that I had to get really fit so that I would be strong at the end of races. He said it was possible to win a race in the last couple of laps when your rivals are beginning to get tired. At the time I was a little overweight, largely because I used to enjoy my beer, but I knew John was right so I stopped drinking there and then. I have been a teetotaller ever since. I also got very fit by going to the gym and running several miles every day. In actual fact I hated running, but I forced myself to do it because I knew it would pay off.

The season was going well and I worked my way up to being a leading contender for one of the national Formula Ford Championships. Because we had no money, Rosanne and I used to sleep in the back of a van at race meetings. We borrowed it from Alan McKechnie who was John Thornburn's partner in the wine business, so ironically, although I had given up the drink, I went to sleep every night with a stale smell of booze hanging in the air. Not only that, but it was freezing cold in the van and the condensation from the ceiling and the windows used to drip on our sleeping bags. Combined with the wind to which circuits like Silverstone and Snetterton are often exposed, neither Rosanne nor I had ever experienced such extreme cold.

But we didn't think twice about it. It wasn't a hardship, it was reality for us at the time. Rosanne and I have a saying: 'What you've never had you never miss.' If we had had a better life up until that point and then had to do that sort of thing, it would have been a hardship. But the fact is that this was our life. It was how we had to live in order to achieve what we both wanted. It was unpleasant and looking back on it now with all the creature comforts we have today, then it does seem like a terrible hardship, but at the time it was necessary and whatever was necessary we did without a second thought.

Both of us were working overtime to pay for the racing. Rosanne was working for British Gas as a demonstrator and took on evening assignments to get as much money as she could. At times she was working up to eighty hours a week. It was a tough situation. We had very little spare time and certainly couldn't contemplate taking a holiday. We saw less and less of our friends and our families. Deep down we knew what we were doing was right, but many of the people around us had serious doubts.

We tried to keep our distance from them. It wasn't a case of cutting them off, we just made a personal commitment to ourselves that we didn't need negative people in our company, telling us that we would never make it, that we shouldn't take the risk and how stupid we were to try.

When you want to turn the tables and be successful in an environment which is already tough enough, you can do without that kind of negative influence. Everybody's entitled to their own opinion, but if it's really negative, then it is far more constructive to keep it to yourself. It doesn't help anybody to come out with that sort of thing.

There were people whom we hardly ever saw, but if something went wrong they would come up to us and say, 'I could have told you about that. I could have told you that wouldn't work.' It's amazing how many people we've run into with that attitude.

If they were more constructive in their approach and came to us saying, 'Listen Nigel and Rosanne, we love you a lot, but we're concerned about what you're trying to do and that you might get hurt,' and maybe even make a few tactful suggestions about other ways of going about things, then I can respect that kind of opinion. As it turned out, our true friends were fabulous and kept us going, while gradually the ones who didn't believe in us dropped away.

I have always been a positive thinker and I have never been able to tolerate people who are negative. Perhaps that is the root of my problem with some of the motor racing journalists I have encountered over the years. In any case, it is something to which I really hardenened my attitude during those difficult early days in Formula Ford.

Meanwhile, things began to look up. A guy called Mike Taylor offered me a newer car, on condition that I used my own engine. I jumped at the chance and drove down to his workshop to fit my engine into his car. It was very late when we finished and I only managed a couple of hours sleep before I had to go to Thruxton to race it. Although I was exhausted, I won the race, which was immensely satisfying. It was to prove a major turning point.

The car was made by a company called Crossle, which was based in Ireland. When John Crossle heard what had happened at Thruxton he called John Thornburn and said, 'Tell me honestly, John, how good is this bloke Mansell?'

'Well from a Formula Ford point of view,' John said, 'he's the best there's ever been. But he's got no money.' Crossle thought for a second and said, 'I suppose I'd better give him a car then.' To which John replied, 'Well, if you don't someone else will, because he's going to win whatever he drives.'

Crossle sent a car over and we managed to persuade one of the top engine tuners to work on the engines for free. Things were beginning to come together and at this point I made the biggest decision of my life.

I was in the position of manager at Lucas, even though I was only twenty-two, and it was a well paid job. The problem was they wanted me to make myself available to work Saturdays and Sundays if the workload required, but they weren't prepared to pay any overtime. At the time I was racing most weekends during the season and winning a lot. I pointed this out to my boss and he said, 'Well, Nigel, you've got to decide whether you're going to be an amateur playboy racer or a mature man in a sensible job.'

That night I went back to Rosanne and told her about my conversation at work. We thought about it until late into the night and agreed that we would only be young once. If we didn't at least try to make it in racing we would have to live with the regret for the rest of our lives. Every element of the discussion brought us back to the same answer – we had to go for it.

The next day I went into the office and handed in my notice. My boss almost fell off his chair. He really hadn't expected it. I said to him, 'Look, I'm young and I've got to give racing a try. I've got all my engineering qualifications, so if it doesn't work out I can always come back here or to a similar place.'

He was quite good about it and I think he could see that I meant it. So I walked out of the door and left my job behind me. There was no turning back, we had taken the plunge. I was now a professional racing driver. It was a strange feeling as I drove home that night. I was satisfied knowing that I had made the right decision, and nothing would shake me from my belief that I was going to make it. But I knew it was going to be tough and I had just given up a healthy source of income. When I told Rosanne we smiled at each other. We had taken charge of the situation. From now on it was down to us.

Three weeks later I broke my neck.

Many people are faced with that difficult choice between doing something they love or playing it safe and going for the secure, tried and trusted route. Some decide, like we did, to go for it. Others choose the safe route and perhaps encounter a degree of regret later in life. I don't know what advice I would give someone faced with that choice. It depends on so many things. You must have the talent, of course, and you must be able to focus totally on one objective. But more important than that, you must believe in yourself. When Rosanne and I look back we wonder what gave us the strength to carry on believing at times.

I broke my neck in my first race with the new car. It was at Brands Hatch and the chequered flag had fallen to end the qualifying session. I was on my slow-down lap when I came up behind a car going much more slowly. The track surface was mostly wet, but there was a single dry line which we were both using. Rather than hit the slower car I swerved and immediately the car became loose on the slippery surface. I went off backwards and in the ensuing accident I broke two vertebrae in my neck.

The accident at Morecambe had been pretty frightening, but this was worse. I was actually paralysed for a few hours and the fear you experience when you cannot feel your arms and legs is truly shocking. I looked at the X-rays of the broken vertebrae and shuddered. The doctors had very serious expressions on their faces as they told me that I was lucky not to have permanent paralysis.

Rosanne went back to Birmingham, because she had to go to work the next day. I think that the shock hit her quite badly. She was tired and despondent. We had been burning the candle at both ends to support ourselves and now we were left wondering whether it was all worth it.

I hated being so far away from her and the rest of my family. The hospital was in Kent, over 200 miles away from my home. I felt isolated and depressed. I couldn't wait to get out of there and get home. After a few days, I tried sitting up and the following day I told one of the nurses that the doctor had said I could walk to the toilet if I felt strong enough. He hadn't said anything of the sort, of course, but I wanted to speed up my release from the hospital. The short walk to the toilet and back took nearly an hour. I was roasted by the doctor when he found out. He said that I should be flat on my back for several months, not walking around. Didn't I understand how serious an injury I had?

The walk to the toilet had been like rolling in broken glass, but it gave me the confidence to discharge myself, much to the dismay of the specialists. I'd had enough of lying around in the doldrums, I wanted to get going again. I was in a position to win the Formula Ford Championship and I couldn't do it from a hospital bed.

Back home again, things didn't look too bright. With me having quit my job a few weeks before, we had only Rosanne's salary to live on. The situation only served to harden our resolve. The accident had been a setback for sure, but we were not going to let it get in the way of our objective. As the weeks passed I took longer and longer walks every day and gradually my neck began to feel better. Seven weeks after the accident I was back in a racing car.

I had missed a few rounds of the championship and had dropped a few points behind the leaders, but I managed to pick up the pace when I returned and soon began winning again, although in my first race back I had a bit of a scare. On the second lap I took off over the back of another car and flew through the air for a short distance. Luckily I got away with it.

As the season wound to a close I was back in contention for the title. My main rivals were Trevor van Rooyen and Chico Serra, the much fancied new Brazilian driver. Both had well-funded teams and plenty of equipment. Van Rooyen always seemed to have a few more horsepower than the rest of us and although everyone suspected that he had something special in his engine we could never prove it. Before the last race at Thruxton, which would decide who was champion, John Thornburn asked the stewards to announce that they would seal the engines of the top four finishers after the race and take them away to be checked. They agreed.

To win the championship I needed to get pole position, win the race and get the extra point for fastest lap. It was a tall order. Luckily van Rooyen didn't seem to have any advantage on the straights that day and through qualifying and the race I was able to pick off my objectives one by one. I started from pole. It was a very close race, but my determination saw me to victory and I became 1977 Formula Ford Champion.

It was hard to believe that only a few months before I had been flat on my back with doctors giving me little chance of racing again that season. It was not the first adversity I had encountered in my racing career and it certainly wouldn't be the last, but I had overcome it. I had set myself an objective and achieved it, which was immensely satisfying. In all I had competed in 42 races that year and won 33 of them. I felt that I had proved something to the people in the business who were watching. Rosanne and I allowed ourselves a little time to enjoy the satisfaction before turning our attention to the next step.

I wanted to drive in Formula 3, so I became a window cleaner and then we sold our house.

It is hard to imagine, looking at all the rewards I have around me now, that I was once a homeless window cleaner. I didn't have to do it, no-one was forcing me, but racing will make you do some crazy things once you get hooked.

Although I had a firm offer on the table for a well-funded works drive in Formula Ford for 1978, I knew that I had to move forward into Formula 3. That was the stage on which true talent was often recognised and I was confident that, given a fair shot in a decent car, I would be spotted by a Formula 1 team owner. The problem was that the stakes were much higher in Formula 3. It would cost several times my old salary just to compete for a season and I didn't have access to that kind of money.

I took a job with my friend Peter Wall, who had an office cleaning business. I did a little administrative work, but mostly I cleaned offices after the workers had gone home for the night. My speciality was window cleaning. It was actually great fun and quite satisfying when you saw the sunlight gleaming off a freshly cleaned window. The only problem was that the business was based down in Cirencester, some two hours drive from home, so I often had to stay at Peter's house overnight, away from Rosanne.

I spent the rest of that winter looking for sponsors to help foot the bill for my move into Formula 3. Despite sending hundreds of letters I got nowhere. It was a fruitless search and although I learned a lot from it, I was still no closer to a Formula 3 drive and the 1978 season was approaching fast. So that's when we did what any right thinking people would do under the circumstances – we sold our house.

It was a tough decision, but as we could see no other way of raising the money we were left with no alternative. Rosanne was still working long hours as a demonstrator for the gas board and her salary supported us as we moved into rented accommodation. It was sad to let our place go as we had been happy there, but we both knew that it was the right thing to do.

We raised £6000 from the sale of the house and added another £2000 from the sale of some personal items. We were staking everything we had. I took the money to March, who had promised to help me if I could get enough cash together to start the season. They were confident that they would pick up enough backing along the way to mount a challenge.

The season started well. I was on pole position for the first race and came through to finish second behind Nelson Piquet. Little did we realise at the time that our careers would become closely linked in years to come.

On race morning I was practising standing starts on the Club straight when I was approached by two people. One of them I recognised as Peter Windsor, an Australian journalist working at the time for *Autocar* magazine. Peter introduced the other man to me as Peter Collins, another Australian, who had a job at Ralt cars, but who was soon headed for the Lotus Formula 1 team as assistant team manager. We chatted for a while and I think that they were both impressed by my single-mindedness. They told me years later that they had never encountered anyone at that stage of his career who had such a clear focus on where he wanted to get to. We hit it off immediately and they said they would keep an eye on my progress. It was to prove one of the most important meetings of my life so far.

The Silverstone race was an encouraging start, but after that, things went downhill fast. It was a very poor car and although I'd been able to hustle it around Silverstone for that first race, I couldn't get it going quickly anywhere else. March blamed me. I knew that it wasn't me who was at fault. I did four more races and picked up some minor placings but all too soon I was told that the money had run out. They had found no backing, so that was it. End of season. Close the door on your way out.

Rosanne and I were devastated. We had blown everything in six weeks and there was nothing left. We had hit rock bottom.

John Thornburn, Nigel's team manager in Formula Ford: 'Alan McKechnie and I had decided to take a break from motor racing after a bad experience with a sponsor. Then Nigel showed up. When I realised that he was winning races with a car which we knew had a twisted chassis, I decided to go and have a look at him racing. I went down to Thruxton and stood on a couple of corners and it was obvious that he was very special. He was beating everybody in an old nail of a car. So we decided to help. We used to turn up with the McKechnie Wine Company van with the race car on a trailer behind it and he'd go out and beat the pants off all these kids in state-of-the-art cars with huge transporters. It was brilliant.'

Peter Windsor, journalist on *Autocar* magazine: 'Nigel is unbelievably competitive and always had this incredible desire to succeed. When I first met him he was running ten miles a day in army boots and firing off five letters a day to sponsors. He had total commitment and talent. To my mind there was no way that the guy would fail to make it. He was always looking forward. I covered Formula 1 for Autocar and Nigel used to ask me lots of questions about how Grand Prix drivers operated, how they travelled, whether they had managers and so on. Then he'd say something like, "I'm going to be winning Grand Prix races soon and I'll have a house in Spain." It wasn't a romantic notion, it was the way he wanted to live.'

7

ROSANNE

Nineteen-seventy-eight was without doubt the worst year of my life and by far the lowest time in my racing career. I had been given a lot of false promises and told I would get a lot of support and help which wasn't forthcoming. I was bitter about it, but there was nothing I could do. In many ways the frustration was the worst part; I felt as though I was powerless to stem the flow of disasters and body blows. I wanted to take control of the situation, but I couldn't see a way forward for my career. We needed money before we could begin to look for any solutions.

Rosanne had been the bread-winner ever since I had turned professional the year before and now I had to lean on her even more. She had a very good job and she put in all the hours that God sent. Although a lot of my time was spent looking for drives and for sponsors to pay for them, I carried on working for Peter Wall down in Cirencester, so Rosanne and I were forced to spend time apart, which put a strain on our marriage.

Although we were both very committed to getting on with what we had decided to do, namely my racing career, the awfulness of our situation began to put that commitment into question. When we were together we talked long into the night about the future. Should we abandon our plans? Should I forget about trying to be the Formula 1 World Champion and go back to engineering or should we stick to our guns, tough it out and hope that someone, somewhere would give us a break soon?

We reminded ourselves that what we were trying to do was something you can only do when you are young. We knew that eventually we would want to have children and so we needed to make the most of the opportunities now. In most jobs, you go to your office or place of work each day, do your job and if you like it and the company is happy with your work, you can do that job up until the day you retire. Before I left Lucas I would occasionally thumb through the magazine which the company sent out to all its employees. There were always photographs of people who were celebrating their retirement after years of faithful service. Sometimes the magazine would honour an old gentleman who had been with the company for 40 years. I used to look at the faces of these people and wondered how they could spend almost half a century doing the same job.

They had made their choices of what they wanted to do with their lives and, with Rosanne's support, I had made mine. Motor racing was calling us and we knew that although we had hit rock bottom, if we didn't dedicate ourselves even more at this time to what we believed we could do, then all the money we had lost and all the sacrifices we had made would be for nothing. It would just be a bad memory for the rest of our lives. I have never wanted the word 'regret' to be part of my vocabulary.

I know how competitive I am and could see that if I stopped racing now I would carry a chip on my shoulder about it for the rest of my life. We turned the situation around by looking at it in a different way. We drew positive lessons from the negative experiences we had suffered. The disasters and the knocks spurred us on to succeed and made us all the more determined not to give up.

I'm sure that there are a lot of people who, if placed in the same situation, would have given up. They would probably have stayed low for years and would have carried that bitterness and sadness through the rest of their lives. But in Rosanne I had a pillar of strength and together we managed to turn things around.

Unfortunately, renewing our commitment to racing did not put food in our mouths. This was a lean time financially. We had only Rosanne's salary plus the few quid a week that I earned from my office cleaning sorties to Cirencester. We were caught in a trap. We had only enough money to live on and to pay the bills on our rented apartment. We so badly wanted to take a holiday or just go out for a night to cheer ourselves up, but we couldn't afford to do anything. In the early days of our marriage, before most of the funds were channelled into racing, we used to take holidays abroad. That was out of the question now.

There was maybe an afternoon or a week during this period where we had a great time, but it was so infrequent that you almost couldn't remember it. And usually it was something which was free, like going swimming in a lake. We had sold almost everything so we didn't have any possessions we could enjoy. We used to spend a lot of time walking my parents' dog on a great big park called Umberslade. We would walk for hours, chatting and playing with the dog. It became a big part of our routine because it didn't cost anything and we could spend some quality time together relaxing, away from people and the pressures of the telephone and life in general.

Rosanne was so strong. She was just as committed to my racing career as I was, even though she had no family background in racing and had only become aware of it properly when she met me. She did not regard my goal of winning the World Championship as a pipe dream, as I'm sure many wives would have done under the circumstances. She believed in my talent and she knew as well as I did that if I could just get one decent shot at it, I would make good. We had only been married for three years, but she gave me all the support a man could reasonably ask of his wife and far more besides. It makes us appreciate what we have now all the more, because we have not forgotten those times when we had nothing.

Rosanne came into my life when I was seventeen. She is a year younger than me and we were both students at Solihull Technical College near Birmingham. Although we were not in any of the same classes, I had seen her around the college and she had really caught my eye. She looked bright, confident and strong and I knew that I wanted to meet her.

My chance came one morning while I was driving to college. I had passed my driving test and bought a second-hand Mini van. I saw her walking along the road, so I pulled over.

'Hey, you're going to the college, aren't you? Do you want a lift?'

She hopped straight into the car. She told me later that she only did that because she thought I was somebody else – a neighbour of hers – and that if she had realised it was a total stranger offering her a lift she would never have got in. As she has said since, 'It's funny how things happen in life, isn't it?'

It was only a short drive and we talked in general terms about this and that, but she made a major impression on me. We ran into each other more and more frequently at the college and before long we started going out together. It was a good relationship from the start and we made sure that we saw each other every day.

She was the youngest of three children from a loving family. She knew nothing about motor racing when I met her. Her brother watched the occasional Grand Prix on television, but didn't consider himself a fan.

I introduced her to karting and I think she could see immediately how important it was to me. What impressed me about her was how willing she was to muck in. Although I took her on some exciting nights out, we also had plenty of long nights in working on the kart and she became quite handy with the sandpaper and the plug spanner. She always used to stick around and help me and we developed a deep bond. Although karting was thrust upon her and she much preferred horse riding, she was behind me from the start and came to almost every race with my family.

Then came the Morecambe accident and she began to see the other side of racing. She was always nervous about watching me race – she is to this day – but Morecambe gave her a nasty shock. She was there when the priest gave me the last rites. She had never seen anything like that before, let alone when someone she cared for was the victim. It was her first experience of the dangers which motor sport can bring. It was a worrying time for her and, being fairly young at the time, she found that she was having to be very mature when dealing with a different side of life.

She could have tried to persuade me to stop after that, I'm sure many girlfriends would have done, but she could see how much it mattered to me and I suppose she could also see that my competitive instinct would always need an outlet. If it wasn't karting it would have been something else.

As well as being highly competitive, I have always been very aggressive and very physical. As I matured as a racing driver I channelled these characteristics into positive aspects of my driving, but before I met Rosanne I used to like raising hell with my male friends.

I don't scare easily and I was never afraid to get into something with someone bigger than me. Having said that I was pretty large myself at that time. As we all know, beer is very fattening and by indulging my taste for it my weight shot up to almost 200lbs, which is a lot for a man of 5ft 10in. It was all pretty pointless, but when you're a teenage male there is always pressure to be tough and to look after yourself. We used to dare each other to do daft things like jump off motor bikes at 30mph. That escapade landed one of my friends in hospital.

Rosanne was always a cut above all of that and I did not want her to get involved with that group of friends. In the early days of our relationship I would enjoy a civilised evening with her and then after I dropped her off I would go out again and hit the town with my friends. Gradually I changed, broadened my horizons and took more of an interest in the things which interested her. We would go on day trips in the car with a picnic, or visit stately homes and art galleries. She was really into horse riding, so I went along with her on rides. We enjoyed each other's company so much that it became second nature to me to want to do these things. After all it was only fair; she supported my karting and helped me work on the karts. We were happy and very much in love.

Rosanne and I had been together for four years when Lucas Aerospace asked me to go and work in America. They wanted to send a group of engineers to Englewood, New Jersey for nine months. The jet engines on the Tristar planes were experiencing problems with flame-outs and I had been specialising in the reheat side of the aircraft which is where the problem was.

We talked it over and decided that I should go, because the extra money that I would be paid would come in very useful. It was a very difficult decision. I would only be gone nine months, but when you are in love nine months seems like a lifetime.

Twenty-four hours before I was due to fly out, the managers at Lucas changed their minds and decided that it would be cheaper to send all of the faulty units back to England to be worked on. I was all packed up and ready to go. Rosanne and I had prepared ourselves mentally for my departure. When we learned at the last minute that it was cancelled, it made us look at each other in a different light.

I told Rosanne that secretly I had been thinking that I would die in America without her. It made her realise that we meant more to one another than the teenage lovers we had been for the past four years. We were so focused on what we wanted together and we realised that we both wanted to make the commitment to each other to spend the rest of our lives together. So we got married. I was twenty-one, she was twenty.

Between us we were earning good money at that time, so we put down a deposit and got a mortgage on a small house near where I used to go to school at Hall Green. It was the first of many big commitments we made together.

Getting married has all sorts of connotations but the most important thing is that you are best friends. At the heart of my relationship with Rosanne is a very good, very solid friendship.

We all feel low at times and at other times we feel strong. Sharing your life with someone is all about keeping a balance. Where Rosanne and I complement each other is that when I am low in a certain area she is like a bulldog and is incredibly strong and conversely when she is down in some way, I help her. That's how the chemistry works between us and we help each other out tremendously.

Of course it hasn't all been wine and roses. We had some major bust-ups in the early days before we were married, as we felt each other out. We are both strong-willed personalities and both quite stubborn. I had had several girlfriends before Rosanne and was always the dominant partner. From the word go Rosanne gave as good as she got; we even split-up a couple of times. We were only teenagers and you make some big mistakes when you're a teenager.

We don't agree on everything, but we have developed a friendship and an understanding which has carried us through the most trying times of our lives. We came from the same part of the world, we grew up together and we have an understanding, which is very important in a marriage.

At the beginning of 1979, Rosanne's mother died of a heart attack. She was only 54. It was an unbelievable blow. After the year we had just had it seemed like the knocks would never cease. Rosanne had lost her mother, with whom she was very close and I had lost a good friend. She was like a second mother to me. She was a marvellous woman and always a great arm of support to us in our struggle for success in racing.

The tide changed at this point. Instead of Rosanne supporting me financially, mentally and morally, I had to support her. She was devastated. It took her a couple of years to get over the loss. Rosanne's father was so distraught that I ended up making all the arrangements, handling the death certificate and so on. It was a harrowing experience.

Not long after the funeral I heard about a paid Formula 3 drive which was available. At the time most drivers had to bring sponsor money and pay the teams to drive, so a paid drive was almost unheard of. Unipart had gone in with Dave Price Racing and was offering £25 per week plus the use of a Triumph TR7 sportscar. It seemed too good to be true. I put on my brown chalk-stripe suit and went down to Price's headquarters in Twickenham, near London to talk him into giving me the job. After all the adversity we had recently endured I was very highly motivated and I was determined to make the drive mine.

Price already had one driver, a New Zealander called Brett Riley and was looking for a second driver who was British. He had heard about my Formula Ford success in 1977 and was also aware of what had happened to me with March the following year. Price is a laid-back Cockney and we had an amiable chat, although I'm sure I came across as very intense. I worked hard to persuade him that I was the man for the job. He seemed to agree and offered it to me without interviewing any more candidates.

I was back in business.

Dave Price, Formula 3 team manager: 'I'd studied the form and he'd obviously had a good career in Formula Ford. I had already made up my mind that Nigel was the bloke for the [Unipart] drive before I spoke to anyone else. At the time there were not many other talented British drivers around. It must have seemed like the deal of the century.'

8

THE BIG BREAK

I threw everything into that Formula 3 drive. I had to. When you're down and out and you get an opportunity like that it seems like the deal of a lifetime.

I said to myself, 'I've got to grasp this chance with both hands and not let go.' Whatever was required of me, whatever commitment was needed from me, I would do it. Brett Riley and I were able to make a little extra money by doing some work for Unipart, visiting dealers and so on and I always did everything that was asked of me. The word 'No' wasn't in my vocabulary at the time. Price couldn't believe the enthusiasm I had for everything. Only later, when he realised what I had been through before getting the Unipart drive, did he understand why I was so committed and so focused. I was grateful to him then as I am grateful to him now. He and Unipart were giving me the one thing which I had always strived for – a chance to race.

Although the March debacle had ended prematurely, I did compete in a handful of other races in 1978. My efforts with the March had not gone entirely unnoticed and I was given a Grovewood award of a one-off race in a Formula 2 car at Donington. My car, a Chevron, was to be run by Creighton Brown's Ardmore Racing team, with backing from petrochemical giant ICI. My team-mates were Elio de Angelis, a wealthy driver from Rome who I would become close to in years to come and Derek Daly, who went on to race in Formula 1 and IndyCars and is now an IndyCar commentator for ESPN television in America.

The car was not too bad and I liked the extra power it had. I went out in practice to get the feel of it. I felt quite comfortable and was quietly optimistic about what I would be able to do with it. I worked up to the pace in first qualifying but in second qualifying a car blew up in front of me, leaving a patch of oil on the track just over a blind brow. There were no oil flags out and I was travelling at top speed as the car shot through the oil, swapped ends and slammed into the barriers. It was a big accident. The team did not have a spare car so that was the end of my weekend.

I also did a couple of invitation races, driving a BMW saloon car in the BMW County Challenge. I enjoyed it tremendously, although I am much happier racing open wheel single-seater cars than covered wheel cars. At Silverstone I had a classic battle with Martin Brundle. He had been competing in the series and had his own well-sorted car, while I was the guest driver in the rather beaten-up 'celebrity car'. We got away from the others pretty quickly and had our own scrap, passing and repassing each other, which lasted the entire race. He was really good in those tin-tops and he beat me in the end after I tried an all or nothing move into the last corner. Terrific fun. I was understandably optimistic about my paid drive in F3. Here was a chance for me to show everybody what I was capable of.

I realised quickly that the situation, although a shot in the arm, had some serious drawbacks. Chief among these was the fact that as part of the Unipart deal we had to use Triumph Dolomite engines. My detractors in the press have filled many column inches over the years with claims that I used to 'whinge' about getting inferior engines to Brett Riley. The truth of the matter is that there was no such thing as a good Dolomite engine. As Dave Price put it, 'They were all crap.' The horsepower figures on the test bed at the factory were encouraging in theory, but in practice, when the engines were installed in the back of the cars, they were nearly 20 horsepower down on the Toyota engines used by our main rivals. It was a very difficult situation. Formula 3 is so competitive that a deficiency like that is almost impossible to make up.

From the word go I tried to make it up with my driving and often that meant pushing the car beyond its limit. Riley was a laid-back individual, one of those guys who likes to win the odd race, but wasn't too worried about it if he didn't. I was the opposite. I couldn't accept our power disadvantage and I wanted to win. I used to try to make up the difference by taking off some wing, thus reducing the car's drag and making it quicker in a straight line. Of course, the catch was that the car was harder to drive around the corners because there was less downforce pushing it down to the ground. To get around this I would turn in to the corners early while I was braking, carrying a lot of speed into the apex of the corner and by responding quickly to the car's attempts to slide, hustle it through the corner.

At the end of March we found ourselves back at Silverstone, where my 1978 season had started so well. It poured down on race day, but I managed to get into an early lead, ahead of Italian Andrea de Cesaris. He passed me, but he also missed out the chicane and was penalised one minute, which meant that, although he crossed the line first, I won the race. I was elated. Rosanne had brought her father along and it was his first ever motor race. Although it was only a couple of months after his wife's death and he was still in a state of shock, it seemed to cheer him up. It certainly cheered us all up. For Rosanne, who was still quite numb, it was a glimmer of light at the end of the tunnel of gloom and afterwards she told me that she was thankful for it.

The rain helped us that day as it helps anyone driving an underpowered car. When it's wet a small horsepower deficit doesn't matter as much. It's the skill of the driver that counts. That became clear at the next race. It was dry and the Toyotas were able to run away from us, which set the pattern for the rest of the season.

Being a laid-back person, Price liked to run a laid-back race team. He and the mechanics used to like to mess around, play tricks and make fun of each other. I'm all for playing a joke and having fun, it's a vital part of maintaining the equilibrium in a successful race team. But when it's time to get down to business, I am a very serious person. If you race to win you have to be serious. There is a time and a place for everything and much as I liked to let off steam occasionally, I always knew where I wanted to get to: the Formula 1 World Championship. Perhaps they were not conscious of that, which I suppose is understandable. On paper, the chances of me making it were miniscule, but I didn't see it that way. They were having fun racing F3, but I was completely focused on where I was going. At times they were perhaps too frivolous in their approach. We could all have done a better job if we had been a bit more serious.

The mechanics used to try to wind me up at the most bizarre times. One evening I was leaving the circuit when I heard one of my mechanics say to another, 'Dab a spot of oil on that brake nipple, would you, so that Nigel thinks we've bled the brakes.'

They had bled the brakes, of course, and they were just trying to have a laugh, knowing that I would hear them and react. But to me, as a driver, there is nothing funny about brakes that don't work. It's not a good subject for a joke.

We did have some good fun away from the track. We quite often stayed in rooms above pubs during a race weekend and, although I had stopped drinking, I used to go down to the bar in the evening to eat and relax with the team. Once I was playing darts with Dave Price and, as usual, I was playing to win. Price had hysterics because I was throwing the darts into the board so hard that he couldn't pull them out.

Our programme with the Unipart team took us not only to races in the British championship, but also to some European events. One of these was the traditional F3 race during Monaco Grand Prix weekend. Rosanne and I were both excited about going to Monaco. I had watched the Grand Prix countless times on the television and was looking forward to my first street race.

Hotel rooms are both rare and expensive in Monaco at Grand Prix time, so we borrowed a camper van and drove it down through France. The van was very old and well-used, but it was quite cosy and we were grateful for it. The drive down to Monaco seemed endless because the van was rather low on horsepower. We became very conscious of the contours of the road. Downhill it was fine and we gathered momentum, but we really struggled up the hills.

When we got to Monaco we couldn't find anywhere convenient to park. Monaco is a tiny place at the best of times, but when most of the place is fenced off with armco, it becomes very restricted. In the end we parked the van in the Formula 3 pits and operated from there. It worked fine, although we didn't have any shower facilities, so Dave Price let us use his room at the Beach Plaza Hotel to shower in. Every year when we went back to Monaco to race Formula 1 we stayed at the Beach Plaza and often used to laugh at the memory of us borrowing Dave's shower.

Neither Rosanne nor I are easily impressed. The ostentatious wealth of Monaco, the multi-million dollar yachts in the harbour, and the glamour of the Grand Prix scene didn't have much effect on us. The Grand Prix cars were impressive, though, and I was aching to drive one. To control one of those 600 horsepower machines around the twisty, armco-lined track, taking care not to let the car slide out too wide as you planted the power exiting the Casino Square – now that was a challenge.

The Unipart cars had failed to qualify for the Monaco race the year before, but we made up for it and I finished the race 11th. Over the years to come I would return to Monaco many times and have some of my best drives in a Grand Prix car there. It is my kind of circuit, one which demands a perfect blend of attacking, but controlled driving. Nevertheless over the years I became convinced that I had a permanent jinx on my driving there. I led at Monaco many times, but never won. Whenever victory was in sight, something always came along to trip me up.

Back in England, we continued to struggle for power against the opposition. I came in fourth at Brands Hatch, but apart from that, the results did not come. I tried everything I could to make that car go faster, but to no avail. I knew that I was as good, if not better than the guys who were winning, but without equal equipment, there was no way to prove it. It was frustrating.

Then something happened which was to change not only my career but also my whole life.

The British Grand Prix in mid-July is the biggest day in British motor sport. Traditionally over 100,000 people turn out, usually in blazing sunshine, to watch the big stars of Formula 1 and a host of support races, including F3.

During the weekend, Peter Collins, whom I had met at Silverstone the previous year and who was now the team manager at Lotus, came to find me. 'Come with me,' he said. 'I want to introduce you to somebody.'

I followed him into the Formula 1 paddock and he lead me to where the Lotus transporters, with their distinctive black and gold colour scheme, were parked. Lotus had totally dominated the World Championship the year before, taking their seventh Constructors' World title, and Mario Andretti had become their sixth World Champion. For 1979, Andretti had been joined at Lotus by another of the top names in Grand Prix racing, Carlos Reutemann.

Peter introduced me to the owner of the team and one of the real legends of motor sport, Colin Chapman. He looked just like photographs I had seen of him, with a sharp face, white hair and moustache, and his black cap. He said he was pleased to meet me and asked me about my season. We chatted for a while and he told me that he would be watching my race. As we parted he wished me luck and then said something which really stuck in my mind: 'It's about time we had another British driver at the top in Grand Prix racing.'

I was very honoured to meet Chapman and as we went away from the meeting his words echoed around my mind. Peter, who by now was obviously a firm believer in my ability, told me that there might be the possibility of a test drive in a Lotus if the 'Old Man' saw anything in me. He explained that Reutemann would be joining Williams for 1980 and the team wanted to find a new number two driver to partner Andretti.

It was not one of our most competitive weekends. I qualified 13th, one place ahead of a young Frenchman called Alain Prost, but was quickly able to move up to sixth place in the race. Watching my progress from a vantage point above the Woodcote chicane were Chapman, Collins and Peter Windsor. Two of them championing my cause, the other listening and watching silently.

Shortly afterwards Collins phoned to say that he had a job for me. Sadly it wasn't a Grand Prix drive, but he was looking for a trained engineer to visit the factories of the teams' suppliers and inspect the quality of their products. He would give me a basic Ford Escort to use and would pay me a basic salary plus fuel costs. As the Lotus headquarters was in Norfolk in the Southeast of England it would mean making an eight-hour round trip three times a week from my home in Birmingham, plus all the travelling to the suppliers. But it would leave me time to keep fit and to race for Unipart at weekends. More important, Peter said, it would give me a chance to learn about Formula 1 and to meet the 'Old Man' on a regular basis. I accepted his offer on the spot.

I began my new routine and despite being tired a lot of the time, it worked out well. Unfortunately, our competitiveness in F3 did not improve and we showed no signs of repeating the win with which we had started the season. Then things took a sudden and unexpected turn for the worse.

In September the championship brought us to Oulton Park in Cheshire. Oulton is a picturesque circuit, with a rolling track set among trees and hills. I had won there several times in Formula Ford and found the circuit challenging.

In the race I was locked in a tough fight with Irishman Eddie Jordan, who now owns his own Formula 1 team, and Andrea de Cesaris. Approaching a fast downhill corner called Cascades I was behind Jordan with De Cesaris in my mirrors. It did not occur to me that he might try anything through Cascades, it just wasn't the sort of corner where anything was ever going to be on without putting the other driver at risk. But try it he did, making a desperate lunge down the inside of me. It was a crazy move. The nose of his car lifted me into the air and once the wind got underneath my car it took off, somersaulting end over end. It seemed to go on for ever, before it finally came to a stop, upside down. It was such a horrific-looking accident that many spectators and some of the drivers thought I was dead.

When the rescue crew eventually got me out of the car I was in agony. My back was killing me and although I was relieved that my old neck injury hadn't been aggravated, I was worried about what could have happened to my back.

The X-rays showed that I had broken two vertebrae in my back and the doctors told me once again that I was lucky not to be paralysed. It was painful, but I had more mobility with this injury than with my neck. So I discharged myself as quickly as I could from the hospital and went home.

I was forced to miss a few races and once again the weeks dragged on with the boredom of injury. The specialists prescribed some pain-killers, but I didn't take them, because I wanted to be able to tell when I was getting better, in order to make a swift return to the track. After a couple of weeks I decided that I was well enough to begin training again. I had rigged up a makeshift gym at home and I got some huge blow-up photographs done of my accident. I stuck them up on the walls so that I could look at them while I exercised. It was highly motivating.

When you are feeling down, you only have to look at certain things and they bring you back to reality and help you to find your balance and your focus. That's what I did with the photos of my accident. It had put a big hole in my season and if left to fester inside me, the demotivating force of injury and despondency could have taken away my focus and my competitive edge. After the struggle I had gone through to get my career to this stage, there was no way I was going to let that happen. I was completely single-minded. The training was very painful, but it had to be done.

Two weeks later I got a call from David Phipps at Lotus. He told me that the team was going to be at Paul Ricard in the South of France the following week testing possible second drivers for 1980. He said they would also be looking for a full-time test driver. There was a shortlist of four drivers and my name had also been suggested by Peter Collins. Would I be interested in driving the car?

I nearly fell off my chair. I said that I would love to drive the car. We talked briefly about the test and then he said he had heard that I had been in an accident and was badly hurt. I said that I did have an accident but that his information was wrong if he had been told that I was hurt. He said that was alright then and he would look forward to seeing me next week.

As soon as I put the phone down I picked it up again and called my doctor. He didn't like the idea of me driving a Formula 1 car so soon after my accident, but I told him that nothing was going to stop me driving that car and if he wouldn't give me painkillers then I would get them from somewhere else. I think he could hear in my voice how determined I was to do this, so he relented and prescribed me a plentiful supply.

When I got to Paul Ricard I had a good look at the competition. There was Elio de Angelis, whom I had met during my one-off Formula 2 race in 1978. He had a full season of Formula 1 behind him, driving for the Shadow team. Then there was the American, Eddie Cheever, and the Dutchman Jan Lammers, both of whom also had F1 experience. Finally there was Stephen South, an Englishman who had a good reputation as a test driver and who had shown a great deal of talent in F3 and F2 and had received a lot of publicity in the British racing press. I was very much the outsider of the bunch.

Lotus had two cars available. South drove the development car and the rest of us drove the test car. The others drove all day and I was itching to be called forward to get my chance. The afternoon wore on and still there was no sign of when my turn would come. While I waited, Colin came over and we chatted for a while about my Formula 3 season and my aspirations in Formula 1.

At around 5.30 pm, with the light fading fast and the shadows lengthening over the track, I was asked to get into the car. The engine and transmission had been driven hard all day and I was informed that the crown wheel and pinion had begun to fail, so the car was jumping out of gear. They told me that I should just go out and get a feel for the car.

I went out and the first thing that struck me was the awesome power of the engine. As I exited the pit lane and planted my right foot on the floor I felt a sharp kick in the back and the acceleration was breathtaking. Ricard has a long straight, which is known as the Mistral Straight, after the famous Mistral winds which blow over Provence to the Mediterranean. In a Formula 1 car you reach over 200mph on that straight, before going into a blindingly fast long right hand corner called Signes, where you can really feel the g-forces tugging on your neck.

Going along the straight for the first time I told myself that, faulty gearbox or no faulty gearbox, I was going to make this test count. It might be the only chance I would ever have to drive a Formula 1 car and I should make the most of the opportunity. I pushed harder on the second lap and as I searched for the car's limits, I spun. I kept the engine running and did another slow lap to think about what I had just learned, then I began to push again. When I finished, after 35 laps, it was dark and the team had the lights on in the pits. While I had been driving I had blanked out the pain in my back, but now, as I got out of the car, I winced. My back was killing me.

At the end of the test I was quicker than Lammers and as quick as Cheever, which I was pleased with. My run had been cut short because it was dark and the car was worn out, but I had made my point.

De Angelis, the most experienced of the five drivers, had impressed the team with his knowledge about the car and his smoothness, so he was offered the Grand Prix drive. Colin and Peter wanted to give me the test contract, while others in the camp thought it should go to South. South queried some points in the contract, so Colin offered it to me straight away. He told me that I would be the team's official test driver and that if everything worked out, I would get to race in three Grands Prix the following season. I was in.

Rosanne Mansell: 'After he was injured at Oulton Park, Nigel had to stay in bed for weeks. I had to go to work every day because I was afraid that if I took time off to nurse him I might put my job with British Gas in jeopardy. I called home at every opportunity I had and used to bring him meals, but most of the time I just left the back door unlocked and friends and family would drop in to see him.'

Patrick Mackie, Ardmore Racing Formula 2 team manager: 'Creighton and I went to meet Nigel at the Grovewood Awards evening and he still had his neck in a brace from his Formula Ford accident. I remember wondering whether he'd be able to race a F2 car. But in practice he was scintillating, very impressive. He was some way off the pace to start with and we changed all kinds of things on the car but it made no difference. Then he went out and started taking half a second a lap off his times until he was right on the pace. He came into the pits and I remember him sitting there saying, "It's alright, don't change anything on the car, it's in me. I've found it now." I felt then that he had the determination and focus to be a World Champion. He had what it took to do a superhuman lap. It was a shame that he wasn't able to do that race.'

Dave Price, Formula 3 team manager: 'Anyone who sells their house to go motor racing has got to have a screw loose, but it worked for Nigel. It wouldn't work for most people but it did for him because he's got that much more – I don't know how you'd describe it really – I suppose the word is commitment. He is completely single minded – I've never met anyone who had so much belief in himself. It's incredible. If he could bottle it and sell it he'd make a fortune.

'He always put a lot of pressure on himself and it seemed worse because his team-mate Brett Riley was so laid back he was almost horizontal. Nigel felt, probably quite rightly, that he should be winning, whereas Brett was happy to make the best of a bad job. Nigel could never accept that the engines were all bad and that we couldn't win with them. He tried to make up for the lack of engine performance himself and he overdrove at times.

'I never thought that he was anything special at Formula 3 level, but you've got to give him credit for what he's achieved. He's done what no-one else has done; won the World Championship, the IndyCar Championship and 31 Grands Prix.

'My wife Carol doesn't come to the races as she hates them, but she always met the drivers I ran over the years and she still to this day says that Nigel was the nicest person I ever hired. She never worked with him, of course, but she found him polite and friendly and normal. One of his greatest strengths is that he hasn't changed at all, he's still completely normal and so is Rosanne. I can talk to them today and if I close my eyes it's just like going back to 1979. They're really nice people. I think if he has changed it's that he's more at peace with himself now because he's done what he's done.'

9

COLIN CHAPMAN

Colin Chapman's motto was 'In adversity we strive'. After what I had been through in the past few years it was a motto I could readily identify with. From the beginning we had the right chemistry and as we got to know each other we found that we had a lot in common. It meant a lot that a big name like Colin Chapman believed in me. He was the first person of real power in Formula 1 who saw that I had talent.

In retrospect, what he did was incredible. There are not many people at the top in Formula 1, then or now, who would take a penniless unknown over all 'The Chosen Ones' available at the time, and put him on the road to success. He not only did that but he stuck with me and supported me as I learned the game. He taught me a lot, not just about racing cars, but about life. If it hadn't been for Colin Chapman I would not have achieved what I have in my life. And if he had lived longer I know that he would have made me World Champion a lot sooner.

Chapman was a dogged, determined fighter. He oozed charisma and confidence and he was a brilliant designer. He had a real passion for technology and things new. When he wasn't working on a new idea for a racing car he would probably be designing a futuristic boat or a microlight aircraft. He adored flying, as do I, and we had many long conversations over dinner during race weekends about flying aeroplanes and helicopters. Occasionally we flew together and had some terrific fun away from the pressures of Grand Prix racing. Colin was a superb motivator and he taught me how to get the best from the people around me. He taught me to keep the pressure on everybody and to keep the engineers looking for ways to improve the car. A driver who just drives the car is less likely to be a champion than one who motivates everyone to give that little bit more and focuses the team on the goal of winning.

Colin was the founder of Lotus and one of the new breed of British racing car designers who revolutionised Grand Prix racing in the late fifties and early sixties, by putting the engines in the back of the cars and changing the whole way the chassis was constructed. He will be remembered as the great innovator and the man who gave the modern Grand Prix car its shape.

He was always ahead of his time, always looking for an edge over his rivals. In the late fifties he introduced the first fully adjustable suspension systems and brought in the idea of tuning the chassis to suit the demands of each individual circuit – set-up, as it is known today. Before that, Grand Prix cars were pretty much the same from circuit to circuit; there was hardly any adjustment to be made. If it was raining you would let a few pounds of air out of the tyres, but that was about it. The driver just had to do try his best to tame the beast he was driving and hope that his chassis was better designed or that his engine had more power than his rivals.

Colin was fascinated by aerodynamics and in the late sixties he pioneered the use of wings on Grand Prix cars to create downforce and increase cornering speed. In the late seventies he pushed the boundaries of aerodynamics out further when he introduced ground-effect, which increased cornering speeds even more by literally sucking the car down to the ground. Enzo Ferrari believed that the engine was the most important part of the racing car; Colin believed it was the chassis. He was a supreme designer and this was central to the success of the team because for most of his Formula 1 career most teams used the same engines, so the chassis was critical. Any edge you could develop over your rivals gave you a better chance of winning races. Time and again the other team owners would shake their heads in dismay as they caught their first glimpse of the latest Chapman innovation. Their designers would then be dispatched to the drawing boards to copy the idea.

Colin worked around the limits of the rule book and the history of Grand Prix racing is littered with examples of his pioneering genius. Ironically his last great innovation, the twin-chassis car, was just too radical for the governing body and the other teams to stomach and they banned it.

His success is the stuff of legend. In the early sixties, Lotus and the late great driver Jim Clark took the Grand Prix world by storm, winning two World Championships and narrowly missing out on three more. Who knows how much more they might have achieved together if Clark had not been killed in 1968? Clark's record of seven wins in one season lasted for over twenty years. It was a great honour for me when I won the World Championship in 1992 to be able to move that mark up to nine wins in a season.

I felt I had come full circle. When I was nine years old I saw Jim Clark race a Lotus and it made a deep impression on me. Growing up, the names Lotus and Jim Clark to me were synonymous with success in Grand Prix racing. You can imagine, therefore, how I felt when I found out that Chapman was telling close friends that I was the best natural talent he had seen since Clark.

To go from having no-one believe in me to drawing comparison with Clark was almost unimaginable. But it was important not to get carried away. There were still many people who didn't share Chapman's belief. I was an outsider who had to prove himself. I had to be 100% better than them just to prove myself in the eyes of my detractors. I had always believed that I had the talent to win Grands Prix and Colin's supportive hand on my shoulder really strengthened my self-belief.

I'm not easily impressed. I take people as I find them and I'm not wowed by stature. If someone is honest with me and the chemistry is right between us then I can get on with them, whether it's a big name or a nobody. But Chapman was something special. He was a fairy godfather to me. Some people say that he liked me because he saw himself in me; a fighter, single-minded and determined to succeed. Perhaps he identified with me because we both came from modest backgrounds with a burning desire to make something of our lives.

Whatever our spiritual affinities, the important thing was that he appreciated what I could do in a racing car. He liked a driver who would take one of his cars and wring its neck, a driver who always gave everything he had and more. He was a respectable racing driver himself and was very sensitive to what his drivers told him about a car's behaviour. He used his understanding of the driving side to tune the chassis. He was especially keen that his drivers should be on the limit in testing. To him there was no point driving at nine-tenths in a test because that wouldn't tell how the car would behave when it was driven flat-out in race conditions. If you haven't set the car up on the ragged edge then you will be stepping into unchartered territory when you push hard in the race.

Chapman taught me that if the driver is always at 100% then it is easier to tell whether an adjustment improves the car or makes it worse. It's a very simple equation; if you change something then go out and test it and if the lap time is slower, it's worse. If it's faster, it's better. Both driver and engineer can save themselves a lot of headscratching by working this way.

We took to each other immediately and within a year of working together he told a television interviewer that I was a future World Champion. Mind you, early on in our relationship I thought I had blown it.

The race team had had a mixed start to the 1980 season. Elio finished second in Brazil, but by the fourth race at Long Beach that was still the only points finish. Long Beach was a disastrous weekend for Lotus. Mario Andretti crashed out of the race on the opening lap and three laps later Elio was out too.

A few days later I was chatting with Peter Collins in his office when in walked Colin. He still looked edgy and preoccupied after the weekend of mishaps. I said hello, but he didn't reply, so I said that I was sorry about what had happened at Long Beach. He looked at me blankly and said nothing.

I said: 'You know what the problem was in Long Beach don't you?' He frowned,

'No, what was it?'

'I wasn't driving for you.'

As I said it I felt a wave of both elation and despair. Elation at having been so bold and despair when I realised that I might have made a huge mistake.

He turned on his heel and marched out of the office without saying a word. I looked at Peter, 'I've blown it, haven't I?' He raised his eyebrows. As it turned out I had hit Colin's sweet spot. He liked people who were cheeky without being offhand and he adored enthusiasm. The chemistry got better and better.

The job of test driver in those days was much more vague than it is today. Nowadays a test driver spends almost as much time in the car as the regular drivers. The Grand Prix schedule is so punishing and the cars are so physically tiring to drive that a team is only too happy to spread the workload onto a third driver. The top teams, Williams, McLaren, Ferrari and Benetton wouldn't dream of starting a season without a test driver. Back in the early eighties some people said that a test contract wasn't worth the paper it was written on. Rene Arnoux had had a Lotus test contract and had never even sat in a car, but I knew that Colin would give me a chance sooner or later.

A few months after the incident in Peter Collins' office I was called for my first proper test at Silverstone. I was told that both Mario and Elio were unavailable so I would be the only driver. The Lotus team, mechanics and engineers would be there just to work with me.

Because the test driver role was less secure in those days I knew that any mistakes I made would probably lead directly to the sack. This was no time for heroics. I needed to establish myself and no more. It was a bright, crisp day and the conditions were perfect for testing. Before I went out for my first laps of the circuit, the engineer Nigel Stroud told me to feel my way into the car, not to push too hard too soon. The main purpose of the test, he said, was to prove some aerodynamic modifications but there was no point in trying them until I could lap in the 1m 14.5s range. I got the impression that he didn't believe I was the man for the job and that he was mildly resentful of being sent to do a test like this with a raw Formula 3 driver.

I took it reasonably easy for the first few laps, feeling the car out, refamiliarising myself with the power of the engine and the braking capabilities. I looked around the dashboard to locate the temperature and oil pressure gauges and the rev counter. Then I began to push.

My fourth lap felt pretty quick and I crossed the line flat-out to start my fifth lap. The car felt fine, it turned in well to Copse corner carrying a lot of speed and the the grip was fantastic. The engine responded sharply as I planted the throttle coming out of the corner. The rest of the lap felt the same way and the speed was utterly exhilarating. I flashed under the Daily Express bridge at over 170mph before braking hard for the Woodcote chicane. A flick right, then left, just riding the kerb with the left front wheel, then right again. Power hard down across the start line. Instinctively I looked to the pit wall for a signalling board showing my previous lap time but the engineers were standing still on the wall. They had nothing to tell me.

Mystified, I carried on. Next time through there was still no board. As I roared around the circuit the thought crossed my mind that my last lap had only seemed fast to me and that in reality I was hopelessly off the pace. How could I be so far away from what the car should be capable of around here? I was pretty sure that with a few adjustments I might go a fraction of a second faster, but it would be only a fraction, no more. On top of that I was tired. I had been concentrating hard and the effort was exhausting. Was this it then? Was this where I would discover that my limit was way below Grand Prix standards?

I brought the car slowly down the pit lane, blipping the throttle to keep the spark plugs from fouling at low revs. I switched off the engine and raised my visor. I looked at the faces of the mechanics and Nigel Stroud. They looked slightly perplexed and Stroud looked positively white. I wondered what had happened. Was I really that disappointing? The mechanics pulled me silently back into the garage and began to inspect the car. Presently Stroud bent down and said, 'I suppose you think that you're bloody clever don't you?'

'Why? What's up?' I said.

'That lap you just did was a 1m 12.5s,' he said with a frown.

It was the fastest lap ever around Silverstone by a Lotus.

When I got home I rang Peter Windsor, who had given me a lot of information and encouragement before the test. He had been unable to make it on the day. He had been waiting for a call.

'How was it?' he asked anxiously.

'Terrible,' I said.

'Why, what happened?'

'I stuffed it into a wall.'

I heard him sigh over the phone. He was probably thinking that I would almost certainly be fired.

'I didn't really,' I added. 'I did a 1m 12.5s, the fastest they've ever had. I would have been on the second row of the grid for the last British Grand Prix with that time.'

The following week Elio tested at Silverstone and went a couple of tenths quicker. We went on to test at Brands Hatch and I took three tenths of a second off his best lap time there. For the second time in only a few weeks I had shown that I was as quick if not quicker than the regular drivers. I was ecstatic. The ball was really rolling now. Back at the Lotus factory Colin was quietly impressed. He congratulated me on my performance and said that he could see no reason why I shouldn't get a chance to do a Grand Prix. He had plans to take three cars to the Austrian Grand Prix in mid-August.

Although I felt I deserved a chance after the pace I had shown in testing, I still couldn't quite believe that it was really going to happen. After all, it was only four years after my first season of Formula Ford, just two years since I had been in despair after the March deal ran out and just one year after I was in hospital with a broken back. Now I was on the verge of breaking into Grand Prix racing. It seemed so bizarre, so erratic, so different from the steady rise to the top which you read about in the racing magazines. When the rumours began to circulate that I would make my debut, one of the leading British motor racing weekly magazines ran a short piece which said that they had heard that Nigel Mansell was in line to drive a third Lotus in Austria, but hoped that this was not true because there were many more deserving drivers. And this was in a British magazine, supposedly devoted to promoting British talent!

My car would be a Lotus 81B, a development car based on the 81 campaigned by Elio and Mario but with some modifications. The wheelbase of the 81B was seven inches longer than the 81, which was proving a difficult car to get up to speed and had been uncompetitive of late.

I knew that, like all of the big tests I had been put to along the way, I had to grasp this opportunity and give it everything I had. There would be no prizes for failure. Five days after my 27th birthday I flew with the team to Austria.

I was extremely nervous, but not overawed. I was well aware of the dangers for young drivers coming into the top level of the sport and making fools of themselves on the track. I would be mixing it with some of the great names, people I had looked up to and admired for years like Jacques Laffite, Alan Jones, Carlos Reutemann, Gilles Villeneuve, Didier Pironi, Emerson Fittipaldi and Jody Scheckter. There were four World Champions in the field and thirteen Grand Prix winners. These were very experienced guys and they were tough, hard fighters. On occasions, as I was quickly to learn, they could be real 'bastards', but there is no doubt that this was a crop of outstanding Grand Prix drivers. I knew that I could not let myself be psyched out by them and spend the whole weekend looking in my mirrors, hoping not to get in their way. It was clear that our cars were not going to be the fastest out there, in fact it would be touch and go qualifying the untried 81B.

The Osterreichring was an incredible place. It was the fastest circuit on the 1980 calendar, with an average lap speed of over 145mph and there were a couple of corners, especially the Bosch Curve, which demanded absolute commitment if you were going to get any sort of lap time. The cars were very unforgiving due to the ground effect, which basically took away most of the suspension movement. It was a brutal ride and the car gave you precious little feel. There was hardly any warning when it was about to get away from you. One second it could be fine and the next you could be gone. I struggled with the car in qualifying. The handling was awkward and the engine developed a misfire. I was headed for non-qualification, but ten minutes before the end of the session Colin put me into Elio's car and with only a couple of laps to work with I managed to take half a second off my previous best. More important, my time was only half a second slower than Mario's, which, given that I only had a couple of laps in the car, pleased me enormously. It knocked Jan Lammers' ATS-Ford off the grid and got me into the race in 24th place.

I was not carried away with the excitement of starting my first Grand Prix. I was nervous, of course, but I didn't have any bouts of self-consciousness, suddenly realising where I was. I took it all in my stride. I felt I deserved to be there and although I was grateful for the opportunity, I wished I had a more competitive car for the race.

Sitting on the grid I composed my thoughts. I would run as quickly as I could without taking any unnecessary risks. The important thing was to finish as strongly as possible, there was no point in trying to be a hero. I needed to learn and to get some racing miles under my belt.

With a few minutes to go before the start, the mechanics put the final touches to the car, which included topping up the fuel tanks using a gravity feeder. I began to feel an intense burning pain in my backside and down my legs. I wondered for a second what it was before I realised that it was fuel, which must have spilled over. I told them what had happened and they asked me if I wanted to get out of the car. I couldn't believe it. Minutes away from my first Grand Prix and I'm being asked if I want to get out. I told them that I needed another solution, so they tipped a bucket of cold water down the back of my seat to try to dilute the petrol. It felt lovely and I forgot about the burning feeling.

The start was incredible. Coming off the pace lap everyone took their places on either side of the track. I was the last to come to a stop. Seconds later the lights far off in the distance went red and then green. There was an explosion of noise and smoke and colour and I leapt off the line and accelerated up through the gears as hard as I could, driving into the heart of the jostling and the confusion. Everyone funnelled into the first corner and the race was on.

I was totally absorbed and completely focused on my driving for the first ten laps or so. Then I began to feel the same burning sensation in my seat, which spread down to my legs. The water had clearly been a placebo and not a cure. The pain grew increasingly severe. I really noticed it on the straights, where I allowed myself a brief rest and cast a quick eye over the dashboard. It became unbearable, it was like being slashed with a knife. The torture lasted until lap 40, when the engine blew up and I coasted to a halt. I have to admit that I was relieved to be put out of my misery. I could hardly walk when I got out of the car as my hamstrings had been shortened. I had the burns dressed and watched the rest of the race. Colin was happy. I had driven well, without incident, but the fuel spillage had rather dominated proceedings.

I went home and spent the night of my first Grand Prix flat on my front in Birmingham Accident Hospital having the blisters on my backside attended to. Grand Prix racing is so glamorous!

Two weeks later I got another chance. Colin wanted me to run the 81B again in the Dutch Grand Prix at Zandvoort. Once again I had problems with it, this time slightly more worrying. On the first day of qualifying one of the wishbones in the suspension broke. I was having a torrid time in second qualifying when the engine blew up. With 17 minutes left in the session, Colin said, 'Put him in Elio's car.' There wasn't even time to change the seat. Once again I had to do the best I could in the few laps remaining. It felt fantastic to get into a car that worked. It was the first time that I saw how the drivers could do the quick lap times and what sort of car was needed to qualify further up the grid. I'm sure that if I had had a little more time to get used to the car and my own seat I would have gone quicker, but after three laps I managed a lap good enough for 16th on the grid.

Once again I was encouraged to find that my time looked good against my team-mates. Elio was only two-tenths of a second quicker and Mario only three-tenths. I was happy with my speed. It had been a delicate balancing act of controlled aggression. Of course I had to go as fast as I could, but if I had crashed I could have been booted out. After all, I was still only the test driver. But I was touched by Colin's compassion in giving me a chance in Elio's car. In the race itself I lasted only 16 laps before the brakes failed and I was forced to retire.

My third appearance would be in the European Grand Prix at Imola. Unfortunately I went off the road in the first qualifying session and couldn't get the spare car going fast enough to qualify it for the race, so I had to sit that one out. Colin said that I could have another try at the United States Grand Prix, but the week before we were due to leave, Mario had a huge accident in Canada and wrote off his race car. He would be forced to use my car in America so I was told to stay at home. It was a big disappointment, especially as the memories of Imola still rankled.

Mario told Colin that he would be leaving for Alfa Romeo at the end of the year. Elio would become the number one driver and the team needed a number two. Naturally there was plenty of speculation about who Colin would choose. He was keen to have a British driver in the car and he told me that I would get the job, but that he could not announce it for a while until he had persuaded the sponsors to take me. At the time Lotus was backed by Essex petroleum company, which was run by a flamboyant character called David Thieme.

Thieme used to wear ornamental sunglasses and a black felt Spanish hat and invited lots of 'beautiful people' to Grands Prix. He was the only person who was ever allowed to smoke a cigar anywhere near Colin. He loved the idea that Elio was an Italian aristocrat racer and after the Ricard test in 1979 he had insisted that Elio get the drive, because he would fit in well with Essex's jet-setting guests at Grands Prix.

He was less keen on having me as a number two in 1981. He was quoted in one of the weekly magazines as saying that there was no way I would get the drive. The press wrote that Jean-Pierre Jarier would be announced soon as Lotus' new driver. Curiously, considering that I was the test driver and had already done two Grands Prix for the team, no-one linked my name with the drive. I kept my silence. It was agony not being able to tell anybody while reading all these stories, but I never believed that Colin would let me down. He had told me that the drive was mine and I would just have to wait. Just before the start of the season Colin made the announcement. I was now officially a full-time professional Grand Prix driver.

I would be paid £25,000 for the year, but out of that I had to pay my own travel expenses, hotel bills, hire cars and so on, all of which were very expensive. We would be going to Argentina, Brazil, Canada and twice to America as well as all of the European races. I would only be able to afford to bring Rosanne to a few races, which was a real shame. I hated the idea of leaving her behind after we had both worked so hard to get to this point.

One of the most touching moments in my experience with Colin came on the eve of the Monaco Grand Prix that year. I had qualified third on the grid in only my ninth Grand Prix weekend and that night we all went out to dinner. I was pleased with my performance, but I was a little subdued because it looked as though this would be Rosanne's last race. Colin picked up on my mood and asked what the problem was. I explained the situation and said that I would love for her to give up work and come with me to all the races because she gave me such a lot of motivation. Colin thought for a second and then tapped his glass with a fork. He said, 'Nigel did an outstanding job in qualifying today and I want everyone to know I've doubled his retainer so Rosanne can come with him to all the races.' And that was it. Colin came from an era when drivers didn't make the huge demands they do today and it was up to the team owner to make them happy. Everything Colin did he did because he felt it was the right thing to do at the time.

The following year, for example, I wanted to earn some extra money by racing in the Le Mans 24 hours sportscar race. When I asked Colin, he immediately refused permission. I said: 'In the contract you can't unreasonably withold permission and he replied: 'I haven't just invested £2.5 million in you this past year, just for you to get yourself wiped out at Le Mans.'

He sat me down and explained that out of the 100 or so drivers at Le Mans every year, only 20 or so were real professionals, and the rest were club drivers or once-a-year drivers. He said that the difference in speeds between the faster cars and the cars in the lower classes was horrendous and that a lot of accidents happened because of the lesser quality drivers competing. I explained that I'd been offered £10,000 just to drive and that was a lot of money to me.

'I don't really want to do it, ' I said, 'But it's a lot of money. I don't get paid much. I'm not complaining about that, because I'm very grateful for this opportunity, but that's the way it is. I need to earn some more money.'

Colin said, 'I want you to stay at home that weekend. I will pay you ten thousand just to stay at home. That's how much I care about you, okay?'

When Colin died of a heart attack at the end of 1982 the bottom dropped out of my world. Part of me died with him. I had lost a member of my family. He was only 54 and had always seemed to have so much vitality and so many ideas. At the time of his death he was working on a design for a microlight which he believed would change the face of personal air transport. We will never know what other miracles of engineering he might have come up with, nor what successes we might have had together, if he had lived a little longer.

I cannot overstate the influence he had on my career and my life. He was my guru. He taught me about the importance of money and the value of kindness. He took me from a penniless Formula 3 driver and within two years made me a millionaire in Formula 1. He was the first person who showed me that the belief that I had always had in myself and my talent was entirely justified.

In Colin Chapman I knew a very warm and very loving human being who was at times kinder and more understanding than my own father.

Peter Collins, Lotus team manager: 'What Chapman liked about Nigel was that he was a risk-taker and a racer and he was determined; all the things the Old Man was. He had a lot of respect for him and I think that he could see a lot of himself in Nigel. When Nigel finished third in only his fifth race and then qualified third for the next race in Monaco, Chapman realised he had something special on his hands and he made sure he didn't lose him.'

10

TAKING THE ROUGH WITH THE SMOOTH

My first full season in Formula 1, 1981, was one of the most turbulent years in Grand Prix history. The governing body, the FIA, was concerned that the cornering speeds were getting too high and wanted to ban the aerodynamic skirts which gave the cars the ground effect. But a ban on skirts would put the emphasis back on engine power and would handicap the British constructors like Lotus, Williams and Brabham, most of whom were still using the Ford Cosworth V8 engine. These teams, under the banner of the Formula One Constructors Association (FOCA), wanted to ban the immensely powerful and expensive turbo engines which had been introduced by Renault and picked up by Ferrari.

The sub-plot to the story was the power struggle for control of Formula 1 between the FIA, led by Jean-Marie Balestre and FOCA, led by Brabham team owner Bernie Ecclestone. The FIA sided with the manufacturer-run teams in an attempt to topple Ecclestone. It was to be a very trying year and one of the principal victims of the political turmoil was Colin's latest innovation, the twin chassis Lotus 88.

Colin and his team of engineers had developed the 88 in great secrecy. The idea was to have one stiffly sprung chassis, which would have little or no suspension movement, but which would maintain constant aerodynamic characteristics. In a separate chassis, the driver and the fragile parts of the car would be isolated from the bumps which the lack of suspension in the primary chassis would cause. In other words there would be two separate chassis with two separate suspension systems. It was a brilliant idea.

Unfortunately the other teams didn't see it that way. Although there was no specific rule in the FIA regulations which made the car illegal, the establishment and the other teams didn't want it. When

Colin had introduced ground effect a few years earlier and blitzed the 1978 World Championship, all the other teams had been forced to spend millions on wind-tunnel research to copy him. They were not willing to go through it all again to copy the Lotus 88.

At the first race of the season in Long Beach the car was passed by the scrutineers, but protested by almost all of the teams, who threatened to pull out of the race if the 88 was allowed to run. I qualified seventh on the grid in a conventional Lotus 81, the previous year's car, while Elio tried to qualify the new 88. He was given the black flag, ordering him to return to the pits. There was a long meeting and the car was thrown out. Colin was shattered. He would spend a lot of money on lawyers and court cases to try to prove the car was legal but the others just wouldn't let it run and the saga would carry on for race after race.

Long Beach was only my second ever street race and my first in a Grand Prix car. I made a mistake in the race, clipped a kerb and slammed into a wall, damaging one of my rear wheels. I was forced to retire.

The next race on the calendar was the Brazilian Grand Prix in Rio de Janeiro. After all of the aggravation at Long Beach we were looking forward to a few days in Rio to relax. One afternoon I was on the beach with Rosanne, Elio and a few of the team. Peter Collins was trying to bodysurf, but he misjudged the tide and got dragged out by a rip current. He tried to swim back to shore but found himself going nowhere. He waved to us for help and at first we thought he was just fooling around. Then I realised he really was in trouble, so I went in after him.

When I got to him he was in bad shape. He was tired and I think he had given up. I grabbed hold of him and shouted at him in the hope it would keep his adrenalin going. I headed for a point further down the beach and the waves brought us around. He said that I had saved his life and certainly the incident brought us closer together. He had been one of my biggest supporters and without him working on Colin to give me a chance I might never have been driving Formula 1 cars so soon. It was a frightening incident, but it was nothing compared with the horror of Belgium.

I remember the 1981 Belgian Grand Prix at Zolder as much for the accidents which killed one mechanic and seriously injured another, as I do for the elation I felt when I stepped onto a Grand Prix podium for the first time.

The weekend began disastrously. In the pit lane a mechanic from the Osella team fell between the wheels of Carlos Reutemann's Williams and died the following day from head injuries. The paddock was rocked. It had been a long time since a mechanic had been killed.

The start of the race was delayed and rather chaotic. In the ensuing confusion Riccardo Patrese stalled his Arrows and a mechanic jumped over the wall to restart it. The green light was given and Patrese's team-mate Siegfried Stohr drove straight into the mechanic, sandwiching the guy between the gearbox and rear wing of Patrese's car. I was right behind them and watched this horror show play out in front of me. I was sure the guy was dead and I thought he'd probably been chopped in half.

I was numb in the car, my legs wouldn't work, my arms wouldn't work and I felt rigid with fear. I felt sick and I was crying my eyes out inside my helmet. I didn't know what we were doing there. I thought, 'We're driving these machines that kill people. That's two people this weekend.' The race was stopped immediately and by the time Nigel Stroud came to my car I was in quite a state. He suggested I should get out of the car and try to get it out of my mind. I said, 'Nigel, if I get out of this car I'll never get back in it again.'

Rosanne came over and tried to calm me down. I told her that I had never seen anything so horrific in my life. She talked to me calmly and before long Nigel came back to tell me that the mechanic was not dead. He had only broken one of his legs and the doctors said that he would be alright. He had been very lucky.

I'm sure that I would never have got into a racing car again had I stepped out of my Lotus that day. It was not the only time that I have ever been frightened in a racing car, but it was one of the most extreme moments of fear that I have ever experienced.

But you just have to deal with it and put it out of your mind. The race was restarted and I got into a rhythm and was lapping quickly and making up places. For most of the race I had Gilles Villeneuve in the Ferrari breathing down my neck and I held him off for lap after lap. It was a really terrific fight. Gilles was so brave and committed. He was one of the fastest drivers ever to sit in a Grand Prix car and certainly one of the drivers I most admired. Beating him that day was another important milestone in my development as a Grand Prix driver.

It began to rain and as the downpour got heavier the race was cut short. Carlos Reutemann was declared the winner with Jacques

Laffite second in the Ligier and I was third. I felt on top of the world. It was an overwhelming experience. The swing of emotion I had experienced in two hours, from the shock and paralysing fear at the start to the ecstasy at the end, was enormous. I climbed the podium, collected my flowers and my first Grand Prix trophy and looked at the faces in the crowd, which had surged onto the track. I looked at Carlos standing on the top of the podium and wondered how long it would be before I would stand up there. The Argentinian national anthem was played for Carlos and then the British anthem was played for the winning constructor, Williams. Although it was not being played for me I felt a lump in my throat. It had been quite a day.

The momentum carried through to the next race in Monaco, where I qualified third and Colin doubled my retainer. I began to feel that I really belonged and I learned that some of the other team owners had begun to take an interest in me. Some, like Mo Nunn of the Ensign team, had made enquiries to Colin about the nature of my contract and whether he would be interested in letting me go. Colin refused. I also heard that Patrick Head, the Williams designer was talking about me. He, like Colin, was known to like a driver who pushed a car hard and I was told that he was asking a lot of questions about me around the paddock. All of this was gratifying, but I had experienced enough let-downs, dashed hopes and broken promises to know that there are no guarantees in this sport.

I retired from the Monaco race with suspension problems, but bounced back at the following race in Spain, where I finished sixth and scored another point. Many drivers don't score a single point in their first season and I already had five, including a podium. I was anxiously looking forward to my first British Grand Prix at Silverstone. The circuit had brought me a great deal of success over the years and it was the first Grand Prix track which I didn't have to learn from scratch. It was to prove one of the most bitter disappointments of my career up to then.

The RAC Motor Sports Association had cleared a modified version of the Lotus 88 in pre-race scrutineering and it looked as though Colin's baby would get its maiden outing. Unfortunately, the other teams protested against the car on the first day of the meeting and it was again thrown out. Because they had been given assurances by the RACMSA that the car would be eligible, Lotus had not anticipated this and only had one 87 on hand, which was given to Elio. My outlawed 88 was taken to pieces and converted into an 87. The mechanics put in an incredible effort, working all night to make a car for me to qualify in the next day, but it was never really on. They ran out of time and although I gave it everything I had, I could not get the car going quickly enough to make the cut. I was crushed. I have always been extremely patriotic and I had seen my first British Grand Prix as an opportunity to show the rest of the world what Britain can do. I was still relatively unknown, although my third place at Zolder had created a minor stir in the press and I was aware of a small group of British fans who were behind me. I could not quite believe that I hadn't qualified. My career had begun to gather pace in recent months, but now it felt as though one of the wheels had come off.

A few hours after qualifying Rosanne and I were in the paddock feeling miserable when Colin came over and put his arms around us both. 'I'm so sorry about this,' he said. 'You're just the victim of some crazy politics.' He knew that we were hoping to move house, but were short on the mortgage. He asked me how much we needed and I told him. He got out his cheque book and a pen and wrote a cheque on the spot for the full amount, which was £40,000. 'I hope this goes some way towards making up for it,' he said with a tense smile.

We couldn't believe his generosity. Colin had seen his most radical and brilliant design banned without anybody being able to produce a valid article in the rules which the car was supposed to have contravened. He had spent hundreds of thousands of pounds on developing the car and almost as much again on lawyers and court cases to appeal against FISA's decisions, but here he was compensating us for our disappointment. His heart must have been breaking. He had been so incensed after the 88 was thrown out in Argentina that he issued a smouldering statement which ended, 'By the time you read this I shall be on my way to watch the US Space Shuttle, an achievement of mankind which will refresh my mind from what I have been subjected to in the last four weeks.'

We soldiered on with the Lotus 87 for the remainder of the year, but there was little joy until the last round of the championship, around the car park at Caesars' Palace in Las Vegas. I qualified strongly in ninth place and had a good race to finish fourth, just ahead of Nelson Piquet in the Brabham, whose two points for fifth made him World Champion. I was later to find out that my performance had caught the imagination of Frank Williams, who had won the championship the year before with Alan Jones. He asked Colin if he could take me to replace Jones, who had decided to retire. Colin said that he would rather give up Grand Prix racing than let me go. Little did I know it then but, over the next fourteen years, my involvement with Frank was to become part of Grand Prix folklore.

Over the winter of 1981 I reflected back on my first full season of Formula 1. Despite the backdrop of political turmoil and the distraction of the whole Lotus 88 saga, it had not been a bad year, although in some ways my third place at Zolder had come too soon. I was left with the feeling that I could have done better. I had outqualified Elio five times in thirteen races and my third place qualifying performance at Monaco had been a real turning point. I felt that I had thrown my hat into the ring and enough people were talking about me to make me feel that I had at least made my mark in Formula 1.

I looked forward to 1982, but it was to be a disastrous year with more tragic overtones.

The first thing that went wrong was that Colin hired a new team manager, Peter Warr, who had been with the team before, but who had spent the last couple of years with Keke Rosberg at Fittipaldi. Shortly after that Peter Collins, one of my main pillars of support, left the team. Although Colin was still in charge, the rot set in when Warr arrived. Warr's whole style of management seemed to be to put all the emphasis on the number one driver and make the number two feel that he had no confidence in him. It was as if you just didn't exist and you certainly weren't in a position to make any demands.

My whole philosophy of life and racing relies on having a small group of people around me who believe in me and share the same desire for success. As my career has progressed I've been able to set things up the way I choose, but in the early days when I was still very much the number two driver, I had to put up with what I was given.

Warr is without doubt one of the most provoking people it has ever been my misfortune to meet. He is one of the 'old school' types and although he was in the Royal Artillery for a while, he had a warped idea of respect and authority and he was obviously used to barking orders at people and having them treat him with respect. He didn't seem to grasp that in motor racing the way you motivate people is quite different. He thought that he knew more about driving racing cars than anybody else and used to try to tell Elio and me what to do.

Right from the off he took a dislike to me because I had such a clear idea of what I wanted and how I was going to get it. He wanted me to take orders from him, which was never going to happen, and he could also see that I had developed a very close rapport with Colin which made him jealous. When Colin offered me a new contract Warr got very upset. He told people behind my back that I didn't deserve that kind of attention and that I had a lot to learn. He thought that Derek Warwick was a future World Champion and badly wanted to get him into the team. But Colin wanted me and put his name to a three-year deal to prove it.

Incredibly, given the state Rosanne and I had been in just three years before, the deal Colin was offering guaranteed to make me a millionaire. The difference between the two situations couldn't have been more different. It was as if 1978 had been in another lifetime. It was a great feeling when I realised that, after all the heartache and the pain and the endless months when we couldn't afford to do anything, I was about to become a millionaire. I knew that if I managed the money wisely, it would guarantee financial security for myself and my family for the rest of my life.

I remember that when the contract was first put in front of me I wouldn't sign it. Colin was flabbergasted. 'What's wrong with you?' he said. 'I'm making you a millionaire!' I told him that there were certain things in the contract with which I didn't agree. Colin got angry and said that I'd never drive for anyone again if I didn't sign. I was only 28 years old and a veteran of a mere seventeen Grands Prix, but I was sure of what my heart was telling me.

'You've got to understand, Colin,' I said, 'I've always believed that if you don't feel right about something, you can't sign a document and commit yourself.'

He went crazy and said I was ungrateful, but I said, 'Look, you might be 100% right, but I'm willing to walk away from this and from Formula 1 if that's what it comes to because I don't feel right about this contract. There are things in here which don't sound right.'

My career might have ended there, but because of the nature of my relationship with Colin, he calmed down and asked me to explain what I wasn't happy about. It didn't take long. The way the contract read it was very commercial and described me like a commodity. I wanted it to be made more human, to reflect the fact that I am a human being, not a piece of property. When I'd finished explaining he said, 'You are a funny bugger, aren't you? If I change a few tiny things you'll be happy, is that it?' I nodded.

'And you were prepared to walk away from a million-plus deal for this?'

Once I discovered kart racing as a child, I was hooked. All my spare time was taken up working on my kart and travelling to events. Here I am age 11 at an early driver's briefing (above left). Note the motorcycle-style leathers which kart racers wear for extra protection. I won a lot of trophies during my junior karting years (above right) and began to race internationally. An early 'off' (below) but nothing broken. Note the racing number.

I continued to race karts (above) until I was 21, then, against the wish of my parents, switched to single seaters. It was tough, but with the help of good friends like John Thornburn (below), I won a national Formula Ford Championship in my first full year of racing despite a broken neck.

Oulton Park 1979 (above). This is one of the photos of my back-breaking Formula 3 accident which I had enlarged and pinned to the wall of my gym to motivate me as I trained to get back to strength. It was a frustrating year, with only one win (below, with team mate Brett Riley) at Silverstone.

I have always been aware of the history of our sport. I would love to have seen Juan Manuel Fangio race (above far left). I saw Jim Clark (above left) race a Lotus in the sixties and it made a huge impression on me. In the 1970s I rooted for the gutsy Ronnie Peterson (top) and for Jackie Stewart (main pic). In my own time Gilles Villeneuve (above) was one of the greats and a close friend.

The late, great, Colin Chapman (above and main pic) shakes hands with Brian Wray of JPS, watched by Elio de Angelis and David Thieme of Essex Petroleum at the launch of the Lotus team in 1981. I would never have achieved what I have without the generosity and wisdom of this extraordinary man. (Below) My first taste of Monaco in a Formula 1 car in 1981 was sweet. I qualified third for only my ninth Grand Prix and Colin doubled my retainer.

Keke Rosberg (above left) a great World Champion and a good friend. Elio de Angelis (above right) was my team-mate at Lotus for four seasons. He was a gentleman and a gifted human being. A great pianist. He sadly lost his life at Paul Ricard testing. (Below) My first Grand Prix win came at Brands Hatch in 1985 and was the first of five wins on home soil. A moment of tranquility (right) in the Isle of Man, our home for ten years.

My first spell at Williams lasted four years and yielded 13 wins. One of the sweetest was the 1986 British Grand Prix at Brands Hatch (main pic) where I beat my team-mate Nelson Piquet (left). Nelson was furious that there were no team orders. Williams has always prided itself on engineering excellence, thanks to people like David Brown (below left) and Patrick Head (below right).

The moment of heartbreak (main pic). Adelaide 1986 and the tyre blow out was without doubt the biggest disappointment of my entire life. The fans helped me to pick myself back up (top left) and gave me strength to take on the top drivers of the time: (from left) Ayrton Senna, Alain Prost and Nelson Piquet.

I loved being a Ferrari driver, although at times the politics were frightening! I began my Ferrari career in the best possible way with a win in Brazil 1989 (main pic) in a car which had proved totally unreliable in testing. I had the great honour to be the last driver to be signed personally by Enzo Ferrari (top right) before he died. My team mate in 1989 was Gerhard Berger (above right). Lifting a wheel at Monza in 1990 (left). The 'tifosi' get behind their man (right) at San Marino.

I have been very fortunate that my job has allowed me to meet and become friends with champions from other sports. Former motorcycle World Champion Barry Sheene (above) is a great character and can always make me laugh. I have known golfer Greg Norman (below) since 1986 and we developed a close friendship both on and off the course.

'Yes, I was,' I said. 'It just didn't feel right.'

He made the changes, we signed the deal and hugged each other. I was going to be a Lotus driver for the next three years.

At Monaco Peter Warr and I had our first serious bust-up, which set the tone for our future relationship. He was in his dictator mode and got on his high-horse with Elio and me about what tyres we should use, how we should set the cars up and so on. I had enjoyed another podium finish earlier in the season in Brazil, where I came third, and with my new contract in my pocket I felt more settled and more self assured. I was comfortable that I knew what I was doing. I was regularly running towards the front with the big names, I believed in myself and I was doing the best job I could. Colin made me feel that I had been right to believe that I had a lot of potential. I was convinced that with the right equipment I could do as well as anyone else in the field.

But as far as Peter Warr was concerned I didn't have a clue. To listen to him you would think that he knew it all and had achieved more than Colin and the engineers put together, when in reality most of what he had achieved had been on Colin's coat-tails. I know that I wasn't the first person that he had wound up. John Thornburn told me that Jim Clark was once so irritated by Warr that he and Graham Hill had thrown him into a river! So I was in good company.

Things came to a head in Monaco when I was sitting on the phone waiting to do a live radio interview, which had been set up a long time before. Warr wanted me to go and talk to some sponsors and I said that I would be right there after I'd done the interview. He stood there, staring at me and said, 'I'm telling you to talk to the sponsors now.' That got my back up and I said, 'Unless you want to move me physically I am going to do what I've promised to do and then I'll talk to your sponsors. Anyway this interview is for their benefit.' When I did see the sponsors I apologised for the wait and they said they quite understood.

But Warr had stormed off to find Colin, who summoned me to come and see him. Warr was sitting there already and Colin wanted to know what was going on. He told me what Warr had said and asked for an explanation. I said, 'Listen Colin, as far as I'm concerned and Elio as well, the way he acts you'd think that he's the best engineer we've got and the best tyre technician in the business. I don't know why you don't put him in the bloody car, because he must be the best driver as well. I can't understand why you bother to employ Elio and me because he wants to do everything. The situation is a complete joke. If he does what he's supposed to do then I can live with that, but I can't stand him telling me how to drive the car. It's doing my head in.'

Warr smashed his fist on the table and shouted, 'That's not fair, that's not fair.' The situation needed defusing and Colin tried to calm us both down. He told me that I had to do what I was told and I said, 'Colin, I have signed a three-year contract with you and you know that I would do anything in the world for *you*. But if you want me to take orders from him then I have no alternative but to leave.'

It was a relief to get all this anguish off my chest. Being young and impulsive I stood up and said, 'Right, I'll go then. I won't drive tomorrow.' Colin sat me down and explained that if I had any problems, I should deal direct with him. But I should understand that Warr was very experienced and there was no reason why we shouldn't work together. I'm sure he could see that Warr was being unreasonable, but he clearly had a lot on his mind and wanted some peace. I shook hands with Warr and we agreed to start again, but inside we both knew that the relationship was doomed.

From that moment on Warr seemed to take every opportunity to bad-mouth me behind my back. He did me no favours when it came to my relationship with other people in Formula 1, especially the press and the other drivers. For the next three years he undermined my confidence and any driver will tell you that, along with talent, confidence is the most important commodity you have. Once you start to question your own ability, you are in for a really tough time. It was the beginning of one of the most difficult phases of my life.

Another major problem was the new car. The Lotus 91 was cleaner and lighter than the 87, but it didn't have the development behind it to make it really competitive. Because all of the effort in the last couple of years had been focused on the twin-chassis car, the engineers were well behind the opposition in other key areas of development. Elio and I were in a no-win situation. The car handled well on fast circuits like Silverstone and the Osterreichring, but we didn't have a turbo engine so we were left behind on the straights and it was awful to drive on tight circuits, where our nimble Cosworth engine would have helped us. Elio managed to win at the Osterreichring, beating Keke Rosberg's Williams by a fraction of a second, but only after most of the turbos had retired.

Having gone on to drive some of the best Formula 1 cars ever designed, I can say without hesitation that I don't think I drove a good

Lotus Formula 1 car. I joined the team as it was beginning its decline. Things go in cycles in motor racing. No team can stay on top for long. After the glory days of the sixties and the domination they enjoyed in 1978, there was no getting around the fact that Lotus was in the doldrums in the early eighties.

There was also a lot of tragedy in 1982. It began with the death of Gilles Villeneuve in qualifying for the Belgian Grand Prix. Gilles death was a tremendous shock to everybody and his loss is still deeply felt to this day. I admired and respected him as a friend and as a racer and it was a great honour when I joined Ferrari in 1989 to be given Gilles' number 27 to race under.

The following month Riccardo Paletti was killed in a start line accident in Canada. Before the race was restarted we were told that he was alive, but we knew that he was dead. When the race got going again I was caught behind Bruno Giacomelli's Alfa Romeo when he suddenly backed off. With no time to avoid him, my car climbed the back of his and as it took off I watched my hand go round and round in the steering wheel. It turned out to be badly broken and would take months to heal.

Later that summer Ferrari suffered another tragedy when Didier Pironi was severely injured in practice for the German Grand Prix. It was pouring with rain and the visibility was zero. The drainage is bad at Hockenheim and because the long straights pass through forests, the water hangs in the air like a curtain. Like the rest of us Didier was driving blind into a ball of spray at 180mph, when he hit a car he hadn't seen and had an enormous accident, breaking both his legs. It was the end of his Formula 1 career.

These events left a very bad taste in my mouth. People were dying and being badly injured all around me and it made me look at my sport in a different light. Villeneuve especially had been my friend. Now he was gone. It reminded me that this is a very dangerous sport and not one to be taken lightly. You must do it properly, or not at all. You must race to win, not to make up the numbers. You must make as much money as you can and chase after all the success you can get because you never know when your number is up. If just being a Grand Prix driver is satisfaction enough then you are a fool. You must come to terms with the risks, then go out there and make it count.

I have often been described as a 'brave' driver, meaning that I do things in a racing car and pull off manouevres which require a lot of courage. Some so-called experts have even suggested that I have more bravery than talent, which is an absurd suggestion. Surely you need more talent to be able to run on and sometimes beyond the limit and consistently get away with it.

I don't think that there's a driver alive who isn't fearful of his own safety at times. If there is he's a real idiot. Some of the people who came into Formula 1 in the last few years were really surprised when Ayrton Senna was killed because they didn't realise that anyone got hurt in Formula 1. Because my career spans a long time I've seen a lot of life and death. When I take risks they are calculated.

As 1982 wound down, I wasn't thinking too much about the season just gone, more on the season ahead. Then suddenly, just before Christmas, Colin was gone. He had been in France on a business trip and had flown back to Norfolk in the evening. The following morning we got a phone call to tell us that he was dead.

All of a sudden the comfort zone I had around me vanished. I didn't have to prove anything to Colin. He believed in me and knew that the results and the success would come when everything in the team came together. When he died there were few people in the team who believed in me. Some, in particular Peter Warr, tried to make me pay dearly for the embarrassment he had suffered when Colin was around. I always got the feeling that he was really jealous of me and had no desire to see me succeed; in fact he had a bigger desire to see me fail so he could say 'I told you so.' That is no way to go racing.

After all the hope and promise of the past two years, things were about to get tough again.

Nigel Stroud, Lotus engineer: 'Nigel would always set a car up on the ragged edge, like Senna used to. He didn't like to work below the limit of a car. If you can do that it's the best way to go, because then you really find out what your car is capable of, but there are not many drivers who can do it. I remember Nigel as a driver of tremendous enthusiasm, who was always prepared to try new things out on a car, to give something a go.'

11

THE WILDERNESS YEARS

I lost my way after Colin Chapman died. I had no support and there were forces within the team trying to pull me apart. My experience of life had made me pretty tough, but no matter how strong you are, when you add that kind of pressure to the already massive stress involved in competing in Formula 1, cracks begin to appear in your armour.

I tried too hard and at times I overdrove. It wasn't anger that made me go to extremes, nor the 'Red Mist', which some people said that I suffered from. With Colin gone, I lost my reference point in the team. Warr clearly didn't believe in me. He subjected me to the real number two treatment and by giving me no firm basis of confidence, made me feel as though the ground was falling away from under me. I was desperate and that is no way to succeed in Grand Prix racing.

If I made the slightest mistake, I would be criticised upon my return to the pits. If there was a new development part to go on the cars, Elio would get it first and it could be a long time before it found its way onto my car. I was a second class citizen.

Not long before he died, Colin had done a deal with Renault for a supply of their potent turbo engines in 1983, but for the first half of the year they were available only to Elio. I had to make do with the old Ford Cosworth DFV. The engine had been the backbone of Formula 1 for many years, but by 1983 it was massively inferior to the increasingly reliable turbos. It wasn't a question of a few horsepower here or there, the difference was measured in the hundreds. If you didn't have a turbo engine, you were racing in division two and I was not in Formula 1 to make up the numbers.

Elio and I had taken a couple of years to get to know each other; we came from completely different backgrounds with completely different experiences. In my first year at Lotus, as I learned the ropes, I had been no real challenge to him. But by the second year I outqualified him a few times and beat him in races and a real edge of competition came into our relationship. I knew that I was not in a car which would win races, so the main goal was to beat my team-mate. He is the only real yardstick by which you can measure yourself because he is using the same equipment. In theory at least.

As I became closer to Elio, we both began to realise that Warr was telling us different things and playing each one off against the other in the apparent hope that I would come unstuck and leave the team, thus allowing him to be fully in charge, rather than the caretaker of a team established by Colin. Elio and I decided to work together a bit more, to pool our information and help each other out. This annoyed Warr no end.

The car with which we started the 1983 season was a disaster. It was not until the seventh round, the Detroit Grand Prix in June, that I scored my first championship point. Luckily we were joined early in the year by the French designer, Gerard Ducarouge who went back to the drawing board. The redesigned car was ready for the British Grand Prix at Silverstone, where I would also get a turbo engine for the first time.

When I drove the car, the difference in power was startling. Although the turbos had been refined over the past few years, they still acted like an on-off switch. You'd put your foot down and one moment there would be nothing, the next there would be over 1000 horsepower hurling you down the track. When I had been given Elio's car to qualify at Zandvoort in 1980, I saw again what a competitive package could do. I felt that my chances had to be improved by the addition of a turbo. They were.

Although I had a few problems through practice and qualifying at Silverstone, I had a good run in the race and came through to finish fourth, which got the momentum going again. I followed up with fifth place at Austria and then had my best result of the year in the European Grand Prix at Brands Hatch.

I qualified third and Elio put in a spectacular effort to take pole position. In the race I finished third behind Prost and Piquet, who were going for the championship. It was my third podium finish in Formula 1 and it felt good to be competitive again. The car had been getting better as the second half of the season had worn on and it did my confidence a lot of good to stand on the podium at Brands. As at

Silverstone a few months earlier I was aware of a much greater section of the crowd who were behind me than before. Around the circuit I noticed many more banners and Union Jack flags with my name on them. I was beginning to reach these people. It felt wonderful. It was a shot in the arm.

Unfortunately my relationship with Peter Warr did not improve as a result of my run of points finishes. If anything it deteriorated even more. At Monza he laid into me for backing off on the last lap and giving away my seventh place to Bruno Giacomelli. I explained to him that the reason I had backed off was to avoid hitting a group of Ferrari fans, who had poured onto the track to celebrate Rene Arnoux's second place. I was in the wrong place at the wrong time and had no alternative but to slam on the brakes. If I hadn't I would have killed several people. If I had given away a win or a points finish I could understand his anger, but to drop from seventh to eighth was hardly the end of the world.

After my performance at Brands Hatch, John Player Special, the main sponsor of the team, had told Warr that they wanted me to stay for 1984, the third year of the contract I had signed with Colin. Warr did not want me to stay. I knew that he had been talking to other drivers all season and he refused to put me in the picture about where I stood. The 1983 season ended and still I had no idea what was going on. I had heard nothing from Warr and as Christmas approached I felt I needed some answers. I telephoned him and he told me that there were other drivers on the list and that I had no guarantee of a drive. He also told me that even if I did manage to hold on to my seat, there was no way I could be paid what I had been before. It was thoroughly demoralising and in retrospect I should have left the team there and then. There was interest in me from a few people and I had had some further discussions with Frank Williams about the possibility of joining his team.

I decided to carry on with Lotus partly because of my attachment to the memory of Colin and partly because I was determined that after all the knocks I had taken, I would maintain a positive attitude and be what I was – a professional – and I wanted to turn the situation around. I would remain loyal to Lotus. It was a big mistake.

Nineteen-eighty-four was a year of great sadness. Just before I went out to Dijon for the French Grand Prix, my mother died of cancer.

I didn't tell anyone about it. I was so cut up. Many people thought that I was being unpleasant because I didn't want to speak to anyone.

I can remember every single second of the weekend in vivid detail. It was so horrible to have to go through all the practice sessions, debriefs, the warm-up and the race after someone so close to me had died. It was one of the worst weekends I have ever had in racing and the sadness in my heart, that tugging sense of grief and the bewildering sense of loss stayed with me, even in the race. But I got on with the job and brought the car home in third place for my first podium and points of the year.

Nobody knew until the Monday that I had been wrestling with grief all weekend. I chose not to tell anyone because I knew that if I had encouraged people to come up to me throughout the weekend, offering their condolences, I would have collapsed into an emotional heap.

The next morning I put the flowers that I had won in France on my mother's coffin and drove the hearse to the cemetery.

The race following the funeral was Monaco. After our strong performance at Dijon I felt confident that another good result was on the cards. I always felt strong at Monaco and the car felt good in practice and in qualifying. I was in contention for pole position, but Prost eased me out by a tenth of a second. Nevertheless I was quietly confident for the race.

But on race day the heavens opened and as the rain showed no signs of letting up, it became one of the wettest Grands Prix in history. Prost led from the start in the McLaren and I followed him. On lap eleven I spotted my chance, passed him and took the lead of a Grand Prix for the first time. I was much quicker at this point than any of the opposition. I had the lead and was pulling away. I was using Goodyear tyres, while Prost and most of the other front runners were on Michelins and the French company was acknowledged to have a vastly superior wet weather tyre. The next Goodyear runner was a long way back. I knew it was going to be a fight, but I had grabbed the ball and although it was bobbling like crazy in my hands, I felt that I was going to win this one. Unfortunately, I was too pumped up and I was going too fast.

The track in Monaco uses public roads, which are marked with white painted lines. In dry conditions they do not pose much of a threat, but in wet conditions they are treacherously lacking in grip. Everybody knows that and makes sure to avoid them whenever possible. Five laps after I took the lead, I was climbing the hill towards Casino Square when I lost control of the back end of the car. I was on the wrong part of the circuit and I had put one of the rear wheels onto a white line and lost it. The car slewed into the barriers and as it went off I felt an incredible sinking feeling. The race was stopped a few laps later because the conditions were just too awful. If it had been stopped a few laps earlier I would have won, but that's the way it works. Some race tracks come to you, like Silverstone always has for me, while on others you can throw your all into winning, but they will always catch you out somewhere along the line.

It was entirely my mistake and I was devastated. I had thrown away the lead of a Grand Prix I felt sure I was going to win. When I was asked by reporters what had happened I told them that I had lost grip when I hit a white line. Unfortunately, they interpreted this as me complaining that the white lines were only there for me, which is not at all what I was saying. I was dismissed as a 'whinger' and came in for some quite vicious criticism from the press. The core of journalists who were convinced that I would never make it now turned to their colleagues and said, 'I told you so.'

Perhaps some of the criticism was justified. Perhaps I should have said, 'It was my mistake, I lost control' and left it at that. But I was angry with myself and I gave an honest answer, which is the only way I know. Unfortunately for me it was taken to mean something completely different. At the time it upset me a lot, but nowadays I am more philosophical about it. Some people are going to criticise you no matter what you do. That's life.

What the detractors didn't mention was that some of the big names at the time, like Didier Pironi and Niki Lauda, had similar accidents. At least I got myself into a position to win.

I was down for quite a long time after that. Although I played the film of the accident through my mind several times and could see where I'd gone wrong, it didn't make it any easier to accept that I had thrown away the lead of a Grand Prix. To be the best in this sport you must continually push your limits and try things out. If you really push hard in pursuit of your goal, you are inevitably going to make a few mistakes. You just have to accept this and chalk it up to experience. Monaco was different. I was not used to making big mistakes and it had a profound effect on me.

Because the environment around me at Lotus was so hostile I had no-one in the team to talk it through with. I needed someone to act as a buffer and, without one, I felt incredibly isolated. Colin would have helped me to deal with it. We would have sat down in a quiet corner and talked it through and I would have learned from my mistake and put it out of my mind. Peter Warr wasn't that kind of person. Behind my back he worked on the press and others, fuelling the criticism and ridiculing my white line 'excuse'. It was enough to make you crack.

I bounced back in the only way I know how – on the track. I let my driving do the talking. At Dallas in July I scored my first pole position, with Elio alongside me on the front row. It was the first time since 1978 that Lotus had annexed the front row.

It was a strange decision to hold the Dallas Grand Prix in July, because the temperature was well over 100 degrees fahrenheit. The track surface melted under the heat and after two days of running Grand Prix cars around it, the surface began to break up. To prevent any more damage, the race day warm-up session was held at the crack of dawn, before the sun got really hot. It was so early that Jacques Laffite turned up in his pyjamas! Niki Lauda led the other drivers in a protest to the organisers that if they didn't sort out the track we would not race. Some heavy machinery was brought in and quick drying concrete was laid over the damaged areas. This would change the grip levels considerably, especially where the track changed from asphalt to concrete. It would be extremely unpredictable.

I took the lead from the start and held it for half of the race. I quickly found out what grip was available and adapted my lines through the corners to suit. I ran comfortably at the front, but we had opted to run on full fuel tanks and my tyres began to fade around half distance. I was caught by Keke Rosberg in the Williams. We had a marvellous scrap, but once he got past I just couldn't live with him. I had reconciled myself to the fact that I wasn't going to win and then suddenly, half way around the last lap, I lost drive though the gearbox.

I couldn't believe it. I'd sat on pole, led half the race and now the bloody transmission had broken half way around the last lap. I coasted around to the last corner, in sight of the finish line and I thought, 'I'll be buggered if I am going to lose points because of this.' So I got out of the car and tried to push it over the line. After a hard race in 110 degree heat, I was already exhausted and dehydrated before I began pushing. The heat was unbelievable and it didn't help that I was wearing black overalls. I heard the crowd roaring me on, then everything went blurred and I fainted. When I came round I found that I had been classified sixth. I had salvaged one point.

Behind the scenes Warr was working to bring Ayrton Senna into the team for 1985. Senna had entered Formula 1 at the beginning of the year with the Toleman team, after winning the British Formula 3 Championship. I knew that Warr wanted him in and by mid-season it was clear that I was out.

At Zandvoort in August, Warr made the announcement that Senna would join Lotus. I had found out about it months before through the sponsors and had begun looking around to see what drives were available. Jackie Oliver made me an uncomplicated offer to join the Arrows team, which I appreciated. I also had several meetings with Frank Williams and he told me that he had a shortlist of three or four drivers to replace Jacques Laffite. He would let me know at the British Grand Prix in July. That weekend came and went and so did the German and Austrian Grands Prix. Still there was no decision.

It was most frustrating. Williams seemed like an ideal move for me. It was a top team and it was embarking on an ambitious engine programme with Honda. Like me it was looking to make a fresh start. I knew that Frank had been interested in me since Las Vegas in 1981 and my cause was being championed by my old friends Peter Collins and Peter Windsor, both of whom were now working for Frank. So why couldn't he make a blasted decision?

I knew that Warr would announce Senna at Zandvoort and I had said to myself that if Frank hadn't made his mind up by that weekend I would count Williams out of the equation.

I approached Frank during the weekend and asked him what the situation was. He said that he hadn't decided yet and needed more time. I told him that I would make his decision easier. I said, 'I'm tired of all of this messing around. If you really wanted me to drive for you, you would have signed me up by now. I have to safeguard my future. Thank you very much for your interest, but you can take me off your list.' And with that I walked away.

I don't think that he could quite believe it. He wasn't used to having drivers turn *him* down. Williams was a top team. They had won the World Championship twice in the last four years. They had some of the best mechanics and some of the best equipment in the business and here I was telling him that I wasn't interested in being treated like an idiot.

My thought at the time was that I was either going to change teams or retire. The two ideas had equal strength in my mind. After Colin died my experience at Lotus sapped my confidence. I was tired of the politics and the messing around. If I was going to race I needed to be somewhere where I could have some good people around me and I would be appreciated. I had also lost a good friend in Gilles Villeneuve and several of my colleagues had either died or been badly injured. Rosanne was about to have our second child and I could quite easily have retired to a blissful life as a businessman and golfer on the Isle of Man. If I was going to stay in Formula 1, it had to be the right situation.

One of my strengths is that I'm never afraid to walk away. I don't kid myself. I don't want to be anywhere that I'm not invited or wanted. I believed that I had something to offer which none of the other drivers had. If Frank didn't choose to see that and to snap me up then that was his choice, but I wasn't going to sit around waiting.

About two hours after my chat with Frank, Peter Windsor came to me saying, 'I don't know what you told Frank, but it seems to have worked. He wants you to call him on Monday when you get home.' I said, 'I told him before I wasn't interested and I'm still not. Tell him to forget it.'

This is where my stubbornness sometimes gets in the way of making sensible decisions. I had entrenched myself in the idea that I was upset with Frank and told myself that I was not going to drive for Williams after all the messing around.

With this going on in the background I was fired up for the race and I had a really good Sunday afternoon. The race was thoroughly enjoyable and the car, although no match for the McLarens, was pretty competitive. I passed Elio for third place and as I stood on the podium afterwards I felt fabulous. It had been a mind-sapping weekend, but once again I had done my talking on the track. That evening, Peter Collins appeared at my hotel and worked on me for about an hour. His basic message was, 'Don't be such a fool. Call Frank tomorrow.'

When I got back home, I told myself that maybe I had been an idiot and that I should call Frank. After all, if there really was a drive for me it would be a very good move and I would be foolish to miss such an opportunity – me, whose golden rule had always been 'Grab every opportunity with both hands and don't let go.'

I resolved that if he jerked me around I would put the phone down on him. I dialled the number. Luckily for me and for him and for the Formula 1 record books, he didn't mess me around. Our conversation was cordial and professional and he gave me the drive with the money I wanted.

With a deal in my pocket guaranteeing me a fresh start I looked to the end of the 1984 season with optimism. Ironically the last race of the season, in Portugal, illustrated the hell I had been put through in the last two years.

My style of driving demands very good brakes because I brake harder and later than most drivers and turn into the apex of the corner while still braking. So I always use the biggest set of brakes available. In Portugal we had the cars running strongly in qualifying and things looked promising for the race. But there was only one set of large brake pads available for the race and Warr decided that Elio should have them. My mechanic told him that there was no way I would be able to finish if I didn't have the large set and he got into something of a row with Warr, who said, 'Do as you're bloody well told.'

The promise we had showed in qualifying continued in the race and with eighteen laps to go I was running very strongly in second place, heading for my best result so far, when my brakes went. I was beside myself with anger, but Warr made no apology, in fact he didn't say anything about the brakes. It summed up the man.

That was the end of my career at Lotus. When I left the team Warr was quoted in the press with two sayings which have since become legendary. The first was, 'Mansell has reached the extent of his somewhat limited abilities' and the other was, 'Mansell will never win a Grand Prix as long as I have a hole in my arse.'

John Thornburn, close friend: 'Throwing the Monaco Grand Prix away just after his mother had died had a profound effect on Nigel. He thought he had it in the bag and he made a mistake. He wasn't used to making big mistakes and it got to him. I think he wanted to win that race for his Mum and he felt he blew it. He needed a buffer and at that time at Lotus it was very difficult because Peter Warr wasn't that kind of team manager. He didn't give him the emotional support he needed from within the team. Colin would have done that.'

Chris Hampshire, close friend since karting days: 'Nigel was very down for a long time after the incident at Monaco. He has had some amazingly unlucky things happen to him. Most people would have just given up, but because of his incredible determination, he's picked himself up and fought on.'

12

'I'M SORRY, I WAS QUITE WRONG ABOUT YOU'

Keke Rosberg had won the World Championship for Williams in 1982. When I joined three years later it was still very much Keke's team and he made no secret of the fact that he didn't want me there.

'If Mansell comes here I'm leaving,' he told Frank Williams when he heard that I was about to be signed. At the Italian Grand Prix towards the end of the 1984 season he held an informal press briefing at which he publicly reiterated his comments. He had heard that I was trouble, a disruptive influence within a team and he didn't want me anywhere near his Williams set-up. My detractors in the press loved Keke's stance and quoted it enthusiastically. Frank reminded Keke that the cars carried his name, that he was the boss and that he would decide who drove his cars.

On the grid before the final race of 1984 at Estoril, Keke came over to my car with seven minutes to go before the off and suggested that we should talk about next year. I expected him to talk tough, but he seemed to want to be positive and we had a constructive, if rather brief discussion about our relationship to date. I was under no illusions about my position. I had been taken on as number two to Keke. He would have principal use of the spare car. This didn't worry me unduly because in a decent team, you can make do with one very good car and some fast working mechanics. I think Keke could see how enthusiastic I was about moving to Williams.

I wasn't the only one who was enthusiastic about it. Frank badly wanted me in the team and so did the chief designer Patrick Head. For the 1984 season Patrick had had two non-technical drivers in Rosberg and Jacques Laffite. Both had limited testing ability: Jacques never extended himself beyond 90% in a test and Keke was not particularly interested in the subtleties of set-up. As long as his car was reasonably balanced he'd drive the wheels off it and that was that. Patrick knew that in 1985 he would have a difficult car and a difficult engine to work with. He would be in trouble if he didn't have a driver with a solid technical understanding, especially of engines. Having driven the more sophisticated Renault turbos, I was well placed to help develop the Hondas.

Now entering its second year, Williams's partnership with Honda looked promising, the engines seeming to get more and more powerful by the week and Patrick knew he needed someone who would run the car on the limit and give good feedback to the engineers. He could see that I was a real trier and there is nothing that Patrick loves more than to see someone grab one of his cars by the scruff of the neck.

With me alongside Keke he would have two real triers and hopefully a strong development programme as well. Keke was dubbed 'the fastest driver in the world' by *Autocourse*, the Grand Prix annual. In my first season as number two driver at Williams I would outqualify him seven times.

But that lay in the future. For the moment, as the 1984 season drew to a close, I was somewhat at a loss as to why Keke was taking this aggressive stance towards me. We had had a minor bust-up over that battle in Dallas earlier in the season, when he accused me of blocking him, but it was only something said in the heat of the moment and I knew that he didn't really mean it.

When someone pointed out that Keke had been with the Fittipaldi team before joining Williams, I realised that he must have been asking his old friend and former team manager Peter Warr about me. It all began to fall into place. No wonder he didn't want me in the team. He must have thought I was the devil incarnate. He had also spoken to Elio, one of his closest friends in racing, at a time when Elio and I were at loggerheads.

Pre-conceived opinions are generally a bad thing. I have always taken people as I find them and prefer to let my instinct guide me. I knew that I wasn't going to get through to Keke in a hurry and I certainly wasn't going to do it by talking him around, so I resolved to show him that his ideas about me were wrong by being a thorough professional and treating him with politeness and courtesy. In the meantime I would continue to do my talking on the track.

Moving to Williams was a breath of fresh air. I had become so used to the stagnant atmosphere at Lotus and I knew as soon as I went to the Williams headquarters at Didcot that this was a serious racing operation. The welcome I got from everybody in the team was incredible. Frank and Patrick did all they could to make me feel at home from the outset. The mechanics from the race team and the test team, with whom I would spend many days endlessly pounding through testing developments, were kind and helpful. Even the tea lady at the factory, Brenda, gave me a warm welcome and plied me with mugs of hot tea.

When I signed for his team, I told Frank that all I wanted was a chance to show what I could do in decent equipment. Frank assured me that I would have the best of everything and the full support of the team. I would be the number two driver, but Williams prided itself on making sure that it produced equal cars. There was no favouritism at Williams. If I was good enough to win for them, then I would be allowed to win.

After the mental torture of the past seasons at Lotus I felt my enthusiasm and passion for racing return. This, I told myself, was where I would make my mark.

Williams had endured a difficult few years and although Keke had won the championship in 1982, the team had not won more than one race per year since 1981. The last season with the new Honda engines had been particularly trying. When I had my first test for the team at the end of the year I could see why. The Williams-Honda FW09 was an awkward car to drive. It understeered very badly and was not particularly responsive to changes in set-up. Also, with the Honda turbo engine you either had no power at all or all of it at once; there was no such thing as a power curve and the usable rev range was tiny.

The engine was derived from the Formula 2 unit on which I had done much of the development work back in 1980 when I drove in four F2 races with the Ralt-Honda team. Now adapted into a turbo engine, it dominated the poor chassis, which couldn't handle the sudden surges of power. The tail of the car would step out of line in a lurid fashion everytime you floored the throttle.

The engine's other major fault was that it lacked rigidity, which is a big problem in a Grand Prix car because it means that the back of the car is prone to flexing. Keke told me before I drove it for the first time that the car was unwilling to follow the front wheels around corners and I could see his point. The most effective way to drive the car seemed to be to pitch it into the apex of the corner and try as best you could to control the tail on the throttle.

The car was Williams' last aluminium-honeycomb monocoque design. For 1985 Patrick was to build an all carbon composite car, which in addition to being much safer to drive, would be more rigid. The FW10 was launched in December in London, when it was also announced that the team would be sponsored by Canon. I attended the launch, but Keke missed it as he was busy in Arizona passing his test to fly a Lear Jet.

In the new year we went to test in Rio, where I spent a tough week working on the Honda engines, doing a lot of long distance testing. Honda had done their homework and came up with a more reliable, stiffer and slightly more user-friendly version of the 'D' engine, although it still behaved like a switch. We were told that before half-season a new engine would be ready. By the first race at the beginning of April, I was pretty optimistic. It turned out to be an absolute disaster.

We qualified well, with Keke second and me in fifth in place. On race day, as the outside temperature soared to around 100 degrees I got a fantastic start and carved my way past the two Lotuses of De Angelis and Senna to challenge the polesitter Alboreto into the first corner. As I came across to claim the corner, my rear tyre was clipped by Alboreto's front and my car rode up into the air and spun across the grass. I got going again, at the back of the field, but the accident had damaged the exhaust diffusers and eight laps into the race I was forced to retire.

I was extremely embarrassed. I had crashed on the first corner of the first lap with my new team and it was tough to take. The team had every right to think, 'What on earth have we got here?', but to their eternal credit they stood by me. My critics went running to Frank to say, 'I told you so', but Frank told them that they were wrong. It had been a racing accident and I had the team's full support. This meant so much to me. If it had been the year before I would have been ridiculed within my own team and the incident would have been used against me. As it was, my new team took it on the chin and the incident was never mentioned again, although I got hell from the press.

The next race in Portugal also began disastrously, but it turned out to be one of the most important and formative races in my career.

During the first qualifying session I was caught out by a rain shower on my first fast lap, so I backed off immediately. In my mirrors I saw the two Alfa Romeos of Riccardo Patrese and Eddie Cheever bearing down on me, looking as though they were trying to push each other off the track. I went off line to give them plenty of room, but to my amazement Cheever's car cannoned off Patrese's and into mine, sending me into the guardrail with a massive thud.

My mechanics spent twenty-four hours rebuilding my car and the next day I qualified ninth, held back by problems with a broken exhaust diffuser.

The rain poured down on race day and as we set off on the warm-up laps my engine developed a misfire. It was a tricky situation. I gave the throttle a stab to try to clear it, but all the Honda's 900hp kicked in at once and threw the car into a slide, damaging the nose and the rear suspension against a guardrail.

I was very upset and for the second time in two races, very embarrassed. To have an accident on the warm-up lap is probably the most embarrassing thing a driver can do, even if it is pouring with rain and your engine has a narrow and volatile power band. I had all the excuses I could have wanted but it didn't make it any less distressing. The fact that I had gone off was pretty awful, but at least I managed to drive back to the pits and the mechanics were able to fix it before the start. While the mechanics worked, I talked to Peter Collins and he reassured me that everything would be fine for the race and that I should keep calm.

Having been attacked by some sections of the press for my mistake in Rio and now having crashed on the warm-up lap, I could have been excused for feeling pretty het-up as I waited to start the race in the pit lane. This was going to be a very difficult race. I loved driving in the wet and knew that I was one of the best drivers in Formula 1 in wet conditions. But it would be no fun with such an unpredictable engine to control. Starting from the pit lane, I had to wait until the rest of the field had gone before I could go. No racing driver likes to sit stationary and see the pack disappear into the distance. It's torture, you feel so powerless. As I waited for the green light I cleared my mind of all the tension I was feeling and resolved to keep control of the car and of myself and to have a strong finish.

I set off after the pack and before long I was passing cars and making up places. Keeping the engine under control was like balancing a piano on a pin. On every corner of every lap I knew that if the power surged, the car would lose traction and I would slide. It required a blend of fire and delicacy, determination and patience. Psychologically, it was without doubt the hardest race I had ever had up to this point in my career. Many cars spun off, including Keke's.

Coming around the last corner before the pits, his Honda cut in with full power and he lost control of the car. He had a big accident, slamming into the barrier backwards and breaking a bone in his hand as the steering wheel whipped around.

The conditions went from bad to worse, but I held on to finish fifth. Ayrton Senna won the race, his first Grand Prix victory.

It was a good result for me and it gained me a lot of respect from people in Formula 1. But more important than that it was a real turning point in my development as a Grand Prix driver; I learned a huge amount that day about controlling my emotions. The year before I had crashed while leading in Monaco, trying to go too fast. This time I had put the pressures of the Rio incident and crashing on the warm-up lap out of my mind to deliver a mature, controlled and fast drive in treacherous conditions.

A racing driver has to have speed, racing instinct, physical strength and determination built in to him. Without these skills he is nothing. But what divides a good driver from a really great driver is what goes on inside his head during a race. To perform at the pinnacle of the sport you must have tremendous strength of mind and the ability to master your emotions. When your heart beats at up to 200 beats per minute your body produces the most enormous amounts of adrenalin and it's easy to get carried away, especially if something goes wrong. Motor racing is full of frustrations, dashed hopes and embarrassing setbacks. You've got to get over those hurdles, because if you don't they can easily pull you down.

It's pretty depressing when you've only done a few races for a team and you suffer setbacks. If the team climbs on your back, as they had done with me at Lotus after Colin died, it can soon erode a driver's self-confidence. This is what happened to Michael Andretti, for example, when he tried Formula 1 with McLaren in 1993. His mistakes started a spiral, which led to a loss of confidence both on his part and on McLaren's. He drove with increasing desperation and in the end was forced to quit. It can easily happen at the top level of the sport, such are the pressures.

I was relieved that Frank and Patrick were supportive and gave me a chance to redeem myself and didn't sack me or criticise me in public. After the race Patrick said that when I came in with the damaged car on the warm-up lap, I looked as though I expected to get a right dressing down. Perhaps I was conditioned to expect it from my Lotus days. In turn the team was impressed by my commitment and by the fact that I had kept the car on the island while Keke had crashed. It brought me closer to the team and they had more respect for me. The turnaround had begun.

I picked up further placings in the points over the next few races and in Detroit I qualified second. In the race, Patrick took a flier on the settings of Keke's car and it worked, Keke winning the race. I was not so lucky. My brakes were diabolical and after 26 laps they caught me out in Turn Three, where I slammed into the only section of concrete wall not covered by tyres. The impact was quite severe and I was concussed for a while and jarred my thumb. But I was very pleased with Keke's result. It showed that the team was on the right track and that the new Honda 'E' engine, which had made its debut the race before, was a winner. I quickly forgot my injury. But two weeks later at Paul Ricard I had an accident which would give a whole new meaning to the word concussion.

In France my wrist was still hurting and had to be sprayed with pain-killer each time I went out. On the first day I qualified seventh, so the following day I was looking to improve my time by at least a second and a half to make the front of the grid. With the ever increasing horsepower available from these amazing turbo engines, speculation had been mounting for weeks about what speeds we would reach on the Mistral Straight. It would be over 200mph, no question, but we wondered how much over.

Our answer soon came and it was staggering. After qualifying on Friday the speed trap read-outs told us that we were doing over 210mph on the run down to Signes corner. It was more like a land speed record attempt than a motor race.

On Saturday morning I was working on setting the car up for the race, running with a full load of fuel and the harder compound Goodyear tyres. Blasting down the Mistral Straight my left rear tyre suddenly exploded. Travelling at over 200mph, I had absolutely no control over the car. I was a passenger and everything happened unbelievably quickly. The tyre disintegrated and destroyed the left rear suspension, which in turn took the rear wing off. I watched as the car rushed head-first for the guardrail. Then the left front wheel caught a plastic catch-fencing post, breaking the suspension and sending the wheel backwards, catching me full in the face, knocking me out. After that the car slammed into the guardrail before eventually coming to a halt, totally destroyed.

Unconscious, I was flown by helicopter to Marseilles hospital.

When I came around I was told that I had severe concussion, but amazingly I had sustained no major injuries. I had a splitting headache, which lasted for about ten days. I was told that I wouldn't be allowed to race the next day and instead, while the race was on I flew back to the Isle of Man to try to get myself fully recovered for the British Grand Prix in two weeks time.

For the next week I sat in a darkened room, wearing sunglasses and avoiding all light and loud noises. For the first three days I saw no-one and spoke to no-one. I lay in complete solitude and thought about the accident and wondered whether it would harm my love of racing. When you are recuperating from a big accident you think about things like that. It had been the biggest accident of my career but, unlike the ones in Formula Ford and F3, where the construction of the cars was not up to scratch, I had not broken anything. I was very lucky and I knew it.

I had high blood pressure as well as a headache and I was under observation from doctors. Once again Rosanne was a pillar of strength, nursing me back to recovery and keeping away all visitors. The accident looked absolutely terrifying on the television and I knew that it had chewed her up inside, but she didn't make a fuss. She knew how important it was to me to do well at Silverstone and that was our clear target. My little daughter Chloe came into my room from time to time, wondering why I was sitting in the dark. I must have looked quite funny, but I certainly didn't feel it. I felt like a zombie.

After the first week I had made good progress and even got out of the house to play golf. In fact I won a local tournament, shooting a round of 73, so maybe the accident helped my game!

I made it to Silverstone, where the team had built a new car for me to replace the one written-off in France. I still felt pretty awful and wasn't fully with it all weekend. I shouldn't really have driven, it was actually quite dangerous. My mind and body were not in perfect harmony and around Silverstone, which is a faster circuit than Paul Ricard, that is not a good state of affairs. I had no problem with my vision, but the messages from my brain weren't getting through to my body quickly enough and the whole weekend was a real struggle.

In the first qualifying session I concentrated on getting used to the car again and went out on race tyres to do as many laps as I could. My progress was halted by an exploding clutch. But on the second day I felt ready to mount a challenge and hurled the car around to lap only a second off Keke's pole position time. It was an incredible concerted effort. I have never had to concentrate so hard on each corner because things didn't seem to be happening as quickly as normal inside my body. It seemed to react slowly to things. My brain wasn't as fast as usual; the delay was slight, but I could feel it and I had to allow for it. When I saw my reference point for braking into a corner, I had to allow myself a fraction of a second longer than normal for my brain to tell my body to begin braking and turning in to the corner. It was a strange and rather unpleasant sensation and I was very glad a week or so later, when it went away.

Keke had showed how much progress our car was making by setting pole position with an average lap speed of over 160mph, the fastest lap ever recorded by a Formula 1 car at a Grand Prix meeting. My effort was to prove a major turning point in my relationship with Keke. He knew what an enormous accident I had had and he respected me for qualifying so well at Silverstone. Equally, I stand in awe of what he did in qualifying, setting the first 160mph lap.

Our relationship had been rocky for the first three months, as Keke persisted with his idea that I was going to cause trouble in his team. But after that things began to improve and we became closer. After my qualifying lap at Silverstone he came over to me and was very complimentary. He couldn't believe that I had been able to come back from such a massive accident and set such a competitive time. He said: 'Nigel, I was quite wrong about you. That was really magnificent. After what you've been through that was a very brave lap.' At least that's what he told me he said, when we discussed it some weeks later. I had no recollection of it at all. He told me that I had completely failed to acknowledge that he was even in the motorhome talking to me! Looking back, I can't believe I drove the next day in that condition.

Being the true gentleman and sportsman that he is, Keke went to the press and repeated what he had said to me. He told the journalists that my performance had been 'magnificent' and that he now saw that he had been wrong about me.

I ran strongly in the early laps of the race, but was forced to retire from third place when my clutch went. I had mixed feelings about this. On the one hand I was annoyed not to have been able to get a decent result in my home Grand Prix, but on the other hand I was quite relieved it was over. I shudder to think what I would have said in the press conference if I had finished the race!

In the middle of the season we struggled with the reliability of the engines, mostly bottom end problems. It was so frustrating. We knew that the performance was there. We were leading races, setting fastest laps and qualifying strongly. All we needed was the reliability and I knew that we could win races. Things began to shape up at Spa in Belgium, where I finished second, my best result to date.

I felt we were making real progress. The Honda engine seemed to have rediscovered its reliability and was certainly delivering a lot of power. The next race would be the Grand Prix of Europe at Brands Hatch. Alain Prost looked certain to clinch his long-awaited first World Championship at Brands. After a very productive test at Brands Hatch in the week leading up to the race I felt that I had as good a chance as I ever had of my first victory.

When you test, if you can find an improvement of a couple of tenths of a second then you usually come away happy. At Brands we found half a second thanks to a redesigned transmission and new rear suspension. We also lowered the rear of the bodywork to improve the airflow to the rear wing. This didn't give us any more power, it just improved the handling a great deal. When you make such a large step forward you are entitled to feel you're in good shape for the next race.

After the problems with Lotus, it had taken time to get my confidence back again and to reach the level of professionalism necessary to do the job. Going into Brands Hatch I had taken part in 71 Grands Prix without winning. I told myself that it didn't matter too much because I had been in a winning situation several times before, both at Lotus and in the early part of 1985 at Williams. The wins had simply escaped me, but I knew that sooner or later I would catch one. In my career I have won thirty-one Grands Prix, but there are probably twenty more that I should have won but didn't for various reasons. You think you've got the race under control and then a wheel nut comes off, or the gearbox dies or the engine blows up. That's motor racing. I was not worried. I was relieved that I was on my way.

At Brands Hatch I got a great start and tried to go around the outside of Senna into Paddock Hill bend. Ayrton forced me onto the dirt. I recovered, but Keke dived up the inside into Druids and I understeered off line, which let Piquet through into third place. My car was better than Senna's through the faster corners, but Senna was able to brake deeper, so I knew he would be difficult to pass. Keke tried many times and on lap seven he went for the inside at the Surtees left hander. Senna took his line and they touched, sending Keke spinning. He was hit by Piquet, who retired on the spot with bent suspension. Keke rejoined and headed for the pits to change tyres. I had been following Piquet and managed to avoid the accident, so slipped by into second place behind Senna.

A couple of laps later, Keke came out of the pits in front of us, just as Senna and I crossed the line. Going through Bottom Bend, Senna went right to try to get past Keke, I went left and squeezed through into the lead. I have always believed in being an opportunist. I'll take any chance I can get and with drivers of the calibre of Senna you don't get too many chances. I could hear the cheers from the crowd when they realised that I was leading. Perhaps this time?

I immediately set about opening as big a gap as I could. By half distance I had over 18 seconds on Senna and had the race firmly under control. Thanks to the pit signals I knew where everyone else was so I would be able to respond if anyone looked like threatening me. Sitting out front in the lead was such a good feeling. I told myself with each lap that passed that I just had to keep cool, keep control and keep the pace up. No-one was going to catch me. It was going to be all right. The concentration was incredible.

As the end of the race approached I could feel the 75,000 crowd willing me on, reaching into the car and pushing me down the pit straight. On the last lap I prayed that the car would hold together, that the engine would keep singing behind me. I was not worried, I felt strong. I safely navigated the demanding left hander at Stirlings, accelerated up through the gears into Clearways. 'I could switch it off and coast in from here,' I smiled to myself. The crowd was going wild as I entered the pit straight and crossed the line. The chequered flag was waved on my right and Union Jacks waved on my left in a blur of colour and movement and cheering. When I saw the sheer joy of the people in the stands outside Paddock Hill Bend I knew that I had won my first Grand Prix. The relief was enormous. All the way round my slow down lap I was crying.

Rosanne was in tears too. When I got out of the car I clasped her and my young son Leo to me and we celebrated finally reaching one of our lifelong goals. I had been racing for twenty-three years, nine of them in cars, the rest in karts. I had broken my neck and my back, lost a fortune before I ever had one to lose, fallen out with family, lost touch with friends and put my wife through hell. Now it was payback time and boy, was it all worth it. I always knew that I could win Grands Prix. Only a handful of people had ever believed me. Now I had proved it to everyone. I was a winner again.

Two weeks later in South Africa I won again, this time from pole position and this time I left no-one in any doubt about my credentials. All weekend I was riding on a wave of confidence and I got into a terrific rhythm for my qualifying lap of over 148mph. The most impressive corner, Sunset, was taken flat and it felt so quick it was almost frightening.

The lap could have been better, but I had to fight a nasty understeer at one corner. As I was on a flyer I decided to try to drive through the understeer and keep my foot hard down, trying to get the front of the car to dig in and provoke the back end to come around. Unfortunately it didn't quite work and the car just understeered more and put me up onto the kerb, heading for the wall. I kept my foot in and accelerated up through the gears, just nudging the wall, but finally managed to get it back onto the track. Once you get on a wave of confidence you feel you can do extraordinary things like that and it certainly was one of my best qualifying laps up to then.

The race served to further justify my confidence. I got a good start and led comfortably for the first six laps until Keke caught me up. He was obviously desperate to get past and I didn't want to get into a fight because I wanted to conserve my tyres. On this track the cars generated less downforce than normal because the air is thinner at high altitude, so they slid around more. With the intense heat it was crucial to look after the tyres. As it turned out, letting Keke through was the right decsion for another reason.

As we approached the first corner a backmarker blew up massively, spreading oil all over the track surface. There were no warning flags and Keke suddenly lost control of his car, which sailed off the road and into the sand trap. I was fifty yards behind him, so I had time to brake and drive around the oil, although I caught the corner of it and had a scary moment of my own. But I was through into the lead again. Luckily for Keke, he was able to drive out of the sand and set off in pursuit of me. It was a thrilling race and for most of it I held off Prost and a charging Keke to take the flag. I was ecstatic. No-one had won back-to-back races that year and this one meant just as much to me as Brands because I had had to keep two of the top names behind me and had succeeded.

I was where I wanted to be at last. An established front-runner.

Keke Rosberg, team-mate, 1985: 'It is true that I went to Frank Williams when I heard that Nigel was joining the team and said that I would leave if he came. Frank held me to my contract and so I stayed. The reports I had heard about him [Nigel] were very negative and at the time we had a nice balance in the team with Jacques Laffite and I saw no need to change a good team. Nigel worked hard to prove me wrong and he succeeded. It took about three months for me to realise that I had been wrong about him and from then on we worked very well together. His performance in 1985 was remarkable from the outside, but from the inside it was no more than I expected from him. He was prepared to go flat out all the time.'

Peter Collins, Williams team manager, 1985: 'Nigel went through a period in the early 1980s when his self-belief was brought into question in his own mind because his position was being undermined by his team manager at the time. The turning point was Portugal 1985, where he crashed in the warm-up and was obviously expecting a massive bollocking, but he went out and had one of his finest races in a very difficult car that day. That was the start of the turnaround.'

Patrick Head, Williams Technical Director: 'Right from the start Nigel was hugely positive and wanted to make the most of the situation. He didn't get a lot of testing in the previous year's car because he didn't fit in it; it wasn't big enough for him. He wanted to make his relationship with Williams work and it was clear that he had had a tough time at Lotus. We were impressed by how committed and positive he was.

'It's always a pleasure to have a driver like Nigel, like Alan Jones or Keke Rosberg, who you know will always give it one in the car. If they turn up at a race they're only there for one thing and that's to win. If drivers like this are off the pace it's because the car isn't quick enough. There is nothing the mechanics love more than a driver who wrings a car's neck. Nigel was always like that so they would work hard for him.'

PART THREE

WINNING

*'I was like a starving man who has just worked
out how to get into the fridge ...'*

13

MAKING IT COUNT

After those first wins at Brands Hatch and Kyalami I never looked back.

Perhaps the trials and tribulations which had gone before had served to shape me, to give me depth and sophistication as a driver. Perhaps I needed experiences like Portugal to learn more about control and self-restraint, which are sometimes as important as sheer speed. Throughout the 1985 season I had felt more and more certain that a win was around the corner. It was so important to me to be a winner. Now I had made the breakthrough and I looked forward to many more victories.

Some people said that Brands Hatch was a turning point in my career because it was there that I learned how to win. This isn't true, I'd done plenty of winning over the past twenty-three years. What changed after Brands was that the window of opportunity to make good in Grand Prix racing opened up wide before me. I was now in a position to win a lot of Grands Prix and I fully intended to focus even more single-mindedly on this task.

My long-held dream to be the champion of the world also seemed closer, or at least more realistic. I could see how, with reliable equipment, plenty of application and a little luck, a championship could be won. I finished the season in sixth place with 31 points, but more important, I had scored 24 points in the last quarter of the season. I knew that if I could maintain that scoring rate in 1986 the World Championship might be on. I could see how Prost had done it. He had won his first title that weekend at Brands, after coming close on three previous occasions. It was quite fitting that on the same day we should both attain such long sought after goals.

I was thirty-two years old at this point and although my mood was one of overwhelming optimism for the future, I couldn't help but think what a shame it was that I had spent some of the best years of my life in second rate cars, unable to show my talent. I was not bitter about the years I had spent in the wilderness. You have to go through your apprenticeship and make the numbers up for a while in F1 before you are put in a position to win. And, let's face it, most drivers never get into that position. I realised after the wins at Brands and Kyalami that I was now in that position and should make the most of it.

Although my standard of living had improved dramatically since the Formula 3 days, I was also aware of what some of the other drivers were being paid, which was in the millions of dollars per year. Driver retainers were beginning to take off and the big names at the top were demanding serious money for 1986. I wasn't bitter about this, but I remember telling myself after Brands that if I got myself into a position where I was successful and a race winner of some significance, then I would be able to command that kind of money because I would be a household name, an ambassador for the sponsors and I would deserve every penny. But until that time I would have to continue my apprenticeship.

One of the big differences between Formula 1 when I came into it and today is that many of the young guys today don't understand this concept of paying your dues. In 1992 when we steamrollered everybody and won the championship they said, 'He's got a better car than me.' When I heard this I thought, well what about all those years from 1980 to 1985, five whole years where I paid my dues, suffered all manner of horrors in poorly built cars, sweated blood just to qualify in the middle of the grid, watching the front-runners pull away from me with ease in their more powerful or better handling cars, patiently waiting for a winning opportunity? I didn't whinge about it. I just got on with it and worked hard to get myself into their position. That is what getting to the top in Formula 1 is all about, or it should be.

If the guys slugging it out at the front have been around for a few years and have built reputations and become household names then surely that makes for a better level of competition and a greater occasion than a group of young drivers, some of whom haven't even done 100 races in their lives jumping straight into the best equipment.

In 1985 some of the great names of the sport were still around and I had broken into their winners' circle. The window of opportunity had opened up, but it wasn't a foregone conclusion even over the winter of 1985/86 that I would get to the very top. Still, I was happier in that I was able to say that I had achieved and I had won races. I approached every year from then on thinking that it might well be my last, so I was determined to enjoy it and make the most of it. I should make as much money as I could and win as many races and championships as possible; any of them could easily be my last. Making up the numbers was not part of the equation. From now on I was going to make everything count.

The tragic death of Elio de Angelis the following year would really cement that philosophy. The most uncertain sport of all is motor racing. Any one of a thousand things can go wrong. Some you get away with, some you don't. It's not like being a tennis player or a golfer.

There are maybe ten things that a golfer can do wrong, including slicing the ball, topping it and so on. If he's a top professional golfer he shouldn't be doing any of them in a tournament. With a racing driver you've got to do your job, all elements of the car down to the smallest bolt have to do their job, as do the mechanics and engineers. It is very complicated and immensely difficult to coordinate. When you hit the sweet spot you've got to grab the opportunity and make it count. And, as I was to learn to my cost over the next six years, you need just a little bit of luck.

One guy who certainly knew how to take advantage of his position was Nelson Piquet, my new team-mate. He had negotiated a fabulous retainer with Frank for two seasons with the team. The deal was signed in the summer of 1985, before I won at Brands, after Keke told Frank that he was joining McLaren for 1986. Frank thought he needed a number one driver to replace Keke and Nelson was ready to leave Brabham after seven years. I did not begrudge him the money, which was light years away from what I was being paid, nor his number one status. He was a double World Champion and, now that Niki Lauda had retired, probably the biggest name in the sport. I had won two races. But I had no fears about racing alongside him. I had shown up well against one World Champion and had no doubts that I would do likewise against this one.

I didn't expect it to be easy though. Piquet had a big ego and would not want to be shown up by his number two driver. He would have first call on the spare car and would doubtless try to get any mechanical advantage he could. I knew him a bit and didn't much like what I saw. He had sloppy values and his sense of humour was of the irritating kind, but as long as we were both professional about it I didn't think it would be a problem. How wrong I was.

From the word go he tried to unsettle me by getting under my skin. Early in 1986 we went testing in Japan and we were travelling on the bullet train with Frank. I had fractured a couple of ribs and was still in some discomfort and Nelson thought it would be funny to poke me in the sore spot. He kept prodding me, saying, 'How are your ribs, then?' and laughing. Presumably he thought Frank would find it funny too and think he was clever. I put up with it for a while, trying to be polite, but it was painful and he wouldn't back off. He just kept prodding me and laughing. It was clearly time to take action.

I stood up and said: 'If you do that again I'll break a couple of your bloody ribs and we'll see how funny you find that.'

He left me alone after that, but it was always his way, to try to niggle and annoy you. It was his way of unsettling a rival and putting them off balance – but it wouldn't work with me.

As we geared up for the new season, things looked very good indeed. The FW11, a development of the FW10 with which we finished 1985, had the hallmarks of a very strong car. The monocoque was a little longer and quite a bit lower than the FW10, allowing better airflow over the rear wing. It was a terrific car and I loved it from the first time I drove it. Honda had come up with a very powerful and fuel efficient engine, codenamed 'F'. Some people claimed the F stood for 'frugal' and certainly with new rules reducing the fuel allowance from 220 litres to 195, the Honda's good fuel efficiency was to prove a tremendous advantage. At both the Williams headquarters in Didcot and the Honda base in Waco, Japan, the momentum which we had built up at the end of 1985 continued. Our package looked as good if not better than the opposition and winter testing suggested that we were the favourites for the championship.

The press made Nelson the pre-season favourite to win the drivers' title and he certainly seemed to agree. He boasted to the team and anyone who would listen of how he was going to win the title. I kept quiet and focused on getting myself into peak physical condition. I did a lot of running up and down the hills in the Isle of Man and spent hours pumping iron in the gym. I felt good; I knew that I could win races and Nelson had shown nothing in testing that I didn't feel I could match or even beat. I knew I was as quick if not quicker and I knew I had the wherewithal to challenge for race wins.

Our final test, a week before the first race at Rio, was at Paul

Ricard, a circuit by now steeped in bad memories for me. The test went well, like most of them that winter and as Frank left for the airport with Peter Windsor we were all in a buoyant mood. Everything was in place and we were in the best possible shape for the start of the season. Shortly afterwards a man came running down the pit lane, shouting, 'Come quick, Frank Williams has had an accident.'

Nelson, Frank Dernie, our aerodynamicist, and I jumped into a car and raced to the scene of the accident, which was about fifteen minutes away. We discovered Frank and Peter in a field, both out of the car. Peter seemed all right but Frank was in bad shape, bleeding profusely. An ambulance arrived and I volunteered to ride in the front alongside the driver, to keep everyone calm and make sure Frank got the best treatment. His injuries looked bad so we decided to take him to Marseilles, which had the best facilities in the area.

We waited all night for news, but all we knew was that Frank was fighting for his life. After a few days we learned the good news that he would live, but also the bad news that he had damaged his spine and had no use of his arms or legs.

It was a huge blow. Everything had seemed so right, so perfectly set up for a great season. After losing its leader like this, the team could so easily have gone into decline like Lotus did after Colin died. That it didn't is a tribute to the strength in depth of the team that Frank had built up with his partner Patrick Head. Amazingly, we were able to carry on that year and to win the Constructors' Championship and score 141 World Championship points. Patrick took overall control, while each of the departments within the team looked after themselves. Sheridan Thynne took care of the business side and the sponsorship, Dave Stubbs ran the race team, Alan Challis saw to the mechanics and Peter Windsor looked after the public relations side. The team showed incredible integrity.

The first race at Rio saw me off the track on the first lap yet again, but this time it certainly wasn't my fault. At the Australian Grand Prix in 1985 I had experienced a coming-together with Ayrton Senna and although that was a racing accident I had seen him try some dangerous moves and was rather worried about him. He didn't seem to have much respect for the other drivers and I thought it would be worth talking to him about it before the new season.

In the Rio test several weeks before the first race, I found him and we had quite a long talk. I said that it was obvious that he and I were both going to be quick in the coming season and that we should both try to be professional as well and that meant that if one of us had the line into a corner, the other should let him go and try to pass at the next opportunity. There was no point in us having each other off. Ayrton agreed and we shook hands.

On the first lap of the race in Rio I got a good start and thought I had done enough going down the straight to pass him down the inside into the fast left hander. I got alongside, my right front wheel level with his shoulder and began braking, but he suddenly came across and hit me. I braked hard to avoid an accident, but his left rear wheel hit my right front and sent me off the road into the armco, tearing off my left front wheel.

We did not talk about it afterwards, but I learned an important lesson about racing against him that day. If I hadn't backed off we would both have hit the armco and it could have been a serious accident. As it was I came off worse and it would not happen again. His tactic was to intimidate and I refused to be intimidated.

I made my point at the next race, the Spanish Grand Prix, where Ayrton and I shared the closest finish in Grand Prix history. Ayrton led from the start with Nelson second and me third. I was getting rather worrying information from my fuel consumption readout so I decided to drop back a bit and see how things worked out. It worked; by lap 19 the readout said that I was on target again and I put in some hard laps to try to make up some of the ground I had lost. I passed Nelson for second place on lap 34 and forced Ayrton to get boxed in behind a backmarker just long enough for me to pass. I opened up a lead of around four seconds and held it until, with ten laps to go, I realised that I was losing grip at the back. The rear diffuser panel was coming loose and one of the rear tyres had picked up a slow puncture. It was maddening, I only had ten to go and a tyre stop would certainly drop me well back.

Ayrton attacked down the pit straight, trying to get me on the outside into the first corner. I held my line and forced him to lock up, smoking his tyres. He kept trying but I wouldn't have it, although the back end was all over the place by now and I knew that I would have to change tyres. I let him past and dived into the pits, where I took on new rubber, and blasted out again some 20 seconds behind him with Prost between us in second place.

I drove my heart out to close the gap, taking as much as four seconds a lap off him. I caught Prost easily, but passing him was really hard. He turned the boost up along the straight so it took me far longer to get past him than it should have done and in the process I lost nearly a second to Senna.

When I got past Prost I had only four laps left to catch Ayrton, who was now six seconds ahead. Going into the last lap I had reduced the gap to one and a half seconds. He was on the limit and so was I. Under-braking for the final hairpin I was too far behind to try to pass, but coming out of it I was right on his gearbox. He weaved, but I wasn't going to be deterred and I kept my foot in. We raced for the line like 100m sprinters ducking for the tape and although I passed him half way down the straight, he had crossed the line first by 0.014s, or 93 centimetres. If the finish line had been five yards further down the road I would have won. And those four extra points would have made a big difference at the end of the year.

Afterwards Prost came up to me and apologised. He said: 'I thought that Ayrton was too far ahead for either of us to catch him. If I had known you could do it I would have let you past!' We had a laugh about it. I couldn't blame him though, after all he was defending his second place.

It was a fantastic race and although Ayrton had won it, he knew that I had made a point to him. I was not going to be intimidated. If he wanted to beat me he would have to fight me every inch of the way.

The next two races at San Marino and Monaco gave me three points and then I got my first win of the year at Spa. It was another superb race, which I won thanks to being crafty and level headed with the boost switch. But I wasn't in a mood to savour the win. Just a few days before the race my friend Elio de Angelis had been killed in testing at Paul Ricard.

I will never forget that day at Ricard as long as I live. Elio had left Lotus when he realised that he had become number two to Senna. As I had found, Lotus wasn't capable of running two good cars, so Elio had had some tough times in 1985 and switched to Brabham for the 1986 season. By this time Elio and I had become good friends. It took me a couple of years to get to know him, because we were so different and came from totally different backgrounds. Once I got to know him, we shared something really special.

After I left Lotus he had a lot of problems with the team and began to understand some of the problems I had had and sympathised with me. It drew us closer together. At one point in 1985 he came to a Goodyear test at Donington and said he wanted to talk. We took his plane down to the South of France, and I stayed with him in his father's house, a fabulous place in St Jean Cap Ferrat. I was due to go to the big test, ironically, at Paul Ricard the next day, but he had been told by Lotus that he wouldn't be needed as Senna would do all the work. He was really upset, particularly as he was ahead of Senna in the points table at the time.

I listened late into the night as he told me about how he was being sidelined within the team, how Peter Warr only had time for Senna and that he might as well not exist. We talked about how the same had happened to me. It opened his eyes. For the first time he appreciated my sincerity. The next day he decided to go to Ricard anyway to watch, so we drove down together and I made a point of going with Elio to the Lotus camp before going on to Williams because I wanted to embarrass Peter Warr and to let him know that I was fully aware of how he was treating Elio. It was disgusting. They didn't put Elio in the car all day.

So the following year we were back at Paul Ricard for a test between the Monaco and Belgian Grands Prix. Elio was out on the track in the Brabham, his engine note rising and falling as he negotiated the track, when suddenly it went silent. The car had somersaulted the barriers and landed upside down, on fire. I was in the pits at the time and I saw the smoke rising. Everybody was rushing around calling for fire extinguishers. There didn't seem to be any marshals around and what track officials there were did not have fire suits on. I ran to the scene of the accident, but it took me several minutes and I couldn't believe that Elio was still in the car and that no-one was doing anything.

Alain Prost and I tried to get him out but the car was crackling and exploding and there was just no way. We couldn't get close enough to undo his belts. He was trapped in the car for eight minutes and then there was quite a long wait for a helicopter to take him to Marseilles hospital. Poor Elio had no chance. He died in the hospital.

He was a lovely man, a real Italian gentleman, a very talented piano player and a great racing driver. His death was the reason why Keke Rosberg retired at the end of the year and it was certainly a turning point in my career. Rosanne and I talked about the risks and decided that if we were going to continue in this occupation we were going to make it pay. I wasn't talking just from a financial point of view, but in the sense that I was even more determined to be successful at it, not make the numbers up. If it ever looked as though that was happening I would stop.

I followed up my win in Belgium with a dominant win from pole position in Canada, which hoisted me to second place in the championship, two points behind Prost, who had won San Marino and Monaco in the McLaren.

Canada was another race won by clever fuel strategy. Nelson kept saying things like, 'This is my favourite track, I'm quick here,' but in reality he was nowhere near me all weekend. After I won and he finished third, his face was a picture. He had realised that he wasn't going to have things all his own way, and he knew damn well that he had been blown off by his team-mate – and everybody else knew it too.

At the beginning of the year Patrick had decided that he would be my race engineer and Canada was one of those races where we got it absolutely right and won by brilliant teamwork.

I had a good lead in the early stages, but I realised that I was getting slightly behind on fuel so we turned the boost down. The hardest thing was letting Keke and Alain in the McLarens catch me up. The temptation to drive as hard as possible was overwhelming, but I knew that I would have no fuel at the end if I did that and as the saying goes, 'To finish first, first you must finish.'

Keke got past me by turning his boost right up and in the process put his own fuel consumption four litres in defecit. I got onto the radio and swore at Patrick. His response was 'Yessss.' He didn't say 'Shut up' or 'Get lost' or anything like that, just a very earnest, 'Yesss. Position one on the boost, Nigel.'

We had four positions on the boost control. P1 was the real economy mode, two and three were racing modes and four would give us an extra 50-60hp for overtaking; only to be used when absolutely necessary. In general, P2 burned slightly too little fuel for racing and so didn't give optimum power over a race distance, while P3 burned slightly too much. So in most races we had to juggle between two and three in order to survive the distance at a competitive pace.

But here Patrick was adamant that I had to run on P1 and conserve fuel. I pushed as hard as I could on low boost, trying not to let Keke increase his lead, which was now four seconds. On lap 20 Patrick came on the radio and told me I could switch to P2. I said 'Oh thank you.' And pretty soon I was up with and past Keke again. After that no-one saw me for dust. It was a question of driving as hard as I could within the fuel allowance and at the end I won by over 20 seconds. It was immensely satisfying and a great piece of teamwork between Patrick and I.

It was not an ideal way to go racing, but having to temper your driving to conserve fuel in those turbo days was a good discipline. It made drivers better managers of a car; far better than you need to be to drive today's Grand Prix cars. There was far more to it back then than just driving fast. You had to be on top of everything. You always knew to the half-litre how much fuel you had. It was down to you to be sensible as well as fast.

I loved the turbo era in Formula 1, they were a lot of fun to drive and the management side of it fascinated me. The big problem with the early turbos was the delay in response. But by controlling the boost switch you could also control the response of the engine. The more boost you had the better the response, but then you'd risk running out of fuel. If you turned the boost down you had worse response and you would induce the car to understeer. You could never get it perfectly balanced and you always had to compromise. Driving the car was the easy part; managing the systems was hard work but great fun.

With Canada in the bag, I had now, including my two wins in the previous season, won four of the last ten Grand Prix races. My career was really gathering momentum and my confidence was high. In France I was back on top with another commanding win, although when I arrived at Paul Ricard and thought about the terrible associations it had for me I wondered whether the circuit had some sort of jinx on it.

I didn't indulge in these thoughts for long. You have to put such things out of your head or they'll drown you. You have to just get on with the job you're being paid to do and forget about everything else. This is where single-mindedness is an absolute must. Whatever else is going on around you or inside your head, you mustn't think about anything other than the job in hand.

I had now won three races to Nelson's one in 1986 and it obviously irked him a great deal. Here was this big shot being paid over $6 million and he was being left behind by me.

Psychologically he knew that the pendulum had swung in my favour and at the British Grand Prix he was desperate to regain the initiative. At Brands Hatch he dug deep in qualifying to set pole position, being the only driver to break the 1m 7s barrier. It was a great lap and it really raised the stakes for the race. I very badly wanted pole for my home Grand Prix, but after an engine blow up, a water leak and a high speed misfire I had to settle for second place. I hoped for better in the race and indeed it was to be one of the greatest races of my life.

The build up to the British Grand Prix that year was unbelieveble. After my win at Brands the year before and my form so far in 1986, the British public clearly felt that a home win was on the cards. As the weekend approached I was inundated with requests for interviews for television, radio and newspapers, some of whom I had never even heard of. The interest in Formula 1 was spread far and wide and the sense of expectation was overwhelming.

For the first time since his accident, Frank came to see his cars in action. He appeared in his wheelchair and got a wonderfully warm response. He even held a press conference where the journalists gave him a standing ovation.

The crowd on race day was over 115,000. The whole place was gripped with Grand Prix fever. It was incredibly exciting. The first start was a disaster. I got the jump on Nelson and then as I went for second gear a cv joint in the driveshaft exploded and I lost all drive. I couldn't believe it. I thought my race was over. I coasted through Paddock Hill Bend and pulled over as the field rushed past me. I hadn't felt dejection like it for years.

Then the red flags came out and I realized that the race had been stopped. Behind me on the track, poor Jacques Laffite had been the loser in a multicar pile up going into Paddock and had broken his legs. It was his 176th Grand Prix start and it would be his last.

I was very upset about Jacques, he was a good friend, but his loss was my gain. The race would have to be restarted and I had a chance to get into the spare car. The only problem was that it was set-up for Nelson. Not only was he a different size and shape from me but the car had not been running well all weekend and on Friday the turbo wastegate had been playing up, which meant a loss of power. I had driven it briefly on the Friday and didn't like it. When everything is going well, you spend the qualifying days tuning your own car in to the circuit, so that on race day it is the best it can possibly be for the conditions.

The most important thing a driver can have is confidence in the car, to be able to trust it when you try a manoeuvre and to know that it isn't going to do anything unpredictable when you really push it. When you jump into a car that you don't know, you throw the form book out of the window. You can't have confidence in the car, because you don't know anything about it. You just have to drive on blind faith and instinct. I was grateful for the second chance but was somewhat pessimistic about the car.

At the restart I decided to play myself in slowly and learn the unfamiliar car. I didn't try anything brave at the start and let Nelson take the lead. Gerhard Berger nipped past into second place in the Benetton. I wasn't too worried, I needed to learn. Nelson had set the car up and it handled quite differently from mine. It was not set up the way I like my cars set-up. The turn in wasn't as good and the spring settings were different. The seatbelts were set too tight and the seat didn't fit. Worst of all there was no drinks bottle. Brands is a very hard circuit and dehydration would be a big problem. It was very uncomfortable, but I experimented with new lines and adapted my style to suit the car. It wasn't going to be easy, but after a couple of laps I began to feel more confident and decided that it was time to get going.

I passed Berger on lap three and closed to within a couple of seconds of Nelson. We opened up a clear gap to the rest of the field and the race became strictly between the two of us. By lap twenty I had closed right up on Nelson and was looking for a way past. I expected a fight, but on lap 23 he handed me a gift. He missed a gear going down into Pilgrims' Drop and I was through. I knew that we were approaching the tyre stops and psychologically it is always an advantage to be in front when the pit stops happen. There was always a chance that the race would be won on the pit stops, but the mechanics handled Nelson's stop on lap 30 and mine two laps later flawlessly. Now it was just him and me. Forty laps. Best man wins.

As I came out of the pits he got really close and I had to defend my position carefully through that first out lap while my new tyres got up to temperature. Nelson had pitted before me hoping to get back the lead through the pit stop sequence, but it hadn't worked. Almost, but I was still just ahead. Into Surtees he tried the inside but I was able to close the door. All around the lap we were nose to tail.

As soon as the tyres were up to temperature I knew that I would be able to pull out a second or so just because they were really fresh. I did that and then was able to protect that lead, not making any mistakes, until I broke his will. He tried turning up the boost but that didn't work.

It was a classic race and very hard mentally. When someone's breathing down your neck all the time it's a huge strain. It's far harder to lead all the way than it is to run a close second and then pinch it at the end. If you are running second you can always use the car in front as a brake. You don't have to concentrate quite as hard when you follow someone as you do when you're running your own race and setting the pace. When you're in front you've got to cover all the corners and you know all the time that if you make a simple mistake then the other guy will pass you, as I passed Nelson when he missed a gear. It was flat-out racing all the way, by far the fastest race I had ever driven.

I was absolutely exhausted and totally dehydrated at the end. But the roar from the crowd lifted me up. The reception the year before had been special but this was something else altogether. We had entertained them royally and they let us know their appreciation. My euphoria was heightened when I realised that now, for the first time in my life, I was leading the World Championship. I had a four point lead over Prost, whom we had lapped on his way to third place!

Nelson looked grave on the podium. I had beaten him in his back-up car and he knew it. It was a great win but even more significant because it was his car. The circumstances had been against us but we got the job done. I had now won four of the last five Grands Prix and six of the last twelve.

I took a lot of race wins away from Nelson, which he couldn't take. He was the number one and always had use of the spare car, but I had proved that I was able to beat him and outpace him and he didn't like it. I made him look less of a driver than he thought he was. Nelson always needed to have something more than you to be able to turn up the heat and beat you.

Nelson had a bunch of friends around him, of the kind no racing driver needs, who gave him appalling advice. They convinced him that he was a quicker driver than me, so if I was beating him then it must be because Williams was giving me a better car and I think that, Brands notwithstanding, he really believed it and began really stirring things up. Because of Frank's accident, Patrick was in charge but he was so wrapped up in engineering, which is what he loves and is best at, that he was not capable of getting on top of the situation which Nelson was creating.

Nelson went to Frank and accused me of reckless driving at Brands. He complained that as number one driver he should have been allowed to win and that Frank should have instructed me to let him through. To his credit Frank was unmoved by Nelson's whingeing. There were no team orders, Nelson had number one privileges like the spare car, but out on the track we were racing.

One of the things Nelson used to do was to deliberately mislead us in technical debriefs. I would have an idea about an adjustment which I thought might improve the car. We would ask Nelson and Frank Dernie, his engineer, what they thought and they would say, 'Oh no, we tried that and it doesn't work,' when in fact it gave a significant gain. Because in a team you rely on saving time by running parallel programmes, we believed them and it was some time before we realised that Nelson was tricking us.

In Hungary Nelson used a new differential in the car which I could have had if I had known that it was that much better. He kept quiet about it. If I had been in his position perhaps I would have done the same thing, who knows. At the time Nelson was a dab hand at keeping things to himself and with good cause. He knew that if I had had the same piece of equipment I would have given him a really good run for his money and probably beaten him. But you would think that the engineers in the team would be professional enough to tell me about it.

When the press enquired why Nelson was suddenly much faster than me in Hungary, Patrick Head denied that he was using a different differential and suggested that I wasn't driving fast enough. It was ridiculous, but it was also classic Patrick. He sometimes says things before he knows the full story. I have a lot of respect for him, but he does respond prematurely to things and develops a picture of what he thinks is the case when often it's not. He's a very clever man who is short on time because he has a lot of pressures on him. Consequently he makes decisions before he has all the facts at his disposal, which can be unfortunate.

I was under quite a lot of pressure from both Frank and from Honda that weekend to sign a new contract for 1987 and 1988. But I was in no hurry as I was in demand from no less a team than Ferrari.

After Brands I had been invited to Maranello to meet Enzo Ferrari himself. As I have said I am not easily impressed but meeting the great man was an amazing experience. He told me how much he admired my driving, 'You drive with your heart,' he said. He had obviously read up about me as he seemed to know a bit about my background. We had lunch and I signed the minutes of the meeting with a proposed outline of a contract for 1987 and 1988. It was all very flattering and the sums of money involved were staggering, but it was hinted to me by certain people at Williams that if I did a deal with Ferrari, my championship hopes for 1986 might suffer. My desire to win the championship made it my absolute number one priority, so two weeks later I re-signed for Williams. I had a seven point lead in the World Championship with five races to go.

Shortly after half distance in the Austrian Grand Prix I coasted to a halt. It wasn't the first time I'd retired with mechanical failure but this one was special. I had been leading until the pit stops and although Prost had got in front during my stop, I had six points in the bag, maybe even nine if I had caught Prost. Instead I had nothing and it would cost me dearly at the end of the year.

For the whole of the second half of the 1986 season I led the World Championship points table. I dominated the Portugese Grand Prix, winning by 19 seconds, my fifth victory of the year and with two races to go, Mexico and Adelaide, I led by 10 points.

What happened next has been well catalogued and talked about, but it just goes to show that nothing is ever certain in motor racing. No matter how much preparation you do, anything can happen. I didn't feel under any special pressure as the championship went down to the wire, as I've said I control the pressure from within. With 18 points available for two wins, there were two drivers who could beat me for the title, both of whom had contested, and won, championships before. Prost was eleven points adrift and Nelson, who had won at Monza with me second, was only ten away.

On the Friday evening in Mexico City I went out for dinner with some of the BBC Television crew to celebrate Murray Walker's birthday. We had a great evening, Murray was on full song as usual, telling jokes and stories from his long and remarkable life. Unfortunately I made the mistake of ordering some rather rare meat and the next morning I was visited by what the locals call 'Montezuma's revenge', which meant that I had to keep trotting off to the toilet at regular intervals. The mechanics even painted a line from the pits to the toilet. My stomach was in knots all weekend.

I qualified third, but the start was little short of a nightmare. As the field lined up on the grid, I went to select first gear. The lights turned green, I dropped the clutch and nothing happened. I couldn't understand it at all. A momentary panic flashed into my mind as the field flooded past me, would anyone hit me up the back? Miraculously no-one did. I jammed it into second gear and crept away from the line, but by this time everyone had gone. Two days of slugging my guts out to qualify at the front had gone down the pan in three awful seconds.

I drove as hard as I could and managed to salvage two points for fifth place. As it turned out I would have to drop these points anyway, because the championship was calculated on your eleven best scores and this was one of my lowest. So effectively I came away with nothing. It could have been better, but it could also have been a lot worse, particularly if anyone had hit me.

Before the final race at Adelaide Rosanne and I considered the situation. I had a six-point lead over Prost. As long as I finished third or higher I would be World Champion. It was a thrilling thought. We talked about the percentages and it looked really good. I thought that I was on the threshold of my first World Championship. I felt that I had put in the hard work and paid my dues and was about to reap the rewards. I was very confident that I would do it.

We were on the brink of realising our lifetime's ambition.

Even today I still cannot believe the way that the 1986 Championship was lost. Williams made such a terrible mistake in not letting me come in for tyres. I wanted to change them, there was no reason not to pit, but they told me to stay out.

When I finally brought my convulsing car to a stop at the end of the long back straight after my tyre exploded it suddenly struck me like a thunderbolt that the World Championship had gone. I had been a mere 44 miles away from clinching the title. Everything had been going fine. The car felt good, I was comfortable in third place, I could have pushed for second, but I didn't want to take any risks. Now it was all over. I was destroyed. I felt a deep sense of despair in the pit of my stomach. It was without doubt the biggest disappointment of my entire life.

The psychological pressure had mounted throughout the weekend. I knew that it would, so I had gone home to the Isle of Man after Mexico to relax and be with the family before going back into the lion's den in Australia. As usual Rosanne was a pillar of strength and she came with me to Australia to help soak up some of the tension.

In the early stages of the race Prost had a puncture and was forced to make an early stop. His team-mate Keke Rosberg was leading, but on lap 63 out of 82 his tyre blew and he retired from his last ever Grand Prix. Before the race I had wanted to make a tyre stop at half distance, but after Nelson radioed in to say he didn't think he would need to stop, the team told me that it wasn't necessary. The Goodyear technicians, they said, assured them that the tyres would go the distance.

I had seen Keke's car at the side of the road, but if I had known what had happened to him I would have stopped for tyres whether the team wanted me to or not. I was untroubled in third place with over a minute in hand over Stefan Johansson in fourth. Even a slow and careful pit stop would not have lost me that third place. But the team said no, stay out there.

On lap sixty-four as I pulled sixth gear approaching 200mph, the left rear tyre exploded and with it went my championship. It took nearly a quarter of a minute to bring the car under control, the thing was pitching about all over the place. When it stopped I slumped. It was so hard to take.

My whole life I had waited for this opportunity. Ever since my earliest days in karts buzzing round the allotments in Birmingham I had wanted to win the World Championship. After all those endless hours of work, the sacrifices, the injuries and the stubborn refusals to give up, my goal, which so many people, including my father had told me was impossible for a lad of my background, had been within reach of my fingertips. I had touched it briefly, but then it was gone. My head was full of a million 'what ifs', but none of them meant anything at all. Motor racing can be kind to you, but it can also be incredibly cruel. I had lost and that was that.

It wasn't just personal disappointment. I felt sorry for Rosanne, who had stood by me through some terrible times, for my friends and family and for all of the British fans who had woken up in the middle of the night to watch the race live on television.

I walked back to the pits and was moved by the response of the crowd, who applauded me all the way and shouted things like, 'Never mind, Nige.' I watched the last few laps on the television monitors and saw Alain Prost cross the line first to become the 1986 World Champion. He was gracious in victory. He said, 'I would like to say how sorry I feel for Nigel. Twice I lost the title at the last race and I know how he must feel. He deserved to be World Champion this year.'

Prost's feelings were echoed by many thousands of people who wrote to me over the winter of 1986/87. I got countless letters which said, 'In our eyes you are the champion, because you were the best. You are the moral victor. I doesn't matter that you didn't win it. You are the people's champion.' It was touching, but I found it hard to look at it that way. I wouldn't have the number one on the car and that, along with the right to defend the title the following year, were the things which really mattered.

It had been a momentous season and I received many accolades which went some way towards making up for the disappointment. The Isle of Man government gave me its prestigious Sword of State and the BBC Television viewers voted me Sports Personality of the Year.

The accolades and the tributes provided a balm, but the aching went very deep, I was down for ages and it took me a long time to bounce back. I thought about retirement, after all I had lost one of my best friends in 1986 and when something like that happens it focuses your mind on the risks. I had enough money now that I didn't need to continue racing if I didn't want to. It was only my desire to win the World Championship and to compete at the highest level that persuaded me to continue. Rosanne put no pressure on me. She said that she would back me whatever I decided to do. I said that I would go for it. Having caught half a glance of the greatest prize in the sport I desperately wanted to be the champion. I did not want the tyre explosion in Adelaide to be the defining moment of my life, the single instant when everything that was there to be gained, had all been lost.

I am a winner and losing was not what I wanted to be remembered for when the history of the sport was written. I had lost the World Championship in 1986 through bad luck on the track. Politics and behind the scenes intrigue involving Honda would contribute to me losing the next two championships.

Anthony Marsh, track commentator: 'Nigel and I had a lot of fun together. He always used to like to introduce me to people as his grandfather. He was about thirty at the time and I was only sixty. Normally I conducted the press interviews at Grands Prix, but in Mexico a local chap thought he'd do it. He didn't really speak English and Nigel realised that it wasn't a very serious exercise so he drew attention to me in the press seats and said, "Give a big hand for my grandfather!" All the press thought it was funny and roared with laughter, but afterwards a girl from the local paper came up and said, "You must be so proud of your grandson and I wonder what your wife thinks? May we do an interview for the Mexico City paper?" I told her the truth, but Nigel said I should have gone through with it and had this ridiculous story in the papers. In Australia, just before the start of the race which would decide the championship, I went to the back of the garage to wish him luck. He was talking with a young couple I didn't know and he called me over and said, "This is my grandfather.

Isn't he marvellous, he's 84." And then he picked up his helmet and left without saying another word. So there I was with these two people who thought I was indeed marvellous for 84. That's the kind of thing which gives him enormous pleasure.

'Another time, at Brands Hatch I was recording some interviews to broadcast over the public address system during the quiet time on Thursday before the action started. I asked Nigel if he'd help and we started recording. The first thing he said was, "Take your hands out of your pockets and stop playing with yourself", which I wasn't, but I had to rewind the tape and start again. He did this three times and a group of marshals standing nearby were having hysterics. After the third time I rewound the tape, but he said, "You haven't rewound it far enough." I said, "Yes I have," "No, you haven't," he said. So I checked and he was right. There was "Take your hands out of your pockets ..." on the tape. Good job he made me check it before it went on air!'

14

KEEPING A SENSE OF PERSPECTIVE

Grand Prix racing can be all-consuming. There are sixteen races a year and a heavy test schedule over the winter and during the season. The stresses and pressures of being a front-line Grand Prix driver are immense; not only do you have the livelihood of all the team members hanging on your results, you also have pressure from sponsors and engine manufacturers to do well which helps them sell more of their products. On top of that the sheer intensity of the competition and the physical act of driving hard is very stressful and wearing.

To counteract this it is crucial to have other interests which give balance to your life. When you suffer huge disappointment, as I did after losing the title in Adelaide, it is important to have other areas of your life to turn to which help you regain strength. My family has always given me emotional strength, but my passion for golf and karate has helped me a great deal in keeping things in perspective.

Golf has been a dream of mine for over twenty years. The game has given me a new lease of life, broadened my horizons and provided another outlet, away from the race track, for my competitive spirit. To get the ball into the hole in as few shots as possible with all the elements and hazards on a golf course is a terrific challenge.

I have many friends among professional golfers, especially Greg Norman, after whom we named our youngest son. Greg and I go back a long way and although we don't see as much of each other as we would like we have a close bond and when we do get together we have a lot of fun. He is an accomplished person in many areas and when we muck around on boats and jet skis he gives as good as he gets. He likes to enjoy himself and if that means pushing the limits he's quite capable of that.

I had admired his game for a long time and when I took part in a pro-am tournament in Australia before the 1985 Australian Grand Prix, playing with such a great golfer as Greg helped me to relax before the race. We struck up a friendship and spent a lot of time together that weekend, and we have been firm friends ever since.

A couple of years later I achieved an ambition by playing in the Australian Open. I would love to dedicate a lot of time in the future to golf to see if I could compete in other major tournaments, but at the same time I can see it's going to be a struggle, mainly because of the injuries I've sustained over the years, especially breaking my back and neck and the surgery I had after my Indycar shunt at Phoenix.

In golf you've got to have a good solid consistent swing and at times I swing well and at others I swing badly, depending on my back. I'd love to compete at the highest level. I could perhaps get down to a handicap of one or two and maybe if I'm lucky I might be able to play scratch. But I don't know whether I can get good enough to realise my dream of 20 years – to qualify for the British Open. I may well enter one year. It would be lovely to try.

The difference between me and the top professionals is that I am not yet able to play every single round in par or better. The great thing with golf is that it's not your style or technique which counts, but how many shots you take on your scorecard. So if, like me, you haven't got an orthodox swing, as long as you shoot par or birdies it doesn't matter. I'm working at the moment on being able to play consistently on or below par. The way I'm doing it is unconventional – but I guess that what's good for me and my back is probably no good for anyone else.

Being so in love with the game of golf, having my own course had been a dream for a long time and I was delighted to be able to acquire one in the summer of 1994. I had put the feelers out for some time and over the years plenty of courses have been made available to me, but when Woodbury Park, near Exeter, was offered to us by the local agents it seemed the right choice.

The course is set in some 400 acres plus on the west side of the Exe Valley. It was designed by the well known golf architect, J Hamilton Stutt and has an 18 hole Championship course, called the Oaks and a nine hole scratch course called the Acorns. The Oaks is 6707 yards long with a scratch score of 72 and is already capable of hosting an international tournament.

In August 1994 I became the owner and immediately set about

building a clubhouse and indoor sports centre, with swimming pool, tennis courts, gymnasium and squash courts. And over the winter of 1995 we expected to extend the yardage of the Championship course to almost 7000 yards. It's a fantastic place and I am very proud of it. Only time will tell if it is the right one, but it's an exciting project, one of many I hope I will be involved in for the future.

My other great passion is for karate, in particular the Okinawan style, known as Uechi Ryu. I did several years of karate when I was a teenager, but only picked it up again properly when I moved to America. I found a teacher in Clearwater called Ric Martin, who is a Sixth Dan in Uechi Ryu. He runs a dojo and gym quite near to where we lived in Clearwater and I began going there every day for a work out.

Uechi Ryu is all about inner strength. It's about having the ability to understand and listen to what your heart is telling you. Pureness of heart and mind is the goal and trying to keep life in balance. There is no question that at times my life is totally out of balance and out of synch, like a lot of other people. It's a big challenge to get yourself back on target and back in focus. You are not only training the body, but the mind and the heart as well. What you get in return for the training is peace of mind. After a hard training session you feel relaxed and at peace with yourself. Although the movies make out that karate is a violent activity, the true way of karate is to be humble, well mannered and gentlemanly.

The style is based on Katas, which are forms, moves and techniques. The core position of Uechi Ryu is San Chin, which is the first Kata that you learn and its principle goes right through to the eighth Kata. San Chin is all about balance, focus, centre of gravity, breathing and internal strength. As you progress through each belt, you learn a new Kata, you learn more techniques and there is a certain curriculum which you have to follow before you can get upgraded to a higher level. Each Kata is harder than the last. Through continuous practice it becomes second nature.

Another important part of the training is conditioning, which is toughening up your exterior muscles to take the blows so that instead of getting hurt by them, they bounce off you like a shield. It is like building a body armour.

I found that it helped a lot with driving a racing car, not just from the physical side, but the mental side as well. You learn to manage your strengths and your weaknesses a lot better and you turn negatives into positives. Overall, it's a wonderful art and a great way to enjoy yourself and benefit your spirit and your mind. Karate has been fantastic for me from the point of view of fitness and suppleness. I studied hard and Ric worked me hard, making no allowances in our training sessions.

After a year of intensive training up to seven times a week – the equivalent of three years training for most – I went over to Okinawa, Japan in December 1994 to try to qualify for my black belt. It was really nervewracking. I had to go before a panel comprising the masters of the style, the lowest was a fifth dan and the highest a ninth dan! We were tested on the Kata, free sparring, and knowledge of the history of the style and on techniques. They also test you on San Chin, where the examiners punch you, testing your stomach and arms, and generally assess your strengths, both internally and externally.

Achieving the black belt was a lifetime's ambition and it was a very special feeling to receive it in Japan. What made it even better was that same week, my *sensei*, or tutor, Ric Martin won the full contact World Championship.

I've got a dojo at home and there's also one at my golf club. I'm committed to karate and before I finish I'd like to get my second and third degree black belts and become a third dan. It would be nice to fight in the World Championships one day, but perhaps I am too old and have too many injuries!

Karl Ayliffe, Uechi Ryu full contact World Champion 1992 and 1993: 'If Nigel wants to do something he'll do it. Getting a black belt in twelve months is quite an achievement, normally it takes two to three years. But the average person trains two to three times a week, whereas Nigel trains five or six times per week and puts a lot of effort into it. He committed himself and was dedicated to it because he'd made his mind up that he really wanted a black belt. He was well received over there in Okinawa, which is a traditional, peaceful place and I think that the Uechi Ryu fraternity would like to see him back there one day.

'I went up to him just before he was due to be tested and I said, "You're not nervous are you?" He said, "I'm ten times more nervous than I ever was before the start of a race." Because when you get out there you are testing your ability and there's only yourself to be tested – there's no car – and you have to rely totally on yourself. He passed with a very high standard. He knows that the black belt is really the start of learning in martial arts. From there it goes up to tenth dan and the higher you get the better you are. First dan, or black belt, is just the beginning.'

15

BAD LUCK COMES IN THREES

The statistics tell it best. In 1987 I won six races, twice as many as anybody else and I had eight pole positions. I was on the front row for every one of the fourteen races I started that year and I led twelve of them. And yet I still didn't win the World Championship.

The main reason I didn't win it that year was because of four inexplicable technical failures, which robbed me of four more victories. In Monaco I was running away with the race when the exhaust broke, something which quality control should eradicate. In Hungary I had the race in the bag with six laps to go when the wheel retaining nut came off, a freak accident, but frustrating as hell.

In Germany and Portugal strange engine problems took me out, handing 15 points to my team-mate Nelson Piquet. I missed the last two races after I crashed in practice in Japan, so Nelson won the title by 12 points which ensured that when he went with Honda engines to Lotus the following year, his car would carry the number one.

At Monza in September, Honda confirmed that they were dropping Williams to join McLaren for 1988 and two weeks later in Portugal my engine was obviously down on power and eventually died on me. But when the mechanics got the car back it fired up first time and burst into life. It rather summed up the season. Not to put too fine a point on it, there were some very suspicious things happening with my engines in the second half of 1987.

Early in the season, Nelson had a huge accident in practice for the San Marino Grand Prix in which his car spun on the exit of Tamburello and hit the outside wall sideways on at 180mph. He had concussion and hurt his foot, but luckily it was not more serious. The next day he came to the track and wanted to race but the medical officer, Professor Syd Watkins, refused to let him race so he

180

commentated for Brazilian TV. I'd love to know what he said when he saw me win the race, which gave me the lead in the championship!

Senna finished second that day and in the next race at Spa he and I would have perhaps our most serious confrontation yet. I managed pole with Piquet alongside and Ayrton third. I got a marvellous start and was tearing away when the race was red flagged for a first lap accident. At the restart Ayrton barged through and led into the hairpin. I wasn't too worried about this as there would be plenty of time to pass him later. I shadowed him around half of the lap and then coming out of the Pouhon corner he suddenly slowed and there was a flame-out from his exhaust, which meant he had lifted off the throttle. I thought at the time that he was in trouble, but it was not beyond the realms of possibility that he was trying a dirty trick on me, dabbing the brakes to unsettle me. In any case I moved left and drew alongside him on the racing line to pass.

It wasn't a place I would normally try to pass, but given that he had slowed and handed me the opportunity I took it. Next thing I knew I was being hustled off the track. With anyone else I would have made it, but I think he had it in his mind that this was a make-or-break corner. He later said that he hadn't slowed and that I must have hit my boost button to pass, which isn't right.

I kept going for a little while but the handling was all cockeyed and I scared myself silly trying not to go off the road. By the time I was forced to retire I was absolutely furious that I had been put out of a race that I had felt quite capable of winning. Another win on top of San Marino would have given me a good start to the championship, with Monaco, one of my favourite circuits, coming up next. It wasn't the first time that he had done something like this and I felt it was time that someone had a word with him.

My critics have said that some of my best charging drives in Grands Prix have been fuelled by a 'red mist' of anger, but this is quite wrong. Anger is not and never has been part of my driving, even in the bad times at Lotus. I can honestly say that the only time I have ever got the 'red mist' in my entire career was when I got out of my car at Spa in 1987 and decided to go and talk to Senna.

I found him in the Lotus garage and I went over to him, grabbed him by the overalls and pushed him up against the wall. He wore loose overalls in those days and I pulled the zip up beyond his chin to just below his nose. 'Next time you do that,' I said, 'You're going to have to do a much better job.'

Needless to say the press made a big deal of it and I was painted as the bad boy, although the reports did not mention that the accident had been forced upon me. He had slowed and I had to pull out to get past him or I would have hit him up the back. After that he had no chance of getting through the corner at that speed and on that angle.

To this day I don't condone my actions and I am not trying to justify them. I would certainly never do anything like that again, but in those days Senna would do anything to win, and he needed to learn that there was one man out there on the track who would not be intimidated by him. He knew that when we were side by side, I wouldn't give an inch and he couldn't scare me off.

The problem was that he and I were both incredibly competitive creatures, cast out of the same mould, if you like. We were both fast and both determined to win and that meant that we would frequently occupy the same piece of road. To both of us winning was everything, but the difference was that I have always played by sportsman's rules, Ayrton wanted to win at any price. At least we both appreciated how quick and talented we were as drivers. I think that Ayrton only had that with one or two opponents throughout his whole career – probably just Alain Prost and myself.

After Spa we developed more of a mutual understanding and he didn't give me any more problems for quite a while. But of course the press stirred it up, splashing the incident at Spa across the headlines and getting all pompous about it, saying that I should have been fined for bringing the sport into disrepute. But the governing body, FISA, took no action. By this time I had become quite used to good and bad publicity and was quite able to rise above it. It did not put me off my stride and in qualifying at Monaco I had the rare pleasure of taking pole with a perfect lap.

Consequently I went into the race feeling supremely confident. The car was working well and was nicely balanced, the engine responsive. I took off at the start, running half a second a lap faster than anyone else and by lap 20 I had a ten second lead over Senna. Everything was looking perfect for that elusive Monaco win, but then on lap 30 I lost all turbo boost pressure. Later I would learn that a weld on one of the pipes to the wastegate had fractured. It was unbelievably frustrating. As I sat on the sidelines and watched Senna win and Nelson take an easy second place I reflected on the last two races; both were certain wins, but I had come away with no points from either. It was still early days from the point of view of the championship, but I felt frustrated that I was already the dominant force and yet I languished in fifth place in the driver's table.

The pendulum began to swing my way at the French Grand Prix at Paul Ricard, which I won, my second victory of the year. By the time we arrived at Silverstone a week later my confidence was high. I had won at Brands in 1985 and 1986 and thanks to the run for the championship in 1986 I had become a household name in Britain. The fans turned out at Silverstone in their hundreds of thousands and the media pressure in the build up to the race far outstripped the year before. In the midst of it all Nelson did his bit to spoil the party, saying that he'd already won two World Championships while I had lost one. He was looking to unsettle me. After all, here he was getting seriously upstaged by his supposedly junior team-mate.

Nelson and I hardly ever spoke to each other, even professionally, by this stage. And if he thought Brands Hatch the year before was humiliating, he was about to have the shock of his life.

The British Grand Prix of 1987 was hailed as one of the greatest Grands Prix of all time and it is certainly right up there in my mind as one of my very best wins ever.

In the course of my long career in motor racing I have had to push hard in many races, running the car right on the limit for prolonged periods. But it is impossible to run every lap of a two hour race with the concentration and commitment you put into a single qualifying lap. Neither the body nor the mind can stand that kind of pressure for long.

By far the hardest I have ever pushed in a race was the 1987 British Grand Prix at Silverstone, when I was faced with 29 laps to catch Nelson who was 28 seconds in front of me in a similar car to mine. Every single one of those laps was driven at ten-tenths, with absolute commitment into every corner, even going off at some corners such was the speed I was carrying. I caught Nelson and passed him with two laps to spare and it is a memory I will treasure for the rest of my days.

Nelson had never really forgiven me for humiliating him at Brands the year before. He had complained to Frank, but Frank had said nothing. At Monza when Nelson passed me at the Lesmo he turned into me deliberately, pushing me out for one scary second towards the fence. 'That makes us quits,' he told people after the race.

Now 12 months after Brands the situation going into the Silverstone race was similar. He needed to prove himself – I had won twice that year and he had yet to win – and to reassert his number one status. At Paul Ricard the week before he had made three major mistakes. He had spun, run wide when I was pressuring him and stalled his engine on his final pit stop. Once again he resolved to get his revenge in front of my own people in Britain. Frank knew that the rivalry would again be intense, but he gave no team orders. His only instruction was, 'Don't take each other off.'

Nelson took first blood, edging me out of pole position by seven-hundredths of a second. It was a good lap. A new chicane had been installed at Woodcote Corner, which led onto the pit straight. As with all chicanes, the idea was to slow the cars down, but I didn't like this one much. Nevertheless I was clocked at 189mph over the finish line, so it didn't slow me down too much!

A few drops of rain could be felt on race morning, but by the time the race got underway, the threat of rain had receded. The crowd was immense. All around the circuit there were banners with encouraging messages for me and when I brought my car onto the grid it was engulfed by a mass of television crews and photographers and radio broadcasters. It was a special occasion. When the time came, I donned my balaclava and my collar, which I have worn every time I have driven a car since my Formula Ford accident. I tightened the strap on my helmet and took one last look at the crowd which packed the grandstands. I was determined to win and I knew that if I had a chance to do it, they would help me.

These last few years, nobody could touch me at Silverstone. But back in 1987, although I felt good about the track, I had yet to win a Grand Prix there. I sat in my car waiting for the flag to send us on our parade lap. The radio crackled into life. It was Frank. He said, 'I've only two words to say, Nigel. And they are: "Brain Power". Have a great race.' Maybe he sensed that this was going to be a maximum adrenalin afternoon, or maybe he just wanted to avoid a first lap collision between Nelson and me.

Prost made a demon start and led into Copse, but both Nelson and I got past him on the first lap and started to pull away. At this stage Nelson was slightly faster than me because I had opted to run with less wing than him, knowing that I would be slower at the start when the car was heavy with fuel, but hoping that at the end of the race I would be easier on the fuel consumption. As long as I could stay in touch while the fuel load lightened I should be alright. But on lap 12 I began getting a lot of vibration through the steering wheel. A wheel balancing weight, basically a piece of lead with adhesive backing which balances the weight of each wheel, had come off.

As the race continued the vibration got worse and it started to blur my vision. Goodyear had told us that it would be possible to go the whole race on one set of tyres, but I knew that I would have to stop to fix the vibration. On lap 36, while five seconds behind Nelson, I pitted. The entrance to the Silverstone pit is twisty and narrow, but I flew down it and stopped for tyres. I was stationary for just over nine seconds during the tyre change and then I was on my way again, now 28 seconds behind with 29 laps to go.

I think that the Williams team probably thought that the race was settled at this point, although they said nothing. There were never any team orders. Nelson would not be stopping for tyres and as far as they were concerned I should be able to hold Senna off and keep my second place. I had other ideas.

The mathematics were simple. I needed to take at least a second a lap off Nelson, but of course he would respond once he realized he was being caught, so nothing less than flat out laps would help me. I pushed quite hard on the first laps on my new tyres and immediately did a lap half a second faster than anything I had done on the old tyres. I put the hammer down once the tyres were fully up to temperature, pushing harder and harder. Nelson saw that I was catching him and responded, lapping faster than he had before to try to maintain his lead. I was giving it everything I had, running wide on the exit of some corners, getting a wheel on the grass here and there, running the car on and even beyond the limit.

Inside the car I was totally focused. With every lap that passed, I could read the gap from my pitboard and with about 12 laps to go it began to tell me the story I needed to know. Nelson's tyres were clearly losing their edge and he was struggling. I had risen to the challenge after the tyre stop, not knowing whether it held any hope of success. Now I could see victory beckoning me on. I was getting closer and closer. The gap fell to seven seconds with 10 laps left. I began to get a visual fix on him. As I came onto the Hangar Straight I could see Nelson in the distance taking Stowe. The crowd could sense that this thrilling chase might be about to bear fruit. Their cheers and encouragement grew lap by lap as the margin came down. The excitement around the track was electrifying. I felt as if a giant hand was pushing me down the straight and through the corners. The team held out a pit board to me saying 'FUEL'. It was true that the meter was showing nearly empty, but I was not going to let that stop me. I had no choice, if it ran out of fuel then so be it, but in the meantime I was going to try to win this race.

The speed was mesmerising. I didn't think about anything else but the chase for all of those 29 gruelling laps. The force of my will and determination drove me faster and faster. I was completely at one with the car; it felt as though it was a part of me as it went around the corners and down the straights. I was using all of the road and more, straightening corners and shortening straights.

When we started lap 58 Nelson was 6.5s ahead, the length of the pit straight. I pushed harder, squeezing everything out of the engine, the car, the tyres, and myself. When we started lap 59 I was half the length of the pit straight behind, having set the fastest lap. Four laps later I followed him into Copse a few car lengths behind. I knew I had him now and he knew it too. I shadowed him through Maggotts and Becketts, thinking about where I might pass.

I wanted to do it as soon as possible, to keep this fantastic momentum going and use it to carry me past him. If I allowed him to hold me up, I might lose the initiative. I swerved gently to his left and then to his right so that he could see me looming large in his mirrors. He knew I had chased him down and I wanted to maintain the psychological advantage by keeping him guessing what I was going to do next. As we swung out onto the Hangar Straight I lined up right behind him, in his slipstream, disappearing momentarily from view in his mirrors. I knew what I wanted to do – I was going to sell him a dummy. I was watching his hands and his head from behind, I knew that they would tell me when to make my move.

I went right, not to pass him, just to make him act. He had his head inclined to the right and was watching in the mirror. Immediately he moved right to cover the line. Straight away I went left, this time a bolder, more aggressive move to make him think that this time I was trying to pass. His head swung frantically to the left to check his other mirror. He bought it and decided to block, his hands turning the wheel well over to the left and his head decked over. This was it. I shot out from his slipstream and made for the inside line into the right hander at Stowe. Too late, he realised his mistake and tried to cover for it.

He came over on me, but I had the momentum. We were both doing about 190mph into the braking zone for Stowe, but I knew I had the corner. He tried to chop me, but nothing was going to stop me now and I never even lifted off the throttle. I was too pumped up after 25 flat out laps to be intimidated by that sort of thing. If anything he had to back off and I sailed into the apex of Stowe ahead.

Both of our engines were screaming during this battle, but they were drowned out by the cheers from the grandstands. It was like a football stadium. The noise was deafening. As I came away from Stowe I could see the fences and earthbanks at the side of the track moving with the blur of colour as people waved flags and held their arms aloft. When I crossed the line the place erupted. Driving down the vast expanse of the Silverstone pit straight felt like walking into a small room on your birthday. I was overwhelmed by people power.

With two laps to go the fuel meter on my dashboard told me that I was out of fuel, in fact it said that I was two litres in the red. I carried on, not pushing now, just maintaining the lead and praying that I wouldn't run out of fuel. As it turns out I did, but not before crossing the line for the 65th time and taking the chequered flag. I had won my 10th and most important Grand Prix victory.

When the engine died at Club Corner the track was engulfed with fans and I was swallowed up by them. It was an unashamedly emotional moment. They were as much a part of it as I was and they were in a mood to celebrate.

In the press conference after the race Nelson shook my hand and we were polite about each other. He said his tyres had gone off in the last ten laps and I said that if he had changed tyres earlier, I doubt whether I would have won, but it was all academic. I had won and once again I had beaten him.

It signalled the end of his relationship with Williams. He felt that Frank should have told me to hang back and let him win, but Frank was having none of it. We had been in a race of our own, lapping everybody else at least once, but there were no free rides at Williams. Best man wins.

David Brown, Nigel's Williams race engineer: 'Nigel is very well disciplined in a car, in terms of getting the lap times, so once he's ahead he settles down into a rhythm and just counts off the laps. That's the secret to it, to be that much in control of what you're doing, and only the really top drivers can do that. At Paul Ricard Nigel was obviously enjoying himself; he was reeling off the laps towards the chequered flag and he suddenly started singing down the radio!

'At Silverstone the fuel meter was reading close to empty two laps from the end. Luckily it was reading wrong, but he crossed the line on fumes.'

16

HONDA

Certain things happened with my engines in the second half of 1987 which shouldn't have happened. Whether they were orchestrated or whether someone made a mistake I have no idea. But I couldn't do anything about it and it was very disappointing.

At Hockenheim, I had the race in the bag when the engine died. Prost inherited the lead, but he broke down four laps from the end and Piquet lucked into his first win of 1987.

Two weeks later in Hungary, Nelson announced that he would join Lotus for 1988. He and Frank had been unable to agree on his status within the team. He wanted Frank to force me to play a supporting role and Frank declined. Nelson would take Senna's place at Lotus alongside Honda's own Japanese driver Satoru Nakajima, while Senna would move to McLaren, who would also get the Honda engines.

The background to all of this was that Williams was about to lose Honda engines a year before the end of the contract. Frank's deal with Honda was due to expire at the end of 1988, but there was an option whereby Honda could buy themselves out of the contract a year early. Honda very much wanted to continue with Senna, but he was unhappy with the set-up at Lotus and with the uncompetitiveness of the 99T chassis. Honda therefore took the opportunity to go with him to McLaren with Prost.

Honda offered Frank a deal with a big payout as compensation for terminating the contract. Perhaps if he had been prepared to take Satoru Nakajima to drive alongside me, he might have been able to hold on to the Honda engines, but he was not interested in pursuing that avenue.

In the short-term, from my point of view it was very bad, because we had a dreadfully uncompetitive season in 1988, with a normally aspirated engine against the turbos, and it really upset me because having won thirteen of the last thirty-eight Grands Prix I felt that I deserved a decent crack at the world title. As a number one driver, with full support from the team and carrying the momentum we had built up over the past three years there is no question in my mind that I could have won the World Championship in 1988.

As it turned out, the Honda turbo pulverised the opposition that year and Senna and Prost's McLarens won 15 out of the 16 races. I am quite sure that with the same engine in a Williams chassis I would have beaten them and taken the title. But having said that, I don't run Williams and as long as they were happy with their decision that's their business.

I knew from the moment I heard that Honda was pulling out, that the odds against me winning the championship in 1987 had reduced dramatically. After all, Nelson would be staying with Honda in 1988 and it made good business sense for them to have the World Champion on board. Clearly they would not be going out of their way for a driver who would not be using their engines the following year.

The official announcement was made at Monza, shortly after first qualifying. Ironically, the driver who had most to lose from Honda's decision, namely me, had just put their car on provisional pole, ahead of Piquet. Honda's managing director of F1, Yoshitoshi Sakurai was asked at the press conference whether he could confirm that for the rest of the season I would get the same equipment as Nelson.

He said: 'The engine settings will be completely the same. Of course the driving styles of Mansell and Piquet are different, so there is something we change a little bit in the setting, but basically the fuel economy and performance are the same.' There would be times over the next few weeks when I would seriously wonder about that.

Third place at Monza left me 20 points behind Piquet with five races to run. I needed a good result in Portugal to have any chance, but all weekend my engines were way down on power. Just before Estoril I had tested the new active suspension car at Brands Hatch and recorded some very fast times with it. I was a bit suspicious of active suspension, having done a lot of development work on it at Lotus in the early days. Being highly experimental, it had a habit of failing in very unpredictable ways, often at high speed and I didn't like scares like that. Nevertheless the Williams system seemed alright and it was clearly a lot better than the passive car.

The principal of active suspension is that it maintains optimum aerodynamics by controlling the ride height, so it would be advantageous to have it as the fuel tanks got lighter, at which time a passive car rises on its springs. I had to win in Portugal to have any realistic hope of taking the title and I knew Nelson would run the active car, so I decided to go the same way.

On Friday in Estoril my engine felt down on power and I set my time, good enough for second on the grid, in the passive car. I asked Honda to change the engine in the active car. They refused, saying that there was nothing wrong with it. I didn't want to seem paranoid, but there was no question in my mind that it was not as crisp and that it dragged on the straights compared to the normal units. Honda's refusal to change it caused some bad feeling within the team and even Frank had a few words with them to see why they were so reluctant to change the engine.

Finally they did change it on Saturday night ready for the race, but when I took the car out for the warm-up on Sunday morning the new engine didn't feel any different from the old one and was still less crisp and had less top end than normal.

There was a major pile up in the first corner, which I nearly went into when I came round to start my second lap. The race was duly stopped and Nelson, who had damaged his car in the accident, was able to get it repaired in time for the restart.

At the restart I got into a battle with Gerhard Berger in the Ferrari for the lead. It lasted until lap 14 when my engine suddenly began misfiring badly and then died altogether. I was out. Prost went on to win with Berger second and Piquet came in third a minute behind Prost. Once again a win had escaped me. When the mechanics got the car back to the garage it fired up first time.

I was upset, but reasonably philosophical about what happened in Estoril, but at the Spanish GP the following week I became convinced that something strange was going on. I had been working on the active and passive suspension cars and had taken provisional pole on Friday in the passive. But what I hadn't realised was that Nelson had been sandbagging that day, lapping slower than the maximum in his active car. So, when towards the end of Saturday qualifying he put in a lap some six-tenths faster than anything he had done before to snatch pole position from me, I had no time to respond.

I called a meeting with Mr Sakurai of Honda and Frank and I told them that I felt that Honda were not treating me fairly. I knew that

Honda had been upset with Frank for missing out on the drivers' championship in 1986 and for not letting Piquet win at Silverstone and I told them that I regretted causing some of the problems between them. But while they had given Frank a big payout for losing the engines, they had made none to me. I had been loyal to Honda and had made a commitment to Williams for 1988 based on them having Honda engines and now that wouldn't be happening. I felt that I was at the end of the pecking order behind Piquet and Senna and that Honda were being disloyal to me. Sakurai said that I was a good driver and that I might be able to drive for them in 1989. Big deal.

The way things were going, I felt that the support wasn't there any more from the team and I was ready to leave. I felt it was a no-win situation for me and I told Frank that I would leave the team if it was in the best interests of all parties. He said that he wanted me to stay.

I decided to stay with the passive car for the race, but I knew that I would have to get ahead of Nelson early. Overtaking at Jerez is extremely difficult, but I passed him where he least expected it and took the lead on the first lap. He was fooled by it, but he later made out to the press that I had put us both at risk with my maneouvre. Once again the press didn't bite. I had him fair and square and that's what they wrote. I pulled away from him and led until the chequered flag. He drove a ragged inconsistent race and messed up his chances by letting his foot off the brake in his pit stop to prevent the rear wheels from spinning. He finished fourth and his lead in the championship was 18 points with three races to go. It was a real long shot, but I hadn't given up yet.

A vitally important skill to have in a race is the ability to get into a rhythm at high speed and be consistently fast. In some of my best Grand Prix wins I got the lead after ten or fifteen laps and then just switched onto auto-pilot, lapping consistently at optimum speed and just ticking the laps off. I didn't want to push the envelope any more than that, there was no need to over-extend myself, so I basically 'put myself to sleep'. You go onto auto-pilot and you simply manage the car; you change gear at the same points, you have all your braking points programmed into your mind, you don't have to judge anything, as long as an oil flag doesn't come out, or you have to struggle passing a back marker, you don't have to wake yourself up. You go into every corner the same as the lap before.

I used to tell my engineer to 'wake me up' if he noticed anything, like someone catching me up or an incident ahead which I was likely to run into. If you can do it, it's a great way of conserving energy, which can often come in handy if you get into a fight at the end of the race, when, after ninety minutes of flat-out racing, everyone is tired.

It doesn't always work, though. Once I got into the lead in Spain, I told David Brown, my engineer, that I was 'going to sleep' and that he was to 'wake me up' after 20 laps. Two laps later I was woken abruptly when the wing mirror flew off and hit the side of my helmet!

In Mexico the Honda situation got really silly. With a huge amount of commitment and a few close calls I managed to get pole, my eighth of the year. But amazingly the timing beam on the main straight showed my top speed to be 15mph slower than Nelson and yet I was far faster exiting the fast 180 degree Peraltada, which leads onto the straight. I asked Honda how this was possible, but they just shrugged. So on the Sunday morning warm-up, when I was still slower on the straight, I decided to prove that my engine was slower.

I came into the pits and had my wings changed to lower settings than Nelson's, which would give less downforce and therefore I should have been quicker in a straight line. I went out again, but all I got was an improvement of 1.2mph. I came back in and showed the figures to Honda and to Frank and Patrick. It was obvious what was going on. I was very upset about it and I demanded that it be put right. A chip was changed in my engine and when I went out again I was suddenly 10mph faster down the straight! I was still 5mph slower than Nelson, but at least I had shown that I was not going to sit there and be cheated.

All weekend I had been at full stretch and had put in a superhuman effort to compensate for my lack of straightline speed. I tried to take the Peraltada flat on the Friday and nearly did it, but the car got away right at the end of the corner, sending me backwards across the line at 160mph in a huge slide which ended up in the pit wall at the far end. On Saturday I had a massive accident when a part in the right front suspension collapsed over a bump in a high-speed left hander. The car slammed a wall sideways on and was too badly damaged to race. The mechanics had to build a hybrid from the spare car and various spare parts.

I won the race. Now I was 12 points behind him with two races to run. Prost retired in Mexico, so he had no chance of winning the title.

We will never know what might have happened at those last two races in Japan and Australia because my season ended when I crashed heavily in first qualifying at Suzuka. The car swapped ends on me in a fast right hander and I slammed the wall backwards at 140mph, jarring my back. It was the most extreme agony I have ever felt.

To this day I have no idea what happened. I was taken to the circuit medical centre and from there to Nagoya hospital for overnight observation. The doctors were worried about a build up of fluid between my heart and my lungs. They were afraid that I had damaged my aorta, but thankfully they were wrong. Honda, to whom the home race was as important as the British is to me, panicked a bit, putting out press statements that I would race, but the medical officer, Syd Watkins ruled me out and to be honest I ruled myself out. I knew I was badly hurt and I just wanted to go home to the Isle of Man.

I had a very black night in Nagoya hospital, my mind spinning over a whole range of horrible subjects, from the accident to the thought that I might have internal bleeding. I was delirious and I wondered whether I should carry on racing. This wasn't the first time I'd been in hospital; did I need to inflict any more of this on myself and on Rosanne? This championship had been out of the question ever since I found out that Honda were leaving and next year looked like I would be making the numbers up. The next morning I loaded up on painkillers and flew back to Europe.

The season played out without me. Nelson didn't finish either in Japan or Australia but still took his third World Championship. I was bitter about what had happened with Honda, but I knew that I had done a good job and shown that in equal cars I could beat Nelson.

In early 1988, he made certain comments in Brazilian *Playboy* magazine about us. He called me an 'uneducated blockhead' and called Rosanne 'ugly'. He also said that Ayrton Senna was 'gay' and Enzo Ferrari 'senile'. I don't mind what anyone says about me, I'm a public figure and therefore I stand in the firing line. I am paid to do a job and to a certain extent you expect to hear both praise and criticism. But for him to attack my family, which is the private side of my life and has nothing to do with my job was out of order. I think it says an awful lot about the sort of person he is.

During the winter I had a good hard think about the situation. On the plus side I felt that I had proved myself to the doubters and the critics who had said that I did not have what it takes to be a consistent Grand Prix winner and a champion. Over the past three seasons I had established myself as a front-runner in Formula 1, I had twice been runner up in the World Championship and no-one could take away from me my 13 wins and 12 pole positions. I had shown that, given the right equipment I could do the job and do it consistently. Using established drivers like Piquet, Rosberg and Prost as a measuring stick, I had come out well.

I had been elevated to that category of driver who can make something out of nothing, someone who wins a race which his car does not deserve to win. You spy an opportunity, which doesn't seem from the outside to exist, you take it and you win. There aren't more than a couple of drivers in Formula 1 at any time who can do this. It's one of the things which marks out a great driver from a good driver.

But it is important to remember that you are only really as good as your last race and that motor racing is a very fickle business. One minute you could be on top of the world and the next you could be in a wheelchair. That's why you should always make it count.

I felt that my success had made me a more mature and a more complete person. We had suffered setbacks in the past and we continued to suffer setbacks, but we had also enjoyed real success and what motivated me to pick it up again after the shunt in Japan was the desire for more success.

Unfortunately 1988 was a very disappointing year. After all the promise which had been shown by the last three years at Williams and all the momentum we had built up with 13 Grand Prix wins, returning to the ranks of the also-rans was hard to take.

After the tragedy of Elio de Angelis' death I had promised myself and Rosanne that I would make my racing count, not make the numbers up. Yet here I was, through no fault of my own, relegated to following the turbo cars, a year after I had qualified on the front row fourteen straight times. We were competitive at only a handful of places and then only because of massive commitment in the cockpit. It was galling, but I consoled myself with the knowledge that we were at least moving forward with the new car.

With the FW12, Patrick Head and his team came up with the first in a new generation of Grand Prix cars, which would be the norm once the turbos became obsolete at the end of the season. Fully integrated and with built-in active suspension, it had a compact transverse gearbox and was beautifully packaged and prepared. In fact the car had everything except the power to do it justice. It worked well on the tighter circuits like Monaco, Hungary, Portugal and Spain where it had a lot of grip through the corners, which meant high g-forces on the driver's neck but which at least gave us the chance to run with the McLaren-Hondas occasionally.

The active gave me some nasty scares, however. Patrick and his team had committed a lot of effort to the design and manufacture of the active and were determined to get it right. Ultimately of course the system would bear fruit and when finally I won the World Championship in 1992, it was at the wheel of an active suspension Williams. But that was some way off and in 1988 we had a different type of system, which had a nasty habit of surprising its drivers.

Because you were never quite sure what would happen next, it made you somewhat wary when pushing your car to the limit in a high speed corner. To go really fast in any racing car you must have confidence in it and frankly it was hard to have confidence in the FW12's active system. During the course of the year it dumped several times and broke three top wishbones, one of them during the French Grand Prix.

I was, I felt, quite right as a driver to voice my concerns about the system, but the engineers were less willing to accept them. I'll never forget Frank Dernie, who had been Nelson's engineer, saying to me in Mexico, 'I've looked at the computer and as far as I'm concerned everything looks fine. There's nothing wrong with the car.' My new team-mate Riccardo Patrese and I were driving our hearts out in these things and swearing blind that they were awful. But here's an engineer, who never gets out of the pit lane and certainly never drives the car, telling me that the car is fine!

As the season progressed it became increasingly obvious to me that I had to move on to maintain my career. When Enzo Ferrari made me another offer, I agreed to a deal and signed it the day after the French Grand Prix in July. I was sad in a way to be leaving Williams, with whom I had made that important transition from Grand Prix driver to Grand Prix winner, but I felt that I needed a fresh challenge and I desperately needed to win again. Watching Senna and Prost blast off into the distance with the Honda engines behind them, scooping 15 of the 16 races, was more than I could take at times. Williams agreed a deal with Renault for a supply of its brand new V10 engine for 1989 and although I was sure it would come good in time, I wanted to move on.

I had a very scary moment that year when I almost went off a cliff on a four-wheeler motor bike. I was not far from my home in the Isle of Man, returning from a day's rabbit hunting, with my rifle slung across my back and having a fine time breezing through the heather along the coastline, when the four-wheeler struck a boulder hidden behind a heather bush and sent me flying. I ended up ten feet from the edge of a precipice while the bike went over it and fell 200 feet into the sea. It was a very close shave.

On the track we suffered a string of retirements largely due to engine problems and, incredibly, when we arrived at Silverstone in July, I still had no points on the board.

I had won the last two British Grands Prix, but on the face of it I wasn't going to be able to give the crowd much to cheer about this year. The active had been worrying me and when it failed in the race at Paul Ricard the week before I had had serious second thoughts about it. In qualifying at Silverstone I had three mighty scares when the active dumped on me. I ended the day 13th and was not at all happy. I had told Patrick Head on previous occasions that I wanted to run a passive car, but he had told me that the FW12 was built around the active and that it wasn't possible to convert it to normal springs. But after the scares in qualifying we decided that it had to be changed in the interests of safety, so Williams began one of the most remarkable cobble-togethers in racing history.

The team worked around the clock to convert the cars to passive suspension. My car was ready for practice and I was immediately a second and a half quicker. The difference, I told Patrick was 'like night and day'. In the afternoon I went out and improved my time by almost two seconds, but could still only qualify 11th. Silverstone is, after all, a power circuit.

The weather on race morning, however, brought a smile to my face. It was good old British rain. The advantage of the turbo cars would be greatly reduced in the wet and as long as I kept it smooth and attacked at every opportunity, I felt that a good result might be possible.

I drove hard from the start and by lap 15 I was up to fifth place. The visibility was very bad, but the crowd was fantastic as always, cheering me on every time I made up another place. I was on a real charge, determined to salvage something from this dismal season. I had a great scrap with Alessandro Nannini in the Benetton and I passed him going into Club with a swooping dive, which he obviously did not expect because he backed off suddenly and got into a spin.

Now I was closing on Michele Alboreto in third place, the man I would be replacing at Ferrari in 1989. I caught him on lap 22 and passed him easily going into Club corner, but not long after that found I had Nannini back on my tail. He dived past going into the Woodcote

Chicane, but lost it three laps later and spun off into a gravel trap. Senna was leading, with Berger losing ground in second. On lap 50 I passed Gerhard and the crowd went barmy. They really wanted me to get my British Grand Prix hat-trick and I kept charging, but it was never on.

Senna had the race totally locked up, driving to the fuel gauge and perfectly controlled in the wet. At the end he was 20 seconds ahead, but I had finished second in a car which had been cobbled together overnight. It was a great result for the team and it gave us a much needed boost. I knew that there would be other days for me at Silverstone.

But it wasn't like winning and it was all fairly academic as far as the championship was concerned. Senna won his first World title in Japan and he and Prost and Honda finished the season with 199 points between them. I was ninth in the championship with 12 points from those two second place finishes. It had been a dismal year and a massive disappointment after the three years I had enjoyed with Honda-engined cars.

I knew that I could have won the championship if Williams still had Honda engines, but that's the way motor racing works sometimes and that's why, although I love it dearly, I also hate it too on occasions.

Chris Hampshire, close friend: 'Nigel invited my wife Carol and I over to the Isle of Man one weekend in the summer of 1988 and when we got to the island airport he was there to meet us. He had a chartered plane standing by and he said, "Hop in, we're going to Scotland." Once we were airborne he said, "Hope you don't mind. 'We're going to Gleneagles for Jackie Stewart's clay pigeon shoot." We'd come all the way from London and now we were on our way to Scotland. That's the sort of man Nigel is.

'When we got to Scotland the security was incredibly tight because the Royal Family was there; Princess Anne, Prince Andrew and Prince Edward, as well as King Husein of Jordan. In fact it was like *Who's Who,* because there were huge stars like Steven Spielberg, famous soccer players and so on.

'The police Special Branch were very worried about security. They didn't recognise me, of course and I didn't look as though I had come for a weekend's shooting in Scotland. Worst of all I didn't have any identification on me, so they picked me up! Nigel thought this was hilarious and kept winding them up about me.

'When we got to Gleneagles, it had been a bit fraught so Nigel said, "Come on, we'll go and have a swim and a jacuzzi". So we put on our swimming shorts and a towelling bathrobe and we were just on the way out of the door when the phone rang. It was Jackie Stewart. He wanted us to get measured up for the shooting clothes and boots and so on. So Nigel and I set set off down there and we were standing there in this hall wearing nothing but bathrobes trying wellies on when Jackie Stewart comes over and starts introducing us to Lord So and So and all these famous people. I just wanted to shrink into the woodwork, but Nigel loved it. He thought it was all a huge joke.'

Murray Walker, BBC television commentator: 'After Nigel won in Austria, he banged his head on an iron girder as he was being driven along in the winner's car. When he came into the interview room he had an enormous bump on his forehead. "Nigel," I said, "You've got a colossal bump on your forehead. Take your cap off so that viewers can see it." And, misjudging the distance between us, I proceeded to stick my finger right into the middle of it! It must have been excruciatingly painful, but he hardly even flinched. If there had been any repeat fees, I'd have made a fortune for the number of times that clip has been shown since.'

17

FORZA FERRARI!

Enzo Ferrari was very much his own man. And that's why we got on. I was the last driver to be personally signed by the 'Commendatore' before he died in August 1988 and that honour remains one of the greatest in my entire career. He said that he considered me to be one of the finest drivers he had ever hired. I was a real fighter, he told me, a driver with courage and passion, who knew how to win races. He said he admired me both as a person and as a family man. He had read a lot about me and knew quite a lot about my life.

I'll never forget the experience of having dinner with him. He was very majestic, a real gentleman. But the power of command he had over his entourage was astonishing. When he wasn't speaking there was general conversation around the table. But the instant he opened his mouth or raised his hand as if he was about to speak, everybody else fell silent. Even if someone was half way through a sentence they would just clam up immediately when the master spoke. That was an indication of the respect everyone had for the man and for what he had achieved. He certainly left a very lasting impression on me.

It was an extraordinary occasion. Because I was there at the instigation of Enzo, people treated me with enormous respect too. It was a very enlightening experience. It showed me what real power is and I must say I felt very glad to be on his side. He was a fascinating man, a giant whose motor racing history stretches back almost to the dawn of the sport. He drove himself in the days of the long road races, when riding mechanics sat alongside the drivers, but he retired into a manager's role in the 1920's. I was reasonably knowledgeable on the history of the team before I met Enzo and signed a deal with him, but over the next two years I became much more aware of what he and his team had been through and of some of the great drivers of all nationalities who had raced for him over the years. Until you drive for Ferrari you don't really appreciate how much magic goes with the name. Not just in Italy, but across the world you are acclaimed right away because you are a Ferrari driver.

Enzo seemed to have a soft spot for Englishmen and he respected the courage and commitment of the 'British Bulldog' attitude. He had been particularly close to two English drivers, Peter Collins, who died in the German Grand Prix of 1958 and John Surtees, who won the World Championship for Enzo in 1964, having already won several titles on motorcycles. Mike Hawthorn, the first Englishman to win the World title in 1958, did it in a Ferrari. I felt honoured to become part of such a noble tradition. It was a shame that I didn't get to work with him for a few years before he died.

It meant a lot to me that the two greatest names in Grand Prix racing, Colin Chapman and Enzo Ferrari believed in me. Their influence on Formula 1 stretched back over decades and they both had a great many drivers and champions pass through their hands. That both of them considered me to be one of the most talented drivers they had ever employed means as much to me as any of my trophies or awards. I'll take the opinion of two such men over the army of so-called experts in the press and the pit lane any day.

I first met Enzo in 1986, when I visited his headquarters in Maranello shortly after that classic British Grand Prix at Brands Hatch. At the time I was flattered to be offered a drive by what was surely the greatest team, historically speaking, in Grand Prix racing. The Scuderia Ferrari had been in motor racing since before the war when Enzo and his small team entered Grands Prix using Alfa Romeos from 1929 to 1938. After the war Alfa offered him the chance to run its factory team, but Enzo decided to go his own way. In the late forties he began building his own cars and ever since 1950, the year that the Formula 1 World Championship began, Ferraris had been at or near the front of the grid.

The factory reeked of history. Feelings oozed out of the walls, the floors and the ceilings. Photographs and paintings covered the walls, echoing memories of past drivers many victorious, many long dead. You had the feeling that this was a place where Grand Prix racing wasn't just a business, it was a tradition. Every mechanic and engineer, right down to the guy who swept the floor, regarded it as an immense honour to work for the Ferrari racing team. In Italy the fortunes of the Ferrari team are second only in importance to the

Pope. Driving one of the shiny red cars, you carry with you the hopes and dreams of an entire nation.

It was interesting to see the reality behind the imposing facade of Ferrari, but back in 1986 I decided that the time was not right for a move there. At the time my decision was motivated not by any reservation about competitiveness, but by the thought that I was signing to drive not just for Williams, but for Honda. When finally I did sign for Ferrari in mid-1988 I could neither forgive nor forget the disappointments of the past two seasons and the departure of Honda, but I was looking for a fresh start and a new challenge, as Williams had given me in 1985.

It was the right thing to do. Going into the 1989 season I was more excited about Formula 1 racing than at any time in my career so far. When I joined Ferrari I was thirty-five years old and a far more mature racer than the man who joined Williams just four years earlier. I was more happy and contented than at any point in my career and I was enjoying my driving far more because I felt that I had got the fire, which had always burned so strongly inside me, under control. My competitive spirit still raged, but it had also been matured and refined by discipline.

Looking back, I could chart my development as a Grand Prix driver to this point; through the early Lotus years, learning the ropes from Colin, then the difficult years when no-one believed in me and I strugged to control my emotions and my aggression. Then the move to Williams where I learned to control my feelings, to become more measured and more considered and to become a consistent winner and a top rank qualifier.

As my success curve increased I naturally came to need and demand different things. In 1980 I was grateful to be there and to have the opportunity to race. In the first three years at Williams I had been the number two driver who did a lot of winning and should have won two championships. Now I had thirteen wins under my belt and as my expectations of myself grew, having the right set-up and the right support from a team became even more important.

At Ferrari I felt I had that support and also their respect. I had always been my own man, not someone who tries to be something they are not just to please someone else. Enzo had signed me because I was an individual and, looking around, I had to say that I was one of the few drivers who stood out for who they were and what they were trying to achieve.

Of course, there were some doubts in my mind. Ferrari had a reputation for being a hotbed of political intrigue and politics is my least favourite aspect of Formula 1. I was aware of the risks going into the project and I decided I would simply have to deal with them head on as and when they arose. For the most part I intended to do my talking on the track.

For the first year, being a Ferrari driver was a fairy tale. I was like a little boy in a sweet shop. You are asked what you'd like and you say 'everything' and you get everything. There is no team like it in terms of looking after its drivers. On one of my early visits I noticed a Ferrari Testarossa in the car park and mentioned to my host how much I admired the car. We chatted for a while about the car and resumed our business. The following week a Testarossa arrived at my home in the Isle of Man.

Another time I admired a Ducati motor bike which was parked in the factory and three weeks later an identical bike arrived at my home. I caught on to this and mentioned to one of the management how much I admired the Falcon 900 private jet, but sadly one of those never arrived at my home! But generally, any little thing that they could do to please you or make you comfortable they would do. It was like a family and it was a real honour to drive for them. It also did a lot for my bank balance. I had a multi-million dollar deal with an option in my pocket for 1991.

Working with Ferrari was also a lot of fun. Every year the team would take a group of Italian journalists for a press conference and skiing trip. I was not too steady on skis, but I'll always give anything a go. On one run at Sestriere I was going far too fast and got hopelessly out of control. As I hurtled towards the finish line there were some anxious faces among the large group of journalists and onlookers. Unable to stop, I ploughed through the throng and collided with a large cart, which was being used to dispense parmesan cheese to spectators!

Whatever Ferrari did they did in style. They had so many sponsors on hand and you were always showered with gifts. We came away from Sestriere with so many presents that we couldn't fit them all in to the helicopter, so we had to hire a van to get them home!

When I joined Ferrari I really thought that I was on the verge of winning the championship. It was long overdue for Ferrari, who hadn't won the drivers' title since 1979 and I'm a romantic anyway so I thought it would be fabulous to do it in a Ferrari, as my countrymen

Mike Hawthorn and John Surtees had done. And when I joined, the opportunity genuinely seemed to be there.

I didn't expect to do it the first year. Even though I had been in Formula 1 for nine years, I knew that 1989 would have to be a building year, putting in lots of hard work ready for an all-out assault on the title in 1990. Part of the reason for this lay in the rule changes. At the end of the 1988 season the turbo engines were banned so everyone reverted to normally-aspirated engines. John Barnard, who had joined Ferrari as chief designer after stunning success with McLaren in the mid-1980s, came up with a totally new concept in Formula 1 design, the 639/640, which featured all new aerodynamic styling, a brand new V12 engine and a revolutionary semi-automatic gearbox, operated by 'paddles' on the back of the steering wheel. Being a totally new car with a lot of electronics, it would need a lot of development. Barnard believed that the car should be raced in the second half of the 1988 season, so that all the bugs would be out of it by the start of 1989 and a challenge for the championship could be mounted properly. Competitiveness would perhaps have to be sacrificed in the second half of 1988 to ensure the challenge in the long term.

Barnard didn't get his way. In the turmoil after Enzo's death in August of 1988 the new management felt that the team should stick with the 87/88C turbo car and put in a thorough test programme on the 639. The car obviously needed a lot of work. Gerhard Berger and test driver Roberto Moreno tested the car in late 1988, but the internals of the new gearbox kept mashing into one another and it had a habit of throwing alternator belts. Many tests ended in frustration after only a few laps.

I first drove the car before Christmas on a rainy day at Fiorano, Ferrari's own test track at the factory. It was a freezing cold day, but I was very excited to be driving a Ferrari for the first time. Everybody in the team was immensely friendly and cheerful and there was a real feeling that we were embarking on a special mission together. It was a wonderful feeling when I first put on my red overalls with the famous Prancing Horse logo and was strapped in to the bright red car.

Because of the conditions, it was hard to tell much about the car, but the new V12 engine seemed very driveable around Fiorano, which is mostly corners. It was only when we took the car for a longer test at Paul Ricard that I realised how short of breath it was down the straight. It had about 600bhp at the time. Clearly we needed a lot more to keep up with the Hondas. On the up side it was without doubt the crispest, most gorgeous sounding racing engine I had ever heard.

The gearbox caused me a few problems too. On the back of the steering wheel were two levers, which controlled the gearbox. The one on the right controlled the seven speeds up, just like a motorbike, and the one on the left controlled the speeds down. The first time I drove it I pushed the left button instead of the right, went down instead of up and locked the rear wheels. Unfortunately I was going down the straight at the time and the car slid backwards across the grass, getting covered in mud and frost. It was terribly embarrassing. The guys had spent half an hour polishing the thing before I went out and as I sat there I was thinking, 'You really don't need this, Nigel.'

At Ricard I had another moment. Braking for a corner and going down through the gears, clunk, clunk, clunk, I put my foot down hard on the throttle and to my enormous surprise found that I was in seventh instead of first! The gearbox was quite tricky to get used to at first, especially the way that you had to rethink when you had full lock on the steering wheel. It was a tremendous advantage to be able to change gears in mid-corner, but you had to remember which paddle was which when your hands were upside down.

The gearbox had other advantages. Changing up through the gears was quite a bit faster than a conventional transmission, because the drive from engine to wheels was broken for a minimum amount of time. From the point of view of fatigue it was definitely better over a long race than changing gears with clutch and lever, but there was also one big disadvantage; you had to go through every gear when you were downshifting and that lost you time. Going from a straight into a low gear corner in the Williams, I would brake hard and late, jam the lever from sixth into second and hit the power. On the Ferrari I couldn't do that.

I wanted to keep a clutch for starts. Barnard was keen to dispense with the clutch altogether. He had come up with a system where there would be two buttons on the dashboard and just before the red light you would engage one, get the revs right and when the lights went green you would just flick the lever and go. Maybe in time it would be the way to go, but I was worried that if you screw up, you go nowhere and that would not only be disastrous for competitiveness, but also extremely dangerous if you were stuck on the grid.

As the new season approached and the testing continued, it was clear that it would be some time before we had a reliable car. I gave an interview before the first race where I said that although positive about the challenge, I felt we had a mountain to climb. I was to be proved right in time, but not before one of the most extraordinary and romantic results of my entire career.

Against all the odds and with a car which broke down in three of the four practices sessions at Rio, I won my first Grand Prix for Ferrari.

Gerhard Berger, 1989 Ferrari team-mate: 'Nigel is a very special character in this business. It is very difficult to understand him because he has two sides to his character. On the one hand he has a soft side, which is too sensitive and too soft and on the other side of him there is this incredible fighter. He can create unbelievable power when he feels that he has to fight. It's like he flicks a switch in his head and he gets superhuman power. This makes him difficult to race against because he's so strong. I saw it as much outside the car as in it.

'I think that before he came to Ferrari in 1989 he asked around about the team and about me and I think that he got the wrong information, because I felt that he never trusted me. He was very polite and we got on well, but he was very careful and I could feel it. I never gave him any reason not to trust me, but when he arrived we went into a competition and I felt that he didn't trust me.'

18

THE IMPOSSIBLE WIN

On the grid before the race in Rio I met the captain of the British Airways flight BA244 which would be leaving Rio at four thirty that afternoon for London Heathrow. The race was due to start at 1 pm and I had booked seats for myself and Rosanne, believing that my car would probably last 10 or 15 laps before breaking, so with a quick helicopter hop to the airport we should make the flight. 'If we're running a little late, might you be able to hold the plane for a few minutes if I phone you?' I asked the captain. 'Yes,' he said smiling. 'But not for too long.'

It seemed a pretty safe bet. In the two days of qualifying my car had failed to last more than five laps in a single run without breaking. Several times I stopped out on the circuit, which was not a safe place to be. Because of my problems with Senna and Piquet, the battles on the track and the things said off it, the Brazilian fans were none to friendly towards me and as I sat on a guardrail after the first of my breakdowns they started throwing coins and bottles at me!

On Friday morning I had a hydraulic pump failure in the gearbox. When we did get the car going, in first qualifying, I was pushing hard when I was badly baulked by Piquet in the Lotus. I had to brake so hard I almost spun. On Saturday I had two more pump failures and ended up with sixth place on the grid. My team-mate, Gerhard Berger had an easier run, although not without breakdowns and was able to clock third fastest time, behind the two McLarens of Prost and Senna.

On Sunday morning, as the temperatures soared to 106 degrees and just as I thought things couldn't get any worse, my car broke down after one lap in the warm-up. The only ray of sunshine on the horizon was the prospect of getting out of Brazil early on the British Airways flight.

Senna fluffed the start and as Patrese and Berger went either side of him into the first corner they touched, Gerhard spinning out and Senna losing his nose cone. I tucked in behind in third place as Patrese led from Boutsen in the second Williams. Prost was behind me.

The car felt alright and on lap three I passed Boutsen and closed up on Riccardo. Lap 10 came and went and on lap 15, by which time I had imagined I would be done for the day and heading for the airport, I lined him up down the back straight. Riccardo came across to keep the inside line into the left hander. I went right and simply drove around the outside of him. I was now leading and couldn't quite believe that the car was still in one piece. The gearbox seemed fine, the engine was pulling well. How extraordinary.

After the tyre stops I was second behind Prost, but unbeknown to me he was nursing a car with no clutch. I passed him easily and once again settled into the lead. Lap after lap I was just waiting for the car to break. In the middle of the race I was feeling pretty annoyed because I had missed my plane and surely the thing would break soon and it would be the worst of both worlds. But as the laps passed I began to think that it might be alright and that I might be about to win my first time out in a Ferrari.

Then all of a sudden, around lap 40, trouble struck. But it wasn't the gearbox or the engine; the steering wheel was coming off in my hands! The thing had somehow worked itself loose and I had to do almost a full lap before I came in for a new one. I screamed down the radio to the team to get a new one ready and when I came in I threw the old one out before I even came to a halt. Quick as a flash, the mechanic pushed the new one onto the steering column, locking it on with such force that he broke the radio button. For the rest of the race I would have no communication with the pits.

I went back out and three laps later overtook Prost again for the lead. By now I had realised that he had a problem and was nursing his car. So now with eighteen laps to go it was just a question of whether my car would last. I was praying so hard, because the car was running fabulously. We had got the set-up just right and the engine was running well and I was winning. I thought, 'This is too good to be true. Please, please, please keep going.' And it did.

The whole team went crazy, and being Italian they were quite emotional about such a remarkable win. The only down side to the whole thing was that when I picked up the trophy, the handles were like razor blades and as I held it aloft Cesare Fiorio asked me why I had blood running down my wrists. I looked up at my hands, suddenly realized what was going on and dropped the trophy. My palms and fingers were slashed!

That win was as close to a fairy tale as anything I have ever known. Rio was definitely one of the races in my career which I had no right to win, but somehow fate had decreed that I would win on my debut for Ferrari and it couldn't have been a better start. I dedicated my triumph to the memory of Enzo Ferrari.

It was Easter Sunday. Back in Maranello the church bells rang late into the night and the local priest, I later found out, received a message of congratulations from the Bishop of Modena giving thanks not only for the Resurrection of Christ but also for the resurrection of Ferrari. The day after the race, huge queues formed for tickets to the next Grand Prix at Imola, only an hour away from Ferrari's home in Maranello. Within hours all the grandstand seats were sold out. The circulation of the leading sports papers and racing magazines soared and my victory appeared on every television news bulletin. The whole of Italy went crazy.

In 1988, when we raced at Monza shortly after news broke that I had signed for Ferrari, I had been aware of a surge in support from the *tifosi*. But when we arrived at Imola a month after Rio, it was unbelievable. I had been nicknamed *Il Leone*, the Lion, and all around the circuit were banners saying: 'WIN FOR US, LION NIGEL'. It was tremendously moving.

Wonderful as that win in Rio had been, I knew it was a flash in the pan. We had been very lucky to win. Examining our competitiveness, it was clear that the gearbox was still not fully reliable and our engine was at least 50bhp down on the Hondas. There was a lot of euphoria in the air; team manager Fiorio had also won on his first time out with Ferrari and had acquired the nickname 'Hollywood'. Everybody in the team got very excited about the result in Rio, but I knew we wouldn't win like that again in a hurry and at Imola the dominance of the McLaren-Hondas would once again be demonstrated.

The extent of their superiority was put into sharp focus in qualifying at Imola. I managed a lap good enough for third on the grid. I kept going, looking to find some more time. The second lap was really hairy, I had to overtake five cars along the way, but I was so committed I just kept my foot in. At the end of it all I had improved by a tenth of a second. But I was still nearly a second and a half behind Prost and Senna.

To this day the memory of that race brings me out in goosebumps. At the start Senna led Prost, with me third, Patrese fourth and Berger in fifth. Gerhard was anxious to get past Patrese and run with me. On lap four, going into the flat-out left hander at Tamburello at around 180mph, his car went straight on into the wall and burst into flames. He was trapped for what seemed like ages before the fire crew put out the blaze and pulled him out. He was then taken to the track hospital. As the accident had happened behind me, it was not until I saw it on televison that I realised how horrific it was and how lucky Gerhard was to be alive.

After the race was stopped, there was an incredibly tense and emotional atmosphere. Everybody was afraid for Gerhard's life. Everyone in the team was very upset and some of them were actually crying. We had no idea at that point why the accident had happened. It was unlikely that he had made a mistake, something probably broke on the car. But what? And would it break on my car when the race was restarted?

A discussion broke out as to whether I should take the restart and it got very heated. Naturally, John Barnard was devastated by the accident and he was being pressured by Cesare Fiorio to make a decision; would my car be safe or not? Of course, there was no way he could answer that. It was far too soon to make a snap judgement of that kind, especially when it could be a question of life or death. Imagine if the same thing had happened again.

I was mortified by the accident and by what I witnessed among the team afterwards. I knew that I could not make a personal decision until I found out more about Gerhard's condition. I went to the hospital only to be thrown out, but I managed to get in round the back and up to Gerhard's room. He was conscious and we talked briefly. He said he had no idea what had happened, but mercifully I could see that his injuries were not fatal. He had second degree burns on his hands, a broken rib and a fractured shoulder blade.

Coming away from the medical centre I met his father and told him that Gerhard was alright. I felt a lot happier, but I also felt as if I was in a kind of dream. As I made my way back to the motorhome, people were talking to me, but I didn't see them or hear them. I do recall running into James Hunt who said that there was no way I should drive as it was too dangerous. I went inside the motorhome and it was like a madhouse. All kinds of wild things were being said and in the middle of it all Barnard was being put under this impossible pressure.

I couldn't listen to any more of that, so I came away and made the decision that I would restart. I knew it was very risky, given that we didn't know why Gerhard had crashed, but from what I had heard, I felt that if I didn't give Barnard the vote of confidence, then the team would suffer in the long term.

I didn't feel particularly brave, although I might well have thought someone else stupid for doing the same thing. You just have to judge the situation as it appears to you and let your instincts guide you. I thought that if something similar happened to me as had happened to Gerhard, I would be able to do something about it to recover the situation. I might still have an accident, but at least I would give myself more margin for error than Gerhard. He had not really been on the racing line before he went off and once the car went, he didn't try to brake or steer out of it, he just 'made himself small in the cockpit' as he put it.

It wasn't easy to get back in the car, but once the race got going again I treated the Tamburello with a lot of respect. Every time I've been there since I have treated it with care. I make sure that I'm in exactly the right place on the track going into it and all the way through the corner my body is hyper-sensitive to the movement of the car, feeling for changes in attitude or slides or anything at all. Tamburello was in the news five years later when, in a similar accident to Gerhard's, Ayrton Senna was killed there. It was a truly horrendous corner.

In any case, after 23 laps my gearbox broke and I coasted to a halt. Although I never like technical retirements, it was something of a relief. I had put my head into the lion's mouth and luckily emerged unscathed.

After examinations of his car, it turned out that Gerhard's right front wing had collapsed and the sudden loss of downforce had stopped the car from turning. Some attributed the breakage to Gerhard's habit of hitting the kerbs as he went through corners. I wasn't so sure, especially after the same thing happened to me in practice for the next race, at Monaco.

I was approaching Casino Square, going uphill flat in seventh when I heard something metallic go 'clink'. My instant reaction was that perhaps it was a drain, you pass over them from time to time on the Monaco streets. I changed down to fifth and turned in to the corner and nothing happened. Luckily because my style is to turn in early, I had a bit more time to deal with the problem. What saved me was that

I braked harder than normal, which transferred a fair amount of weight to the front. But I was running out of road on a bad camber. After I brought it under control, I realised that the same thing had just happened to me as had happened to Gerhard at Imola, except that, luckily for me, I hadn't being going as quickly. The wings had been beefed up since Gerhard's shunt and yet mine had broken just like that. I suddenly felt physically sick.

The day before I had had a heart-stopping moment when the left rear suspension broke. I put the two episodes out of my mind and squeezed everything I could from the car, but it was only good enough for fifth fastest. In the race the gearbox played up terribly and ceased working altogether on lap 27 after some lurid episodes when it selected neutral at just the wrong moment.

The Rio result faded further and further into the distance as reliability wiped out some competitive performances in the first half of the season. In Mexico, where Gerhard made his comeback, I was in second place and closing, swapping fastest laps with Senna, when the gearbox suddenly stopped working altogther. In the US Grand Prix at Phoenix the same thing happened when I was in third place.

By the middle of the season, though, things were really beginning to look up. I was second in France and at Silverstone, third at Hockenheim and then scored one of the best victories of my entire career in Hungary.

I might have won in France had my race car not been damaged in the spectacular start line accident of Mauricio Gugelmin. I made a good start and was just turning into the tight first corner when the blue Leyton House car landed upside down on my rear wing, destroying the back of my car and causing my head to thump the roll bar. I was forced to use the spare car which was in fact Gerhard's race car, discarded by him because it had an oil leak! The mechanics feverishly set about fixing the leak, but the delay meant that I would have to start from the pit lane – a far cry from the beautifully set-up car and second row grid position with which I started. I was mortified. My race car had been possibly the best set-up car I had had all season and I really felt that a win was on the cards. The McLarens were well within range in qualifying and warm-up and I was feeling very confident. Nevertheless, I finished the race in second place, and the fact that I did so in a car with considerably less grip than my own was promising.

In the British Grand Prix I had a really good battle with Alain Prost, but I picked up a puncture and lost half a lap nursing the car back to the pits. I fought back, urged on as always by the massive Silverstone crowd, but I couldn't make up the gap. I would have to settle for second behind Prost. 'Next year,' I told myself, 'when we've got this car right, I will come back and win this race and the championship'. Little did I know then that the man who beat me that day, whom I believed a sportsman and a fair competitor, would not only prevent me from winning the following year, but would cause me to announce my retirement from the sport.

By the time we arrived at Hockenheim the speculation was rife that Prost would be joining me at Ferrari in 1990. He had held a press conference during the Paul Ricard weekend to announce that he would be leaving McLaren after six seasons during which he had won three World titles. It seemed that he could no longer stand being in the same team as Senna. It appeared that the two of them had made an agreement in San Marino that there would be no overtaking on the first lap and Senna had broken the deal. The politics had got completely out of control.

My deal with Ferrari stipulated that I would be the number one driver in 1990, with use of the spare car. It was the deal I had longed for all through my apprenticeship years and when I was number two to Piquet. Then Ferrari asked me whether I would be prepared to re-negotiate my deal to allow Prost to join the team as equal number one. I wasn't enthusiastic about it, but I was open-minded.

Ferrari had made me feel very welcome. The way they treated me and motivated me was very special and I felt that I had the support I had always longed for from a team. It was visible in my driving. I think at this stage I was driving better than at any point in my career up to then. I felt a much more mature driver and knew much better what I could and could not do. I was relaxed, focused, comfortable and highly competitive.

The prospect of having Prost as a team-mate did not worry me. I'd always had quick team-mates and had beaten two World Champions in the same equipment, so I was quite confident that I could beat Prost too. He was clearly the best all-rounder in Formula 1 at the time and the most complete racing driver, having won 38 Grands Prix by stealth and cunning. I thought him a fair sportsman. In all of our battles on the track he had always been very fair. We had enjoyed some close duels and he never tried anything dangerous nor had he tried to take me off.

I badly wanted to win the World Championship the following year and to me the whole 1989 season was dedicated to gearing up for that challenge. I could see that with the right development, the 1990 Ferrari would be the class runner of the field. The championship was beckoning.

I could also see that Ferrari badly wanted Prost in the team and that they would probably sign him anyway, so it was in my best interests to get the best deal I could for myself in the circumstances. They made certain promises and Prost himself made certain promises about the way things would be in 1990. It was a situation I would not have chosen, but I didn't feel that I had anything to fear. Winning the championship by beating him in equal equipment would really mean something. I was sure I would have the team's support. How naive I was.

My victory in the Hungarian Grand Prix of 1989 was not only the high point of the year, but also one of the best all-round wins I had ever achieved. I triumphed through a combination of sheer opportunism, flat-out driving and careful, disciplined preparation of the car for the race, which included throwing away any chance of qualifying at the front.

We had arrived in Budapest just a few days after my thirty-sixth birthday and I was feeling pretty confident about our prospects for the race. I didn't like the Hungaroring very much, I don't think many of the drivers do. It's not what I would call a real drivers' circuit in that there's nowhere to overtake. Nevertheless, I thought that our car would be strong on the track. The premium on engine power was less than at many of the power circuits we had been on, like Paul Ricard, Silverstone and Hockenheim, and the Ferrari 640 generally handled well on this type of circuit.

I worked hard setting the car up on qualifying tyres, but I just wasn't getting anywhere. The car had a dreadful understeer which we just couldn't get rid of. It led to some rather heated words with some of the management, who saw Gerhard in sixth place on the grid and couldn't work out what I was doing. I discussed it with my engineer Maurizio Nardon and we decided to go our own way for the afternoon, to scrap the idea of qualifying and just concentrate on getting the race set-up perfect.

While everyone else was doing qualifying runs, I honed down the race settings, running on full and half full tanks to get the balance as good as possible across the range. By the end of the session, I had a reasonably good race set-up, but I had slipped down to 12th on the grid and I still wasn't happy with my car. I knew that I needed more downforce at the front for it to be really effective on turn in. Designer John Barnard said that I had the maximum wing available. I sat down with Maurizio and we thought it through carefully. We came up with the idea of making a Gurney flap to add onto the front wing to give us the extra downforce we needed.

It was made overnight and fitted before the warm-up on Sunday. Immediately, the car felt better and I was a second a lap faster than before and easily the fastest car of all in the warm-up. The problem now was that I would be starting in 12th place on a track where it was notoriously difficult to pass. I would have to do the bulk of the work at the start and then take whatever chances came my way.

I have never been more psyched up for the start of a race. I felt that a win was possible, but I would need to be supremely aggressive on the first lap if I was to stand any chance. I stared at the lights without blinking, made double sure I was in first gear and waited. I was on the inside lane, nearest the pit wall, with not too much room for manoeuvre. 'Probably have to go left,' I thought to myself. The instant the red light disappeared and the green began to come on, I floored it. Two rows in front of me Modena had got a poor start, so Martini, directly in front of me, jinked left to go around him and headed down the middle of the grid. I had no alternative but to follow. But he wasn't as fast through the gears as me and I jinked further left and passed him. I took the outside line as we sprinted down to the first corner, then I went around the outside of the cars in front and exited the corner in eighth place. I had passed four cars before the second corner!

After that I had to be patient and choose my moment carefully to pick off the others. I was also being very careful with my tyres, not putting them under any unnecessary strain while the heavy fuel load lightened. The last thing I would need would be a tyre stop. I sat in eighth place until lap 12 when Nannini pitted and things started to move. By lap 30 I passed Berger and then ten laps later I sped past Prost when he least expected it, I was now third with half the race still to run.

On lap 52 Senna passed Patrese for the lead down the main straight and through the second corner I followed him. I was now second with Senna only a few car lengths ahead. The next time we crossed the start/finish line I was glued to his gearbox, but he left no room for me to pass into turn one. That was the main passing place, there really wasn't another, unless the driver in front made a mistake and then you just had to be ready to act. I had been in this situation with Senna before and I knew that he would make it extremely difficult for me to pass. He could be quite ruthless and wouldn't think twice about cutting you up. Sometimes when following him like this in the past he had suddenly braked where you would expect him to accelerate. It was also possible that he would try to put me off if I tried a lunge down the inside. My senses were never as highly tuned as they were when I was racing him like this.

There were 21 laps remaining and no reason to do anything hasty. I would pressurize him at every turn and be ready to pounce if he made any mistake or showed any hesitation. He knew that I had the car to do the job and he also knew that I would never give up trying. I decided that if a chance came up I would take it and I'd hold my ground whatever he did to try to stop me. It was a battle of wills.

My chance came sooner than expected. As we went down the hill five laps later we came upon Stefan Johansson in the Onyx. Although we didn't know it at the time, he had gearbox problems and was struggling to select. He saw us coming and kept to the left of the track, but Ayrton hadn't realised that he was travelling abnormally slowly. We were both absolutely on the limit coming out of the right hander and he had left no margin. Senna backed off slightly as he got boxed in and that was all I needed. I flashed right and passed him. It was the only time that anybody overtook him on the track all season.

Of all the races I have won and all the moves that I have pulled, that is one of the most celebrated. The move to pass Piquet at Silverstone in 1987 was sweet, but also inevitable. He was never going to resist me that day. The move around the outside of Berger at the Peraltada in Mexico in 1990 was also extraordinary and some of the moves on the Indycar ovals were unprecedented, but I think that manoeuvre in Hungary was the best because it set me up for a great win and because it relied on pure opportunism and instinct.

Many people have asked me, 'How did you do that?' The answer is, by instinct. You cannot plan a move like that and you certainly don't have time to think about it; it's all instinct. What you can do is plan to be ready for anything. You just have to be ready to take the opportunity when it comes. If I had been ten feet further back from Ayrton, he would not have got boxed in like that and would have sailed past Johansson without trouble. The secret was that I was right there and forced him into making a split-second misjudgment, and when you're fighting against people like Senna that's the most you are ever likely to get.

After I passed him he fell back and the fight seemed to go out of him. When I set the fastest lap, some seven-tenths of a second faster than anything he'd managed, he realised that he'd been beaten and lost interest. No-one could deny that Senna was one of the greatest drivers of all time, but he wasn't always very good at being put under pressure. Because of the clever way he positioned himself within the McLaren team, he was often able to demonstrate his speed and ability, but it was not often that he was put under intense pressure or challenged seriously in a one-on-one fight. He tried to avoid them either by going faster in a superior car or by outpsyching his rivals.

I was one of the very few drivers who ever put Senna under this kind of pressure and he didn't like it. He knew that I was the only one he couldn't outpsyche and that I would fight him all the way.

I won the race by almost half a minute and it was one of the most incredibly satisfying wins of my whole career. I had started the weekend with a big problem, but I drove around it and won. I still have the car today. It has pride of place in my Golf Club, Woodbury Park in Devon.

Gerhard Berger, Ferrari team-mate: ' It was a difficult year for me. I decided half way through the season to join McLaren for 1990 and naturally all of the team's support went to Nigel. He wasn't manipulating it, it's just the way the team shifted its focus. A year later when he was having trouble with Prost he came to me at Silverstone for a chat and he said, "Now I know what it must have been like for you last year," because the team was throwing all its support behind Prost.

'He went through so much. In 1990 everyone was saying that he couldn't win the World Championship and I think that he started to believe it himself, so he decided to stop. It was only when Frank persuaded him that he could win the title with Williams that he changed his mind. He came back, won the title and became one of the greatest drivers in the history of Formula 1, and I am so happy for him that he was able to show people that.'

Cesare Fiorio, Ferrari team manager 1989/91: 'I really enjoyed working with Nigel. It is very important for him to build a human relationship with the people in the team he works for and he expects the same in return from the team. He makes you feel very involved in his success. In modern Formula 1 this is not very common. Most winning drivers nowadays forget what the team has done for them. They thank the team, but they don't really mean it. Nigel always does.

'Nineteen-eighty-nine was a fantastic season for Ferrari. Nigel won in Brazil which was fantastic, but basically the car was totally unreliable. So we put in a major reliability programme to improve the car and Nigel worked incredibly hard on this. He was very involved and interested in the technical side. It was the first year of the electronic gearbox and it did not compensate for the mistakes of the drivers. You had to change at just the right time at the right revs and so on, or it would break. Berger used to get the timing wrong and made small mistakes which would break the gearbox. Nigel did not. He was incredibly sensitive to the mechanical side and never made mistakes. The coordination of his brain and hands and feet was incredible. I think that Gerhard thought that Nigel was getting better equipment, but in fact it was just that Nigel made fewer mistakes. You could see it on the telemetry that Nigel was able to synchronise things to thousands of a second.

'Nigel always drove hard, but he was not hard on his equipment. People who believe that he was are believing a myth. At the end of the race, you could take apart his engine and gearbox and you could tell that they had done some hard work but they were not mangled. With many drivers I have run, you just emptied out what was left of the mechanical parts at the end of the race, but not with Nigel.'

19

PROBLEMS WITH PROST

Although I didn't realise it at the time, my life at Ferrari began to go wrong the day that Alain Prost put his name to a contract, shortly before the 1989 Italian Grand Prix at Monza.

At that point Prost was looking like he might well win the World Championship, but he was upset with life at McLaren and the Ferrari hierarchy were very keen to have the number one on their car the following year. I had never had a problem with him; our battles on the track had always been sporting and he had always been genuine in our dealings out of the cockpit, so I took him at face value. But I had never been in the same team as him, so I had no idea how he operated. The next year would provide me with a first-hand lesson in Machiavellian politics, as the support of the Ferrari team and all hope of me winning the championship disappeared in a maze of intrigue.

In late 1989 I had no idea all this was coming. If anything Prost had my sympathies at the time. He suggested that he was not getting equal equipment from Honda and some of Senna's performances in qualifying seemed to point to Ayrton having a horsepower advantage. After my experiences with Honda over the past few years, I knew how Prost felt. Senna was the driver whom Honda really wanted and he was the one who would be staying in 1990. Prost, having already announced his move to Ferrari, had every right to wonder about whether he was getting a fair deal. It is very easy in these days of electronic engine management systems to have two chips that were not quite equal, but whose differences are almost impossible to detect.

Monza did not give me the result I was looking for. To win for Ferrari at Monza is the dream of every driver and after our win in Hungary, the romantic in me believed that it might be possible. Clearly so did the *tifosi*. The race was a sell-out and all around the track were banners with 'IL LEONE' and 'MANSELL=GILLES'. The passion of these people could be felt everywhere. It was like another British Grand Prix for me.

When I went out onto the grid for the start of the race, the whole place erupted. It was really incredible. I had been fastest in the morning warm-up and although I was third on the grid, I felt that a big day was in store. When I got out of the car on the grid I thought I would have a bit of fun, so I went up to the back of Ayrton's car and gave the thumbs down. The crowd loved it.

Unfortunately, in the race my gearbox failed but Berger finished second and Prost's win, now that he was to become an official Ferrari driver, went down well with the *tifosi*.

The season ended unsatisfactorily for us. I was disqualified in Estoril and suspended for one race after reversing in the pit lane and failing to stop for the subsequent black flag. What can you say about incidents of this kind? The governing body saw it one way, I saw it another. Ferrari contested it, but FISA decided to penalise me. I thought it was a harsh penalty given the state of the championship.

There was no question that we had the measure of the McLaren-Hondas at Estoril. Gerhard got a flying start and led the early laps. I was very comfortable running with Ayrton at the front and passed him for second place on lap eight, pulling away at over a second a lap. I took the lead from Gerhard on lap 24 and everything was looking good. As long as I had a decent tyre stop I would be in good shape to win. Unfortunately, there was confusion in the pits and I overshot my pit stop mark. As no-one seemed to be coming to pull me back, I reversed and made the stop before rejoining the race in fourth place.

The stewards said that they showed me the black flag three times but I never saw it. I was tucked up under Ayrton's rear wing, looking for a way past into the first corner. I found one on lap 48 and got alongside, but he came across on me, his right rear flattening my left front. We were both out of the race. It was only when I got back to the motorhome that I learned I had been blackflagged. I genuinely had no idea. If I had known about it I certainly wouldn't have wasted my time fighting Senna. When you're locked in a fight like that, running right on his gearbox at close on 200mph you don't see black flags. Ayrton himself said that he hadn't seen it and he was in front.

I accepted that I had broken a rule by reversing in the pit lane and, although I didn't see it, I had failed to stop for the black flag. But what happened next was a joke.

Jean-Marie Balestre, president of FISA at the time, convened a press conference at which he announced that I would be fined $50,000 and suspended for the next race, the Spanish Grand Prix.

I was staggered. I knew that I would be fined for missing the black flag, but it seemed that Balestre was making me a scapegoat for ruining the championship as with Senna out of the points, Prost virtually had the title in the bag. It was ridiculous. I tried to get the RAC to convene an FIA Court of Appeal, but I was told that they couldn't get enough people together in time and the appeal would be heard after the Spanish Grand Prix. When it did meet it was unable to make a judgement, but the judges said they thought the penalty excessive. After that the matter was dropped.

The last two races of the year, in Japan and Australia were an anti-climax. The engine let me down at the former, while the rain ruined the race in Adelaide, which should never have been started.

Japan was also the scene of the bitter dispute between Prost and Senna which ended with Prost being crowned World Champion after driving into Senna at the chicane. Ayrton carried on, but was given a $100,000 fine and had his superlicence taken off him. Over the winter the FIA Court of Appeal judged that he was a dangerous driver and the row continued right up to the first race of 1990.

When Prost arrived at Ferrari he was upbeat and positive. He seemed to want to put the bitterness of his wrangles with Senna behind him and concentrate on testing the new Ferrari 641 – a development of the previous year's design. John Barnard, the designer responsible for the car, had left the team to join Benetton and the update had been carried out by Enrique Scalabroni and Steve Nichols.

The car featured a revised gearbox which allowed the driver to accelerate through the gears without lifting his foot off the throttle and which had programmes allowing him to downchange without using every gear. Although that was a facility I missed from the old manual days, I wasn't too keen on having the box initiate such a programme by itself when travelling down a straight, so I treated it cautiously. The engine with which we would start the season was around 70hp more powerful than the one with which we started 1989. That made it still less powerful than the Honda, but I was optimistic that with various developments we would overtake Honda as the season progressed.

We tested very hard for the 1990 season, harder by far than for the previous one. The year before we had been doing bursts of three or four laps before something broke; now Prost and I were both doing Grand Prix distances at every test as well as dedicated engine, gearbox and chassis testing. By the end of February we had done 2500km of testing at Estoril alone, most of it on the gearbox and we really felt that we were moving forward.

My initial impressions of Prost were favourable. He was a meticulous tester, although he didn't run at the limit in testing, preferring to stretch himself only to about 90%. It was clear that apart from Senna, Prost would be my main challenger. I was confident that we had the car to win the championship and I felt that given the same equipment I could match and beat Prost.

It was to be an up and down season. The team transformed from being very supportive of me to being totally supportive of Prost. They brought the World Champion in with number one on the car and they got behind him and gave him everything he wanted – to my disadvantage. I didn't like that. I was trying to do a solid job and given equal treatment I'm sure I would have done, but as the season wore on it became clear that Prost was working things behind the scenes to his own advantage.

I have never had any time for politics, perhaps that is one of my greatest weaknesses, but when you share a team with an expert, you find yourself on the receiving end of them, like it or not. Behind my back, Prost worked on the senior management of Ferrari and its parent company FIAT, telling them that we could not both go for the championship and that he represented their best chance. The effort should all be concentrated on him.

By the time of the Canadian Grand Prix the team's support had shifted away from me and it was quite a blow. Reluctantly I had to admit when asked by the press that Prost was 'not the man I thought he was'.

It was a very difficult period, the ground was shifting fast underneath my feet. The support from the team evaporated and my dominant performances in qualifying turned into retirements. There was always some technical thing which would fail on the car, and it seemed that only one car could work well at any time. I began to feel as I had at Lotus after Colin died. After all that I had achieved in the intervening years, I felt I deserved better than this.

Things came to a head at Silverstone. The week before in the French Grand Prix at Paul Ricard I had taken pole. But when I got into my qualifying car at Silverstone it felt different. So I came into the pits and said to my mechanics, 'This is not my car.'

'Yes it is,' they said.

'I know my qualifying car and this is not it, am I right? Look, we've been together two years now, just tell me the truth. I can take the truth, but please don't lie to me.'

They went quiet and looked at each other, then at me and one of them said, 'You're right. After Ricard, Prost wanted your car so we were told to swap the tags. This is his car you're driving.'

'Fine,' I said. 'I'll beat him in his own car then.' And I proceeded to put his car on pole position!

I was very motivated when I went out to qualify. The engine seemed down on power in the first session, it was 6mph slower down the straight than the Hondas and 2mph slower than Prost.

The team acknowledged that there was a problem with the engine management system on my car and Fiorio admitted it to the press, promising that everything would be alright the next day. It was and I gave it everything I had, lapping half a second clear of Senna in second place and a whole second faster than Prost.

In the race, I was dominating until I discovered I had gearbox trouble. On lap ten it changed from seventh to fourth on the straight and apart from the unpredictability of it, it was over-revving the engine and upsetting the car's balance under braking. At one point it made a change from sixth to fourth in the middle of Stowe corner and on lap 22 it went from seventh to first midway down the Hangar Straight, sending the engine to 16,400rpm, which lost me the lead to Berger. I got the lead back, but by lap 43 the box had a mind of its own and Prost sailed past me to take the lead and what would turn out to be an easy win. I was devastated. As the car rolled to a halt at Copse, I thought once again about the wider picture.

I had seen for some time now that there was a lot of other business going on between Prost and the management and I didn't have the backing of the team. I had grown tired of the politics, a game I had never wanted to play anyway. I had been on the road for ten years now and I had a wife and three young children I would love to see more of. I was in a position financially where I didn't need to race any more if I didn't want to. I wasn't doing it for the money, I was doing it for the satisfaction of winning and ultimately trying to be the best in the world.

I had made the promise to myself in 1986 that I wouldn't make the numbers up and if there was no top drive available which would give me the support and backing I needed to win the World Championship, then there was no longer a place for me in Grand Prix racing.

I could get a drive for plenty of money – Jackie Oliver had offered me a drive with his Arrows-Porsche team – but that wasn't enough. I wanted to win and even if I couldn't get into a championship winning car, at least I wanted to be in one which could win races and where I had the team's full support.

Rosanne and I had talked about it before the race. We explored all the avenues and decided that we were being manipulated. It had been a great career, I had won 15 Grands Prix, had a good time and been sensible by saving our money. We felt we were better than we were being treated. So we decided I should stop. I thought leaving Ferrari at the top of my career was better than going to a lesser team, because I knew then that I wasn't going to drive for Ferrari again. The president of Ferrari, Piero Fusaro had come to Ricard the week before to try to persuade me to stay, but I told him there was no way. So at the end of the British Grand Prix, I announced my retirement.

People said that it was an impetuous decision which I'd arrived at on the spur of the moment when my car broke, but that wasn't it at all. Rosanne and I had looked closely at every possibility, thought it all out over many weeks and we saw that all roads led to one conclusion. With the announcement made, we were genuinely looking forward to my retirement at the end of the year.

I have come in for a lot of criticism for saying that I was retiring and then 'unretiring' at the end of 1990, but perhaps those who criticised were not in possession of the full story. Ever since I left his team, I had been talking to Frank Williams about going back in 1991. When I left I think he was better able to see what he was missing. Although I won thirteen races for them, Williams had treated me as a junior, but when I joined Ferrari they began to respect me more than they did when I was with them.

I had been talking to Frank in early 1990 and as the Prost situation became more unpleasant we talked seriously and agreed the bones of a deal for 1991. But just before the Silverstone weekend, Frank came to me and said, 'I can't offer you a drive next year because Senna's coming to us.' At the time Senna and Prost dictated the driver market and nobody made a move until they had done their deals.

'Listen, Frank,' I said. 'I think that I'm just as good as Prost and Senna, but if that's what you want that's your business.' With no top drive available to me, my mind was clear. I would retire at the end of the year with no regrets.

But the following month during the Belgian Grand Prix weekend, Frank found out that Ayrton had only been using the Williams offer as a bargaining tool with McLaren and Honda to get more money and to strengthen his position within the team. Senna re-signed with McLaren for another two years just before the Belgian Grand Prix and that dropped Williams right in it, because they didn't have a top driver for 1991. They had been interested in Jean Alesi, but he was only just starting out in Formula 1. In any case, he wanted to drive for Ferrari.

I was quite happy about retiring at the end of the year and had settled my mind on the subject. But then Williams' commercial director Sheridan Thynne, a close friend of mine, decided to find out whether I would change my mind. He approached Rosanne first and asked whether I would be receptive to an approach. Knowing that I will look at anything worthwhile, she said, 'Why don't you ask him?'

Frank Williams then came to me and said, 'You've got to drive for us,' to which I replied, 'No I haven't, I've retired.'

'Well, what will it take for you to come back?'

I gave him a list of demands, basically asking for undisputed number one status, with guarantees of support in a wide variety of areas. I stressed that I needed guarantees of each item in writing. A lot of what I was asking involved assurances from sponsors and suppliers that they would do whatever was necessary to help me win the World Championship. Everyone would have to be fully committed. That was the only way to beat Senna and McLaren and Honda. It was a major list of demands.

Frank told me, and subsequently the press, that what I was asking for was 'impossible'.

'Fine,' I said, 'I can happily retire then.'

Three weeks later the 'impossible' had happened and Sheridan came to my home on the Isle of Man with the contracts and all the written guarantees I had requested. Now we had a serious decision to make. Basically, I didn't want to come out of retirement and then fall short of my target of winning races and World Championships. I knew after all those years in the business that I couldn't win on my own and that everybody had to make the commitment.

When we had taken the decision for me to retire there were many good reasons, all of which I felt were correct. Now a new opportunity,

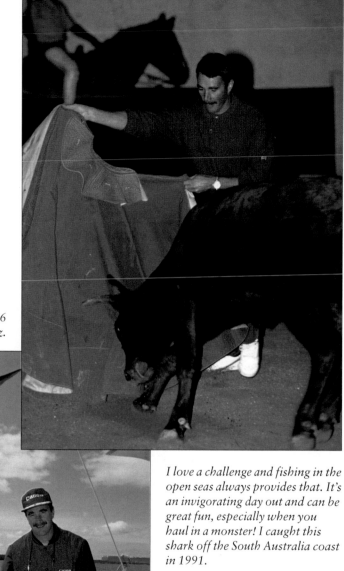

Bullfighting in Spain in 1986 on our first visit to Jerez.

I love a challenge and fishing in the open seas always provides that. It's an invigorating day out and can be great fun, especially when you haul in a monster! I caught this shark off the South Australia coast in 1991.

...AND GOD SAID:
"NIGEL GO AND
WIN!"

I have been very touched by the support I have received over the years from fans around the world, particularly in Britain and in Italy (main pic). At Silverstone in 1990 they wanted a win for Ferrari number 27 as much as I did, but despite dominating the early stages, all was not well at Ferrari and I retired with gearbox problems (left) and announced my retirement. The wheel falls off in Portugal and with it go my chances of the 1991 World Championship (right). Playing soccer in Spain a week later with the journalists and photographers.

Passing Prost at Magny Cours (above) en route to victory in the 1991 French Grand Prix. He was trying even then to take my Williams seat for 1992. With Niki Lauda (left), a three-time World Champion and a man for whom I have the utmost respect.

Riccardo Patrese (above) was a great team-mate and together we got the job done in 1991 and 1992. I saw no reason to change a winning formula. (Below) Testing at Estoril in 1991.

Ayrton Senna was always the hardest man to beat. He and I fought for the 1991 World Championship and it was one of my best years of racing. Millions held their breath as we came down the main straight in Barcelona (main pic). At Silverstone (left) I gave him a lift after he ran out of fuel and at Suzuka I wanted to be the first to congratulate him on his third World title.

The win in Brazil in 1992 (left) made it two out of two. I was on a mission that year. Arguing the toss with Frank Williams (below left). (Bottom left) I gave it all I had after a late pit stop in Monaco, but it wasn't to be. Second place to Senna broke my five-race winning streak.

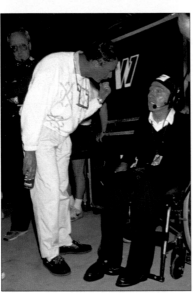

The Williams-Renault FW14B (right) was without doubt the best racing car I have ever driven. Victory number seven of the year at Silverstone in July set me up for clinching the Championship the following month in Hungary.

The expression says it all after winning the World Championship (left). I sought to dominate every race that season, to lead from the front (bottom left) and open up as big a gap as possible. This is the start at Adelaide – what I thought would be my last Grand Prix.

Rosanne and I picked up the World Championship plaque at the FISA prizegiving in Paris in December 1992. That season we ended up with nine wins and fourteen pole positions.

My sensei Ric Martin won the 1994 Full Contact World Championship in Okinawa the same weekend as I got my black belt.

I practised karate as a teenager and took it up again when I moved to Florida. As well as being good physical training it helps to keep a balance in life. Achieving a black belt was a lifetime's ambition.

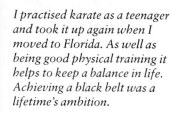

With Rosanne, Chloe, Leo, and Greg in the club house grounds at our own Woodbury Park Golf Club.

Phoenix 1993 (left and right). My first race weekend on an oval and my whole Indycar experience could have ended with this accident. A major operation on my back followed and six months later I clinched the PPG IndyCar World Series with my fourth oval win of the season. It was a real rollercoaster ride.

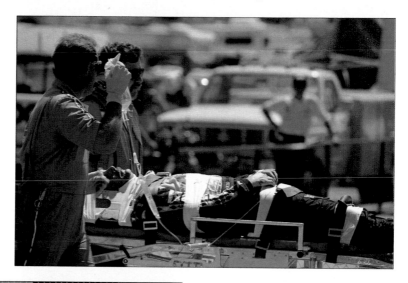

A J Foyt is one of the great characters of American racing and he helped me to get to grips with the ovals.

Sharing a joke with Jim McGee (left) and Roger Penske, two of the cleverest strategists in Indycar racing.

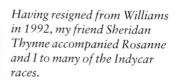

Having resigned from Williams in 1992, my friend Sheridan Thynne accompanied Rosanne and I to many of the Indycar races.

A pit stop en route to the first oval win at Milwaukee. Fast and clever pit strategy is crucial when you race on short ovals. Jim McGee read the race and together we made the key decisions.

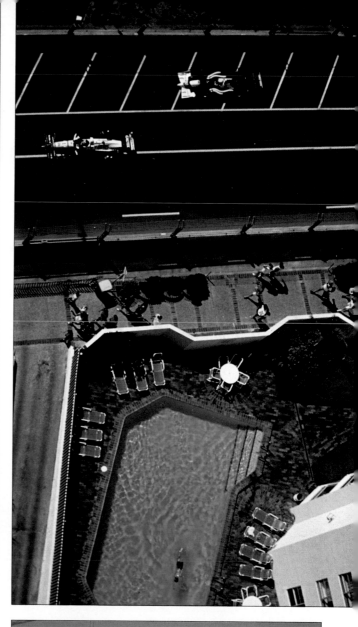

Paul Newman and Carl Haas run an outstanding outfit. Here they are (far left) alongside me as I celebrate with the PPG trophy at Nazareth. Emerson Fittipaldi (left) was my principal challenger for the 1993 title with the Penske team. It had been Paradise the year before when we won on our debut, but in 1994 the race at Surfers' (above right) was the start of an unlucky year. (Right) The fans in the States gave me tremendous support throughout my two seasons in Indy car.

Back in the F1 groove with a win from pole position at Adelaide for Williams in 1994. On the podium Gerhard Berger called me an 'old bastard' for beating him!

The 1995 McLaren-Mercedes was a dreadful car. In the first test at Estoril I realised that it would be making the numbers up, not winning. I chose to stand down rather than compromise myself.

I worked closely with Damon Hill when he was the Williams test driver in 1992 and was delighted when he got the drive in 1993. I had hoped we would be team-mates in 1995, but it wasn't to be.

which hadn't existed before and on a scale not present before, had opened up. It guaranteed my number one status and full support for a crack at the world title. After fourteen years of chasing my goal in racing cars and after ten years in Formula 1, here was a bona fide chance to do the job properly at last.

It was all very well criticising me for retiring and then changing my mind (as many have done), but let me point out that we delivered the goods in abundance in 1991 and 1992; we won the World Championship, won fourteen Grands Prix, took 16 pole positions and scored 180 points. If that wasn't worth coming out of retirement for, I'd like to know what is. The only reason why I was able to do that is because we got the contracts and the guarantees and raised everyone's level of performance.

Ironically, when it became clear during 1991 how the team was shaping up and the huge efforts being put in by Renault and Elf, Prost tried to get me out of the car for 1992. But my contract was so solid, because I had been dogmatic about the wording when it was drawn up in 1990, that they weren't able to get me out. But they tried. People do not realise that what Prost succeeded in doing in 1992, namely worming his way into Williams and pushing me out, he had tried to do in 1991 as well. If he had succeeded then, I would never have won the World Championship.

My mistake with Prost was that I have always believed that everybody's alright until proven otherwise, because let's face it, if you go through life thinking that everyone's going to deceive you, you're in for a pretty miserable life. So partly through my honesty and partly through naivety, I took him at his word and I shouldn't have done. Some of my disappointment was at having been taken in by him.

The Portuguese Grand Prix of 1990 gave me an opportunity to level the score a little with Prost. I had an opportunity to win and I took it.

Going into the weekend, Agip, who had done a lot of research and development work, came up with a new fuel mixture which gave us a little more straight line speed. I comfortably outqualified Prost, who lined up next to me on the front row.

Unfortunately, I made one of the worst starts of my career. I got a lot of wheelspin and the car got out of shape and slid to the right, squeezing Prost out. Senna took advantage of my poor start and led into the first corner. He held the lead until lap 50, when I passed him into the first corner and pulled away. I was lucky four laps later not to be taken out by Philippe Alliot, who chopped across me while I was lapping him for the second time. His right rear wheel hit my left front and sent him off into the barriers, but fortunately my car wasn't damaged and six laps later I was declared the winner after the race was stopped for an accident involving Alex Caffi.

I had my first, long overdue, win of the season. Prost had been unable to pass Senna and finished third behind him. Prost was furious and made a public statement that Ferrari did not deserve the championship and that Fiorio should have ordered me to give him the race.

That win put me level with Stirling Moss on sixteen victories. Throughout his legendary career, Moss never won the World Championship. At the time I was still not sure if I ever would, but eight days later, on 1 October, I signed the deal with Williams which would hopefully bring me that long awaited prize.

Portugal wasn't the only high point of the season. Another was the nail-biting finish in Mexico and my famous scrap with Gerhard Berger. With three laps to go I was in second place, with Gerhard breathing down my neck. As we went down the main straight I tried to make sure that he couldn't make a run at me down the inside and I thought I'd done it, but he came through anyway. It was an ugly move, as he took to the kerbs on the inside and shoved me out of the way. I wasn't too happy about this and was determined to repass him. Gerhard made his car very wide on the next lap, but as we came down the straight leading into the Peraltada, a long flat in fifth right hander, I darted from left to right behind him to keep him looking in his mirrors and wondering which side I was going to come. As we approached the Peraltada I went left and passed him around the outside on the loose surface, snatching second place in the process.

But I had learned my lesson. There is only one driver at Ferrari who can be number one and they choose who that will be. The other driver is unlikely to win a race because they don't have the capacity to run two reliable cars. They've got better at it, but there is still a difference between the number one and the number two. At Ferrari if you are not number one you might as well not bother, you'll just be banging your head against a wall. That's where they broke me because if they had given me the backing they gave to Prost in 1990 – backing I had worked hard for in 1989 – I would have been contesting, and may even have won the World Championship.

When I left Ferrari, I left honourably and on good terms. When

Prost left, before the end of the following year, it was because he'd been fired. At least my two years ended amicably. I think that demonstrated how Ferrari felt about him and the way he had treated them after all that they had given him.

Cesare Fiorio, Ferrari team manager: 'Prost tried to make Nigel nervous. He knew that Nigel was very quick and I think in his mind he didn't want Nigel to be at 100% of his potential. So he was always trying to unsettle Nigel. At the start of the season in Brazil, for example, they worked together in the practice sessions to find a good set-up. They talked together a lot and decided which set-up was the best and had the cars set-up accordingly. But then on the grid, five minutes before the race, Prost got his mechanics to make changes to his car to get a better set-up. Nigel saw this and was very anxious. He said, "What's he doing, what's he doing?" Prost knew that this kind of thing could make Nigel unhappy. After that it was hard to get the two of them to work together. Each one went his own way. It was a turning point and it was a shame because with two great drivers like that we could have cleaned up if they had worked together.

'It was hard for Nigel. He is less complicated than Prost and in his mind he thought that they would work as a team to get the best out of the car and then compete on the track, best man wins. Prost didn't work like that.

'There has been a lot of speculation about the start in Portugal. At that time Ferrari had the best car and the best drivers – with the exception of Senna – in Formula 1. We had both our cars on the front row, with Senna and Berger behind. Everyone said that Nigel deliberately slid across on Prost, but this is not right. The last thing he would want would be to let Senna past. He is not stupid, he is a racing driver and he knew that Senna would be very hard to pass if he allowed him to get through. He did not want to give the opposition a gift like that or to make more work for himself later. He made a mistake and three cars got through.

'We had decided before the race, that if they were running one-two near the end of the race, then Nigel was to let Alain through to win, because Alain was going for the championship against Senna. Nigel understood this and agreed to it.

'The problem was that Nigel passed Piquet, Berger and Senna quite quickly and took the lead, but Prost didn't get past Senna, who finished second. I couldn't tell Nigel to slow down because that would have given the win to Senna, so there was nothing I could do until Prost passed Senna, which he was not able to do. After that race Prost attacked both Nigel and me, but I am 100% sure that Nigel didn't do it on purpose to let the other cars pass.'

20

BUILDING UP FOR THE BIG ONE

My two years at Ferrari were an eye-opening experience and they also did a lot for my development as a driver. When you are at the height of your competitiveness, you get sharper and as the experience gels with the talent and motivation, the result is a better racing driver, both in the car and within the team. You become less willing to accept, and more programmed to question and to push for changes. I was a more rounded and more professional driver after Ferrari.

Although I was getting older – I was 37 when I rejoined Williams – I was even quicker than when I left, because the speed had become more disciplined and more managed. Experience tells you when and where to apply yourself and when to over-step the limits. You learn to conserve mental and physical energy and use it more wisely when you can see that it counts.

Many drivers lose their edge as they get older or when they have children. Something creeps into their minds and takes away the urge for ten-tenths driving. They'll lift off fractionally at a corner they used to take flat, for example. Driving a Formula 1 car is such an absolute business and there are always a lot of good, hungry, young guys coming through that you really cannot afford to be like that. If you feel you've lost your edge, it's time to stop immediately.

My assurance when dealing with my team on a day-to-day basis was also greatly improved by my time at Ferrari. Although I learned to speak reasonable conversational Italian, I handled all technical matters in English and the language barrier sometimes meant that I had to do more work myself and get more involved in making sure that I got what I wanted. Consequently my confidence out of the car became much stronger. It had been an important transitional phase and I felt that I had learned and benefitted from it. Going back from Indycars into Formula 1 at the end of 1994, I felt the same way.

When I changed my mind about retiring in 1990, Williams wanted me to sign a one-year deal, but I wanted two years. I knew how much work had to be done and the experience of Ferrari, where I had done the work in 1989 and not reaped the benefits the following year, was still fresh in my mind.

I explained this to Frank and insisted on two years. What I should have done was push for a three-year deal, because then I might have won two consecutive World Championships. The work had been done and an irresistible momentum had been built up by the time Prost came along like a magpie in 1993 and took my seat. He barely even stretched himself and still he won the championship.

There's no magic in the business, no overnight solutions, there's just lots of hard work to be done. And you've just got to make sure than when you do get it right, you reap the benefits, because there are lots of people, including manufacturers, sponsors and other drivers, who want to take it away from you.

Having got all the contracts and the letters of intent from the sponsors and the suppliers, I committed myself fully to the job of working with Williams. Much had changed in the two years I had been away. For one thing the team had joined forces with Renault and Elf and for another the technical department had been boosted by the arrival of Adrian Newey, a talented aerodynamicist who joined Williams from the Leyton House team.

Williams won two races in 1990 with the FW13B, one each for Riccardo Patrese and Thierry Boutsen. It had been quick at times, but the general feeling was that the team ought to have done better and that the car should have been more consistently competitive. Towards the end of 1990 I went to Paul Ricard to test the car and I saw the problem immediately – the drivers had been too easy on themselves.

Boutsen was the sort of driver who had on-days and off-days. If his car didn't feel right then he would be uncompetitive, but when everything was perfect, he could be fast. He didn't like a car that moved around at all, so it was very stiffly sprung, especially at the rear. I hated it immediately and changed everything – springs, roll bar, dampers, differential, the whole lot – to soften the car up. By the time I'd finished with it, the car was much more nervous and jumpy, but it was two seconds a lap quicker. Maybe some of that time was in me, but I certainly made the car a lot faster. The car rolled around a lot, but it was more supple and it turned into the corners better.

The key point here is that just because a car is more stable and comfortable to drive, that doesn't make it quicker. Invariably a nervous car is quicker, but it's very demanding to drive. It moves around and is never comfortable at any place on the track, so it keeps you working hard for the whole race. That's the way I like a car to be set-up, because even though it's always a struggle, it's faster.

When you go into corners in a car I've set up, it feels as though it wants to step out at the back. But the fact that it's nervous means that it will react quickly to the steering and will therefore turn in quicker to a corner. And that's what I need to be really fast. The car feels like it wants to swap ends on you half way through the corner, but that's something you learn to live with.

I'm sure that a lot of drivers, if they tried to drive a car I've set up, would find it almost impossible to get around a corner quickly. It must be balanced properly. If it's not balanced, then there's nothing you can do with it. A stable, stiff car is reassuring and comfortable to drive, but it's not that quick. If you want the ultimate, you've got to have something which is close to the edge of the envelope.

A lot of work needed doing on the engine and it was clear that the drivers had not put enough pressure on Renault. The RS2 was a good engine with a lot of potential, but it didn't match the Ferrari and had a long way to go to beat the Honda. The drivers had obviously been polite to Renault, when what they should have told them was that they weren't working hard enough and that the engine needed a lot more power.

The fuel which Elf had provided was fairly standard and, knowing the huge power gains which Ferrari had been getting with the developmental fuels from Agip, I knew that Elf had a lot of work to do to catch up. Special fuels could gain you an extra 60 or 70bhp. It was obviously going to be a big growth area in the coming seasons and we needed to get on terms with the others.

I told Renault and Elf straight that their stuff wasn't good enough. I don't think they liked that very much and it didn't endear me to them to start with. I tried to be constructive and positive about it, but the bare facts were that their work just wasn't up to scratch. No one likes to be told that they can do a lot better, even less that they are a long way behind their rivals. Coming from Ferrari, I knew what lengths they were going to in order to increase competitiveness, especially with those power-boosting fuels, and Williams-Renault would need to act quickly if we weren't going to be left behind. Moreover, if we were going to win the World Championship, we would have to beat Senna and McLaren-Honda. It was possible, but to do it we would need to raise our game by several notches.

I think that initially Renault and Elf didn't believe what I was telling them and thought that I was complaining for the sake of it, but after a few months they realised that this wasn't the case and then they started doing something about it. But not before they had complained to Patrick Head that I was putting unreasonable demands on them and Patrick had told me to back off for a while.

The Ricard test gave me a good indication of where Williams and its partners were up to and I looked forward eagerly to my first test in the FW14, which looked impressive on the drawing board. The FW14 was the work of both Patrick and Adrian Newey. Aerodynamically the car was the next generation of design and this was a key element of its success, because in these post-turbo engine days when the horsepower advantages were reduced, aerodynamics became all the more important.

Patrick had tried the 'raised nose' idea in the wind-tunnel, but had seen no significant gain. But when Adrian arrived he created a different front-wing configuration which, when used in conjunction with the raised nose, made a major difference. The FW14 was designed around Adrian's aerodynamic principles, which not only helped the airflow but also benefitted the handling. It was also designed around a new semi-automatic gearbox and, with two years experience on the Ferrari unit, I was able to help a lot with the development of the gearbox.

Many of the problems we suffered in the early stages with the Williams gearbox were similar to those on the pioneering semi-automatic gearbox at Ferrari, in that it would suddenly go into neutral, get stuck in gear or jump unexpectedly out of gear. It was disconcerting, but we all knew that the eventual gain would be worth it. These are just the inevitable growing pains of a new technology.

Although a huge development programme had been carried out, with Mark Blundell as the test driver, we still had some gremlins in the gearbox in the early part of 1991. Those times were difficult for the team and for me because we lost a few races at the start of the season, which handed the initiative to Senna and McLaren. We had to work very hard to make up the lost ground.

One of the most important rule changes in Formula 1 in the early nineties was the one concerning championship points scoring. A win now yielded ten points and all scores counted, so the championship would be won by the man with the most points. Previously it had been nine points for a win and your best twelve results counted.

So the most important thing in Formula 1 became reliability. If you finished all the races you had a much better chance of being champion. You've got to improve the technology, of course, and you can have the fastest and most beautiful car but if it doesn't finish then you are not going to win any races and you certainly won't win championships. There are no shortcuts, you have to go through the pains of getting it right. Naturally we wanted to get it right as quickly as possible and history shows that by mid-season we had a championship winning car. The problem was that the championship began in March, not June.

The FW14 was a fantastic car. It was adaptable and easy to set up according to the individual requirements of each circuit. It worked over a broad range of set-ups and it was quite a straightforward task to hone it down during the various practice sessions over a race weekend. Once the gearbox worked, it was a car you could have complete confidence in and push very hard.

For some reason, the Williams cars I had driven before had always suffered from bad brakes and this one was no different. We really struggled in 1991 before we got to grips with it. The problem was a 'long' or 'soft' brake pedal, in other words you had to push further on the pedal to get the braking effect you required.

As I mentioned before, my driving style demands good brakes. I turn in on the brakes and carry a lot of speed into the apex of the corner, but I also need to slow the car down in the corner. If my brake pedal is soft, it adds a lot onto my lap time. People who drive in the classic style, where they brake in a straight line and then turn in, can put up with the brakes going soft. But when I'm running on the limit, if the brakes are good, I can do my thing; but if they're not there then I go past the point where I need to be and then I'm slower out of the corner. So that was a big problem in 1991. But, as I said, the upside is that, like everything else, we got it right in 1992.

One of the greatest strengths of the Williams team is the speed with which it can react to the changing circumstances of a Grand Prix season. If something is not working technically, then it becomes a priority to seek out the reason and rectify it. The keys to this are the quality of the engineering staff back at the factory and the rapport between the driver and his engineer. The driver has to get on with everybody, but to have the right chemistry between those two people is very important. David Brown and I had worked together in 1987 and 1988 and we learned a lot together. When I returned he was my first choice. He is an outstanding engineer and we came to trust each other explicitly and developed a very efficient working method.

If he said something to me, I knew that he meant it. So I didn't question it. Equally if I felt sure about something, then he didn't question it. Our relationship was very strong, and more importantly we didn't waste time because we were both on the same wavelength. That counts for a lot in racing because you have precious little time during a weekend to achieve your goals. A four-day race weekend might seem like a long time, but when you pare it down to a few hours of practice, qualifying and the race, you realise that it's a lot shorter than you think. An engineer needs to be good in the heat of the battle and to be able to think practically when time is short. It is easy when trying to get the most technically from something as sophisticated as a Formula 1 car to get lost or to go down a blind alley. But the quality of the rapport between myself and the Williams engineers in 1991 and 1992 and the clarity of thought and communication between us ensured that we didn't get it wrong very often. For me, and I'm sure David and Patrick Head feel the same way, that was one of the most satisfying aspects of our success during that period. It was pure teamwork. David and I enjoyed our motor racing together and that is vital.

We worked hard and thought alike. I always liked being the first car out on the track for the morning practice session at every Grand Prix. It helped to out-psyche the opposition and let everyone know that we were there to work hard. That sort of thing shows that you mean business. David made sure that the car was always ready for me when I wanted it.

The FW14 was delayed slightly in production, but I finally got my hands on it in February of 1991. This left us with little time to iron out the teething problems before the first race at Phoenix on 10 March. Because the FW14 was a completely new car with a new gearbox and new engine we were inevitably going to have some reliability problems, but I had my fingers crossed that the difficulties would only last a race or two and then we would be able to challenge. The testing, though brief, was encouraging and we set off for Phoenix and the first race of my new adventure with quiet optimism.

David Brown, Nigel's engineer at Williams: ' Nigel was quicker when he came back from Ferrari at the end of 1990 than before he left. He was better all around; he got more deeply involved in the set-up of the car and the technical operation of the team and he seemed to be more aware of what could be done. He was less willing to accept more, ready to question.'

Sheridan Thynne, commercial director at Williams: 'The period from the evening of the 1990 British Grand Prix after Nigel's 'retirement', until the day he signed the Williams contract was one of the most fascinating of my life. Standing – utterly dejected – by the Williams motorhome at Silverstone that evening, I was convinced by my eldest daughter, of all people, that Senna (whose prospective arrival at Williams had caused Frank to terminate his discussions with Nigel) would not actually join us at Didcot.

'So I explained this to Rosanne, put it to Nigel over breakfast in the Ferrari motorhome in Hockenheim and did what I could to discourage him from taking any steps that would stop him returning to Formula 1 (although he was totally and justifiably sceptical about my 'plan'). Things took a turn for the better in Spa when Senna told Frank that he was going to stay at McLaren, as exclusively predicted by my daughter six weeks earlier. And at Monza, greatly aided by a push from Renault's Bernard Casin, Frank and Patrick took the concept on board and gradually accepted it. After several tiring discussions and a bit of a 'bumpy ride', it finally came together around the Portugese Grand Prix.

'What motivated me? Well I like winning and deeply believed not only that Nigel was the best driver but also that he provided precisely the 'charge' that Williams-Renault and Elf needed to climb the championship pinnacle. But it could easily have not happened, as I was aware throughout those painful weeks during which, I am advised, I was not easy to live with.

'It was worth it!'

21

FOR ALL THE RIGHT REASONS

The 1991 season was one of the best I have had. I didn't win the World Championship, but I proved that I had stayed in Formula 1 for the right reasons. Before the first race there were a lot of people, especially among the press, who doubted my motivation. These were the same people who thought that my decision to retire at Silverstone in 1990 was an emotional and impulsive one. Perhaps if they knew me better and knew the level of commitment I had insisted on from Williams and Renault and Elf, they would have realised that both assumptions were wrong. I finally had the deal I wanted; undisputed number one driver in a dedicated team and I was as highly motivated and fired up for the fight in 1991 as I had ever been.

On top of that, I was boosted just before the first race at Phoenix by being awarded the Order of the British Empire at Buckingham Palace by the Queen. It was a very proud moment, not just for Rosanne and me but for motor sport in general. It said a lot about the importance that motor sport had developed in the public's eye and it was one of those moments of wider recognition which remind you of your place in the nation's consciousness.

I was on a high, but was not without my critics. Many people pointed to my qualifying performances at the start of 1991 as evidence of the supposed lack of motivation. It is true that in the early part of the season I was outqualified by Riccardo Patrese, although I outperformed him in the races. But let us not forget that he was no slouch. He'd been with the team for two years. I had to build up my confidence with the situation. Riccardo had developed the two previous years' cars and so in early 1991 he was more on the pace than me. On top of that, I had the lion's share of the technical problems in qualifying for the first half of the season and that contributed to the statistics. Once I got comfortable I was able to outqualify him and in 1992, when we raced the active suspension car, I was usually a second or two per lap faster than him.

The FW14 showed a lot of promise but we lost out through lack of reliability in the first three races. I felt an increasing amount of confidence in it as a car to drive hard. If we could just get the gearbox sorted out we would be right there. The problem was that while we had no points on the board after three races, Ayrton had a maximum thirty.

In Monaco things came right and I picked up six points for second place. I never like to finish second, but it was good to get off the mark. Ironically, considering how well I have always gone at Monaco, it was my best finish to date on the circuit. The car was far from right in qualifying. It did not inspire confidence, and it's hard to be quick at Monaco if you haven't got complete confidence in your car.

In the early stages of the race the throttle was playing up, sticking open at odd times and behaving like an on-off switch. Of all the circuits we race on I can think of no worse place than Monaco to have that problem. In the second half of the race, however, it cleared and I was able to do my thing. The fault was afterwards traced to a loose sensor in the throttle mechanism. Around the 50 lap mark it fixed itself in one position and luckily stayed there until the end.

On lap 55 I caught Prost and started looking for a way past. I found one going into the tight chicane after the tunnel. I lined the car up down the inside and simply outdrove him. It was a satisfying moment.

At the front Ayrton was away clear for his fourth consecutive victory. After the race he told me that he had been climbing the hill out of St Devote just at the moment when I had passed Prost and had been able to see it on the giant Diamond-vision screen. It had made him smile too.

I wasn't smiling after Canada, however, as I saw 10 points disappear out of the window on the last lap when I was 47 seconds in the lead. Senna had retired and I was set to take a big bite out of his championship lead. I have already discussed what happened with the car going into the hairpin and the absurd suggestion that I switched off my own engine. It was painful enough to have lost the points without the so-called experts weighing in with idiotic ideas like that. It was one of the worst mechanical failures I ever suffered and one of the best examples I can point to of how I am treated by those members of the press who most resent my success.

The statistics were galling; after Canada Ayrton had a 33 point lead in the table, but it could have been 23. There were eleven races to go and we needed to start winning regularly if we were going to have any chance at the end of the season.

We all dug in to forget the disappointment of Canada and to redouble our efforts and it paid off; Mexico was an all-Williams affair, although it was Riccardo who got the first win of the season. I took the lead at the start and opened out a cushion of around four seconds but then my engine began to have problems. Riccardo passed me on lap 15 and pulled away and I fell into the clutches of Ayrton. We ran in close company for a while, as I tried to figure out what was wrong. I fiddled around with the fuel mixture switch and found a richer setting which seemed to solve the problem. By this stage there were only 11 laps to go and Riccardo was 10s ahead. I put the hammer down and my fastest lap was only a tenth of a second slower than the pole position time! It was a tremendously exciting showdown. I took a second a lap off him, but it was just too late. He put in his own personal fastest lap of the race on the last lap and it was all he needed. I was disappointed, but at least we had proved that the car was right and I had another six points.

The momentum was building fast now. We were a long way behind Ayrton in the points, but everyone in the team could sense that our package was coming good and it would be a real challenge to see if we could catch Ayrton and McLaren. The pressure was really on, nothing less than a string of wins would do and in one fabulous month we won three consecutive races, France, Britain and Germany. It boosted the team morale hugely and set us up for a challenge in the second half of the year. At the beginning of July we trailed Senna by 31 points, but by the end of the month we had cut that to 18. On a personal note it was the first hat-trick of my career and the first by a Briton since Jackie Stewart in 1971, when coincidentally he won the same three races.

The win in France gave us a tremendous boost and the following weekend at Silverstone we totally dominated. There was a marvellous feeling of expectation about the whole weekend, a sense that anything could happen. I have often said that racing in front of my home crowd is worth at least a second a lap and with a combination of the warm welcome from the fans and the competitiveness of our package, I felt very proprietorial about Silverstone. It had become *my* circuit.

The track had been changed considerably from the year before. The old Becketts had gone to be replaced by a corkscrew sequence of corners, Stowe was now far tighter and the chute between Stowe and Club now had an area called the Vale, which was designed to improve the show for the spectators and to slow the cars down through Club and Abbey. Most impressive of all was the new Bridge corner; a downhill right-hander taken flat in top gear. It required a lot of bravery to go through there at full speed, but it was one of the keys to being fast on the new layout. After that was the new complex of tight corners, Priory and Luffield, which changed the character of the circuit and made it one of the most difficult tracks in the Championship for which to set up a car because whereas in the past it was a power circuit with few slow corners, now a compromise was called for to accommodate the real mixture of fast corners, straights and highly technical tight corners. I loved it from the start, although part of me missed the high-speed excitement of the old Silverstone.

I got provisional pole on the Friday, but it was clear that the track was much quicker on the Saturday. In second qualifying Ayrton gave it everything to record a lap two-tenths quicker than my best at that point. I knew I was going to have to do something special to beat that. I went out and immediately was plugged into the power of the crowd. I wound myself up on the warming up lap and then went for it. The car felt good, the engine was sweet and I felt strong. It was a tidy and extremely fast lap and I came through Bridge so quick I almost scared myself. The pressure was on, but I had to have pole position here at Silverstone of all places. It was without doubt one of the best laps I have ever managed and I was deeply moved by the standing ovation from the crowd as I slowed down.

I made a poor start in the race and Senna led for the first half lap, but I nailed him into Stowe and never looked back. Before the race, we had studied the tyre wear and the temperatures and planned to do the whole race without stopping. I wanted to open out as big a cushion as possible as fast as possible and after six laps I was 7.6s clear of Ayrton. I kept piling on the pressure and by half distance I had a lead of 21s. I was soon glad I had pushed so hard, because I then hit trouble. I lost two wheel balance weights – the same problem as I had had when fighting Piquet at Silverstone in 1987 – and as the vibrations increased I called the team to get a set of tyres ready for me. We changed the tyres in a little over eight seconds and when I rejoined my lead was a mere two seconds over Ayrton, who was not planning to stop. I pressed hard, using the fresh tyres to the best advantage and broke away from him.

Everything looked good for a win, but in the closing stages my gearbox began to play up. I couldn't believe it was happening. After the problems at the start of the year, we had thought that the box was now reliable and yet here it was missing gears and doing things it shouldn't. I was cursing the thing and I decided not to take any risks, so I left it in top gear for most of the last two laps. There were a few heart stopping moments, but the car held together and I won my fourth Grand Prix on home soil. On the slowing down lap, I realised that the result was better than I had thought because Senna had run out of fuel on the last lap and he would only be classified in fourth place. I could see that the crowd was giving him quite a hard time, as I had been given in Brazil a few times, so I stopped to pick him up. It was the sporting thing to do.

The day after my win I received a very special fax from the British Prime Minister, John Major. It read, 'Congratulations on a splendid victory. You drove a great race and the whole country is proud of you.'

My luck continued in Germany where I not only won the race, but Ayrton ran out of fuel again on the last lap, this time losing all chance of a points finish. The gap between us had shrunk to a mere eight points and Williams were ahead of McLaren in the Constructors' championship for the first time since 1987, which is a good indication of the level to which we had all raised our performance over the past eight or nine months.

After the bruising they took from us in July, McLaren embarked on a huge test programme to improve their car and engine, including one massive session at Silverstone involving five drivers. They were trying all kinds of developments, a potent new V12 engine from Honda, a new semi-automatic gearbox and a variety of new software programmes in a desperate effort to recapture the advantage over us.

I would pinpoint Belgium as one of the races which lost us the 1991 World Championship. Like some of those early in the year it was a race we could and should have won, but lost through mechanical failure. This time it was a crippling electrical fault. When a faulty voltage regulator caused my gearbox to fail and then shut down the engine after 22 laps, I had my fifth retirement of the 11 rounds so far and again I had lost almost certain victory. I had passed Ayrton in the pit stops and was pulling away comfortably, even allowing myself the luxury of changing gears 1000 revs earlier than normal to protect the engine.

To make matters worse, Ayrton collected another 10 points and his lead looked substantial again; 71 points to my 49. At that rate I would have to win three times with him scoring no better than a second and a third in order to get level with him.

The stakes were higher than ever after Spa. Nothing less than wins would serve our cause. The increased pressure was obvious in every area of the team. We knew we had the wherewithal to win this championship, but we had to win every race from now on. If Ayrton scored maximum points again the championship would effectively be over. Only by winning every race and hoping he didn't score could we have any chance. It would be tough, but then we had never expected beating McLaren to be easy. In Monza we got it right and I won my fourth race of the year.

Even though I had left their team, the *tifosi* were fantastic to me all weekend. There were hundreds of well-wishers around whenever I entered and left the circuit and the grandstands were full of banners encouraging me and the team.

During the previous winter a huge package had come through the post from Italy. Inside was a large, expensive looking trophy with the inscription, 'Our World Champion in 1990'. For me, that said it all about my relationship with the Italian supporters. Their passion for this sport is quite incredible and by sending me this fabulous cup they were expressing their gratitude to me for our two years together with Ferrari and perhaps suggesting that in Prost Ferrari had backed the wrong horse for 1991...

In fact the Ferrari team was struggling badly. They had brought out a new car at Magny Cours, where Prost had twice led me and twice I passed him without a fight. The management seemed to be in chaos, Prost had used his influence behind the scenes to get Cesare Fiorio, the team manager, fired and had repeatedly criticised the team in the press. In the end the bosses decided to show him where the power really lay and fired him after the Japanese Grand Prix. For my part I was glad to be out of it. I had committed myself to what I considered a winning package and I knew that there would be no let up in the relentless momentum which would bring us to the door of the World Championship.

Nevertheless, when it became clear that he would not be staying at Ferrari, Prost tried to use his relationship with Renault and Elf to worm his way into Williams for 1992. Luckily my contract was written in stone and he was not able to do anything. The following year I would not be so lucky and exactly twelve months later I would be forced to make a very sad decision at this same Monza circuit.

The pendulum had swung away from us after Belgium, but we improved things a little at Monza. Renault brought an updated engine to Monza, the RS3B, which they assured me was better than the RS3. After running it in practice on Friday I wasn't so sure. In any case I had a problem with the gearbox on my race car, so I spent most of qualifying in the spare, which had a normal RS3 unit in it. It was a titanic struggle for pole, but Ayrton pipped me by a tenth of a second.

I shadowed Ayrton at the start and then allowed Riccardo through to put pressure on Ayrton and hopefully wear his tyres out a bit. They fought it out and Riccardo passed him but then spun and dropped back to third place. At half distance I decided it was time to attack and I went after Senna with a vengeance, putting real pressure on him, just the kind he didn't like. I tried to pass him on the inside into the long final corner, the Parabolica, but he closed the door. I harried him all the way down the pit straight and he made a mistake into the first chicane, locking up a front wheel and flat-spotting his tyre. I knew I had him now and I picked my moment carefully, made sure I exited the second Lesmo bend faster than him and passed him on the chute down to the Ascari bends.

He pitted to replace his damaged tyres and when he came out we studied the gap and his lap time on the fresh tyres carefully. This was a critical time. I had to win this race to have any chance of the championship and a wrong decision about tyres would simply hand the win to him. On the radio to David and Patrick, we decided that my tyres would last the distance and that his new ones weren't giving him enough of an advantage to allow him to catch me. I kept it smooth, stuck to a target lap time and brought the car home for a vital fourth win. The only downside was that Riccardo wasn't around to take a few more points off Senna, who finished second.

If I hadn't won then the next race at Portugal wouldn't have meant anything. As it was the Portugal race assumed monumental importance. There was no doubt that it would hold the key to our championship.

Of all the bizarre, freakish misfortunes that I have suffered over the years, perhaps the worst and most frustrating was the pit lane incident in the Portuguese Grand Prix. To lose a Grand Prix when you are leading is one thing, to lose one as important as Portugal is another, but to lose it because your wheel comes off in the pit lane after a routine stop is very, very hard to take. I blamed no-one. My heart went out to the poor mechanics because I knew how they must be feeling. I was numb with disappointment and I'm sure they were too.

Going into the race, team morale was the best I could remember it in my time at Williams. Everyone was working together and everything gelled, the engineers from Renault and Williams were in harmony, the fuel from Elf was getting better and better and all the hard work we had done and the demands we had made before the season started were bearing fruit.

I knew that I had to do it all at the start, that if I let the two McLarens of Senna and Berger stay in front of me I would have a terrible time passing them later in the race. I was extremely aggressive off the line and passed both of them in the first two corners. I thought I passed them fairly and most people seemed to agree with me, but Senna complained bitterly after the race and the feud would spill over to the next race in Spain.

Once ahead of Riccardo I developed my lead and took control of the race. There was no pressure on us during the tyre stop, but when I received the signal to go, I dropped the clutch and accelerated away. Just then, to my horror, my right rear wheel parted company with the car and rolled off down the pit lane. The wheelnut had not been put on properly ... and that, to all intents and purposes, was the end of my championship hopes.

I have never wanted to dwell on the issue, it's just one of those bizarre things which happen from time to time and which serve to remind me why I believe in fate. The frustration as I sat there beached on three wheels in the pit lane was as intense as any I can remember. I admit that later I was in tears when, after clawing back from 17th to 6th place in 20 laps, I received the black disqualification flag for having my car worked on in the pit lane.

After the wheel had come off, the mechanics had run down to where I was stranded in the fast lane and fitted a new one, which was against the rules. I had gone out and given everything for over 25 minutes, setting new lap records and risking my neck, all for nothing.

Ayrton was still unhappy about my start when we arrived at the new Barcelona circuit and we had a really good go at one another in the Sunday morning driver's briefing. Ayrton always seemed to think that he should be allowed the divine right to barge through and push people out of the way, but when it happened to him he didn't like it and he called it dangerous driving. Much as I respected his ability, that didn't wash with me.

During the briefing, the FIA president Jean-Marie Balestre referred to the incident at the start in Estoril and said that if anyone drove like that here today they would be penalised. I wasn't having this, so I asked why it was that these matters were always raised when I was supposed to have done something wrong, but never when it was Senna, who to my mind had done far worse things and got away scot-free. Ayrton leapt to his feet and said that the FIA should study the tapes of races from the past few years and they would see that I had been involved in far more incidents than him. Then he called me a 'shit' and sat down.

I got up and said to him, 'Ayrton, you don't have a divine right. The rules are there for everybody. If we want to do it to you, then we *will* do it to you.' I stood my ground and I felt that most of the drivers were on my side, because most of them were intimidated by him anyway, but I wasn't having it. We had a few words and then the officials squashed it.

I won the race that afternoon after passing Ayrton down the long pit straight; wheel to wheel for what seemed like an eternity, neither of us prepared to give up. He should have known by now that I would not be intimidated as I had proved again in the drivers' briefing. I held my ground, passed him and went on to win the race. It was some consolation for what had happened in Portugal and meant that to overhaul him in the championship, I would have to score maximum points in the last two races while Ayrton got no more than four points.

As it was still mathematically possible to win the championship, we had not resigned ourselves to losing. But when Ayrton backed off in the middle of the very quick first corner in Japan, putting me off line and into the sand trap, it really was all over. I was glad to escape that incident without injury. I hit the sand trap sideways at close on 200mph and my first concern was that the car might dig in and flip over. Luckily, it didn't.

Despite our differences, I hung around until the end of the race to congratulate Ayrton on his third World Championship. Like the lift I gave him at Silverstone, it was the sporting thing to do. Our conversation was amicable. Having won the championship he was in a mood for reconciliation and we were as friendly as we had ever been up to that point.

The last race of the season in Adelaide was a fiasco and a painful one at that. An hour before the start, the heavens opened and by the time we went out to form the grid the conditions were appalling. It was so bad in fact that the international airport had to be temporarily closed down! The 1989 race there had been wet and everyone remembered how bad the track was in the wet. The drainage was poor and the spray rendered visibility almost impossible.

It was one of those terrible situations, where you know that it is foolish to race, but you are aware that the whole world has turned on their television sets to watch and you don't want to disappoint them. Despite these conditions the start was not delayed and we set off into a ball of spray. I was directly behind Ayrton on the grid and after three laps I managed to pass Berger for second place.

I chased Ayrton hard, but the conditions got worse and worse. As more and more drivers lost control of their cars, debris became scattered around the track and then it became really dangerous. There were several cars parked at odd angles on the main straight. I knew I had passed quite a few on the previous lap, but I couldn't remember exactly where they were. As I came down the straight I was right on Senna's tail and ready to pass. I got on the radio to David Brown with probably the strangest question I have ever asked him.

'David, can you see on the television? Is it safe for me to overtake?' It was a crazy situation and really very dangerous. The stranded cars were there alright, hidden by the spray. I could have hit them and when you look at the video tape of that race, there is a moment when I'm catching Senna, where I very nearly have a big collision with a parked car. Fortunately, I saw it at the last minute and managed to take evasive action.

I was determined to get past him so that I could have a clear track with an uninterrupted view. Unfortunately, as we climbed the slope out of the first chicane my car suddenly snapped sideways and ploughed into the wall. It was very painful. I was helped from the car with what I thought at the time was a badly bruised left foot. It was not until later that I realised what a potentially disastrous injury I had sustained.

I had broken the foot years before and never had it set. In the past few years it had give me a few twinges of pain, but I thought nothing of it. In fact, the foot had become quite deformed and now with the fresh break sustained in the Adelaide shunt, I was in trouble.

Should the race have been allowed to start? Ultimately, it's really only the drivers, or those with past experience of the circuit who are in a position to judge a situation like that. If you cannot persuade the officials beforehand that it is not a sensible idea to give the green light, then you cannot be unprofessional and refuse to start. I think that if I was in that position again I would get all the drivers together and say, 'Look, the officials want this race to start, Bernie wants it to go ahead. It's not an ideal situation, but that's the way it is and we can handle it if we are sensible. We've got to drive this race sensibly and that means everybody. So let's all take it easy to start with, nobody trying to be a hero into the first corner. Let the race settle down for 10 or 20 laps before you try to overtake.'

In other words you go slower, but it still looks and feels like a race. Obviously you need the cooperation of every driver to do it and that's a difficult thing to achieve, but I've been around a long time and know most of these guys, so I think I could prevail upon them to listen.

The season was over and instead of going back to the Isle of Man, it was to my new home that I flew after Australia. We had bought a house in America, a colonial-style property called Century Oaks, because of the two oak trees in the back garden, one of which was reputedly 470 years old. The house, in Clearwater, Florida overlooked the Gulf of Mexico and Rosanne and I had decided to move the family out there to escape the cold of the Isle of Man winters and as few people knew me in America, we hoped we would have a little more privacy.

When I got back to Clearwater I went to see an orthopaedic surgeon, George Morris, who X-rayed my foot. He showed me the results and it wasn't a pretty sight. There was a fracture of the joint and the neck of the bone from the previous injury. George explained that when an injury like the one I had sustained many years ago goes untreated, the body's natural tendency is to throw down extra bone to try to heal itself. Because my foot hadn't been reset, the extra bone had formed a spur the size of an acorn. Now with the Adelaide fracture, I could only walk on the inside of my foot and when it was bad, the only way I could walk at all was in a particular pair of cushioned sneakers.

George said that he needed to operate immediately. The recuperation period would be two months. I wasn't keen. There were only a few short months over the winter and in that time I wanted to test heavily and I needed to get fit for the 1992 season when, I had told myself, I was going to dominate the World Championship. Nothing could be left to chance. I had promised myself that I would train harder than ever before and diet like crazy. I wanted to lose ten pounds and get seriously fit. That was one of the main reasons why I had moved to Florida. It is medically proven that when you are cold your body needs more food and hence it is more difficult to train effectively.

It was a real dilemma. Should I have the surgery and lose two months of vital preparation time for what I knew was my best ever chance of winning the World Championship, or should I try to forget about the injury, train as hard as I could and take each race as it comes? If I didn't have the surgery it would be a painful season and I wouldn't be able to tell anyone about it, because if the FIA found out they might make me have it operated on or find me unfit and suspend my licence. After all the work we'd put in building the team up for the championship, I wasn't going to have it all ruined by a miserable foot injury. I would just have to grin and bear it.

George was surprised when I declined the surgery. 'I'll be amazed if you can walk after a race,' he said. 'Every time you put your foot down it'll be like walking on broken glass.' He was right.

I got to work immediately on the diet and the fitness programme. I cut out all fats, ate a lot of healthy soups, chicken stir fries and salads, and lost some serious weight. Every day I cycled, swam and pumped iron in my home gym for hours on end, while trying not to aggravate my foot by running on it.

I kept in close touch with David Brown and the engineers at Williams as the new car neared completion. The FW14B was the car that would carry me to the world title in 1992. It was basically an evolution of the 1991 car, building on the strengths of that car with the addition of some well-tested electronic wizardry. Adrian Newey had spent a lot of time in the wind tunnel with the FW14 perfecting the aerodynamic package.

Patrick Head had been fully committed to the idea of using active suspension ever since its debut in 1987. After the problems we had had with it in 1988, he and his team went back to the drawing board to come up with a better, more reliable system. After a lot of testing and refinement we had a system which seemed to fit the bill. We knew that we couldn't afford a repeat of the technical failures of early 1991 so the system was put through over 7000 miles of testing, much of it carried out by Damon Hill, at that time the test driver.

We had taken a developmental active car to Adelaide for the final race of 1991, but I drove only 16 laps in it in practice on the Friday, before returning to my normal race car. It was interesting to compare it at that early stage with the 1991 car and although it was some way from being competitive, I could see the potential in it.

I planned to spend December settling in to our new home in America, but in the early part of the month we had a test at Barcelona which was supposed to determine whether the active should be run in 1992. I drove the two cars back-to-back for the first three days and Riccardo drove them for the final two days. Unfortunately, the weather was against us and we didn't get as much clear running as I would have liked. Nevertheless, I told Frank and Patrick that I felt we should go ahead with the active system.

At the end of January I flew to Europe again for an eight-day test at Estoril, the objective being to make a final decision whether to run the active car for 1992.

It was an unprecedented test, the longest and most intensive that Williams had ever done and it was without doubt one of the most productive. We again had two active FW14s on hand and I did two race distances in them. We also had a passive car out there for back-to-back comparison and the difference was phenomenal.

We then tried a little experiment with the tyres. Extra sticky qualifying tyres were to be phased out by Goodyear for 1992, but we had a few sets left over and we fitted them to the active car to see how it would compare with Riccardo's pole time from the previous year in the passive car. I did a lap almost two seconds quicker and we had our answer! It was an immensely positive and morale-boosting test and we confirmed our decision to run the system in 1992.

Having hated the active system in 1988, I came to really appreciate it in 1992. I liked it primarily because I could change things on the car as I went around the circuit, and I felt could manage the car better because I was more in control in the cockpit. I know exactly what I want from a car and if you can change things as you go around then it is almost like you are engineering the car yourself. It was great, although Riccardo had some problems with it, because it didn't give him the 'feel' he wanted.

Unfortunately, not everything went well in Estoril. I had a huge fright when I got hit full in the front of the helmet by a bird, while travelling at 180mph!

Back in Florida, I worked hard on my fitness and psyched myself up over the remainder of the winter. This was going to be my best ever chance of winning the World Championship. I would crush the opposition, take no prisoners and not let up until we had got the job done.

I was on a mission.

David Brown, Nigel's engineer at Williams: 'Nigel liked the active car, the FW14B because he could change a lot in the car with the switches in the cockpit, so he could have greater control technically while on the track. He was tremendously enthusiastic about it and if you were testing with him you might suggest that he try a certain switch on the next run and he'd say, "I've already tried that one ... and this one and this one and this one ..."'

22

WORLD CHAMPION AT LAST!

The momentum which we had built up since late 1990 was irresistible and in 1992 we marched to the World Championship. It was clear in pre-season testing that we had developed a fantastic car and all the hard work of the engineers and the fabricators alongside Renault and Elf over the past eighteen months was about to pay off. We built a World Championship winning package and used it properly to get the job done.

Unfortunately, the competitiveness of Williams-Renault was not lost on Alain Prost, who was embarking on a sabbatical year, having been fired by Ferrari at the end of 1991 and having failed to use his influence with Renault and Elf to get my seat for 1992. Prost was adamant that he had not retired, but that he was merely resting. He wanted to race again and he wanted to drive the best car. Although the saga would not come to a head until September, the first I heard of it was in March, just before the second race of the season in Mexico.

We utterly dominated the opening round in South Africa, where I got pole position and won by 24 seconds from Riccardo with Senna a distant third. It was the first time that the Formula 1 cars had been to South Africa since 1985 when I won my second ever Grand Prix. With the country now fully on the road to reform and apartheid about to become a thing of the past, the country had once again been opened up to the top level of the sport.

I felt strong all weekend and I knew that it was vital to throw down the gauntlet to the opposition early, as if to say 'Look, I am going to win this championship and I'm going to do it by beating you all every time we go out.' Before the action started, I had a personal triumph at Kyalami, because I weighed in 4kg lighter than I had been in 1991 and 2kg lighter than Riccardo. He was absolutely livid and asked for me to be reweighed, but the awful truth for him was that I was lighter. My diet and winter preparation had paid off.

We arrived in Mexico City at the height of a big pollution scare. The air is always bad there because it's so thin due to the altitude and there are so many cars and trucks pumping out exhaust fumes. But race weekend was the worst it had ever been in the city's history. It was like being choked and it left your throat quite sore at the end of every day.

The Peraltada corner had been modified following Ayrton's flip the year before. The banking had been lowered and the track had been resurfaced. If anything the change made the corner even more dangerous because it was now very slippery through there and the absence of any banking made the cars slide away from the apex. The track surface in Mexico is bumpy at the best of times because it's built on reclaimed marshland, so the contours of the track change from year to year. But this year there were added problems because of the dust and smog dumped on the track surface making it unpredictable and slippery. Our active suspension had given us a lot of problems here in 1988, but in 1992 it turned out to be a big help.

I got pole, just a few hundredths ahead of Riccardo and eight-tenths ahead of Schumacher. Things were looking good for win number two. I was chatting to Frank before the race when he raised a very odd subject. He asked me what I thought of the idea of running with Prost as a team-mate in 1993.

Memories of 1990 came flooding back to me, the swapping of the chassis and the influence behind the scenes. I knew that Prost had a good relationship with Renault, because he raced for them in the early 1980s and he had been sponsored for almost his entire career by the Elf fuel company. It was obvious that his nationality and his relationship with the management of the two companies, both of which are controlled by the French government, could lead to the same thing happening again as had happened at Ferrari.

I had come out of retirement to do a job. I had done all the hard work, got all the guarantees of support from all the partners and raised standards through the team. We had built up the momentum through 1991, accepting the failures of reliability and the disappointment of missing out on the championship, all with the belief that our time would come. I had personally staked a great deal on this project and now, just as I was about to reap the rewards for all the hard work, I was being asked if I would like Prost as a team-mate! I told Frank that there was no way.

I had heard rumours that Renault and Elf were putting pressure on Frank to take Prost, but what I didn't know was that when Frank made that first speculative approach to me in Mexico, Prost had *already* agreed terms.

It was not until much later that I would learn this and discover that Prost would be paid in excess of $10 million, plus pensions and a variety of dealerships and petrol stations. The French pressure had won out, but in March, just before the Mexican Grand Prix, Frank couldn't bring himself to tell me. After all, it was only the second race of the year!

On the track the steamroller continued. I won in Mexico, ahead of Riccardo, with Michael Schumacher third. Ayrton failed to finish. It was a great race, with both Riccardo and I pushing very hard throughout and trading fastest laps.

When I got home, I told Rosanne about what Frank had said and she couldn't believe it either. We still didn't know, of course, that Prost already had the deal, we just felt aggrieved that Frank could even consider taking Prost.

In Brazil, I had a coming-together with Ayrton in practice, which said a lot about the frustration he was feeling and the degree to which I had out-psyched him that season. We had stolen the early advantage and had scored maximum points, but Senna and McLaren were not going to let us get away from them. They were throwing everything they had at us and in Brazil they debuted their new MP4/7, which featured a radical new electronic fly-by-wire throttle system. They had three of the new cars on hand as well as the three MP4/6s. It was the first time in the history of the World Championship that a two-driver team had brought six cars to a race. It showed not only the fantastic resources the team had, but also how serious they were about beating us to the championship.

In qualifying I got a perfect lap and snatched pole. It was one of those times when you know that even with another try, you could not go any faster. I was a second faster than my team-mate and a good couple of seconds up on Ayrton. As it was his home race, this was no doubt a major irritation to him. In second qualifying I was coming up to overtake and he indicated that I should go to the left to pass, which meant that I would go around the outside of the upcoming right hand corner. I went left, but he suddenly accelerated. I ran out of road, and clouted the wall hard, badly damaging the whole right hand side of my car, which had to be repaired before the race the following day. It had been a misunderstanding and I said as much to the press.

But what people don't perhaps realise is that I had quite bad concussion from that impact and spent a long time in the medical centre that evening. I got about three hours sleep that night and consequently I was not in the best shape for the race.

I made a terrible start, but ran second to Riccardo in the early laps until the pit stops. I was quicker in the traffic than him and took the lead while he was in the pits. After that I held on to the flag for my third win in a row and our third one-two finish. Meanwhile, Ayrton had retired the brand new McLaren.

I now had 30 points in the championship, while Senna, whom I still considered the most likely challenger, only had four. We were in a strong position, but there is no room for complacency in motor racing and at that stage if there was one team capable of reacting quickly it was McLaren. Their new car had not been the success that they had hoped straight out of the box, but you could never count them out. They would get it right soon and they had a new active suspension system in the pipeline which would no doubt take them a major step forward. The relentless pressure on everyone at Williams-Renault would have to continue.

After Brazil, Frank asked me again about Prost. I couldn't believe it. I said to him, 'Why on earth do you want to change the team? Riccardo and I have just come first and second in the last three races, and everybody's working together fine. What do you need Prost for?'

He dropped the subject after that, but in the next few weeks he became very keen for me to sign a new contract for 1993. I didn't see what the rush was all about and I wanted to concentrate on my driving and on securing the championship as quickly as possible. That was the main focus and that was, after all, what we had been building up to. The whole team was on a high at this time, realising that all the hard work of the past 18 months was paying off. Morale had never been so high and I didn't want any distractions.

In any case I was not going to sign anything until I knew who the other driver would be. I didn't believe that Frank was serious about Prost and I thought that I had made my feelings on the subject perfectly clear. I still didn't know, of course, that Prost already had the contract in his pocket.

There were warning signs everywhere against complacency. In the Sunday morning warm-up for the Spanish Grand Prix, Gerhard Berger was fastest in the McLaren-Honda. Clearly the new car was developing fast. The warm-up, like the race, was a wet affair, making a lottery of all that had been learned in practice.

It was an intriguing race. Sitting on the grid before the start, everyone was faced with some tough decisions. The weather was very changeable and although it wasn't actually raining, it was wet. The rain began to fall just before the off, so most people went for wet weather tyres, but not for full wet weather settings on the chassis. You couldn't afford to do that. Full wet settings involve, among other things, running a lot more wing to create higher downforce and therefore more grip through the corners. But the trade-off is that you are slower on the straight. In the wet that doesn't matter so much, but if it suddenly dried out you'd be passed on the straights like you were going backwards!

I pushed hard in the slippery conditions and opened out a lead quickly. We had started on wet weather tyres and by lap ten there was some quick thinking to be done. The track was drying out fast, but the black clouds above threatened more rain. I stayed out and looked for the wet line around the corners to keep the tyres cool. With only ten laps gone the fuel load was still heavy and I could ill afford to lose time through tyre problems. Shortly afterwards the rain started falling again, but harder than before. Cars were spinning off left, right and centre, largely because, in the uncertain conditions at the start, no-one had opted for a full wet set-up. Everyone was hedging their bets. I had thought that it might well dry out, which meant I had too little wing for the wet conditions and too much fuel in the car for a wet race, but I'm sure it was the same for everyone. It was such a lottery.

Riccardo spun out on lap 19, leaving Michael Schumacher as my main challenger. At the time he was 22 seconds behind me, but he then began a mighty charge which saw him reduce the gap quite dramatically. By lap 50 he was less than five seconds behind me. In the car, I was having a minor panic. I couldn't understand how he was doing it. My lap times were consistent, I was not on the limit, but I was going as fast as I had all along and yet here was Michael reeling me in.

It was an interesting battle psychologically, because I was on top in the championship and I needed to keep winning, so I was driving protectively, not taking any risks and protecting my lead. Michael had nothing to lose and was right on the limit. I knew that I would have to go to the edge of the envelope if I was going to fight him off. I didn't want to do that because the conditions were so treacherous and cars were aquaplaning off the track everywhere. But I had no choice.

I began to get out of shape on some of the corners and I found that there was a lot more grip off line, so I pushed in those areas and suddenly speeded up. In this way I was able to stem the flow and stop Michael from catching me. Then I started to pull away again and when I saw the gap opening up, the feeling of relief in the car was immense. I had been very worried by Schumacher. I pushed until I thought I was safe and eventually won by 24 seconds. It was a satisfying win and a very significant one too.

Spain was the 25th Grand Prix win of my career, equalling the record of my boyhood hero Jim Clark. It was an immensely moving thought that, after all that had happened to me and after all the trials and tribulations, I shared a place in history with the mighty Clark. That night I thought about Jim and about Colin Chapman and reflected on how far we had travelled and all the work we had done to get to where we were.

Some of my detractors were implying that my success was diminished because I had such a mechanical advantage, but the truth was that at times the car wasn't that much better than the rest. Riccardo had the same car and he was struggling to keep ahead of the opposition.

Whatever chassis advantage I had in 1992 I had worked for thirteen years to get and I deserved it. If anything I was adding to it, so motivated was I to dominate the season. Yes, I won easily with no competition, because I drove with all my heart. But because it was me driving everyone said that it was the car which was doing the winning. When Prost and Senna had done the same thing in the past, it had been them.

I dominated in 1992 because I was on a mission. We had the best car, but I pushed it to the limit and that's why we won so many races, got so many poles and won the title in record time. When Prost got his hands on the car the following year he cruised to the title. Along the way he was made to look very humble by Senna, particularly at Donington, and let's not forget that McLaren in 1993 with their customer Ford engines, were certainly not the force that they had been with Honda in 1992.

In San Marino I claimed another piece of history. No-one had ever won the first five Grands Prix in a season. That historic win came after I had clinched my fifth consecutive pole position, over a second faster than my team-mate. It was a fabulous day, one of the best in my career. To realise that I had made history was again very moving. The championship now began to look like a distinct possibility, with Ayrton some 42 points behind me. I wouldn't let up the pressure until the title was mine, but after San Marino I began to think that at last it might come true.

It was at this point that Frank and I began to talk again about 1993. I told him that I was prepared to sign a contract for the same money as 1992, thereby foregoing the substantial fee increase that winning the championship should have brought me, provided that Riccardo was kept on as the number two driver. He asked me what the deal would be if Prost was taken on.

I had given it a lot of thought and it was obvious to me that the team's French partners wanted Prost around. I told him that if that happened I would want compensation, as Ferrari had given me in 1989 when Prost joined. After all, I would be losing my number one status and the dilution of the team's efforts would lead to all kinds of knock-on effects, and the reduction of my earning power. If I was going to win the World Championship in 1992, I wanted to defend it the same way in 1993 and I very much doubted whether that would be possible with Prost in the team.

I said to Frank that if Prost was going to come on board I would need written guarantees from Frank and from all the suppliers and partners that we would have equal status and that I would be given equal equipment, technical support and team support.

On the track, I focused my attention on making it six wins in a row. I was confident that my current form would mean that my Monaco jinx might be broken and throughout practice and for most of the race, it seemed it would. I took pole comfortably and had a 30 second lead with seven laps to go when the left rear wheel suddenly began to feel loose as I drove through the tunnel, the fastest part of the circuit. I thought I had a puncture so I slowed down a little and radioed the pits that I needed fresh tyres. I came in, but getting into and out of the pits at Monaco is such a slow business that by the time I came out, Senna had caught and passed me.

I tried everything I could to get past him for the remaining six laps, but Monaco is so tight and there are only a couple of places where you might try it. Ayrton knew the track like the back of his hand and he knew how to make his car a little wider at those places to defend his position. He also realised that I would try anything and everything to get past. He held me off, as he was entitled to do and we crossed the line a couple of car lengths apart. Monaco had done it to me again.

After the race we learned that my tyre had not been punctured and that it wasn't a wheel bearing failure either. The likely explanation was that the wheel nut had come loose. If I think of the races I have lost because of wheel nuts ...

I was disappointed, but it had been a fantastic race and the most important thing was that I had scored six points towards the championship. I had now scored in all six races and I had to grudgingly admit that it was one of the best second places I had ever achieved.

Ayrton was fair in Monaco but at the next race in Canada, he took me out of the race when I tried to pass him into the final chicane before the pits. The biggest regret I have about that whole incident is that neither the television cameras nor any photographers got a shot of it, so a fair judgment on it will never be made. People took sides afterwards and a lot of ink was dispensed on writing about who was right and who was wrong. I was criticised but as far as I am concerned the only thing I did wrong was to put myself in a position where he could put me out. It was one of those things that Ayrton did from time to time. It was a blow, but luckily Ayrton retired too with electrical problems, so my championship lead wasn't affected.

By the time we arrived in Magny Cours for the French Grand Prix I was hearing strong rumours that Prost had already signed a deal with Frank, although Frank would not confirm this when I asked him. Clearly if this were true then I would have to rethink my position completely.

Although the whole contract business was becoming increasingly distracting, I put it out of my head for the race and won, despite a furious fight with Riccardo who was trying very hard indeed. I had heard that he had been told he wouldn't be needed for the next year and if that was the case then he certainly drove as if to prove a point. The race was stopped for rain, but after the restart I got past him and although the rain fell again in the final laps, I won by nearly 50 seconds. It was our fifth one-two finish of the year and I now had 66 points on the board with Silverstone the next race on the calendar.

France was my 27th Grand Prix victory which put me equal with Jackie Stewart. It was a magical figure, which had stood for so long as the record until Prost, then Senna and then I broke it. No-one else has since come close. After the race Jackie sent me a fax saying, 'Welcome temporarily to the 27 club. I'm sure that you won't be a member for long.'

It was a nice gesture and I agreed with the sentiment. I felt like Silverstone belonged to me and no-one was going to beat me on that 12 July. I was two seconds a lap faster than Riccardo in a test at Silverstone and comfortably inside my own pole time from 1991. I was making everything count; every test, every practice session, every race, every single lap.

I had a good laugh after the test when news reached me that Ayrton had been stopped for speeding on the M25 motorway around London, normally the most congested motorway in Britain. The policeman had flagged down his Porsche, which had been doing 121mph and allegedly said to him, 'Who do you think you are, Nigel Mansell?' Frankly, I was amazed that he had managed to get out of second gear on the M25. I don't think I ever have.

On the Thursday before the British Grand Prix we did a Renault promotional day at Brooklands, the old pre-war race track. I drove a replica of the 30bhp Renault which won the 1902 Paris to Vienna race and Rosanne and I dressed up in costumes of the period, me in a tweed driving coat and period collar and tie, Rosanne in a ladies' driving cloak with a bonnet. It was great fun and all for Renault's benefit. Behind the scenes, however, I was becoming more and more convinced that something had been agreed with Prost and that no-one was telling me about it.

I won the British Grand Prix and it was one of the most emotional and magical weekends of my entire life. From first practice on Friday to the chequered flag on Sunday none of the other cars mattered. I have gone into detail about the race and the atmosphere elsewhere in this book, but I cannot overstate the help that every single one of the 200,000 people who came to watch that weekend gave me. Two laps before the end of the race I put in a really fast lap and lowered the track record by two seconds. I didn't do that for my benefit, I did it for the fans because they deserved it. It was my little present to them to thank them for their loyalty. I knew that with the new rules reducing wing sizes and narrowing tyres for 1993 that lap would stand as a record for a few years and they would know that it was my tribute to them.

As I stood on the podium I was in tears. I had just won my 28th Grand Prix, the most ever by a British driver.

Two weeks later Frank admitted that it was 'likely' that he would sign Prost. It was at this point that I discovered that Prost had had an agreement with Williams all along. I was utterly devastated.

What I didn't know was that in the contract, Prost had a right of veto on the second driver and had already exercised it by saying that he didn't want Senna in the team. It was not until much later that I discovered that Prost had also tried to veto me, but Frank had insisted that I should be allowed to stay. Prost had relented and signed on that understanding.

Although there was an offer on the table from Ferrari to go back there alongside Alesi, Rosanne and I felt we had put in so much work to get to this point and that we should stay on and fight Prost on a level playing field. I had no doubt that in a 1993 Williams-Renault I would be able to beat him in a straight fight, so I went to Frank and we negotiated a deal for 1993.

We sat down and agreed terms during the Hungarian Grand Prix meeting. I would race alongside Prost, we would be equal number ones, with equal backing and this would be written into the contract. I would also get $1.5 million compensation. Having agreed the deal, Frank said that the contracts would be sent to my home on the Isle of Man the day after the race.

I had won in Germany, my eighth win of the season and was now within a few points of the championship. If I could clinch it in Hungary, it would be the fastest anyone had ever clinched the world title, with only two-thirds of the season gone. It was ironic that such a record should fall to me, as someone who had been waiting so many years to win the title!

I had a tough time in qualifying, with a few problems on the car, including a fire in the engine bay on Friday and then I found myself involved in someone else's accident while travelling at 160mph on the Saturday. Luckily the damage to me and to my car was not too serious and I secured second place on the grid behind Riccardo. There would be no team orders for the race. All I needed to be World Champion was a win or a second place.

When I went to bed on Saturday night I turned over thoughts about contracts and about the prospect of racing with Prost the following year. I felt that Riccardo and I had done everything we could have to fulfil our responsibilities and we had delivered the goods in abundance. Over the past season and a half I had won 13 races and scored 158 points while he had won twice and scored 93 points. I could see no reason to change the team we had, but it seemed that commercial pressures had come to bear and, although he had done everything that he was asked to do, Riccardo would be out. I felt sorry for him.

I knew that we were in for a hard race. Seventy-seven laps of the Hungaroring is tough at the best of times. I knew that patience would be required and I hoped and prayed for reliability.

Fittingly the race was the 500th World Championship Grand Prix since the World Championship was established in 1950. In the intervening years there had been 23 World Champions. It was an exclusive club and one I had waited 17 years to join.

At the start, the absence of team orders was apparent as Riccardo shut the door on me, allowing Senna and Berger to go around the outside. I was now in fourth place. With these two holding me up, Riccardo set about building his lead, while I tried to pass Berger. In the cockpit I kept myself calm and told myself that whatever happened it was the championship I was going for today. The record ninth win of the season could wait for another day.

On lap eight I found a way past Berger into the first corner and tried to find a way past Senna. As usual he was very hard to pass. I dodged out of his slipstream a couple of times and made a couple of feints, but there was no way by. After a few laps of this I decided to sit back and wait. I still had Berger breathing down my neck and when I made a slight mistake on lap 31 he slipped past me. I passed him again two laps later and this time stayed ahead.

Six laps later Riccardo made a big mistake and lost it on the off camber left handed second corner. He got going again after some help from the marshals, but by then he was down in seventh place and no longer a threat.

This meant that with Ayrton leading and me in second place, all I had to do was hold my position and I would be the World Champion. I settled in and began counting off the laps. Then I hit trouble; one of my rear tyres was punctured. Luckily it wasn't of the same order as in Adelaide in 1986 and I came into the pits to change tyres. It was a tense moment, but the crew handled it well and I rejoined sixth with 16 laps to go. I pushed as soon as the tyres were fully up to temperature and started making up places.

I gained one place when Schumacher's rear wing flew off on the main straight and he slid out of the race. Then I passed Hakkinen, who was in a battle with Brundle and Berger for second place. I picked off Brundle for third place. I wasn't clear in my mind what the points situation was. Did I need second or third place? I radioed the team and Patrick came back with the answer that I needed second, so with 13 laps to go, I passed Berger for second. In fact, I didn't need second place and third would have done, but by the time I found that out it didn't really matter.

Those last laps were incredible. Every time I crossed the line I ticked off another lap. When we got into single figures I was praying that everything would keep working. I just kept on going.

When I saw the chequered flag on lap 77, I couldn't tally up the points in my head because I was so emotional about finishing the race. I knew that I needed a second place to clinch it, but I couldn't get a clear idea in my head. I didn't know whether I'd wrapped it up or not. When I was told over the radio that I had won the World Championship I was overcome with every emotion you could think of. All the way around the slowing down lap, I was crying tears of joy. I couldn't believe I had really done it. I realised how much pressure I had put on myself to achieve this goal and having achieved it, the relief was enormous. After coming close so many times before and after all the struggles that we had gone through, I was the World Champion at last!

When I came out onto the podium and was greeted by the roar from the crowd, the tears welled up again. I couldn't control the emotions which were pouring from me. In the mass of people which had gathered in the pit lane, directly below the podium I could see Peter Collins, now in charge at Lotus. I could also see my Williams mechanics jumping up and down. It was incredible.

Ayrton had won the race and as I stood on the podium and tried to take in the enormity of it all he came over to me and was in a most benevolent mood. He put his arm around me, hugged me and said, 'Well done, Nigel. It's such a good feeling, isn't it? Now you know why I'm such a bastard. I don't ever want to lose the feeling or let anybody else experience it.'

I'll never forget those words as long as I live.

David Brown, Williams engineer: 'At Silverstone he was already on pole and he decided he was going to go out and give it a bit more. He always regarded Silverstone as his race, which it was. His second pole lap was extraordinary. He was always blindingly quick there and you have to be very brave and very strong for that. The speed he was going into Copse corner was quite unbelievable.'

23
DRIVEN OUT

I began to get worried when the contracts didn't arrive from Williams on the Monday morning after I won the title.

When Frank and I had concluded our discussions the day before in Hungary, the deal was basically agreed. The only minor sticking point had been over the matter of hotel rooms. Frank wanted to drop the provision of three rooms for me and my family at each race. I wanted at least one for Rosanne and myself as a sign of good faith from them, if nothing else.

In the BBC coverage of the Hungary race, commentator James Hunt dropped a bombshell, announcing that Ayrton had offered to drive for Williams for free. It was true, Ayrton had stepped in with that offer, although it was obvious that he didn't mean it quite as simply as it sounded. But it was to confuse things greatly over the coming weeks.

On Monday the press arrived early on the Isle of Man and we got together for photo shoots with the family. I gave an interview to Murray Walker and the BBC, all the time the reality of my situation beginning to dawn on me more and more. Murray is an emotional man and it was touching to see just how moved he was by my success. The magical feeling grew and grew; I was World Champion at last and however confusing the goings-on behind the scenes, I was determined to savour this rich moment.

That afternoon Frank sent me a fax saying that he was sorry about the delay, but that he had had to consult with Renault and Elf. As soon as I had read the fax I called him up. 'Now listen, Frank,' I said, 'You're not messing me around are you?'

'No, no,' Frank replied. 'It's just that there are a few things that need sorting out.' I was nervous about the delay and wary of Senna's emergence into the equation. All sorts of alarm bells were ringing in my head, but I told myself that I was probably over-reacting.

I couldn't see what the delay could be about. We had agreed it all in Hungary, Rosanne had witnessed it and as far as I was concerned I had committed myself to Williams for 1993 to drive, albeit reluctantly with Prost. Team morale had soared as the championship grew closer and when it was clinched there was a real satisfaction at a job well done, not least with Renault, who had been striving since 1977 to win the title. I had now won 13 races for them, more than any other driver, including Prost, and I had just brought them their first world title. Sales of Renault passenger cars were well up in Europe and some of the credit for promoting sales was given to our high profile successes on the track. Nineteen-ninety-three was a done deal, the new car looked very promising on the drawing board and I looked forward to beating Prost in it. Yet still no word from Williams. Why? Was it Senna's offer to drive for nothing which was holding things up?

On Tuesday Rosanne and I gave a press conference at the Castletown Golf Club and not surprisingly the press wanted to talk more about the future and the contracts situation than about the championship just won. I was asked whether I was contemplating retirement. I said, 'That decision is not mine to take. If I am given an opportunity to defend my title and to further my career in the way which I have strived for over thirteen years in Formula 1, then I will continue. If that opportunity is not afforded me, then I might consider retiring, because even more today than before, I am not there to make the numbers up.

'But my first choice is to defend my championship and to defend it in the best and most vigorous manner that I can. I don't want to leave something that I have created with the team, with the sponsors and the engineers and the mechanics for someone else to inherit, and I don't want to have to go off to try to build it all up again with another team.'

I was asked whether I meant that it was a case of 'Williams or nothing'. I looked at Rosanne, she looked at me and we knew. 'Yes,' I said.

The day passed with no news from Frank and I was half tempted to call off an appearance in a golf tournament on Wednesday, but I thought that it might help take my mind off the worry. Half way through the round, my mobile phone went. It was Sheridan Thynne. He said he had been instructed by Frank to offer me a new deal worth half of what we had agreed and he said that I had two hours to agree. Frank said he had Ayrton standing by in Paris waiting to sign if I didn't want the deal.

I was utterly flabbergasted and very angry. I had seen my fair share of chicanery over the years in Formula 1 but nothing had prepared me for a shock like this. I told Sheridan to tell Frank, 'I don't need two hours. If you want Senna, sign him.' I later found out than Senna was not in Paris at all.

I had won the World Championship just four days before and here I was being rejected. It was tough to take. Frank's argument was that he had to look after the interests of his 200 strong work force back in Didcot. Prost's $10 million deal had added massively to the wage bill and he did not have the money for both of us at that price. He didn't want to sacrifice any jobs at the factory. I could understand his feelings about his employees, but I had just won the World Championship! I had finished the job which I had been hired to do and delivered the goods in terms of notching up plenty of lucrative World Championship points for the team. I had worked ceaselessly for the past 18 months. Now as World Champion I should be able, if anything, to *raise* my price, not take a 50% pay cut and accept playing second fiddle to Prost. This was my crowning moment after 17 years of back-breaking struggle, my moment in the sun ... and I wasn't being allowed to enjoy my success.

By the time we got to Spa for the Belgian Grand Prix, the press had fully caught wind of the situation and rumours ran around the paddock. Frank and I had not spoken for a while and stories appeared in the press that I was being greedy and stalling the negotiations and that I was being difficult about hotel rooms. Although I was prepared to say publicly that I felt I was being treated shoddily, I did not want to go into details and the suggestion that I was being greedy about hotel rooms was beneath me.

It wasn't the money, it was the principle that mattered. I couldn't understand why the goalposts kept moving. I knew by this time that Prost had a veto in his contract which prevented Ayrton from being signed, so Frank's call seemed even more mystifying.

For his part, Ayrton was keen to get into a Williams, but he was frustrated by Prost's veto, which he told the press about on the Friday at Spa, thereby dialling himself out of the equation and heightening the furore over the contracts situation.

At least things were going my way on the track. In first qualifying,

I was two seconds ahead of Ayrton and three seconds ahead of my team-mate and when rain fell on Saturday, preventing any chance of improvement, I had my 10th pole position of the year.

I also became aware that weekend that the demands on a World Champion's time are much greater than for normal drivers. As soon as I arrived at the track on the Thursday I was inundated with requests from all sides; for interviews, sponsor requirements and all manner of other demands. It was nice to be the centre of attention for the right reasons, but it left little time for other things. I didn't want too many distractions, after all the championship may have been won, but the effort could not be allowed to drop off within the team. I still wanted to break more records, including most pole positions and most wins in a season, both of which were held by Ayrton.

The race was rather frustrating for me. It was, like Spain, a half-wet, half-dry affair and I looked to have it won when my engine developed a misfire and I lost around 100bhp. The engine would not rev as high as before and I found myself taking the sweeping Eau Rouge corner in fifth gear rather than sixth because it was quicker on the exit. There was nothing to be done about it and I had to settle for second place while Michael Schumacher won his first Grand Prix in the Benetton-Ford.

Riccardo finished third that day and our combined ten points clinched the Constructors' World Championship for Williams-Renault. The Renault management were ecstatic. It was the culmination of many years of trying and within two weekends they had claimed the two highest prizes in motor sport.

Coming away from Belgium that weekend I felt a strong sense of rejection. The signal I was getting from Frank was that he didn't care whether I drove for him or not. Behind the scenes, Bernie Ecclestone, the commercial genius behind Formula 1, was working to patch things up, fearful that he might lose the World Champion from his series next year if something wasn't done. Bernie promised me that if I went ahead and signed the contract, he would personally ensure that my position was not undermined.

It was a kind offer, but there was more at stake than money or status, it was about what I referred to at the time as my 'comfort zone', in other words the respect and welcome which I require from a team if I am to do my job properly. I had said all along that I didn't want to be anywhere that I wasn't wanted and where I did not have the full support of the team. I wanted to defend the title in the same way in which I had won it, it was surely my right after working so hard to get to this point. I warned Frank that if the thing wasn't sorted out soon I would retire. I knew I meant it.

By the time we arrived in Monza for the Italian Grand Prix, it was clear that things were coming to a head. I was tired of the saga, but still listened patiently to the arguments. Prior to leaving for Monza I had been told that a revised offer would be presented to me over the weekend. In fact the goalposts moved again and I made fresh discoveries about things which had already been arranged. We talked throughout the weekend, but it seemed to be getting us nowhere.

On the track McLaren and Senna were highly competitive. I got pole position, but Ayrton was a close second. I drew considerable satisfaction from being the only front-runner to improve my time in the second qualifying session, but the whole thing was overshadowed by events off the track.

I met the president of Elf on Saturday lunchtime and he assured me that his company wanted me to stay. In the early evening I had dinner with Sheridan, Peter Windsor and Peter Collins and we discussed the position as old friends. But my meeting with Frank later that night yielded nothing and I arrived at the track on Sunday morning determined to take charge of the situation.

By now Bernie Ecclestone was getting concerned. When I asked him if I could use the circuit's press office to make an announcement, he threatened to have me banned from the place if I was going to retire. We talked and he could see that I had had enough. I said to him, 'How can I drive for someone who doesn't want me?' He saw my point and relented.

I went up to the press office ready to drop my bombshell. Seconds before I began speaking, a member of the Williams marketing department, Gary Crumpler, appeared at my left shoulder. Frank had sent him at the eleventh hour to say, 'Stop this, we agree to everything.' It was a total climb down by Frank and Renault and Elf. The counter offer presented to me on the golf course was withdrawn and they were prepared to sign me for the original price agreed in Hungary.

But it was all too late. It saddened me to think that I had been ready to sign weeks before when I had thought I had a deal. Then I had found that I didn't and now at the very last minute, it was all rearranged. If they had come to me a day earlier and made the counter offer I would have seriously thought about staying on, but to leave it until now… at that moment I decided that I was not going to be bought and I refused to be treated like that. I started reading my speech:

'Due to circumstances beyond my control I have decided to retire from Formula 1 at the end of this season.

'I have made this decision with some regret, but not without a great deal of thought. Any relationship between a Formula 1 team and its driver is vital for success and partly dependent on money, because it defines how seriously the team and its backers take the driver. Those who know me well understand the importance of the human side and the mutual trust, goodwill, integrity and fair play that are the basis of all human relationships. All these issues have suffered in recent weeks.

'Looking back I feel that relationships between me and the Canon-Williams team began to break down before the Hungarian Grand Prix. A deal was agreed with Frank Williams before that race in front of a witness (Rosanne) and I have to say that at the time I felt very good about racing again with Williams in 1993. Having won the championship I was looking forward to defending the title with what I believed to be a very competitive car. However, three days after Hungary I was telephoned by a Williams director who said that he had been instructed to tell me that because Senna would drive for nothing, I, the new World Champion, had to accept a massive reduction in remuneration from the figure agreed in Hungary. Considerably less I might add, than I am receiving this year. If I did not, Senna was ready to sign that night, I was told.

'Needless to say I rejected the offer and said that if these were the terms, Williams had better go ahead and sign Senna. Since then it is fair to say that relations with the team have not been good, and I am referring here to the directors, rather than the scores of people behind the scenes at Williams. I have listened to many different opinions, some well-meaning, some not and we have heard the public statements made by Senna in Belgium. To say that I have been badly treated is I think a gross understatement.

'Of course, any team owner is free to choose whomever he wants to work for him, but it was the lack of information and sudden changes that I found disappointing. It is difficult to put into words the sort of commitment you need to make in order to succeed in Formula 1. I am aware of criticisms made of my approach to racing, but I am the way I am because I believe in total sacrifice; a total ability to withstand pain and a total belief in myself and my ability. To have the motivation to win a World Championship you must in turn have those commitments back from the team. When I returned from Ferrari I did so with the belief that I had the motivation and the team had the commitment, I don't think that I was wrong.

'Now things are different. I no longer feel that the commitment towards me from the team is there. There are many reasons for this and I have tried to give some idea of how I feel. Other people will no doubt draw their own conclusions. One thing is clear; Alain Prost has been committed to the team for months. For another, I thought I had a deal when I did not and needless to say I do not understand why this has happened.

'In recent weeks, certain people have tried to smooth things over and I respect that and I thank them for their time. But now I realise that it is all too late. To my mind it all comes down to fair play or the lack of it. Money, the trigger for the problems after Hungary, is now no longer an issue for me.

'In finishing I would like to say in the most sincere way that I will always be grateful to Williams and Renault for the support they have given me and hopefully will give me for the rest of 1992. I want to win the remaining races and I am sure that the FW15, from what I know about it, will do the job in 1993.

'As for myself, I know that I am not yet ready to retire from motor racing completely. I still love my racing and I still want to win. So I may look at the IndyCar World Series and see what opportunities, if any, may exist there.'

I folded up my speech and looked at the faces of the assembled press. I was sure that many of them would draw their own conclusions; some would sympathise, others would attack me anyway. Some would say it was a hasty decision, but in reality Rosanne and I had thought about it for weeks and I had warned Frank that I would act if he continued to procrastinate.

I added, 'There is no disagreement between me and any of the sponsors. Frank Williams and I spoke minutes before coming here. I publicly thank him and Renault and all the associated sponsors. We have not fallen out. It was not a question of finance. I think that I have demonstrated that in front of you, which was difficult.'

I got up and left the press room. And that was it. I had retired. I was glad to have made a decision and it was an immense relief to be clear of it all.

When you've come from nowhere, overcome disadvantages and

actually won a World Championship you do not expect to be compromised. What happened with Williams after so much success on the track was an immense disappointment to me.

Of course, many of us are a lot wiser now and everybody regrets what happened. I was standing up for what was correct. What I didn't see was who was manipulating the situation, which I can see now. With 20/20 hindsight I can say that if I had known then what I know now about what was really happening while some of the decisions were being made and if someone at the centre of it had taken the trouble to explain it better to me, then the outcome may well have been different.

Frank had the interests of his workforce at heart, he had commercial considerations and his hands were tied. Prost is a strong politician and he had the backing of Elf and Renault. If I was to keep my seat at Williams, he wanted me to play second fiddle to him, after all the work I had put in to win my first World Championship!

Having worked for the late great Colin Chapman and having seen how he operated I think it would be true to say that Colin would never have allowed himself to be manipulated in the same way that Frank had. It was disappointing to say the least.

If I hadn't worked with Prost before and seen what he did at Ferrari, I might have accepted their last minute offer in Monza. But having been his team-mate I knew what would happen and I thought, 'This is a joke.' I knew I could do other things and fortunately for myself and for the history books I did do other things.

Many people have said that I should have stuck around and taken Prost on in equal cars in 1993 and I must say that I would have relished the chance to beat him in a straight fight in the same car. But I have to ask myself whether they would have been equal cars.

As it was, he stroked his way to the title, driving at eight-tenths for most of the season, without ever really extending himself. On several occasions he was made to look very ordinary by Ayrton.

In hindsight I should have accepted the revised offer whispered into my ear at the Monza press conference, but I have more dignity. I've got no regrets, because I stood by my word under the circumstances as they were at the time. I have always tried to live my life standing up for my beliefs and for what I believe to be correct. You have to be true to yourself. That's not saying that you can't make mistakes, because everyone does, but what mistakes I do make I stand by them and try to make them good.

In my mind I also had the satisfaction of knowing that I was leaving Formula 1 at the top, having set many records and having taken the greatest prize the sport has to offer; one for which I had been striving for 17 years. No-one could take away from me what I had achieved and all those who had said that I would never be a World Champion were forced to eat their words.

I worked for Williams for six years and from the point of view of success we achieved an awful lot together. But on a human level, that achievement seems to count for very little with them. I won more races and scored more points for Williams than anyone else, but they never seemed to appreciate or derive strength and satisfaction on a human level from what we did together, perhaps because the 'family' relationship that I wanted was beyond their scope or understanding.

However, I was both impressed and touched when Sheridan Thynne resigned from his post as commercial director at Williams because of the way I had been treated. It is rare in today's world that a person resigns from a well paid and important job over a point of principle. That sort of integrity is increasingly scarce and I was moved by his support.

Even today the new drivers at Williams are finding that they are portrayed as greedy when they ask for more representative salaries. It is very sad but some people are jealous of success. I believe that Damon Hill will probably find this, because they've given him a chance, picked him out of nowhere and made him successful, yet they will always want to control things.

The greatest bonus for me from the split with Williams was the way that 1993 turned out. I didn't instigate events in 1992, but what happened the following year was like a fairy tale.

Patrick Head, Williams technical director: 'We had some very good times together and we should have handled the whole 1992 thing better. Unfortunately the press got hold of it and it was a fantastic story for them so they polarised the issue and set the two sides off against each other. I don't think the same thing would happen again, because we know a lot more now about how to handle situations like that. I think we all regretted the way things turned out.'

Bernie Ecclestone, FOCA president: 'I made strenuous efforts to keep him [Nigel] in Formula 1 at the end of 1992. The split was unnecessary. It was a litle bit of stupidity on the part of Frank and Nigel. They lost their way in dialogue and because of that it all came to an end.'

David Brown, Nigel's Williams race engineer: 'An incident at Hockenheim proved the sort of calibre of driver Nigel is. After changing his tyres he reported that something felt wrong with the left rear tyre. After exhaustive checks nothing wrong could be found with the tyre and the pressures were consistent, however the tyre in question did have a different date code stamped on it, which suggested a slightly different compound! Only a very sensitive driver who is operating at ten-tenths could have noticed this.'

24

SAYING GOODBYE TO FORMULA 1

Over the years I had received some interesting offers from teams in the PPG Indycar World Series although I knew little about it other than what I had seen on television from time to time. I could see that it was a very competitive series and that some of the great names from the history of Formula 1 like Emerson Fittipaldi and Mario Andretti were racing over there.

I had met Roger Penske, whose team was one of the mainstays of the series and when he invited me over to his base in Detroit in 1991, I went along to have a look. Roger is a man I respect and admire enormously. He has an incredible history of success in motor racing, but that is just a sideline to his multi-billion dollar business empire. When things began to look as though they might not work out with Williams, I called Roger and we discussed the Indycar situation. Roger's main rival, Chicago team owner Carl Haas had made me a serious offer to drive one of his Lolas and Roger said that I should consider it because Carl runs a good team. Twelve months later Roger would wish he had never given me that advice!

There's an incredible network of communication in racing, and often people on the other side of the world know that things are going wrong before you do. Both Carl Haas and his partner, the movie star Paul Newman, romanced me with what could be achieved in America. Both knew that there was a huge gap in salary between what I was being paid in Formula 1 and what I could get in America so we looked for a new way of finding the right retainer. Indycar racing was something that I was interested in and I felt that at that point in my career there were a lot of doors closing in Formula 1 and a lot of people were orchestrating things behind the scenes. So I said to myself: 'Okay, maybe I'll go Indycar racing and see what happens.'

I liked the idea of a spell in the States. I was very happy with our new home in Florida. I liked the freedom it gave me, the ability to take the children for a hamburger or to visit Disneyland as a private person, with no hassle. If I raced in America, the travelling would be much less than with Formula 1 and I would be able to spend more time with my family and see more of my children growing up. I saw no other drives in Formula 1 that I wanted but I knew that I still wanted to race and to win. The motivation for making the move was clear to me. No-one in the history of the sport had ever won back-to-back Formula 1 and Indycar World titles.

The high-speed oval tracks were daunting with their 200mph plus average speeds and were seen by the American establishment as too difficult for a road racer to master quickly. After all, it had taken Emerson Fittipaldi a season and a half to win on an oval and after that he won only three oval races in his first six years of Indycar racing. The challenge was exciting and it captured my imagination as much as it did the public's.

Carl and I discussed a possible deal and kept it bubbling all the time that the Williams saga continued. In September, one week before the race at Monza, we met in London and provisionally agreed a deal for 1993, although I could not sign it until I knew the outcome of my discussions with Frank.

On the Saturday night in Monza I made two phone calls; one was to Rosanne at home in Florida and the other was to Carl. When I announced my retirement on the Sunday I thought seriously about stopping altogether, just hanging up my helmet and trying to live a normal life, but the desire to win more races and to make more history burned strongly.

We put the final touches to the deal and a week later I signed it. I did all the negotiations myself, as I have throughout my career. In the modern era many drivers like to have managers to do this for them; Michael Schumacher is looked after by Willi Weber and my old friend Keke Rosberg has made a second career for himself managing the new Finnish talents like Mika Hakkinen and J J Lehto.

There is no doubt that being my own manager has put an added strain on me throughout my career. But I have found it far better not having someone else acting for me. I could have crashed and burned a few times on the advice I've had from people who wanted to manage me. I've made decisions based on instinct and experience and by and large it has worked out for me. I feel that I am the only one able to say what is right for me and with hindsight it has been fortunate that I haven't had a manager taking 20% of everything I've earned.

The deal completed, I was now officially an Indycar driver for 1993 and the reaction from the British racing public was incredible.

Williams' headquarters in Didcot were inundated with letters from unhappy Formula 1 fans who were livid about the way I had been treated. When I discussed this later with Frank he dismissed it, saying, 'These people don't pay my wage bill.'

The deals may have been done which sealed our divorce, but there was still a lot to be done on the track. For one thing I was still hungry for my record ninth win of the year and I also wanted to get the record for most pole positions and the highest number of points.

On race morning in Portugal the Williams team officially announced that Prost would be driving for them in 1993 and that he would do a three day test in Estoril immediately after Sunday's race. My name tags and Union Jack would be peeled off the car and replaced with his name and the French tricolour. My engineer David Brown would oversee his progress.

In the press conference after the Portuguese race, Ayrton made a scathing attack on Prost saying that he was acting like a coward and that, 'He must be prepared to race anyone under any conditions, on equal terms. He wants to win with everything laid out for him. It is like going into a 100 metre sprint race with running shoes – while everyone else has lead shoes. That is how he wants to race. It's not racing.'

I listened to Ayrton's words, but I felt above it all now. I had just won my ninth race of the year and it had been one of my most dominant wins. At the start I had pushed very hard, driving with the intensity of qualifying laps in order to open out a gap. After two laps I was already over four seconds clear. By the end I had lapped everyone except Berger in second place, who was 38 seconds behind me. The win gave me another record; I now had 108 points, the most ever scored in one season.

I was relaxed and serene. I had won the World Championship and whatever else people tried to take away from me, no-one could take away that honour. I had made my decision not to stay in Formula 1 for all the right reasons and I looked forward without regret to my final Grands Prix in Japan and Australia. I looked at the goings on around me with detachment. I was genuinely glad to be out of it all.

The result wasn't all good, however. At the end of the Estoril race, my team-mate Riccardo Patrese had a huge accident, the biggest for many years in Formula 1 and was very lucky to escape alive. His car took off over the back of Berger's and headed skywards. It flew through the air nose-first, narrowly missing a bridge and for an awful second it looked as though it might do a loop-the-loop. Luckily it didn't and it came crashing to the ground right way up with Riccardo unharmed inside.

Riccardo had been a fantastic team-mate and I wanted to find a way to thank him for all his help and support over the past two seasons by helping him come second in the championship. He deserved to win more races than he had over the past two seasons. It was only because I so badly wanted the championship that he didn't win more. Within the first few races of 1992 he had realised that he couldn't beat me in the same car and conceded that. I think that speaks volumes of his character.

As a racing driver you might think privately that you can't beat someone and you might accept it, but you don't admit it. He conceded it and it improved the team, because there was no pressure on me or on him, we all knew where we stood. The psychological needle, either real or imagined, which exists between competitive team-mates was removed and we could all get on with doing the best job possible. I was grateful for his candour and support and so what happened in Japan was my way of paying him back.

It was a close scrap for second place in the championship between Schumacher, Senna and Riccardo. Before the Japanese Grand Prix, Riccardo and I agreed privately that he should be allowed to win and when I had built up a good lead I got on the radio to ask David Brown what the points situation was if the race finished as it was. He came back with the answer that Senna was out of the race, so if it finished like this with Riccardo in second place, he would have two points advantage over Senna with just the Australian Grand Prix left.

I thought about it for a while and then stopped at the chicane to wait for him to pass. When he did, I followed in his slipstream and chivvied him along a bit. Unfortunately my engine let go not long afterwards and I was out. But he got his win, which pleased him enormously as he looked set for runner-up slot in the points.

As the season drew to a close, there was plenty of activity behind the scenes as the powers that be in Formula 1 struggled to sort out the loss of the World Champion. Bernie Ecclestone did not want to lose me and he approached Carl to see what terms he would want to release me from the contract. But my move was sealed.

Meanwhile I was touched to receive warm messages of welcome from some of my new rivals in Indycar racing. One came from Emerson Fittipaldi, whom I had respected enormously for twice winning the World Championship in the early seventies and who was still going strong with Penske in Indycars. He offered to show me around the circuits in a road car and to give me detailed advice on how to drive on ovals. As a former F1 driver he knew as well as anyone how hard it was to adapt to oval racing and he admitted that it had taken several seasons for him to feel confident on the ovals. Other drivers like Al Unser Jr and Bobby Rahal said how much they were looking forward to me coming over.

Just before the Japanese GP I had paid a visit to Laguna Seca, California for the last round of the Indycar championship and had been impressed by the warmth of the welcome. It was the first time I had seen the Indycars in action and I wondered what it would be like to drive one. Being heavier, they were clearly less responsive to changes of direction than a Formula 1 car and the chassis construction was different. While all Formula 1 cars are made from carbon composite, the Newman-Haas Lolas were made of a mixture of carbon and aluminium to keep the costs down.

One of the things which really impressed me was that the emphasis was clearly on pure competition, with no one team establishing any domination over the others. Any one of eight or ten cars could win a race and it was quite common to win on one type of circuit one week, but be off the pace the following week on another track, which is terrific for the spectators. I liked the idea from their point of view, but I could see that it would lead to some frustration for the drivers. Whereas Formula 1 at the time was pretty free technically, with teams like Williams and McLaren developing intricate electronic systems, the Indycar rules restricted the cars considerably. If any one team was going to get a jump on the others it would clearly be Penske because they are the only ones to build their own chassis, whereas the other teams are all customers.

As a customer team, if you have good engineers and drivers, you might be able to eke out a small advantage over other customer teams, but if you build your own chassis, once you get it right and then refine the design you can make a big gain. At the end of 1992 there was no sign of it, but by mid-way through the following season Penske would be the car to beat and in 1994 they were in a different league.

Sitting by the side of the track in the beautiful California sunshine,

I felt that I had made a good choice. The cars looked fun to drive, but I would have to wait a few more months before finding out.

I arrived in Adelaide for what I thought would probably be my last Grand Prix to hear that James Hunt was criticising me in the British press for leaving Formula 1 and not, as he put it, 'staying in Formula 1 and proving that you are a worthy champion by taking on Alain Prost.'

It was sad to hear James say that. The truth was that there was nothing in what Williams had offered me which would encourage me to stay. I was not 'running away', as James suggested. That was an absurd idea. The fact was that I was not being given a chance to defend my title in a sensible way, so I had chosen to go to America instead.

I was happy that weekend in Adelaide; the championship was won and the season was coming to an end. There was plenty of fun going on with the team during the weekend and we stitched up Paddy Lowe, one of the engineers, a real treat.

Coming out of the circuit compound on Saturday night in our hire cars, I nudged the back of Paddy Lowe's car with the nose of mine. He wanted to get me back, of course, but he got carried away and when we got out onto the street he hit my car, not hard, but enough that it made a bit of a noise. Unknown to Paddy there were two police motorcycles watching this, and as I sped off down the road, I saw him being pulled over in my mirror. Rosanne, who was with me at the time, said: 'Don't you think you might need him tomorrow?' She had a point. I went back and when I got there the two policemen were tearing into Paddy and asking what the hell he thought he was doing. Paddy was quite worried and, worse still, he didn't have his driving licence on him.

I had done some work for the Adelaide police and, although I hadn't met these two, they knew who I was. I asked them politely if I could have a quiet word. I explained to them that it was me whom Paddy had hit and that he was a vital part of our efforts to win the Grand Prix the following day and it would be wonderful if he could be let off on this occasion, but would they mind giving him a *really* hard time first? They kindly agreed, then went to work on Paddy, grilling him and treating him like a naughty schoolboy – all in all they gave him a fantastically hard time! Poor Paddy was speechless and had no idea what was going to happen or whether he would go to jail. The police were brilliant and after we'd had some fun at his expense they let him go.

The race the next day started well and I was enjoying it a great deal until lap 18. I was leading from Ayrton and driving well within myself, doing the sensible thing and not overstretching myself. But then Ayrton hit me up the back and took us both off. It was a sad way to end because I had not yet won in Australia and it would have been a fitting way to leave F1. Ayrton had this belief that if he couldn't win then no-one else was going to. The limits that he pushed himself to were definitely over the edge at times and that was one of those times.

I was angry that he had taken me out of the race, but the stewards didn't seem interested when I raised the matter with them. Rather than cause any kind of scene at my last race I left the circuit and drew the curtain behind me over Formula 1. Ayrton and I didn't speak to each other afterwards.

That was the last time I ever saw him.

David Brown, Williams engineer: 'Nigel came on the radio after only about ten laps of the Japanese Grand Prix, asking me about the points standings. Almost every lap he asked me a different question, and all the time he's pulling away in the lead. Ann Bradshaw, our press officer and Sheridan were frantically trying to work it out and we gave Nigel the answers. He thought about it for a while and then he said, "I'm going to let Riccardo past, David." And I could hear him slow down at the chicane and wait for Riccardo. The radio was still open and all of a sudden you could hear a car come past and Nigel accelerating after it. I thought at the time that if that had been Berger going past instead of Riccardo, then we would have seen something!'

Murray Walker, BBC television commentator: 'I've been interviewing Nigel on TV for over 15 years and for the whole of that time we've had an unspoken, good-natured battle with each other as he craftily strove to keep his heavily-sponsored cap in vision and I struggled just as hard to keep it out. The BBC don't go in for advertising and frame the shot accordingly.

'First he leans confidently forward, jutting his cap into the camera lens as I lean back to block him, whilst the well-briefed cameraman zooms in on his forehead. Then an adjustment of position as he slides slowly down his seat to lower the dominant logo, followed by a sort of rolling lurch into full vision for his reply to my searingly perceptive question. Like everything he does, Nigel works hard at it and no-one could have given his sponsors better value. In the end, I think we came out even!'

25

THE AMERICAN ADVENTURE

Living and working in America had many advantages. Obviously the weather in Florida was one of the best things. Waking up on a freezing cold rainy day on the Isle of Man was never the greatest incentive to go out for a ten-mile cycle ride, but on a bright sunny morning in Clearwater with the temperature in the eighties, nothing could be nicer than to take a mountain bike ride along the coastline with my neighbour and friend Alex Plisko. The children loved it too, spending many happy hours in the outdoor swimming pool or playing soccer with their friends.

In America, everything is at your fingertips. Close to our home there was a good school for the children, a lovely golf course, a fabulous hospital, the Morton Plant, which I would unfortunately come to know very well and a superb dojo where sixth dan and World Champion Ric Martin teaches Okinawa-style karate. Everything was within a short drive. Things come to you in America and there are a lot of facilities for doing just about anything you want.

Travelling around the country was a doddle, everyone speaks English, the hotels are all roughly the same and the food is plentiful and good. It is a fascinating country, not least because of its sheer size and its range of landscapes. Flying across the country from the west coast to the east, you pass over deserts, snowy mountain ranges, lush green prairies, forests and huge sprawling cities – all in the space of a few hours. During our spell in Indycars we had some fun trips to the beauty spots of America and Canada – the Grand Canyon, Niagara Falls and Yellowstone National Park – all of which greatly enhanced our American experience.

Unfortunately, there are plenty of bad things about America too, the worst being that anyone can go into a hardware store and buy a gun. If you live in America you must always realise that and act accordingly. There are plenty of cranks and weirdos around and it is chilling to think that they have access to powerful weapons sight. The country has a lot of problems and when you live there you always have to be very mindful of what you do. Of course, this is the same more or less anywhere you live in the world.

There are also a lot of hidden catches about living in America, things which you only realise once you settle in. There are a lot of hidden taxes, for example, state, sales and property taxes, which mount up dramatically. Insurance is also very expensive and liability is awful. Law suits are rife and people can sue for what their opponent is worth rather than for what is reasonable in the circumstances of the case. That said, we enjoyed our time living in America and the whole extraordinary adventure.

Before my first test in an Indycar in January 1993, I had a hectic winter schedule which began with the postponed foot operation and which then, 72 hours after leaving hospital on crutches with my foot in a cast, took me on a whirlwind tour of Europe with 28 engagements in 11 days. I had promised a lot of people that I would do things once the season was over and now they were all crammed in alongside the awards ceremonies and prizegivings. It was crazy to do it so soon after the operation, but there was no other time to fit it all in, especially since I wanted to be in the best possible shape for the 1993 season. The tour started badly when I hobbled into the executive jet terminal at Heathrow airport. I was waiting for a plane to take me to Italy and as I let myself delicately down into a steel-framed chair it collapsed, sending me sprawling on the floor!

Once we got to Bologna, though, it was all forgotten and I was given a poignant reminder of just how passionate the Italians are about their motor racing. At a ceremony in front of 2000 people at the Madina Palace I was to be presented with the Golden Helmet award, which is voted for by the Italian public. I came onto the stage and was hit by a deafening sound of klaxon horns and cheering. It was like a football match. Up on the balcony I could see a huge Union Jack hanging down with the words, 'THERE IS ONLY ONE NIGEL MANSELL'. I was very moved. I collected the award, thanked the public for their kindness and for voting me the driver of the year and walked off the stage thinking that was it.

Then something really special happened. Two ladies got me back onto the stage and wheeled on a large trolley with a metal cover. The cover was lifted to reveal a huge sculpture, a bronze globe of Europe on a base of Italian marble, with a bronze lion standing on top of it. The crowd surged forward and I was engulfed by hundreds of people.

When everyone finally calmed down I learned that the Italian fans, on hearing that I was leaving F1, had organised a public subscription and raised £50,000. Nine bronzes had been cast and the best one was presented to me. The rest were melted down so that the award would be unique. One of the organisers said to me, 'This is to symbolise that there is only one of you and it is a tragedy that you have left us.'

I was touched by the response from the fans wherever I went. I wasn't sorry to be leaving Formula 1 behind, but I was sorry to be leaving the fans. They had given me so much support over the years and we had developed a great rapport.

In Paris I attended the annual FIA award ceremony where I collected the prize which I had wanted my whole life: the Formula 1 World Championship. There is no doubt that winning the World Championship is the greatest achievement in any driver's life. It is what racing is all about and I had dedicated my life to the pursuit of it. I had come agonisingly close to touching this prize several times before but now it was safely in my hands. I was delighted to have bounced back after the disappointment of 1986 and '87 and from the false hope of 1989 and '90. This time there was no disputing it.

Another engagement I was happy to fulfil was to be guest of honour at the Springfield Boys' Club Christmas party. The club, based in Hackney, East London, is run by my old friend Anthony Marsh and it provides an activity centre for disadvantaged children. As well as speaking to the children, I also joined in a vaulting competition, sitting on the floor while the children flew off a springboard and over us. It was a really fun evening.

Back home in Clearwater we celebrated Christmas and the New Year. I had no resolutions, nor any idea how things would turn out. It was an exciting prospect, but I admit that I was slightly worried about it too. The oval tracks were all new to me; I would have to learn quickly and trust the limits of the cars. The speeds were very high and mistakes would be paid for with a trip to the concrete wall.

In my mind, however, I was still on a mission and would be morally defending my World Championship. I had won it over there against the cream of the Formula 1 drivers; now I would defend it over here against the best of the Americans. Then, with any luck, I would have the coveted number one on the car and defend my Indycar title in

1994. All that was a long way ahead, but I began to feel good about my chances after the first test session on the one-mile oval at Phoenix International Raceway in January.

When I arrived at the track, my initial feeling was, 'What the hell am I doing here?' The place was like the OK Corral, with dust and sand everywhere, and so different from the sophistication of a modern Grand Prix track. Only six weeks had elapsed since my foot operation, but it looked as though the decision to operate early had paid off. We were competitive straight away and during the pre-season test programme we broke the track records at most of the places we visited.

There was a lot to learn. My Lola Indycar, powered by a Ford turbo engine was 50% heavier than the Williams-Renault and consequently a lot less nimble. It did not change direction as quickly as a Formula 1 car, so everything happened a little bit more slowly. The Indycar also created less downforce than the F1 car, so the cornering speeds were slightly slower and the g-forces acting on the driver's neck were lower.

The Lola had none of the high-tech gadgets of its Formula 1 counterpart; active suspension is banned in the Indycar rules as are traction control, carbon brakes and the semi-automatic gearbox. In a straight line with the right gears, the two were probably equal in terms of top speed, although the Formula 1 car accelerates faster because it is lighter and decelerates more rapidly because of its carbon brakes, whereas the Indycar uses steel brakes. Because the brakes were not as good, you had to start braking a lot sooner for the corners and so there was also the added excitement of wondering whether you were actually going to make it around the corner at all!

One of the most important things I had to remember with my new car was the art of changing gear manually. Having driven semi-automatic gearboxes since 1989, I had to teach myself how to use a gear lever again and how to change at just the right times, especially on downshifts. If you change too soon when going down through the gears and let the clutch out, you run a high risk of over-revving the engine, something the semi-automatic box is designed to prevent. My learning curve on the car was quite steep, but it was nothing that wouldn't come with a bit of practice.

Driving on the ovals, however, was a whole new experience. In all my time in Indycars, I never learned to feel comfortable on ovals despite winning four times on them and once winning a 500-mile race.

On ovals you have to commit yourself going into corners at 200mph plus. You brake very gingerly, if at all, and you try to carry as much speed as you can around the corner. All the time you know that if anything goes wrong, whether it be a tyre going down, a suspension problem or just having a little bit of oversteer, you're going to hit the concrete wall on the outside of the track and have a monumental accident. It's actually quite frightening. Some of the corners are really dangerous. When I made a guest appearance for Williams in the 1994 French Grand Prix at Magny Cours I heard some of the drivers in the pre-race briefing complain about how dangerous some of the corners were and I thought to myself, 'If you think this is dangerous, you should see some of the places like Michigan where we have to run.'

Later on in the summer of 1994, I managed a lap on the Michigan Speedway at an average speed of 235.7mph, which was unofficially the fastest ever lap of a racing circuit. Going into Turn One at over 240mph is really petrifying and you find your brain telling your right foot: 'Don't lift off the throttle.' I have a computer printout sheet which one of the engineers gave me afterwards that shows the car's speed and the throttle opening all the way around the track and you can see that for two whole laps, through all the corners and along the straights I had my foot flat to the floor. If anything had gone wrong, it would have been carnage out there.

Although I wasn't ever comfortable, I think that one of the reasons why I was still able to adapt quickly to the ovals and to win on them is because my natural style of driving is to turn in quickly to an early apex and carry a lot of speed through the corner. I found that this technique is fundamental to being fast on an oval. Also, I am quite aggressive and opportunistic in traffic and I rely on my instinct and experience. You have to be able to dodge around the slower cars if you are going to keep your lap times competitive over a 200 or 500-mile race. So although many people were surprised at how quickly I adapted and won on ovals, if you look at the technical side of the driving, it was perhaps not as surprising as it seemed.

Driving on an oval is, however, quite frustrating. You cannot grab the car by the scruff of its neck and throw it about. It has to be driven delicately, almost with the fingertips and you do not venture out of the prescribed envelope. I did it once and learned a very painful lesson.

For oval tracks, the car has a natural understeer dialled into it, which is done by adjusting the front wing. You can do it mechanically but it's better to do it with the wing because you can adjust it during the pit stops if the car's handling isn't right. That's why you see mechanics turning keys on the wings during pit stops, to create more or less understeer. You also have a right rear tyre which is slightly larger than the other to pull the car down to the left. These are safety measures designed to prevent the car getting loose at the back and oversteering into the wall. It takes a bit of getting used to, but it's definitely safer. Balancing the car is of paramount importance and I was fortunate that at least in 1993 Newman-Haas had settings which gave me a car that worked. Getting an Indycar into that sweet spot on an oval is very hard, but once you are there it's magic.

Although the oval tracks may look the same, they all have a distinct character and two corners are never identical. The nearest four corners you find are at the new circuit in Loudon, New Hampshire which is a super track and one on which I won in 1993. The four turns are similar, the only difference being a slight variation in the degree of banking from when the tarmac was laid. You can certainly feel this in the car. You only have to have a small bump in the middle of the corner and you'll feel it in the cockpit when you're running at 180mph.

If Loudon is the smoothest oval then Milwaukee, another track I won on, is the opposite. It's so bumpy there, you feel like you're airborne for half the lap!

Nazareth and Phoenix are different because they only have three corners and they are faster; you average 180mph on them as opposed to 165–170mph on Loudon and Milwaukee.

Then you have the superspeedways, Indianapolis and Michigan, which are 2.5 mile and 2 mile tracks, respectively, with two long straights and four corners, and a couple of short chutes linking the corners. Again, all the corners are different and you take them at different speeds. Turns one and three are taken faster than two and four because obviously you go down the straight a lot faster than on the short chute. Indianapolis is the smoother of the two. Michigan is bumpy because the winters in that part of the country are cold and this breaks up the track. There is one bump going into turn three which is so severe that when you hit it, you lose your vision for a split second.

When you race on an oval you have to be very clever about how you position the car on the track. Dirty air from the car in front is a big problem and if you're in the wrong position with no room to slide out before you hit the wall, you're going to get hurt. If you get too close to the car in front, then you haven't got the necessary air pressure over your wings to maintain the downforce, so you lose grip and hit the wall. It's so important to feel the car at all times and to know when you're going to have problems before they happen.

If you're behind one or two cars, that's no problem. But if you're behind four or five, then you're in trouble. It doesn't matter who you are or how good a driver you are, you cannot get too close because there will be no air left for you and you'll hit the wall. At Indianapolis you get five or six cars in the chain going down the long straights and you can pick up a great tow in the slipstream, maybe they'll pull you along at 250mph, but heaven help you if you get too close into Turn One or Turn Three, because you'll lose all your download and the vortices will upset your balance. When you go out to race on an oval track you've got to know this, and feel it and smell it. If you do lose control, there's nothing you can do except brake like crazy and hope you stop before you hit anything!

Over the course of a weekend and even over the course of a race, circuit conditions can change and this is particularly critical on an oval. At Nazareth towards the end of 1993, for example, I had too much understeer at the start, which took me out to the edge of the track. As I had an opportunity to clinch the championship that day I was worried, but then as the temperature rose and rubber went down my car started to handle more neutrally. The balance became as perfect as you could wish for. The only way I was going to hit the wall then was if all four corners lost grip at the same time, which was unlikely. The car was marvellous, I could drive at ten-tenths and really use the car in all areas of the track, and on an oval, that is the ultimate; when it's up to you how fast you go around the corner because you know that, within reason, the car will allow you to do it. The only thing limiting you then is the width of the track.

So on that day the track came to me purely by chance and it was fantastic. The Penskes started the race with more neutral handling, but when the track changed they became loose and developed oversteer. The only way to correct that problem is to come into the pits and reduce the angle of the front wing. Usually that will fix it, but in my first year I saw some drivers forced to park their cars because the handling was so awful that it was dangerous to stay out there. At the time I thought to myself, ' How can that be? How can the cars be so far off cue that they are undriveable?', because we had settings on every oval in 1993 which were close to the sweet spot.

It happened to me, ironically, at Nazareth the following year and I saw the problem quite clearly. The car feels like it's trying to get away from you all the time, trying to spin itself. You find yourself having to fight the car and at those speeds that's the last thing you want. I came into the pits three extra times that day and in all the mechanics took six whole turns out of the front wing – which basically puts the wing plates down. By rights, in that condition it shouldn't oversteer at all, but it was still doing it. I couldn't believe how bad the handling felt. There was obviously some serious mechanical problem somewhere and my instinct said, 'Get off the track and out of harm's way.'

A week later when the car was back at the factory, the team discovered that the scales were incorrect and that there had been 150lb of pre-load on the wrong side of the car. Without question, that was the cause of the problem.

Luckily there were no such problems in early 1993 during my first tests on the oval at Phoenix. Jim McGee, the team manager gave me a lot of advice before I went out for the first time, telling me what to look out for and describing a few tell-tale handling signs. He described how the car would feel and what to watch out for on the entry and exit points for the corners. Because the camber of the corners was different from what I was used to, I needed to be aware of the characteristics of the corners and ways in which the car would pull when fully loaded. McGee has so much experience and his insight was invaluable.

The tests went well. I came within a few tenths of a second of the track record on the Phoenix oval and I broke several records on road courses like Laguna Seca. I was riding on a wave of enthusiasm and I felt my faith restored by the warmth of the welcome I received from the boys in the team. I was excited by the prospect of my first season in this new formula, but I was especially excited by the team of people I would be working with.

Newman-Haas is an outstanding racing team. The mechanics are good enough to work in any of the top Formula 1 outfits and everyone in the team gave me the support and backing I needed to get the job done. It was a tremendous pleasure to get to know Paul Newman; a legend in his own lifetime and a genius in his field. He's a very pure person, very generous, understanding and warm. When he looks at the racing world he sometimes draws breath and wonders how some things can happen.

I have admired him since I was young, and loved films like *The Sting* and *Butch Cassidy and the Sundance Kid*, and those about racing, like *Winning*. When I got to know him, I found out that he had long been a fan of my driving, which was very flattering. Paul is no mean driver himself, he came second at Le Mans in 1982, and second in the Daytona 24 Hours of 1995 at the age of 69! He genuinely loves his motor racing, both as a driver and an owner.

Paul is incredibly famous and lots of people get overexcited when they meet him. They get all edgy and clam up, which makes him feel uncomfortable, but we were able to relax together and found that we had a lot in common. He admired my ability as a racer and I admired him as a man and as an actor. Paul is a tremendous talker and one of the things we most enjoyed was to sink into an easy chair in the motorhome or in a hotel and just talk. He described it as 'long, easy talkin''.

We found that we enjoyed talking about anything and everything: history, racing, life and its pleasures and disappointments. We talked about the things he's gone through in his career and the things I've gone through in mine. He has had an incredible life. Despite our age difference we had similar views on a many things. It meant an awful lot to me that I could have a relationship like that with someone such as Paul, a man for whom I have the utmost respect.

His partner in the race team and the man who runs it day to day is Carl Haas, the cigar-chewing businessman. I like Carl and his wife Bernie, who is very much part of the Newman-Haas decision-making process. But sometimes I wonder if his wish to govern by consensus leads to tough decisions being delayed or not even taken. Carl's heart is certainly in the right place but when it comes to being hard, biting on the bullet and making a decision that will be unwelcome to some, he's perhaps too nice a guy.

Jim McGee was the perfect team manager. He had been a regular winner in Indycar for years; he has won Indy 500 five times, took the 1989 Indycar title with Emerson Fittipaldi and the 1992 title with Bobby Rahal's team. When Carl finalised the deal with me he hired Jim because he knew that with his easy manner and enormous experience Jim would help me to learn quickly and would be able to make critical decisions on race strategy.

In Indycar, races can be won or lost on pit stops – there are usually three scheduled fuel and tyre stops per race, more in a 500-miler. The timing of those stops is critical and relies on carefully reading the yellow flag caution periods. If there is an incident on the track, the race director will put out the yellow flag to slow the field down while the problem is cleared. If this happens around the time when you are scheduled to stop anyway, there is a lot to be gained by coming into the pits immediately, while everyone is going slowly. It is up to the team manager to tell you the exact time to come in. If you get it right you can make as much as a half or whole lap on your rivals.

Reading the race and knowing when to stop and not to stop, or when to go for a shorter 'splash and dash' stop is a real skill and Jim was a very significant part of my championship success. Also, under him, the human element of the team was tremendous: the mechanics were positive, hardworking and good fun to be with. I have always worked on my relationship with the mechanics, after all they are one of the most important areas of your success, but the boys at Newman-Haas were brilliant and we had a lot of fun together.

Both on and off the track Jim and I had a fantastic relationship. He understood me well and helped me enormously in my efforts to acclimatise. He has a great feel for people and was a wonderful barometer of what was going on inside the team and around the paddock. He's a fabulous man manager because he has a huge wealth of experience and is a very calm person. However crazy things got, Jim always used to say, 'I don't let anything spoil my day'. He gave me a lot of encouragement and advice. He was also very good at marking my card when he saw me being approached by someone who wasn't to be trusted or who had some dodgy history which I couldn't possibly have known about. I knew the ropes in F1, but in Indycar terms I knew no-one. Jim McGee went to the trouble of giving me the background.

Another of the old-stagers, Bill Yeager helped in that way too. Bill is an extraordinary character who has been around Indycar racing for over 50 years and worked with all the greats like A J Foyt and Parnelli Jones. He was a team manager for Parnelli in the mid sixties when Jim Clark and Colin Chapman came over to the Indy 500 and won with their rear-engined Lotus against the front-engined roadsters of the time. Yeager has seen it all and he used to look after me and the family and make sure that we had everything we needed. He was the arch fixer, a good friend and a very useful person to have around.

My race engineer Peter Gibbons had a lot of experience too, having worked with four-times Indy 500 winner Rick Mears at Penske. He and I hit it off pretty well and although it took him some time to understand my way of working, we came to the right technical solutions most of the time.

Going into the 1993 season, the situation looked positive. The balance of characters in the team was good, the chemistry was good, the car looked promising and I was on a high as the reigning Formula 1

World Champion. After our win in the opening race on the streets of Surfers' Paradise, Australia I realised that the championship might well be on. It was a thrilling way to start the season. I took pole position but early on I incurred a stop-and-go penalty for passing under yellow flags, which I didn't realise I had done. When I rejoined after serving the penalty in the pits, I was in fourth place and had to fight hard to get back into the lead.

Once back in front a new concern arose – I was sure I was going to run out of fuel. Sure enough, on the last lap the engine started to splutter and I could hear myself saying, 'Just a few more corners, please. Don't let me down now.' I kept it in fourth gear and crossed the line five seconds ahead of Emerson. As soon as I reached the first chicane on the slowing down lap, however, the fuel ran out. But I had taken the win and the points. It was a great way to start my Indycar career and it was also nice to make history as the first rookie to win an Indycar race from pole. It set the tone for an historic season.

Given all the publicity and my background on street circuits, it was almost expected of me to win at Surfers, but there was no doubt that the first real test would be the 200-mile race at Phoenix, my first oval race.

In the event, it was very nearly my last.

Jim McGee, Newman-Haas team manager: 'Those first tests at Phoenix were amazing. There were over 100 journalists and photographers there from all around the world – for a test session! Nigel went out and within a few laps he was running four-tenths of a second off the lap record on a track he'd never seen before in a car that was totally unfamiliar to him. I was watching this and thinking, "Oh my God. What if he loses it in front of all these people?" But Nigel seemed to rise to the occasion. Like an actor, he always seemed to come forward with his best performance when the pressure was on.'

Bill Yeager, Newman-Haas team coordinator: 'I've been in the Indycar business for fifty years and Nigel is the best I have ever seen; better even than Jimmy Clark when he came over here and kicked our asses, better than AJ Foyt, who I worked with for years. I told Foyt, "If this kid had been around when you were racing, you wouldn't have won jack-shit'. He knew it too."

Mike Knight, Newman-Haas press officer: 'After Nigel won in Surfers', the crowd scenes were incredible. I was trying to steer him through this sea of people. He was so popular and everybody wanted to get near him. I remember saying to myself, "Now I know what it must have been like to work for Elvis…"

26

THE CONCRETE WALL CLUB GETS A NEW MEMBER

According to an old saying in American racing circles, 'There are two types of driver: those who have hit the wall and those who are going to hit the wall.'

I would have quite happily gone through my two-year Indycar career in the second category, but at the beginning of April in practice on the Phoenix oval, I joined the Concrete Wall Club...and it is an experience I will never forget.

Our speed in pre-season testing on the ovals had been very encouraging and I was on a high from the win at Surfers. From the beginning of practice at Phoenix I was running laps around the track record, and going into Saturday's practice session I was comfortably on top of the time sheets. I was going faster and faster, widening my pattern and running higher and higher on the track, which enabled me to straighten out the corners. Then disaster struck.

Going into Turn One at 187mph, the car stepped out at the rear and slid backwards, hitting the concrete wall at undiminished speed. Such was the force of the impact that the casing of the gearbox punched a hole in the five-inch-thick concrete wall.

Why was it such a big accident? Because I was running high on the race track, so when the car broke loose I had no time to scrub off speed. The car got away on the entry to the corner, which is the worst place for it to happen.

The accident was caused by a combination of factors. I was twenty or so laps into a run and there had been a significant heat build-up in the tyres on the right side of the car. In addition to that, I had gone too high in the groove and got out beyond where most of the rubber had been laid down, so I lost grip and that was it. There were some suggestions in the press that I thought I knew better than the engineers and had insisted that they take out the understeer, but this is not true. The car certainly had understeer dialled in to it, but the heat build-up in the tyres gradually changed the handling and led to it becoming increasingly neutral and then an oversteer. The hotter the right rear tyre gets, the more oversteer you get.

I got caught out, but that was the last time it would happen. I had learned a big lesson about ovals. You have to work with the car and tune it delicately, getting it to work for you rather than the other way round, which was what I was used to in Formula 1.

I was used to driving at 110%, but on an oval you need to remain at 95% and not go beyond it. You do not wring the car's neck to get the fastest time you can; instead you work up to a speed, using 95% effort and letting the adjustments you make to the car do the work for you. When you have found the 'sweet spot' where the car is working for you, then maybe you can run one or two laps at 100% driver effort, but no more than that. Once I learned that system then there was no problem on the ovals. I was a wiser member of the Concrete Wall Club.

I was knocked unconscious by the accident and when I came to I was told that the Indycar doctors had ruled me out of Sunday's race on the grounds of concussion, but that was the least of my worries. The real problem was that the full brunt of the shock which travelled through the car from the gearbox and engine had been absorbed by my lower back, and a cavity measuring 12in x 14in had opened up where the fat and muscle had been torn away from the bone and flesh of my lower back. It felt and sounded nasty, and over the coming weeks the severity of the injury would become all too apparent.

Nevertheless, I counted myself fortunate. It could have been much worse. We had spent a lot of time working on the seat, making it a perfect fit for the contours of my back. So when I hit the Phoenix wall the shock waves were evenly dispersed across my whole back. If I had had that accident in a car with an ill-fitting seat, the shock waves could have been focused on one area and that could well have been fatal.

After a night in hospital in Phoenix, I was transferred home to Florida, where I learned that my team-mate Mario Andretti had won Sunday's race, his first win since 1988. The result meant that I was still leading the points, despite having missed a race. I was anxious not to miss any other races and was determined to be ready for the next round at Long Beach, California in two weeks' time.

But the injury was worse than we had thought. Because all the organs fit neatly together inside the body, it is not natural to have large cavities suddenly appear. Faced with this abnormal occurrence the body reacts naturally to try to heal itself and fill the cavity as best it can. Fluid was building up fast and for the next two weeks I had to go to hospital twice a day to have it drained from the cavity. Needles were stuck into my back and up to half a pint of fluid per day was drained out.

My old friend Anthony Marsh was staying with us during this time and in the plane on the way to Long Beach he said, 'Do you really think that this is a good idea, Nigel? I mean, you're terribly hurt and Long Beach is a very bumpy circuit.'

He was right, but it was vital from a championship point of view to do the race at Long Beach. Surfers had shown us how competitive we were and I believed that given a few breaks, I could carry the momentum of the 1992 Championship and clinch a historic double. I badly needed to keep scoring points to keep that hope alive.

In fact, the reality of the situation was far worse than we were able to let on at the time. Because insurance is such a problem in America, if it had been known that I was racing with internal bleeding it could have led to all kinds of trouble with the local authorities and with the circuit's insurers, rather like my foot problem the year before. So we played it down during the Long Beach weekend, and privately I had painkillers injected into my lower back to ease my discomfort, while after every practice session Jim McGee would take me down to the medical centre where Dr Steve Olvey and Dr Terry Trammell, the Indycar medical officers, would drain off the fluid. Greg Norman was with us on race day and he came to the medical unit and watched this procedure. He stood there amazed and said, 'Nigel, are you sure you know what you're doing?'

Quite how we got through that weekend I'll never know. I was in a lot of discomfort with tubes sticking out of my back and everything was aggravated by the pummelling the body takes when you are driving hard on a bumpy street circuit. I told myself that if I was more than a second and a half off the pace I would not carry on, because I'd just be getting in the way. Before practice on Saturday and the race on Sunday I had neat anaesthetic injected into my back to wipe out all the pain. I pushed really hard in qualifying and got the pole, but it was an unnerving experience because, although I was right on the limit, I couldn't feel the car.

When you drive a racing car, your senses are all highly tuned and your whole body becomes a nerve centre. When you are running on or close to the limit, your brain receives information from every part of your body about what the car is doing, how it's handling, what the engine is doing and so on. The expression, 'driving by the seat of your pants' is actually quite accurate. Your lower back and your bottom are very sensitive to the movement of the car, particularly to defects in handling and to slides. When that part of your body is numb, you lose feedback and it's very difficult to get a rounded picture of what's happening. When your lower back is numb, it's hard to tell how the car is handling.

It was an extraordinary experience trying to get my legs coordinated with my arms, so that I could use the pedals and the steering wheel and gear lever in the right way. Because the bit between the arms and the legs was redundant I felt very disjointed and found that I had to think really hard about what I was doing, rather than driving naturally.

The anaesthetic did the trick for qualifying and the race, but I was driving on pure instinct and using my other senses, like eyesight, to a higher level because my backside couldn't feel the car. It was quite useful being numb in the sense that it cushioned the bumps, which are always bad on a street track. At the start of the race, I was numb from the bottom of my rib cage to just above my knees, but I found I drove at my best after about an hour when the numbness began to wear off and I could feel the car and compensate for its faults.

While I was still having to consider my every movement in the car, I got into a collision with Al Unser Jr, who tried to pass me on the outside of a short chute. I was having to pay so much attention to what I was doing that I never considered that he might try a passing manoeuvre there. He tried to jump on the inside, hit my rear wheel and put himself out of the race. It was regrettable and led to some heated quotes in the press but we resolved our differences quickly and over the next two years we became quite good friends.

My gearbox began to play up with about 40 laps to go, leaving me with no second gear, a vital ratio on a tight track like Long Beach, so I used third for the chicanes and hairpins and kept soldiering on. I finished in third place, which I thought was pretty reasonable in the circumstances, and I was very pleased to come away from such a difficult race still in the lead of the championship. Ahead of me on the road, Penske's young driver Paul Tracy had won his first Indycar race.

After the race I flew home and went into the hospital to have my back attended to. Twenty inches of plastic pipe were put in to try to drain it off and seal the cavity closed, but it didn't seem to work. The situation was much worse than we thought and Rosanne and I were beginning to get very worried indeed about it. I rang Jim McGee in the middle of the night to tell him that we had to act quickly or the whole season would be lost.

Jim rang Dr Trammell at his hospital in Indianapolis. Trammell is a legendary orthopaedic surgeon who has a fantastic reputation in racing circles. He agreed to see me, so I flew up immediately to Indianapolis, arriving around ten at night.

Trammell did a scan on my back and it showed up the cavity and the sheer size of it was terrifying. We talked it through with Terry and with George Morris, who had done my foot operation just five months earlier and decided that the only solution was to have surgery. I said, 'Let's do it now,' but Trammell had been working on the operating table all night and was in no fit state to carry out or observe an operation like that after an eighteen-hour shift. We then decided that the operation should be done the next evening at Morton Plant Hospital in Clearwater so that I could be near my home and the family.

With Trammell observing, George carried out the operation, taking out the fat and muscle which had broken away and closing the internal cavity with over 140 stitches. Less than one week later I was lapping Indianapolis at over 220mph.

I had caught my first glimpse of the Indianapolis Motor Speedway during my flying visit to Dr Trammell's hospital. Jim McGee had driven me from the airport to the hospital and as we left we were discussing the Indy 500 and I told him that I had never actually seen the track, so we went there and Jim managed to persuade the management to let us do a few laps in Jim's road car. The sheer size of the place was incredible, the grandstands all along the main straight were simply massive. The track itself seemed quite boring initially, it was just four corners, taken more or less flat out.

Over the coming weeks, as I went through my Indianapolis rookie tests and practice runs I occasionally felt a ping inside as one of the stitches let go. It was a most extraordinary feeling. What kept me going through all this? Why did I race at Indianapolis in such a condition? I suppose that adrenalin had a lot to do with it and a strong desire to race and to win. As my career has shown me many times, you have to be so single minded and dedicated if you want to succeed and you can't allow yourself to be beaten when things don't go according to plan.

For me the greatest achievement in 1993 was being able to bounce back from such an awkward injury, which could so easily have ended my season, to win four oval races and the title. This brings me back to my core point about why I am a racing driver. If you have the spirit of the racer and that thirst for success in competition, then so long as you can walk and get into the car you'll always try your best to win. That's all I did. I tried hard.

Indianapolis Motor Speedway demands a lot of respect from a driver. If you don't respect it, it will bite you. The track is very changeable and any one of a number of things from a small gust of wind to a cloud obscuring the sun can make it feel completely different from the previous lap. It's such a lottery what the conditions will do in qualifying, when each car has to complete three laps alone on the track, the average speed of those three laps being your qualifying time.

I didn't worry too much about qualifying, after all 500 miles is a very long way and it makes little difference whether you are first or fifth on the grid in a race like that. But throughout the month of May, whenever I went out on that track I gave it a lot of respect.

Because of the accident at Phoenix, the Indianapolis 500 would be my first race on an oval, which was not an ideal state of affairs. However, I learned an awful lot in the space of that one afternoon about how races are won and lost on ovals. I could easily have won at my first attempt, having led with only a few laps to go, but unfortunately I messed up.

I make no excuses about it. I was just out of hospital and a little below par, but I made a few mistakes in the race and the win went away from me. I said at the time that the crew had done brilliantly and that only one person lost me that race. But I am proud that at least I got myself into a position to win it. If things had worked out a little differently for me, if the last 15 laps had been green flag all the way, then I would have won it.

The race was yellow flagged because a car was coasting slowly down the pit lane and the officials thought that this merited a caution flag. This allowed Emerson Fittipaldi and Arie Luyendyk to close right up on me, which they might not have been able to do in open racing, and when the green flag was given for the restart, they anticipated it much better than I did and sailed past me down the straight. I was extremely upset. I had the race under control and then everything changed. I was going flat out down the straight, but they passed me like I was going backwards. It was very frustrating, but it's one of the fundamentals of oval racing and a salutary lesson for me. It's a shame that I wasn't able to learn that lesson in Phoenix so that I would have been ready at Indy, but that's history and you cannot change the way history is written.

As I fought to get back on terms with Emmo and Arie I touched the wall at around 220mph coming out of Turn Four, sending up a shower of sparks. I was pushing hard, going slightly beyond the envelope, using all of the road. I remember in the split-second before I hit the wall thinking to myself, 'Get the car square, Nigel. If you hit at any kind of angle, it'll tear everything off.' I was hoping that I might even miss the wall, but you can't fight a car too much in a situation like that, so it hit square with a thump.

My main concern now was the extent of the damage and whether the car would hold together. I was worried about the next corner because you fly into it at around 240mph and if anything let go in that situation I would be in very big trouble. But I was so fired up about losing the lead and so determined not to drop down any further than third, so I just hung on in there and got to the finish. Penske seems to have a knack for setting their cars up so that they are at their best at the end of the race. They have won Indy several times because of this and 1993 was no exception. Emmo's car was really hooked up and there was no catching him once he'd got the advantage. I was disappointed not to win after having the race in the palm of my hand, but that's fate. I consoled myself with the thought that we were leaving Indy with a healthy lead in the points, so it wasn't too bad.

The Indianapolis 500 is a fantastic event, with its month long build up, the 600,000 crowd on race day, the razzmatazz, the cheerleaders and all the American pomp. I'm very glad that I got a couple of chances to race there because I came to see through all the veneer and appreciate what a tremendous amount of hard work goes on. The slow-burn of day after day of practice becomes interminable. One of the many traditions of Indianapolis is that he race lasts a whole month; it feels as though it's never going to end. You need a fair slice of luck to win here. Like anything else, I suppose you make your own luck, but there are a few random elements that the race could well do without and which undermine its status as a world class event.

There are a lot of things which can happen in a motor race which shouldn't happen; sometimes it's your own fault, sometimes it's a mechanical failure, but when you have rank amateurs in the field it's a whole different thing. They have a lethal weapon in their hands and they make terrible mistakes like Dennis Vittolo made at Indy in 1994, when he neglected to slow down for a yellow flag and failed to realise the speed differential between himself and the train of cars, headed by me, going into the pit lane. He hit the last car in the train, took off and landed square on my roll bar. It put me out of the race on the spot and could very easily have taken my head off.

Imagine the feeling of sitting in an open racing car at 30mph, about to make a pit stop which could put you in contention for the lead, when all of a sudden you are hit by a car flying through the air at over 100mph. A few feet in one direction and that would have been it. He could have killed himself and he could quite easily have killed me or someone else.

In no way was Dennis Vittolo qualified to be in a race of that magnitude, he should have been in the grandstands watching it. Look at the chaos he caused; a huge pile-up in the pit lane and the elimination of perhaps the only car capable of giving the purpose-built Penske-Mercedes specials a run for their money. The other possible consequences of the accident do not bear thinking about. If Indianapolis has to open up the doors to people like him in order to make the numbers up, then it's not as big or as attractive a race as they think it is.

The Vittolo incident in my second year of Indycar racing affected my whole thought process about the Indycar scene and it fundamentally affected the way I look at life. Coming only a few weeks after the deaths of Ayrton Senna and Roland Ratzenberger at the San Marino Grand Prix, it reminded me that there is no point in taking futile risks. I am a professional racer and what I do is defined by the boundaries of professional sport. Fate had decreed that I was not killed at Indy in 1994, but the cause of the accident was outside those boundaries and that is totally unnecessary. I thought about what Colin Chapman had said when he stopped me racing at Le Mans. It made me shudder.

Once Indy '94 was finished, it was history. You cannot change what's happened in the past, but you can affect the course of the future by benefitting from your experiences and turning negatives into positives, and being more forceful and stronger. I think that what happened after that incident was another example of something which has occurred throughout my life, where I have taken disappointments and potential disasters and turned them into strengths. This for me is real experience. The more real experience you have behind you, the stronger it makes you as a driver and as a human being.

Since I left Indycar racing I have been asked whether the Indy 500 is a race I feel I have to win before my career is complete. Certainly it would be great to compete again and try to win it, but as a one-off race it does not have as much importance as trying to win another World Championship. That would be the ultimate for me.

I learned a lot at Indy in 1993 and I put it to good use the following weekend in Milwaukee, where I won my first oval race after a late race restart from a yellow flag. This time it was Raul Boesel who closed up under the yellow flag, but I was not going to be beaten again and I held him off and won the race. When the yellow flag was thrown towards the end of the race I thought, 'Oh no, not again!' and I talked to Jim McGee on the radio about what we should do when the green flag was thrown. He revved me up, saying, 'Make sure you get your foot down as soon as you possibly can.' You usually know which lap the starters will decide to 'go green', but you have to anticipate it before you even come out onto the pit straight.

The race went green with only two laps to go. There was just no way I was going to allow myself to be jumped again. I put the lessons of Indy into practice and bunched the field up coming into the final turn, forcing them to slow down and allowing myself the luxury of deciding when to floor it. By the time they reacted I would already be half a second up the road. Boesel got a slight edge on me but I had done a much better job than at Indy and he didn't quite have the speed to pass me into Turn One. I had won my first oval race, the first British driver to do so since Graham Hill won Indy in 1966.

A lot of people's perspectives changed after I won on an oval. It was noticeable among the immediate circles in the Indycar paddock and I was conscious of wider interest around the world. I was conscious of more respect from the old hands in American racing. Milwaukee was the first oval win, followed by Michigan, New Hampshire and then Nazareth. I am tremendously proud of these victories because they are some of the hardest wins I have had.

Oval racing is pure racing; wheel to wheel with an opponent for lap after lap. There is little difference between the cars so it comes down to skill, judgment and improvisation in traffic on the driver's part and a cool strategic head on the team manager's part. When you and your crew win a 200 or 500-mile oval race after a few yellow flags, plenty of high tension pit stops and maybe a few laps spent running in fourth or fifth place, the satisfaction is immense.

After Milwaukee I had 70 points in the championship, ahead of Boesel on 52 and Emerson, whom I considered the major threat, on 51 points. Our Lola-Ford package was good on the ovals and perhaps we had a slight edge there over the Penske-Chevrolet thanks to our engine. But as we got into the meat of the season and the string of road races at Detroit, Portland, Cleveland and Toronto a very different picture began to emerge.

Penske was putting in a massive engineering development programme on its cars and they were rapidly turning a good car into a great car. They had started the season with a transverse mounted gearbox, whereas my Lola used the more traditional longitudinal 'box. The advantages of the transverse are that it improves weight distribution because there is less weight hanging out at the back of the car and this also allows the aerodynamicists to tidy up the air flow around the back of the car.

Lola's development programme received a set-back when the chief designer, Bruce Ashmore left in the middle of the season to join Lola's arch-rival Reynard, another British racing chassis manufacturer which was planning to enter Indycars in 1994. Competition between Reynard and Lola has been fierce for many years; both vie for the same customer business in Formula 3000 and Reynard was planning to come in and take a significant share of Lola's Indycar market.

Lola regrouped quickly and John Travis and Keith Knott, both experienced engineers on Lola Indycars, took over the reins. But it was a distraction and it destabilised the set-up for a while. In that time Penske stole a lot of ground from us. They improved the mechanical grip of their chassis so that it was more stable in the middle and on the exit of the corners on road and street tracks. Paul and Emerson were able to turn into the corner and put the power on earlier, giving them a higher exit speed. Their car also seemed to slide less than ours.

The race in Portland, Oregon gave us some indication of the problem, Emerson won and I was second in a wet race. It was my first experience of driving an Indycar in the wet and it was quite different from a Formula 1 car. Because of all the extra weight, when it starts to slide it takes longer to regain its grip, and when it really lets go and loses all grip, it goes away from you in the wet twice as fast as a Formula 1 car would.

In Cleveland we had a terrific scrap for second place behind Paul Tracy. The Penske by now was really showing its strengths and I had a massive struggle to stay with Emmo, but I think that race showed Indycar at its best. In one lap we passed and repassed each other several times and you could tell how much the crowds were enjoying it by the noise they were making! But there was no mistaking it. The championship did seem to be moving away from us during this spell of road races.

Between Cleveland and Toronto we took the children to Steamboat Springs in the mountains of Colorado, for a three day break. This was at the suggestion of my surgeon George Morris who kept a ranch there. We walked, rode horses, fished and played golf early every morning. We were staying in George's place and the boys – plus Sheridan, who was also with us – had the top floor. One night, Sheridan heard Greg wake up Leo and persuade him to get up, get dressed and go down to watch TV since it was 'nearly time to get up'. Sheridan had the difficult task of explaining to them that at 2.30am it wasn't. Sheridan accompanied us to many of the Indycar races, assisting me with press and sponsor liaison and occasionally, when Rosanne and I had to go to a sponsor's dinner, acting as a babysitter. Greg, who is a natural mimic, entertained us by giving a skilled rendition of Sheridan's very English way of saying, 'Off to bed,' accompanied by a brisk clap of the hands to command their attention.

The season was just over half way through and I trailed Emerson by two points with three oval races and three road races left to run. We stemmed the tide of Penske superiority with a Newman-Haas one-two on the Michigan Speedway, me leading home Mario. It was one of those days when we had the set-ups absolutely right for the conditions and we were able to beat the field comprehensively. I was surprised by this in a way because the track is owned by Roger Penske and his cars test there a great deal – it was there in 1994 that Penske tested the one-off Mercedes stock block engine in secret preparations for the Indianapolis 500.

The banking at Michigan is a lot steeper than at Indianapolis and it launches the car out of the corner and down onto the straight. It's pretty daunting stuff, especially when you think that you go into some of the corners at upwards of 240mph.

Michigan was more tough than it needed to be for me because I arrived there with a nasty bout of gastric flu and that's the last thing you want when you are driving round and round in circles on a bumpy track. On the Friday I was pretty sick, running a high temperature and vomiting. As a result of that I was unable to eat and I was very dehydrated because I just couldn't hold anything down. The symptoms persisted but I decided that it was too important a race to miss. Our set-ups were obviously spot on, as I had been turning fast laps all weekend. I knew I could win it and the way the championship was looking it could be a make or break race for us.

It was sheer hell driving such a tough race in that condition. By half way through I had a splitting headache, which was beginning to affect my concentration. On one of the pit stops I even asked for and was given some aspirins! When I got home I went straight to bed and spent three days rehydrating myself.

The result at Michigan was just what the doctor ordered. I had my championship lead back and I even had an 18 point lead over Emerson, who had failed to score after coming in a distant 13th. We had regained the initiative, but I had also proved to anyone who doubted me, that I could win consistently on oval tracks.

I was aware that winning on ovals in your first season was considered special, but I was also conscious of the fact that there are always plenty of critics waiting to pounce as soon as you make a mistake. There were no grounds for complacency.

The next race at New Hampshire a week after Michigan was one of the finest wins of my career and according to many of the American racing pundits, it was one of the best oval races ever. In truth, I was still learning how to race on the one-mile ovals. I had learned a bit at Milwaukee, but New Hampshire taught me a lot about working with the traffic and taking low and high lines around corners and maintaining momentum. For a while, as I was following Emerson and Paul Tracy I watched their lines and some of the ways they tackled traffic and picked up a few good ideas.

Their cars were working better than mine in the first two-thirds of the race, especially moving through traffic and dirty air. Watching their cars it was clear that they could hold a tighter line in the corners than the Lola. This was true at most of the one-mile ovals, but especially New Hampshire. But what really impressed me was their performance in traffic. While I was slipping around all over the place, the Penskes could blast past the other cars. In other words, whatever percentage of the download we lost through running in dirty air, they were still left with some more besides. They could get closer to other cars in traffic without it affecting them as much as it affected my Lola. In fact, up until 10 laps from the end I had almost told myself that I would have to settle for third place. But I changed my style and won the race.

The lead had changed a few times during the race, but in the closing stages, with no more pit stops on the horizon, it developed into a straight fight between the Penskes and me. Tracy led, Emmo was second and me third. I got past Emerson, but he stayed right with me. Tracy was some way ahead and I had to make an impression on him.

I had thought about a different way of driving the car as the race had gone on and now it was all or nothing so I decided to give it a go. If you turn up the turbo boost on an Indycar, pretty soon you are going to hit the rev limiter, which is a pop-off valve, which slows you down. I needed more power without the risk of popping the valve so I tried changing up to sixth gear from fifth, thereby dropping the revs, and slingshotting out of the corners a bit more, exiting at a higher speed to get the revs up to where they would be if I were in fifth gear without the extra boost. It worked and I was able to haul Tracy in and four laps from the flag I dived past him on the outside and won the race.

That day was also my 40th birthday. As we celebrated I thought about all my years in the business, the highs and the lows and some of the great races. The one we had just completed was very special and I joked with Rosanne that maybe life does begin at forty after all!

Back onto the road courses again, it seemed as though we were going backwards. I finished second to Tracy at Road America, but in Vancouver I was a distant sixth. Luckily both Penskes were behind me so I held the points lead. After the race, Emmo made me laugh. He was telling the press that he had been in deep trouble in the race but he said, ' I take my hat off to Nigel because I could see his car was far worse than mine.' The result meant that I had a mathematical chance of clinching the Indycar title at the next race in Mid-Ohio. It seemed extraordinary to be in this position just 12 months after announcing my retirement from Formula 1 at Monza and eight months after driving an Indycar for the first time. The thought that I might clinch the title weighed heavy on my mind all weekend.

I got the pole, but it all went wrong at the start when Tracy cut across me into the first corner and damaged my front suspension. I had it repaired and hung on in the race, but I had lost two laps and ended up 12th.

I made up my mind that nothing had ever come easy in my life and that this championship would probably go down to the last race at Laguna Seca so there was no point in getting excited about it. I should do the best job I possibly could and go hell for leather in each of the last two races. Consequently I was very relaxed throughout the Nazareth weekend and the result came my way.

The first thirty laps were a nightmare, but then the car came to me and I adjusted my style a little and we were off. Sometimes you have to be patient on an oval and if your car is not working the way it should you have to hold on and wait for it to come around. I had not had much oval experience up to this point, but I had won three of the four oval races I had entered and I called on that experience now to help me through. I told myself that things can change quickly, that even in a mile – in 20 seconds – the car can change and the conditions can change and it can come good. So for those opening laps when it started to look really bad, I didn't panic, I just regrouped and thought it out and with every gallon of fuel that was burned off the handling changed and after a while I had a perfectly balanced car. Then I put the hammer down.

I took the lead around quarter distance and more or less held it for the rest of the race. From my point of view, in the cockpit, I could see that the Penskes were both suffering handling difficulties and struggling to keep the pace up. All I had to do was to keep it on the island and keep running smoothly and fast and the championship would be mine. Scott Goodyear challenged me at several points, but I managed to keep a cushion over him by taking every opportunity in traffic and eventually came home half a lap in front.

It had been the fastest one-mile oval race in Indycar history. On the slowing down lap my brain struggled to work out the maths of the points situation. In my ears I could hear Jim McGee saying, 'Congratulations, you've done it,' but I could not take in his meaning, I wanted to know where Emerson had finished. McGee kept saying, 'You've done it, you're the Champion,' but it wasn't registering.

Then all of a sudden it sank in that I was the Champion. I had pulled off the crazy dream of winning back to back Formula 1 and Indycar world titles.

For the next week, until Prost claimed the Formula 1 title in Estoril, I had the honour of being the reigning Formula 1 and Indycar Champion at the same time. No-one had ever done that before and I wonder how long it might be before it happens again.

Although I would never have said it publicly at the time, I had genuinely believed that the Indycar Championship was on from the first race at Surfers' Paradise. In many ways it had been more difficult than the Formula 1 Championship the year before, because in 1992 I didn't have to bounce back from a huge accident and back surgery. Ironically after 12 years of trying to win the World Championship I had won the Indycar title at my first attempt!

The PPG Indycar awards banquet was an incredible affair. It took place in San Francisco just after the last race of the season at Laguna Seca. All the drivers were there to celebrate and the whole evening built up to a dramatic climax when we collected the trophy. The organisers had done a wonderful job with the set design and the main stage looked magnificent with flowers everywhere, surrounding the giant trophy and my race car, decked out with the number one. I made a speech thanking everyone who had been part of this amazing success. It was a very special night and it felt sensational to be the new champion.

The Americans really push the boat out at award ceremonies and prize givings. There followed some terrific nights all over the country as we were presented with some very prestigious awards. The ESPN network honoured me and in New York I was given perhaps the most special award of all: a blue sapphire ring encrusted with diamonds which is given to the outstanding Driver of the Year, as voted by the American public.

Worldwide, the response to my championship success was overwhelming. Faxes, telegrams and flowers poured in from the most unlikely places and it seemed that my ' American adventure' had really captured the imagination of the racing fraternity and the public on both sides of the Atlantic. When I came back to England at the end of the year to drive a Ford Mondeo in the British Touring Car Championship's TOCA shootout at Donington, a crowd of over 90,000 turned out to say hello. That was a very special feeling. At the end of the weekend, of course, I had a different kind of feeling after I was piled into a bridge parapet at 120mph by Tiff Needell and was knocked out cold! I was also honoured that week to be presented with a special Gold Medal by the Royal Automobile Club.

I was very proud of what we had achieved, in some ways it was more special than the year before. I was happy because no-one could dispute what had been achieved. Even my harshest critics were forced to accept the testimony of the record books and to my mind that was enough to silence all of them. I felt a huge weight lifted from my shoulders. All my life I had been striving to prove to the world that I had the talent to be one of the best drivers in the world. Now I had nothing to prove anymore. No-one could take my success away from me.

There had been so many special moments in the year; winning from pole on my debut in Surfers', emulating Jimmy Clark 30 years on at Milwaukee, winning the Marlboro 500 at Michigan and the New Hampshire win on my 40th birthday. It had been a magical year for all the right reasons, all the sweeter for having been achieved without wranglings and skullduggery behind the scenes in the team.

Jim McGee, Newman-Haas team manager: 'When Nigel got hurt in Phoenix he went home and evidently they had never seen this type of an injury before and they thought that it would heal itself. When he showed up in Long Beach, Dr Olvey and Dr Trammell saw it and they knew he was going to have to have some kind of surgery. After each practice session I had to take him to the medical centre where Dr Olvey would drain the pouch of fluid with a long needle. It was a real nasty deal. The fluid was making this pouch bigger and bigger. He did a hell of a job that weekend, getting the pole and finishing third. To do that in the condition he was in was an incredible feat and for me that was the biggest and toughest thing he did that whole year.

'He recuperated incredibly fast. After the operation, Dr Morris and Dr Trammell said that it would be three weeks before he would be recuperated but twelve days later he was in a car at Indy doing his rookie test! He missed the normal rookie tests and normally the Speedway would not let a driver run; he would have to come back the next year. But we used a few connections and were able to get that waived and they let Nigel do his rookie orientation. Within two hours he was the third quickest driver that day at around 225mph. He took to Indy like it was the most natural thing in the world to go fast there. He knew just how to deal with the traffic and how to place the car on the oval and it was as if he'd been doing it for 25 years. I was Emerson's crew chief when he started on the ovals and it took him years to get used to it.'

27

'YOU'RE COMPLETELY MAD, BUT VERY QUICK FOR AN OLD MAN'

The 1994 season was disappointing for me personally and for the sport as a whole it was tragic. The loss of Ayrton Senna and Roland Ratzenberger in San Marino hit everybody hard and it will be a long time, if ever, before we get over those losses.

It would have been almost unimaginable to predict at the start of 1994 that I would end up as I did winning the last Grand Prix of the season for Williams, but as I have often said, nothing is impossible in motor racing.

It is important to remember that what happened in my life with my return to Formula 1 came about because of the terrible accidents of Senna and Ratzenberger. It had been Bernie Ecclestone's intention for the past two years to get me back into Formula 1, where he said I belonged and 'shouldn't have left in the first place'.

For many years, Bernie and I have talked almost every week on the telephone and that continued after I moved to America and Indycars. He wanted me back in the fold and Renault were keen to have me race in their home Grand Prix at Magny Cours, which I was free to do as it did not clash with an Indycar race. I made the 'guest appearance' in France for Williams-Renault and then followed up by doing the last three races of the season, culminating in that win in Adelaide.

I owe Bernie a lot. What he has done to help me throughout my career is fantastic. Without his support I wouldn't have achieved half of what I have. Even when I went over to Indycars he said, 'Get the job done, go and win,' because it was good for him and for the image of Formula 1 that I was able to go over there and win the championship first time out with new cars and all new circuits. His backing and friendship throughout that whole period was fantastic.

Bernie is a fabulous person who has been a friend for a long time.

He gets things done. Being from the old school, if he gives you his word on something then you know it will happen as he says. Bernie's word is better than any contract. His word is his bond and everything that man has ever said to me has come true. That is one of his great strengths. He has tremendous vision and control. He's able to see the next thing along the way and then to control its destiny and that is what makes him such a remarkable person.

People on the outside don't see the lighter side of Bernie. I'll never forget in Austria in the late eighties when he was play-fighting with my children Chloe and Leo in his motorhome. He had put them on the electric lift and sent them up and down, to howls of laughter from the children.

At the start of the 1994 season I was the reigning Indycar champion, looking forward to defending my title. Things looked promising. The new Lola, now with a transverse gearbox, like the Penske, was at least a second quicker than the 1993 car at most of the circuits we visited during pre-season testing. It was a real pleasure for me to see the red number one on my car – the first time I had ever defended a championship. We were optimistic, but as it turned out, it merely taught us how great an achievement it had been to win the year before, because in 1994 we simply could not get a break.

Several times I was in winning positions but the little bit of luck that you need on your side just wasn't there. With each disappointment came the stronger realisation of how luck had been on our side the year before. At Phoenix, for example, I was leading and throughout the day was the fastest car on the track, but a faulty engine map caused the engine to stall in the pit stops and I lost a lap during my first stop. At Michigan I got the pole and was storming off in the lead for the first 20 laps when my throttle stuck open at 240mph. It felt like someone had hit me up the back when I came off the throttle, because the engine was still going flat out.

At New Hampshire the car was working well and I was challenging the Penskes, but then my team-mate, Mario Andretti, took me out while I was lapping him. At Vancouver, I was six seconds in the lead with 20 laps to go when I made a quick 'splash and dash' pit stop and as I exited the pits the officials put out a yellow flag for a car, which had been stopped out on the track for at least five laps. Consequently, I fell behind the pace car and dropped from first to ninth place.

At Indianapolis, I was given a black flag penalty for passing in the pits. Twelve months later the chief steward came up to to Jim McGee and asked him to pass on his apologies to me. They had looked at the tapes and realised that they had made a mistake! Then, of course, Dennis Vittolo landed on my head. We just couldn't get a break all season and it seemed that we were always in the wrong place at the wrong time. In all, we had six or eight occasions like this, where if the luck had been on our side as it had been in 1993, the season could have turned out quite differently.

It was always a major struggle. Penske had made a much bigger improvement to its car than Lola and the red and white cars simply drove away from us in the races. In qualifying I could sometimes keep up with them and even beat them, but once the cars were filled with fuel in race set-up, I couldn't live with them at all. It was a whitewash.

Al Unser Jr, in his first year with the team, won eight races and blitzed the championship, Paul Tracy won three and Emerson won once. Having three cars certainly helped them in getting the race set-ups perfected and it was typical of Penske to even try to run three equal cars. I admired Roger's commitment. I also took it as a compliment. It showed how badly he had been upset by what we did the year before.

The Penske chassis had us beaten in every department. It was superior on road and oval courses. It had more mechanical grip, conserved its tyres better in a race and was far more driveable in all conditions. At times in some races I had to do qualifying laps just to stay with them. I remember realising how serious the problem was at the start of the race in Detroit, where Al Jr simply drove past me on the short straight. I was flat out coming out of the previous corner but he just breezed past me. All credit to him and his team. He had the car of the moment and he used it effectively to win the title.

Ayrton Senna was killed at the beginning of May and it really shook me up. It made me think very carefully about what I was doing and about the risks involved. It was also tough to explain to my children, who were by now old enough to understand what had happened. Williams approached me about driving in the French Grand Prix, as a guest appearance. Renault wanted me back in the car, as did Bernie Ecclestone.

If I was going to make the commitment to come back into Formula 1, I didn't want it to be just for a handful of races. I wanted another crack at the World Championship, so we negotiated a deal, whereby I would drive four races in 1994 with an option for 1995. The decision to return to Formula 1 would mean a massive upheaval of our lives and it was one we didn't want to make lightly. We were happy and settled in America. We had a magnificent house in which we had invested a great deal of time and money to make it exactly the way we wanted it. The children were happy in their schools and the Florida lifestyle suited us down to the ground. We had made some fantastic friends and we looked at America and Indycar as being our future.

We were enjoying the Indycar series. For sure, we were not having the success so far that year which we had enjoyed the year before, but it only served to remind us how special 1993 had been and I was confident that we would have a lot more success in the coming years. I had talked a lot with Eric Broadley at Lola about the 1995 car and was convinced it would be a winner, as it subsequently proved to be. Mario would be retiring at the end of the year and Carl and I had been discussing candidates for the job of my new team-mate. Texaco, one of the main sponsors of the team were launching a worldwide advertising campaign with me and there were a great deal of structures and contracts in place.

When Bernie along with Frank Williams and Renault came knocking on my door, I didn't think it was possible to get out of all the commitments I had in America – but my world was turned upside down as contracts were unravelled and I was cleared to make my guest appearance at the French Grand Prix in July.

My return to Formula 1 began with a test session at Brands Hatch on the Tuesday before the French Grand Prix and that was probably one of the happiest times of the year for me. I thought that we would have a quiet test, but I never dreamed that there would be over 15,000 people there on a Tuesday to watch one car go around the short circuit. The welcome the fans gave me was really special. Every time I came back into the pits after a run, they would applaud.

It was difficult to step back into a Formula 1 car after a season and a half in Indycars. The Indycars are easier to drive, more forgiving and more solid due to their extra weight. The last Formula 1 car I had driven was the active Williams. Since then, 'driver-aids', like active suspension and traction control had been banned. I felt quite uncomfortable to start with because the car was very pitch sensitive. I had a spin fairly early in the test which helped me to get my orientation back a bit. I thought as the back of the car stepped out, 'That's not a problem' based on instinct of how an Indycar would respond, but of course an F1 car steps out much more quickly and before I knew where I was, it was travelling backwards. Obviously, adapting back to carbon brakes took a little time as well, as did learning to run deeper into the corners. The whole day was a real challenge to try to go quicker and quicker. From the start of the day to the end of it we improved our time by three seconds, and it was clear that we were right on the pace.

Although the French Grand Prix was just a guest appearance, it was also a tremendous challenge, perhaps greater even than going to Indycar in the first place. I knew that I would be under the microscope and that people would say, 'Oh well, of course he's doing it for the money,' or some such line. None of this was anywhere near the truth. The money you get paid in a situation like that is nothing more than a reflection of your market value. If money had been the important factor, I would never have left Williams in the first place.

The truth is that I wanted to show that I was still highly motivated to win at the highest level of the sport. The challenge was to prove it to myself and to others. The race at Magny Cours was a fantastic experience. The critics were saying that I was too old, that I wasn't fit enough, but I put the car on the front row of the grid and almost had pole position for my first race back, only for Damon Hill, my team-mate, to pull out a special lap to pip me at the last minute. He was certainly working harder than he had ever done before to get pole.

The race was a disappointment because I made a mistake on the set-up of the car on race day and I wasn't as competitive as I should have been. I broke my golden rule – never change the car between Sunday morning warm-up and the race. The last time I had been to Magny Cours with a conventional suspension car, in 1991, David Brown, my engineer and I had tried raising the back of the car and it had paid off for us. After the warm-up in 1994 we did the same thing, but it didn't work out and the car was off-balance throughout the race.

I was running in third place and I'm sure that we would have kept that position at the end, but a belt broke in the engine and I was out. There were some fatuous suggestions in the press that I had stopped because I was out of breath! If the journalists concerned had bothered to follow it up with the team they would have been told the real reason for the retirement, but perhaps that's too difficult for them to do.

I gave myself nine out of ten for the French Grand Prix. It wasn't a good race, but I felt that I had got back into the swing of things.

The final three Grands Prix of 1994 offered me a chance to get fully up to speed. It wouldn't be easy, especially after all the transatlantic travel we had been doing, not to mention the fact that I had already done 17 races. In retrospect, to do the European Grand Prix the week after the final Indycar round at Laguna Seca was almost suicidal. It was the craziest calendar I could remember following for years. There were eight hours of time difference to adjust to and I did three days of solid testing as soon as I got off the plane. Then I went straight to Jerez, Spain for qualifying and the race.

I did alright, but got tagged by Rubens Barrichello so I had to change the front wing. Unfortunately, the bolts weren't done up properly on the wing so I was called in again to fix them. In the end I spun out. I was glad to get away and to be able to get back to the USA and have a rest. There was some criticism of me for not testing between Spain and Japan, but after the schedule I had been following, I was worn out. I needed a good rest in order to be ready to challenge properly in Japan and Australia.

Japan was great fun and I really enjoyed the race, although I was sad that I missed out on pole position. I had been quickest in the dry morning session on Saturday, breaking the track record, but it rained in the afternoon so there was no chance of translating that speed into a better grid position during qualifying.

I got a terrible start but soon got involved in a fantastic scrap with Jean Alesi in the Ferrari. I lost out in the end because the race was calculated over two halves due to the weather, and Alesi had a slight aggregate advantage over me even though I managed to get past him at the finish. It was a lot of fun dicing wheel to wheel with him and I think it helped to put some excitement back into Formula 1. At the end of the race we shook hands and had a good laugh. 'You're completely mad,' he said, 'but very quick for an old man!' I thought that I had beaten him, but I had forgotten about the aggregate times. The comeback podium would have to wait another week.

That final weekend in Australia was quite remarkable. I went out determined to get the pole which had been denied me in France and Japan. There was a hairy moment when I came around a blind corner to find Johnny Herbert's Benetton stranded in the middle of the road, but despite this I got the pole on my next lap and wasn't challenged, although Schumacher went off the road trying to beat my time.

In the race I got a good start, contrary to what the press said afterwards. I could see that Damon wanted to come up the inside and I knew that he and Schumacher would be challenging for the championship, not me, so I got out of Damon's way to help him get his attack started as soon and as strongly as possible. I moved off line to let him through and on the second corner I was again off line, so that by the third corner my tyres lost grip and I slid off the track altogether. It was my mistake, I should have allowed for that. The car had been perfectly balanced in the warm up, but the excursion over the kerbs damaged the floor and the balance was affected for the rest of the race.

I had to push hard after Damon and Michael collided and I managed to hold off Berger to win the race. He made me laugh on the podium, calling me an 'old bastard' because he had so badly wanted to win. I wanted to win too and although in some ways it was a lucky victory because Damon and Schumacher took each other out, it was a win nevertheless – my thirty-first in Grand Prix racing.

It was a fairy tale finish to the season for me, but not for Damon. The anguish he must have felt when he looked at his bent suspension and realised that it was all over must have been hard to bear. I know the feeling, having lost World Championships in the past. It's a great shame that Damon didn't have better visibility into that corner and clearly he didn't appreciate as he went to pass Schumacher down the inside into the next corner that Schumacher had hit the wall. If he'd seen the force of his impact with the wall he would have deduced that the Benetton was finished and would have backed off and waited for Schumacher to pull off the track. But that's motor racing. The hard truth is that 'if's and but's' don't count in racing.

I've been asked what I thought about the motives of each driver in that incident. The only conclusion I have come to is that hopefully Schumacher didn't realise that his car was damaged, and went for the racing line. He and Damon collided and everyone knows what happened.

What people don't realise is that in those split second moments, which can be defining moments in your life, it's instincts which take control. Sometimes your instincts are right and sometimes they are wrong. Whatever the nuances, both of them should be congratulated for being in a position to challenge for the World Championship. That takes some doing in itself and it was good that after such an awful year for the sport there was a championship fight at the end.

As we came away from Adelaide I felt confident that I would be driving for Williams in 1995. I had played myself in over the course of the four races and at the end of it the results looked pretty positive. I had a fourth place, a win and a pole position and had proved that I was right on the pace. The 1994 Williams was not the best car in the field, but from what I knew about the 1995 car, I believed that it could well be, and I was later proved right. I was excited by the prospect of a competitive season in the best car. Who knows what might have been achievable?

It didn't cross my mind to retire after the Adelaide win, because when you're winning the last thing you think of is stopping. I know the Williams mechanics and engineers so well and I know how to motivate them because I spent six years and four races with them and we won a lot together. I believe that with David Brown we could take on any race in a half-sensible car and expect to do well as a team.

I was very fired up about going back into Formula 1 full time. We decided that we would make the full commitment to return to Britain, because there was no point in trying to commute across the Atlantic to race in Formula 1. If we were going to do it, then it had to be done properly. It was a huge commitment from every aspect. It is incredible how much stuff you accumulate in a few short years in one place. Rosanne took charge of packing our lives into dozens of boxes and chests ready for the move.

When we returned to the Isle of Man we found that it was still a wonderful place when the weather was nice, but coming back from Florida to an English winter was a big shock to the system. We rented a house for 18 months which was soon renamed 'Fawlty Towers' because nothing worked quite as it should – floorboards creaked, handles kept falling off doors and so on. But even the best laid plans are changed. Following a combination of niggling incidents both for ourselves and the children, we began to have doubts about our future on the island. Rosanne and I sat down one evening and came to a decision that the Isle of Man was not for us and that we should move immediately in view of us needing to find new schools for the children. It was a decision which, while immediate in formation, also had to be, for practical considerations, immediate in its execution.

So we moved in to a temporary house near the golf club in Woodbury and laid out plans for a new house to be built, exactly how we wanted it. We are hoping it will be finished in December and that we can spend Christmas in our new home. It was definitely the right decision. The children are happy to be back home in England and the schooling that we are giving them is very good. Rosanne and I are happy to be back in England too – it is our spiritual home and we have never forgotten our roots and our past. A little piece of England always stayed with us throughout over a decade of tax exile.

At the end of 1994, there were a number of interesting Formula 1 opportunities on the table. I had been approached by Ron Dennis of McLaren during the races at Jerez and Suzuka. At the time, he believed, as I did, that I would be driving for Williams in 1995 and that I would probably not be available, but he registered an interest anyway and told me about his new partnership with Mercedes-Benz, which he was very optimistic about.

Before I accepted any other offers, I waited, along with everyone else, to see what decision Williams would take. Over the run-up to Christmas much was made of the rivalry between myself and David Coulthard for the Williams drive. I believed that my deal would come to fruition and that they would take up the option in my contract. I felt that I had agreed a good deal with Williams and with Renault for the four races in 1994 and for the 1995 season. I have to say, however that looking back now with perfect hindsight, if I had not believed then that Williams would pick up my option for 1995, I wouldn't have done that deal.

Murray Walker, BBC commentator: 'Before the race at Jerez, Nigel had a test at Estoril in Portugal with the other Williams drivers. The Portuguese were so delighted to have Il Leone among them again and they furnished the empty garage next to Nigel's with a carpet, furniture and even a standard lamp!

'After the test, the BBC crew and I were faced with the prospect of a long, hot and tedious drive across to southern Spain. "I'll give you a lift," said Nigel, meaning a two-hour ride in his private jet, with him at the controls. What a way to travel! "I don't expect to go well in Spain," said Nigel, "Because I've still to get up to speed. But I should be there in Japan."

'He wasn't kidding! Suzuka saw that superb battle with Alesi and then that last wonderful pole position and victory for Williams in Australia. If only he'd retired then...'

Sheridan Thynne, close friend and adviser: 'I really enjoyed my trips to America: not just the good racing and the warm friendliness of the senior officials, but the open way in which Indycar racing is managed. Even so, when Nigel's departure became public knowledge, the number of people who came to give their good wishes and said they wanted Nigel to stay (many of whom I didn't even know by name) was astonishing. Perhaps this is partly because they understand more clearly than Grand Prix people that racing has to be a "show" and realised how much Nigel contributes to that "show".

28

THE STAND DOWN FROM McLAREN

Williams went for Coulthard. They didn't have to pay him very much at all and they opted for youth over experience. The decision not to go with me was their prerogative. I was disappointed but it was their call and they did what they considered was in the best long-term interests of the Williams team, which I can respect.

I think it would be fair to say, however, from looking at their performance in 1995 in races like Spain, Monaco, Canada and France that they paid dearly for it because they lost their direction. The Williams was a championship winning car, but the drivers were struggling to get the best out of it, which could not be said of Schumacher and the Benetton. Coulthard had an incredible opportunity to drive the best car in Formula 1 but by mid-season Williams decided to replace him for 1996 with Jacques Villeneuve.

I still don't really know to this day why Williams chose Coulthard in preference to me, because they didn't tell me. The most disappointing thing in all of this was that we found out that I didn't have the drive through the press rather than from Williams themselves. When you hear the true story in the press 24 hours before you hear it from the Williams management, it is rather sad in light of all the great times we shared together. When all is said and done, I did win 28 races for them.

I had mixed feelings after I learned the news. Naturally I was disappointed because I wasn't going to drive what I knew would be a really competitive car and one which might have allowed me to win another title. On the positive side, I thought that perhaps this might be the right time to call it a day, having won my last Grand Prix in Adelaide.

We went through about a week of wondering what was going to

happen, at the same time coming to terms with the fact that we weren't going to be with Williams. Up to that point all the signs had been that it was going to happen. I knew that Renault wanted me while Rothmans, the main sponsor, wasn't too bothered either way. It just came down to Patrick and Frank, and I think that if the truth be known, Renault were probably also surprised as I was, initially, by their decision.

Back in 1994, we had negotiated certain protection elements into the contract whereby I would be recompensed if my option wasn't taken up and Williams followed through correctly on this. At least this time the split was amicable and honourable. It was a pure business decision, which I can respect. A lot of water has passed under the bridge since the dark days of 1992. As far as I'm concerned, Frank can speak to me anytime and I can speak to him. On a business and professional level all the bridges burned in 1992 are now repaired.

At this point, Ron Dennis of McLaren rang me up suggesting that we should get together and talk. We had a number of meetings to thrash out what we might be able to do together. It was really a case of Ron motivating me, saying that McLaren would be capable of winning races, talking up the partnership with Mercedes and the new three-litre engine and so on.

Negotiations over the deal began badly. Ron had formed certain opinions about me over the years, as I had about him, although we both had to respect each other's track record. I knew what he had achieved at McLaren since taking over in 1981 was remarkable — after all, so much of it had been achieved at my expense! It took several meetings before we both began to see that there was more to each other than we had thought. I felt that I needed to explain to him what I had achieved in racing, but he cut me short and said that he was well aware of what had been achieved and that I should be comfortable because it was a remarkable record, mostly achieved at *his* expense. He wanted to talk about the future and once we started sharing our personal attitudes to racing we found we had a lot in common.

From then on the dialogue was relatively smooth and we quickly arrived at a deal for 1995. It may seem extraordinary to some that we should have come together after so many years of apparent animosity, but as Ron said himself, 'So many people in this world are quite different once you get to know them.'

People said it was an unlikely marriage. I think that we certainly respect each other a lot more now than we did before because we know each other better. Whatever reservations may have existed in the past were forgotten because the bottom line is that we are both racers and we are both dedicated to winning.

However, I soon realised that there were pitfalls. McLaren's problem today is that Ron has got involved in so many other business ventures over the past few years that he has increasingly left the running of the Formula 1 team to other people. Although he has some great people in his organisation, some of them are at times living in a fool's paradise and resting on past glories. I think that Ron became out of touch and he only started to realise, early in the 1995 season, just how big a problem he had.

I had never understood why Ayrton Senna left McLaren at the end of 1993, but as my experience of them developed, I realised that he had left because he could see that technically the team was in decline. They had lost the Honda engines at the end of 1992 and although Ayrton performed some heroics in 1993 to beat Prost's Williams to victory five times, he could see that the chassis designs were not maintaining the standards of the previous ten years.

It was tough for me to find all of this out the way I did, but I have respect for Ron Dennis and I have no doubt that given time, he'll get it right and sort the team out. He's got some great sponsors behind him and he has Mercedes, whose past record speaks for itself. As long as he stays in motor racing he'll surely bounce back to the top.

The car McLaren produced in early 1995 was dreadful. My motivation has always been to compete at the highest level – to win and to mount a serious assault on the World Championship. It quickly became apparent that this wasn't going to happen with McLaren. It would be very unprofessional for me to specify exactly what was wrong with the car, but I can put it in context.

I need a car in which I can go into a corner deeply on the brakes and then when I turn the steering wheel, it will react immediately and go where I point it – to the the apex of the corner. Sadly the McLaren couldn't do this at all. So I couldn't trust the car or build a relationship with it and I certainly couldn't drive it on the limit. If I tried to go ten-tenths, the chances of having an accident were very high. It was more sympathetic to drivers who like understeer and who, once they have turned the steering wheel, allow the car plenty of time to turn. Everything I was asking from the car, it wasn't able to deliver.

My team-mate Mika Hakkinen got to know the car better than me, because obviously he did a lot more miles in it, and he just drove through a lot of its problems. He is young and inexperienced and so it was more acceptable to him than it was to me. He doesn't yet know what it takes to win and win consistently and like any young driver, he's prepared to put up with a lot – as I did in my Lotus days. When you've won 31 Grands Prix, and two World titles, your tolerance threshold is that bit lower. You know straight away when you're in a bad car and you have a pretty good idea how much work needs to be done to make it competitive.

I realised that it was a bad car the first day I drove it in testing at Estoril. I went off on the first lap because the car literally jumped in the air and swapped ends for no apparent reason. I should have realised then that we were in serious trouble but I thought I'd be tactful and suggest that it was my mistake and try again. I went out and did some more laps and it was immediately apparent that it had not been my error but that the car was all over the place.

Sometimes the front end would have maximum grip and the rear end would have no grip, then suddenly it would be the other way around – tons of grip at the back and none at all at the front. So you had massive swing from understeer to oversteer in a split second in the middle of a corner. Clearly the car was highly unbalanced aerodynamically and that showed on the stopwatches – it was at least two seconds off the pace on most circuits.

I was hugely disappointed by that first test at Estoril and I could already see that it was going to be a long, uphill battle. Not only was there a major handling problem, but the engine was also down on power compared to the Renault – on the straights we were almost five miles a hour slower than the Williams or the Benetton. Because I'd been in the game so long and had started many seasons with new cars, I knew that the chances of us rectifying the problems in the short term were remote.

When I joined McLaren, I really believed that the team was something special, but in fact they were no different from the other teams I have driven for – Williams, Ferrari or Lotus – in that they are not infallible and they make mistakes. There is no magic ingredient to get things right. It requires sheer determination and hard work and the right people making the right decisions regarding equipment to put on the car.

What I found to my dismay was that some of the people in the McLaren team hadn't got a clue what to do about the problems. That is what really knocked my confidence in the McLaren organisation – they didn't have a quick-fix and although the will was there, the savvy to get it done quickly and properly was not. I could see that until they put some new blood into the team and new direction in the design department, they would be in trouble for some time to come.

The other problem, of course, was that the cockpit was too small, so it wasn't physically possible for me to drive the car. It was a design fault, partially explained by the fact that they didn't think they would be employing a driver of my size when the design was finalised, although I'm not that large. Mika had the same problem, but he is a bit smaller than me and by adapting some of the panels in the cockpit the team were able to make him a little more comfortable. Unfortunately, there wasn't any margin to allow them to do the same for me.

I was cramped in the cockpit and couldn't use my elbows and upper body strength properly. So it really was a recipe for disaster. I found that three or four laps was the absolute maximum I could manage in the car. A decision was taken jointly between myself and Ron that there was no way I could race the car as it was and that a new chassis would have to be built. It was embarrassing for McLaren but Ron certainly took it on the chin in the press conferences. I kept my silence, refusing to be drawn on my feelings about the car and on missing the first two races.

The team set to work building a new cockpit and it must be said they did the job in record time. But it was tough staying at home while Mark Blundell stood in for me in Brazil and Argentina. I found it highly demotivating.

I was not expecting much from my first outing at Imola. The team worked hard and a new chassis was completed in record time. It was ready the week leading up to the race so there was no time for testing and the first time I drove the car was in practice at Imola. I was dismayed.

Other than having more room in the cockpit, the car itself was no different. It had all the same handling characteristics and defects as the original. It was a question of trying to get the best out of it and trying to put in plenty of work to get the car balanced as best I could. I got pretty close to Mika's time in qualifying, but it gave me no satisfaction. We were not competing. We were just making the numbers up, not challenging. There was no way that the package could be considered a challenger for the championship.

Going back to Imola was difficult for everyone after what had happened there with the deaths of Ayrton and Roland Ratzenberger the year before and also the memory of what happened to Gerhard Berger, who laughs and jokes around the paddock nowadays, but who could easily have been killed there in 1989. It's a tough place, Imola.

The changes they had made to the circuit to make it safer were better in some ways, but in a lot of respects it has become uninspiring. There are now six second gear corners – hardly a real drivers' circuit.

Our problems were evident in Spain. You can't go storming into a corner – as I want to – and then have nothing happen when you turn the wheel. I made a lot of alterations to the car, but they didn't make it any better. They merely delayed one problem and created another.

So I was fighting the car all the way and if I was lucky I might be able to get tenth on the grid and that would be a good result with that car. As the Spanish weekend progressed I couldn't believe that things could be so bad, but they were.

In first qualifying I was 1.8s slower than Mika, even though the throttle traces on the telemetry showed that I was on full power 3% longer than him. I picked up a chunk of time in second qualifying, finishing within nine-hundredths of a second of Mika, but I got no satisfaction from it all because we were still so slow. I was only tenth on the grid and we were 2.4s off the pole time of Michael Schumacher.

Ron implied that he didn't agree with my decision to retire the car on lap 18 of the race. But when you're driving a car which isn't working and you drive into a corner and it understeers straight off the track heading for a brick wall and nothing you do makes any difference, then that's pretty stupid. After all I've been through and achieved I'm not going to drive any car, no matter how illustrious the team, which is downright dangerous. If you have to do it because you're young and your career is just beginning, then that's another thing and I've been through that.

Sitting in the cockpit I had no idea what was wrong with it, whether the front wing was broken, whether there was something wrong with the front suspension or if I'd picked up debris underneath the car. I knew that it didn't feel correct and so I had to retire it. Sadly I've had to do that two or three times in my career and you always hate to do it, but it's better to be fit to fight another day than to be in hospital with broken legs or worse. Anybody who criticises a driver for using his intelligence and retiring an undriveable car is being unreasonable.

Inevitably some people said that I had 'given up', others suggested I was only doing it for the money. What I would say to them is that when you get into a racing car, anything over 30mph is potentially lethal. It's like a loaded gun. And whatever money you can get for doing our job, good luck to you. I have never begrudged anyone earning more money than I do. It just means that their salary is the new goalpost.

I am fascinated by the critics. These are people who give the public the benefit of their enormous wisdom, but who have never actually driven a Formula 1 car in anger and have no idea what it's like to drive flat out in a Grand Prix for almost two hours. Do they know what it's like to race wheel to wheel with Ayrton Senna at 190mph? Do they know how it feels to have a suspension breakage going fully committed into a 160mph corner? Would they make the supreme sacrifices, take the enormous risks and push themselves beyond all reasonable human limits?

Why bother? It's so much easier to sit in an office and criticise.

I came back home from Spain and thought hard about it. As a racing driver you have to be able to look yourself in the mirror and say: 'I'm prepared to drive on the knife edge.' Driving a car on the edge means that at certain times you are risking your life. Any driver worth his salt is prepared to do that – and let me tell you there aren't many of those. I am one of the few who was able to do it. But there has to be a good reason.

I had agreed to leave everything I had built in America and a solid contract for 1995 in Indycars to come back to Formula 1 for the Williams team, not for McLaren. I chose to come back for a lot of reasons and after much persuasion from key people in Formula 1. In my mind, as long as I got up to speed in the four races, it was a foregone conclusion that Williams and Renault would take up my option for 1995. But it hadn't worked out that way.

So here was I driving for McLaren and it wasn't working out at all. I had tried to put my heart and soul into it, but the car wasn't up to it. I had to go back ten years to think of a car as bad as this one.

I am an honest person and had negotiated a very lucrative contract for the year. But I saw no hope of the sort of improvement I wanted, and I didn't want to be seen as a journeyman driver getting paid millions of pounds to drive around in eighth place. From my experience, I knew there was no quick fix. It would take the whole year at the very least.

I had a meeting with Ron Dennis and we talked through a whole lot of things. We were both disappointed and frustrated about the car and regretted the way things had turned out, and it was agreed amicably – at my request – that I should stand down. It was one of the toughest decisions I have ever made, but I was happy with it. I could say that I should never have driven for McLaren, but I won't say it because I don't regret the experience of driving for one of the very best teams in Formula 1.

I have since sat on the sidelines and watched developments, and despite hoping that things would get better for McLaren, they obviously haven't. The car was two seconds a lap off the pace at the start of the year and as the season progressed, although they massaged the problem they were unable to fix it.

I have a tremendous soft spot for Formula 1. I always have and I always will. Whatever happens, it's the pinnacle of motor sport. What Bernie Ecclestone achieved over the years is astonishing. There are some super sponsors, great manufacturers and some fine teams as well. There are, however, few great designers around at the moment and to keep on the pace you have to have your own aerodynamicist, spending all of his time in the wind-tunnel coming up with new things to improve the car.

In Formula 1 there is no limit to what you can come up with, no limit to what you can spend. This is one of its strengths. It's also one of its weaknesses because the poorer teams cannot afford it and therefore cannot compete at the same level. So you have a first, second and third division and that's good if you've got three or four equal teams at the top of the tree, but if you haven't got that it becomes very boring very quickly. Formula 1 was stronger a few years ago with some big names, several World Champions and over thirty cars entered for each race.

Times have changed in Formula 1. Today most people are being manipulated and penalised financially, especially the drivers. A lot of drivers are being paid peanuts and at a certain point in your career you have to ask yourself whether or not it's worth putting your life on the line for next to nothing. I am glad that Michael Schumacher was able to break the mould by getting over $20 million for his Ferrari contract. Good luck to him.

Another problem with modern Formula 1 is that there has been a terrible over-reaction to the deaths of Senna and Ratzenberger in terms of circuit safety. When I started out in the early eighties there were numerous fatalities. The circuits were modified slightly but not to the extent that they have been since Imola 1994. The Formula 1 calendar featured many real drivers' circuits, with corners where you had to have guts to be quick. On these tracks you needed a lot of determination, skill and strength to hang on to the car. Since the fatal accidents at Imola, all the fast exciting corners have disappeared. There are now many second and third gear chicanes; even the kerbs have been lowered, so now anybody can just drive right over them and not be worried about an accident because the run-offs are so huge and they know they won't hit anything. In the eighties you didn't drive over the kerbs because if you did you risked breaking the car or being thrown across the track.

In those days you had to be a driver of some standing to get a Formula 1 superlicence. Now it seems anyone can get one. I'm not knocking the governing body, the FIA, because I think they have done a good job with Formula 1 in a lot of ways, but it is so costly now that Formula 1 has to have many drivers who can pay their way, but whose right to a superlicence on merit is debatable.

As 1995 draws to a close, there are numerous offers on the table to do a host of things. We are looking at each on its merits and when we are ready to make a decision, we'll make one. I don't feel that I need to go out there and prove I'm still competitive after the McLaren affair. Let's not forget that I won my third to last race from pole position – my thirty-first Grand Prix win. Like me or not, people have to admit that I am true to my word. I said I would not make the numbers up and when it was clear that the McLaren was far from competitive I stepped down. If I had been in it for the money I could have made a fortune by completing the season, but I preferred to stop and hand back the money rather than waste my time trying to race without any chance of winning.

Do I think I could win another World Championship given the opportunity, with a truly competitive car and a motivated team? I think I could, yes. Do I think I'll get the opportunity to try? Realistically, I don't think so.

To be successful as a driver these days you have to be selfish, single-minded and dedicated. There are no short cuts, no matter how much talent you may have. You pay a heavy personal price for success; marriages may fail, friendships may be broken. I have lost friends, but I am unusual in that I've managed to keep a happy balance a lot of the time, thanks to my family. Perhaps it's not been a perfect balance but

I've kept my feet on the ground more often than not. That isn't to say that I haven't made mistakes and done the wrong thing at times, because I certainly have. When I feel the aches and pains from where my body has taken a hammering over the years, I reflect that it's been a small price to pay.

During my sixteen years in Formula 1 and Indycars, I never had the opportunity to look back and reflect on my experiences and the success that I've had because I was always on the treadmill, and the treadmill goes so fast that if you pause to look backwards you might trip up. So it is only since pulling out of the McLaren deal that I have started to appreciate some of the things which have happened over the years and all the success that has been achieved. I also look forward to some new challenges – making a success out of my golf club, maybe even competition golf, who knows? But whatever it may be, I still want to win.

I have given a great deal of my life to motor racing and it has given much to me in return. But the most valuable lesson I've learned is that life is not a practice run.

Life today is what you have today, and tomorrow it will be gone. The next day you wake up and it's a new day of your life. It's great to chase after your goals and your challenges, but you shouldn't forget that you will never get that time back. So you should make the most of every moment, and if you get really annoyed about something and you've got good cause then that's fine, but don't let it spoil your life. You can only try to control the future, you cannot control the past. Above all, you have to keep things in perspective.

I do ... and I realise that I'm lucky to be alive.

FACES IN THE PADDOCK

The following are background notes to some of the major characters that have appeared in the book:

JOHN BARNARD Chassis designer. *English*.
One of the most successful racing car designers of the last 20 years. His cars have won F1 World Championships, the IndyCar Championship and the Indianapolis 500. Started at Lola before designing the Chaparral Indycar which won the Indy 500 and CART title in 1980. He devised the all-conquering McLarens of the mid-1980s and in 1987 he joined Ferrari, leaving in 1989 to join Benetton. He rejoined Ferrari in 1993, where he is today. Regarded by some as a genius, he has huge confidence in himself and one of his conditions when signing for a new employer is that they establish an office near his home in Surrey.

CREIGHTON BROWN Team director. *English*
A founder director of McLaren International with responsibility for the McLaren road car project, Creighton began life as a farmer. He met Ron Dennis when they were rival team owners in Formula 2 and bought into Ron's team, Project Four, which became the McLaren Formula 1 team (*see Ron Dennis*).

DAVID BROWN Race engineer. *English*
A true-blue Williams employee and one of the most successful Formula 1 race engineers of the last decade. Saw Nigel to 1992 World Championship and engineered Prost to the title the following year. First worked with Nigel in 1987 during the turbo era and was reunited in 1991 when Nigel returned from Ferrari. Shy, but humourous.

COLIN CHAPMAN Designer/Team owner. *English*
Founder of legendary Lotus company, which was split between racing and production cars. One of the greatest racing car designers in the history of the sport and arguably the greatest innovator. His cars won in all categories: Formula 1, Indycar, sportscar racing and the minor formulae. Under him Lotus won seven World Championships and 72 Grands Prix and he also won the Indianapolis 500 twice in the mid-sixties, wins which forced the American racers to join the rear-engined revolution. He won World Championships with Jim Clark, Graham Hill, Emerson Fittipaldi, Jochen Rindt and Mario Andretti. Died in 1982.

PETER COLLINS Team Manager. *Australian*
After arriving in England from Australia, he worked as a storeman at Ralt, before

moving to Lotus as assistant team manager. Left Lotus for Williams. Ran Benetton team in late eighties before taking over the reins at Lotus in 1991. After team folded went into driver management. One of the principal figures who helped Nigel into Formula 1.

DEREK DALY Driver/TV Commentator. *Irish*
Nigel's team-mate for one-off Formula 2 drive at Donington in 1978. Competed in 49 Grands Prix with a best finish of 4th in 1980. Drove for Ensign, Tyrrell, March and Williams teams. Moved to America to race Indycars and Sportscars. Retired from racing to become full-time TV commentator for ESPN network in America.

ELIO DE ANGELIS Driver. *Italian*
Son of a wealthy Italian businessman, Elio was also a concert-standard pianist. Competed in 108 Grands Prix between 1979 and 1986. Team-mate to Nigel from 1981 to 1984 at Lotus. Moved to Brabham in 1986 and was killed while testing at Paul Ricard in France.Won two GP – the 1982 Austrian and the 1985 San Marino Grands Prix.

ANDREA DE CESARIS Driver. *Italian*
A competitor to Nigel in British Formula 3 Championship in 1979, he caused the accident which broke Nigel's back at Oulton Park. Nicknamed 'de Crasheris' because of his frequent sorties off piste, he matured in the early 1990s and gained respect with his performances for the fledgling Jordan team in 1991. Drove in 208 Grands Prix with ten different teams over fourteen seasons. Never won a Grand Prix, best finish was second twice in 1983 with Alfa Romeo.

RON DENNIS Team owner. *English*
One of the most successful team owners of the last 15 years. Has overseen 80 Grands Prix victories, seven Drivers' World Championships and six Constructors' Championships for his McLaren team since 1981. Started as a mechanic on Jochen Rindt's Cooper-Maserati, before moving with Rindt to Brabham in 1968. Started his own Formula 2 team in 1971, called Rondel Racing. Badly injured in a road accident in 1972, he gave up working on cars and went into management. Gained a reputation for immaculate preparation and high standards through seventies. Recruited John Barnard to design the first McLaren MP4 Formula 1 car, and took over 50% of the equity of the McLaren team in 1981. Far more human than robotic, authoritarian image created by the media.

FRANK DERNIE Designer/Engineer. *English*
Joined Williams in 1979 and stayed 10 years, becoming the team's aerodynamics expert. A spell at Lotus as technical director was followed by a move to Ligier and then to Benetton. Was one of the engineers behind Michael Schumacher's 1994 Championship-winning Benetton-Ford B194. Has a quick intellect twinned with a finely-honed contempt for slower thinkers.

BERNIE ECCLESTONE Commercial mastermind of Formula 1. *English*
Son of a trawler captain, Bernie raced motorcycles and Formula 3 cars in the 1950s. Managed several drivers in 1960s, including Jochen Rindt and made a fortune in property development. Bought Brabham team in 1971. Won 22 Grands Prix and two Drivers' World Championships before selling the team in 1987. Formed Formula One Constructors' Association and as FOCA president took on the governing body, the FIA and its autocratic president Jean-Marie Balestre in a head-on struggle for control of Formula 1. Became vice president (promotional affairs). Bernie is credited

with bringing in manufacturers, television networks and major sponsors and turning F1 into a multi-million pound global television phenomenon. Once said, 'I have the most control over everything, I even want to know what colour the toilet paper is.'

ENZO FERRARI Team owner. *Italian*

Known as the 'commendatore'. An accomplished driver in the early days of the sport through to the early thirties, he set up the Scuderia Ferrari in 1929, running Alfa Romeos in Grands Prix as well as sports car events like the Mille Miglia and the Le Mans 24 Hours. One of his first drivers was the great Tazio Nuvolari. After the Second World War he decided to build his own cars, initially for racing and subsequently production versions. Won the World Championship with Alberto Ascari in 1952 and 1953. Since then the team has won a further seven World Championships. There has been a Ferrari on the grid since the second race of the newly established Formula 1 World Championship. Enzo died in August 1988, his surname forever identified with the most glamorous and desirable road cars in the world.

CESARE FIORIO Team manager. *Italian*

Worked for Lancia for 15 years, winning multiple World Rally and World Sportscar Championships. Joined Ferrari in 1989 as Formula 1 team manager, winning nine Grands Prix in two seasons, the best period in Ferrari fortunes since the early eighties. Nicknamed 'Hollywood' by the Italian press because of his flamboyant style and ever-present sunglasses.

EMERSON FITTIPALDI Driver. *Brazilian*

Double Formula 1 World Champion and also an Indycar champion. Emerson is credited as the vanguard of Brazilian drivers, his success encouraging others, like Ayrton Senna, to move to Europe. Contested 144 Grands Prix between 1970 and 1980. Won the 1970 US Grand Prix, in only his fourth start. Won fourteen Grands Prix and the 1972 and 1974 World Championships. Formed his own team in 1975. Did not drive between 1981 and 1983. Moved to Indycars in 1984. Won 1989 Indianapolis 500 and Indycar title and won Indy 500 again in 1993. Has a spendidly laid back view of life and a lupine smile.

A J FOYT Driver/Team owner. *American*

Legendary Indycar driver. Won Indycar title seven times and Indianapolis 500 four times. He is the all-time record holder in wins with 67. Only driver in history to have won the Indy 500, Daytona 500 (stock cars) and 24 Hours of Le Mans (sports cars). Badly injured in an accident in 1990 he retired from driving at Indianapolis in 1993 to concentrate on his own team. A larger-than-life Texan, he also owns a stud farm, America's largest funeral business and has oil interests and a major car dealership. Very much his own man, his motto is, 'My way or the highway.'

CARL HAAS Team owner. *American*

Co-owner with movie star Paul Newman of the Newman-Haas Indycar team, with whom Nigel won the 1993 PPG IndyCar World Series. One of American racing's leading team owners, his cars have been winning for over 20 years. He has run some of the great names of the sport in Indycars, Can-Am and even Formula 1. He is also the importer for Lola cars in the United States. Easy to spot in the Indycar paddock because of the six inch long cigar he keeps, unlit, in his mouth.

PATRICK HEAD Formula 1 designer. *English*

A partner in Williams Grand Prix Engineering, with whom Nigel won 28 Grands Prix and the 1992 World Championship. One of the most respected and consistently successful designers in Formula 1. Often accompanied his father, an Army Colonel who raced a Jaguar in club events. After leaving the Royal Navy he studied engineering and in 1970 joined Lola cars. He worked on Walter Wolf's Formula 1 project for two seasons before joining forces with Frank Williams in 1977. His designs began winning Grands Prix in 1979, and in 1980 won the World Championship, the first of seven Constructors' titles and five Drivers' titles. A tremendous racing enthusiast.

NIKI LAUDA Driver. *Austrian*
Triple Formula 1 World Champion and one of the sport's legendary drivers. Competed in 171 Grands Prix between 1971 and 1985. Drove for March, BRM, Ferrari, Brabham and McLaren and won 25 Grands Prix. Won the World Championship with Ferrari in 1975 and came back from horrific fiery accident at the Nurburgring, Germany in 1976 to win the 1977 title with Ferrari. Switched to Brabham in 1978, but retired suddenly in 1979. Made comeback with McLaren in 1982 and clinched his third World title in 1984. Owns his own airline, Lauda Air and works today in Formula 1 as an adviser to the Ferrari team. Credited with doing much to improve safety for drivers in the seventies and eighties. An unsentimental man, he gave away most of his racing trophies.

JIM MCGEE Team manager. *American*
A veteran on the Indycar scene, McGee has overseen five victories in the Indianapolis 500 and has won the Indycar title on numerous occasions with a wide range of teams including Patrick Racing, Rahal-Hogan Racing and Newman-Haas. A very good psychological manager, he specialises in building a deep rapport with his drivers and giving them a sense of perspective.

ADRIAN NEWEY Chassis designer. *English*
Built his reputation at the March/Leyton House Formula 1 team, before being recruited by Williams in 1990. Was the principal designer, together with Patrick Head, of the Williams FW14 and FW14B cars, in 1991/92.

ROGER PENSKE Driver/Team owner. *American*
One of the giants of American Racing and owner of the most successful team in Indycar racing. Has also won in Formula 1. After a successful career as a driver in the sixties, concentrated on team management and building an automotive business empire, worth billions of dollars. His cars have won the Indianapolis 500 a record 10 times and his team has won the Indycar championship nine times.

DAVID PRICE Team manager. *English*
A successful team owner in the junior formulae and a well respected team manager in sportscar racing. Price's cars have won the British Formula 3 Championship and he has overseen victories for Mercedes-Benz in the Le Mans 24 Hours and other World Sportscar Championship events. Thin, slick and laconic, he is a brilliant racing strategist and something of a wheeler-dealer.

KEKE ROSBERG Driver. *Finnish*
Flamboyant driver with walrus moustache. Won 1982 World Championship for Williams, despite only winning one race that year. Began his F1 career at Theodore in 1978, then raced for Wolf in 1979 and Fittipaldi in 1980 and 1981. Left Williams at the end of 1985 to join McLaren as replacement for Niki Lauda. Retired from Formula 1 at the end of 1986 season after the death of his close friend Elio de Angelis.

Subsequently raced sportscars for Peugeot and touring cars for Mercedes and Opel. Has his own team in German Touring Car racing and a prosperous business managing young racing drivers, including Mika Hakkinen.

STEPHEN SOUTH Driver. *English*
Trained as a dentist. One of the real up and coming men of British motor sport in the late seventies until he broke his leg in an horrific accident.

SHERIDAN THYNNE Former commercial director of Williams. *English*
A close friend and adviser to Nigel. Sheridan joined Williams in 1979 after a career as a stockbroker convinced him that his understanding of the links between business and sport would be well served in motor racing. Widely recognised as the man who talked Nigel out of retirement and back to Williams in 1991, he resigned from Williams himself in 1992 over the way Nigel had been treated.

KEN TYRRELL Team owner. *English*
A fixture in Formula 1 since the late sixties, Ken Tyrrell has never recaptured the glory days of 1969, 1971 and 1973 when Jackie Stewart won three World Championships for his team, once with a Matra and twice with one of Tyrrell's own cars. Tyrrell has a reputation as a talent spotter and has set many great drivers on the road to success.

PETER WARR Team manager. *English*
A former Officer in the British Army, Warr joined Lotus in the 1960s. Worked briefly for Wolf and Fittipaldi teams in the late seventies before rejoining Lotus in 1981 as team manager. Was briefly FIA steward in early 1992.

FRANK WILLIAMS Team owner. *English*
Raced until 1966. Began his own team in 1969 and went through a tough time in the seventies with underfunded team. In 1977 Patrick Head joined him and with sponsorship from Saudia Airlines things looked up. Won first race in 1979 and Alan Jones won the team's first World Championship in 1980. Frank was paralysed in a road accident in 1986.

PETER WINDSOR Journalist/Team manager. *English*
Inspired by a chance meeting with Jim Clark at Sydney Airport shortly before his death in 1968, Windsor returned to his native England and became sports editor of *Autocar* magazine. In his columns for *Autocar* he attempted to draw attention to a young British driver whom no-one else seemed to write about – Nigel Mansell. Windsor helped Nigel find sponsors and advised him on the world of Formula 1. He joined Williams in the public relations department and was a passenger in the car when Frank Williams had his paralysing accident in 1986. He became part-owner of the Brabham team in 1989, before being hired by Ferrari to manage its racing facility in England. He was team manager at Williams during Nigel's second stint with the team in 1991/92. He left to start his own Formula 1 team.

BILL YEAGER Indycar team manager. *American*
Larger than life character in the Indycar paddock. The supreme 'fixer'. Started working in Indycars in 1950. Won the Indianapolis 500 with Troy Ruttman in 1952, the first of many wins at the 'Brickyard'. Has worked with all the legends in American racing – Jim Rathman, Parnelli Jones, A J Foyt, Bobby Unser, Al Unser and Mario Andretti. Nigel was the only 'foreign' driver he worked with. Has seen motor racing 'change' from a hobby into a sport and then into a business.

MY TOP 10 RACES

It's been a thrill to have played a major role in some of the outstanding Grand Prix races of the last decade. The following are a list of my favourites:

1985 SOUTH AFRICAN GP Kyalami, *19 October*
My second Grand Prix win and a harder one than my maiden win at Brands Hatch. It was a tough, gritty fight with my team-mate Keke Rosberg.

1986 SPANISH GP Jerez, *13 April*
I didn't win this one, but it was the closest Grand Prix finish in history. Ayrton managed to hold me off across the line, but I gave it everything in the final laps, after an unscheduled tyre stop had lost me a lot of ground.

1986 CANADIAN GP Montreal, *15 June*
I loved the old turbo-engined days of Formula 1. Fuel strategy was terribly important and a driver had to be a good manager of the car as well as quick. This one was won by great team work with Patrick Head.

1986 BRITISH GP Brands Hatch, *13 July*
One of my real favourites this one and something of a fairy tale. Beating my team-mate, Nelson Piquet in the spare car in front of the home crowd was fantastic. Definitely one of my best days in a racing car.

1987 BRITISH GP Silverstone, *12 July*
What a classic! The most intense race I ever had. Incredible atmosphere at Silverstone, as always. I lost the lead to Nelson Piquet after an unscheduled tyre stop and rejoined 28 seconds behind with 29 laps to go. The rest is history.

1989 HUNGARIAN GP Hungaroring, *13 August*
Ayrton was always the most difficult competitor to pass and you only got once chance, if any. People still ask me about that move today! To win in Hungary from 12th on the grid was also quite special.

1991 FRENCH GP Magny Cours, *7 July*
Prost had taken over at Ferrari at my expense and caused me to retire. Williams then talked me out of it. So to beat Prost the following year in a straight fight in his home Grand Prix was a wonderful occasion for me. I passed him twice into the hairpin and each time wondered what he was thinking.

1992 BRITISH GP Silverstone, *12 July*
I recall this as an extraordinary weekend; a hugely satisfying pole position and a convincing win. Over 200,000 people came to Silverstone to watch and I wanted to make sure they didn't go home disappointed.

1993 PPG INDYCAR RACE Surfers Paradise, *21 March*
Special for historical reasons more than anything else. It was the first time a rookie had won pole in Indycar's 84-year history. It was a fantastic way to start my Indycar career.

1993 PPG INDYCAR RACE New Hampshire, *8 August*
Old American racers came up to me after this one and said that it was one of the best oval races they had ever seen. It was brilliant, pure racing. My fourth oval victory of the 1993 season ... and it happened on my 40th birthday, too!

CAREER HIGHLIGHTS

1963–1975 Karts
1963 (First Competitive Race)	Shennington	Retired (Engine fell off)
1963 (First Win)	Tern Hill	1st

Championships won: Midlands Champion (7 times), Northern Champion

1976 Formula Ford
6 wins from 9 races

1977 Formula Ford
33 wins from 42 races
Championship Standings: Won 'Brush Fuse Gear' FF1600 Championship

1977 Formula 3 (Lola T570)
1 October	Silverstone	4th

1978 Formula 3 (March 783)
19 March	Silverstone	2nd (Pole position)
27 March	Thruxton	7th (Front-row start)
16 April	Brands Hatch	7th
22 April	Oulton Park	7th
30 April	Donington	4th

1978 Formula 2 (Chevron)
24 June	Donington	Did not qualify

1978 BMW County Championship (BMW 320i Saloon)
16 April	Silverstone	2nd
3 June	Donington	1st
30 June	Oulton Park	Retired
26 August	Mallory Park	3rd

1979 Formula 3 (March 783 and 793)
4 March	Silverstone	11th
11 March	Thruxton	2nd
25 March	Silverstone	1st
1 April	Snetterton	8th
8 April	Donington	7th

7 May		Brands Hatch	6th
20 May		Donington	Retired (Accident)
27 May		Monte Carlo	11th
10 June		Brands Hatch	4th
17 June		Cadwell Park	Retired (Suspension)
1 July		Silverstone	8th
14 July		Silverstone	6th
27 August		Silverstone	6th
9 September		Donington	2nd
15 September		Oulton Park	Retired (Accident; broke back)

CHAMPIONSHIP STANDINGS
1. Chico Serra (March 793)   103 points
2. Andrea de Cesaris (March 793)   90
3. Mike Thackwell (March 793)   71
8. Nigel Mansell (March 793)   24

1980 Formula 2 (Ralt RH6/80–Honda)

8 June	Britain	Silverstone	11th
22 June	Belgium	Zolder	Retired (Accident)
20 July	Holland	Zandvoort	5th
28 September	Germany	Hockenheim	2nd

CHAMPIONSHIP STANDINGS
1. Brian Henton (TG280B–Hart)   61 points
2. Derek Warwick (TG280B–Hart)   42
3. Teo Fabi (March 802–BMW)   38
12. Nigel Mansell (Ralt–Honda)   8

1980 Formula 1 (Lotus–Cosworth 81)

17 August	Austria	Osterreichring	Retired (Engine)
31 August	Holland	Zandvoort	Retired (Brakes)
14 September	Italy	Imola	Did not qualify

WORLD CHAMPIONSHIP STANDINGS
1. Alan Jones (Williams)   67 points
2. Nelson Piquet (Brabham)   54
3. Carlos Reutemann (Williams)   42

1981 Formula 1 (Lotus–Cosworth 81 and 87)

7 February	South Africa (non-championship)	Kyalami	10th
15 March	United States	Long Beach	Retired (Accident)
29 March	Brazil	Rio de Janerio	11th
12 April	Argentina	Buenos Aires	Retired (Engine)
3 May	San Marino	Imola	Lotus did not compete
17 May	Belgium	Zolder	3rd
31 May	Monaco	Monte Carlo	Retired (Suspension)
21 June	Spain	Jarama	6th
5 July	France	Dijon	7th
18 July	Britain	Silverstone	Did not qualify
2 August	Germany	Hockenheim	Retired (Fuel leak)
16 August	Austria	Zeltweg	Retired (Engine)
30 August	Holland	Zandvoort	Retired (Engine/Electrics)
13 September	Italy	Monza	Retired (Handling)

| 27 September | Canada | Montreal | Retired (Accident) |
| 17 October | Las Vegas | Caesars Palace | 4th |

WORLD CHAMPIONSHIP STANDINGS
1. Nelson Piquet (Brabham)   50 points
2. Carlos Reutemann (Williams)   49
3. Alan Jones (Williams)   46
14. Nigel Mansell (Lotus)   8

1982 Formula 1 (Lotus–Cosworth 87B and 91)

23 January	South Africa	Kyalami	Retired (Electrics)
12 March	Brazil	Rio de Janeiro	3rd
4 April	United States	Long Beach	7th
25 April	San Marino	Imola	Didn't take part (FOCA boycott)
9 May	Belgium	Zolder	Retired (Clutch)
23 May	Monaco	Monte Carlo	4th
6 June	United States	Detroit	Retired (Engine)
13 June	Canada	Montreal	Retired (Accident)
3 July	Holland	Zandvoort	Did not start due to injury
18 July	Britain	Brands Hatch	Retired (Handling)
25 July	France	Paul Ricard	Did not start due to injury
8 August	Germany	Hockenheim	9th
15 August	Austria	Osterreichring	Retired (Engine)
29 August	Switzerland	Dijon (France)	8th
12 September	Italy	Monza	7th
25 September	Las Vegas	Caesars Palace	Retired (Accident)

WORLD CHAMPIONSHIP STANDINGS
1. Keke Rosberg (Williams)   44 points
2. Dider Pironi (Ferrari)   39
    John Watson (McLaren)   39
14. Nigel Mansell (Lotus)   7

1983 Formula 1 (Lotus–Cosworth 92 and Lotus–Renault 93T and 94T)

13 March	Brazil	Rio de Janerio	12th
27 March	United States	Long Beach	12th
10 April	Race of Champs (non-Championship)	Brands Hatch	Retired (Handling)
17 April	France	Paul Ricard	Retired (Handling)
1 May	San Marino	Imola	Retired (Broken wing)
15 May	Monaco	Monte Carlo	Retired (Accident)
22 May	Belgium	Spa	Retired (Gearbox)
5 June	United States	Detroit	6th
12 June	Canada	Montreal	Retired (Handling)
16 July	Britain	Silverstone	4th
7 August	Germany	Hockenheim	Retired (Engine)
14 August	Austria	Osterreichring	5th
28 August	Holland	Zandvoort	Retired (Accident)
11 September	Italy	Monza	8th
25 September	Europe	Brands Hatch	3rd (Fastest lap)
15 October	South Africa	Kyalami	Not classified

WORLD CHAMPIONSHIP STANDINGS
1. Nelson Piquet (Brabham)   59 points
2. Alain Prost (Renault)   57

3.	Rene Arnoux (Ferrari)		49
12.	Nigel Mansell (Lotus)		10

1984 Formula 1 (Lotus–Renault 95T)

25 March	Brazil	Rio de Janerio	Retired (Accident)
7 April	South Africa	Kyalami	Retired (Turbo failure)
29 April	Belgium	Zolder	Retired (Clutch)
6 May	San Marino	Imola	Retired (Accident)
20 May	France	Dijon	3rd
3 June	Monaco	Monte Carlo	Retired (Accident)
17 June	Canada	Montreal	6th
24 June	United States	Detroit	Retired (Gearbox)
8 July	United States	Dallas	6th (Pole position)
22 July	Britain	Brands Hatch	Retired (Gearbox)
5 August	Germany	Hockenheim	4th
19 August	Austria	Osterreichring	Retired (Engine)
26 August	Holland	Zandvoort	3rd
9 September	Italy	Monza	Retired (Accident)
7 October	Europe	Nurburgring	Retired (Engine)
21 October	Portugal	Estoril	Retired (Brakes)

WORLD CHAMPIONSHIP STANDINGS

1.	Niki Lauda (McLaren)	72 points
2.	Alain Prost (McLaren)	71.5
3.	Elio de Angelis (Lotus)	34
9.	Nigel Mansell (Lotus)	13

1985 Formula 1 (Williams–Honda FW10)

7 April	Brazil	Rio de Janerio	Retired (Accident)
21 April	Portugal	Estoril	5th (Started from pit lane)
5 May	San Marino	Imola	5th
19 May	Monaco	Monte Carlo	7th (Front-row start)
16 June	Canada	Montreal	6th
23 June	United States	Detroit	Retired (Accident)
7 July	France	Paul Ricard	Did not qualify
21 July	Britain	Silverstone	Retired (Clutch)
4 August	Germany	Nurburgring	6th
18 August	Austria	Osterreichring	Retired (Engine)
25 August	Holland	Zandvoort	6th
8 September	Italy	Monza	11th (Fastest lap)
15 September	Belgium	Spa	2nd
6 October	Europe	Brands Hatch	1st
19 October	South Africa	Kyalami	1st (Pole position)
3 November	Australia	Adelaide	Retired (Transmission)

WORLD CHAMPIONSHIP STANDINGS

1.	Alain Prost (McLaren)	73 points
2.	Michele Albereto (Ferrari)	53
3.	Keke Rosberg (Williams)	40
6.	Nigel Mansell (Williams)	31

1986 Formula 1 (Williams–Honda FW11)

23 March	Brazil	Rio de Janerio	Retired (Accident)
13 April	Spain	Jerez	2nd (Fastest lap)
27 April	San Marino	Imola	Retired (Engine)
11 May	Monaco	Monte Carlo	4th (Front-row start)

25 May	Belgium	Spa	1st
15 June	Canada	Montreal	1st (Pole position)
22 June	United States	Detroit	5th (Front-row start)
6 July	France	Paul Ricard	1st (Front-row start; fastest lap)
13 July	Britain	Brands Hatch	1st (Front-row start; fastest lap)
27 July	Germany	Hockenheim	3rd
10 August	Hungary	Hungaroring	3rd
17 August	Austria	Osterreichring	Retired (Driveshaft)
7 September	Italy	Monza	2nd
21 September	Portugal	Estoril	1st (Front-row start; fastest lap)
12 October	Mexico	Mexico City	5th
26 October	Australia	Adelaide	Retired (Tyres)

WORLD CHAMIONSHIP STANDINGS
1. Alain Prost (McLaren)   72 points
2. Nigel Mansell (Williams)   70
3. Nelson Piquet (Williams)   69

1987 Formula 1 (Williams–Honda FW11B)

12 April	Brazil	Rio de Janerio	6th (Pole position)
3 May	San Marino	Imola	1st (Front-row start)
17 May	Belgium	Spa	Retired (Accident)
31 May	Monaco	Monte Carlo	Retired (Wastegate pipe)
21 June	United States	Detroit	5th (Pole position)
5 July	France	Paul Ricard	1st (Pole position)
12 July	Britain	Silverstone	1st (Front-row start)
26 July	Germany	Hockenheim	Retired (Engine; fastest lap)
9 August	Hungary	Hungaroring	14th (Pole position)
16 August	Austria	Osterreichring	1st (Front-row start; fastest lap)
6 September	Italy	Monza	3rd (Front-row start)
20 September	Portugal	Estoril	Retired (Electrics)
27 September	Spain	Jerez	1st (Front-row start)
18 October	Mexico	Mexico City	1st (Pole position)
1 November	Japan	Suzuka	Did not start due to injury
15 November	Australia	Adelaide	Did not start due to injury

WORLD CHAMPIONSHIP STANDINGS
1. Nelson Piquet (Williams)   73 points
2. Nigel Mansell (Williams)   61
3. Ayrton Senna (Lotus)   57

1988 Formula 1 (Willams–Judd FW12)

3 April	Brazil	Rio de Janerio	Retired (Overheating; front row start)
1 May	San Marino	Imola	Retired (Engine)
15 May	Monaco	Monte Carlo	Retired (Accident)
29 May	Mexico	Mexico City	Retired (Engine)
12 June	Canada	Montreal	Retired (Engine)
19 June	United States	Detroit	Retired (Electrics)
3 July	France	Paul Ricard	Retired (Suspension)
10 July	Britain	Silverstone	2nd (Fastest lap)
24 July	Germany	Hockenheim	Retired (Accident)
7 August	Hungary	Hungaroring	Retired (Exhaustion; front row start)
28 August	Belgium	Spa	Did not start (Illness)
11 September	Italy	Monza	Did not start (Illness)
25 September	Portugal	Estoril	Retired (Accident)
2 October	Spain	Jerez	2nd

30 October	Japan	Suzuka	Retired (Accident)
13 November	Australia	Adelaide	Retired (Brakes)

WORLD CHAMPIONSHIP STANDINGS
1. Ayrton Senna (McLaren)   90 points
2. Alain Prost (McLaren)   87
3. Gerhard Berger (Ferrari)   41
9. Nigel Mansell (Williams)   12

1989 Formula 1 (Ferrari 640)

26 March	Brazil	Rio de Janerio	1st
23 April	San Marino	Imola	Retired (Gearbox)
7 May	Monaco	Monte Carlo	Retired (Gearbox)
28 May	Mexico	Mexico City	Retired (Gearbox)
4 June	United States	Phoenix	Retired (Alternator)
18 June	Canada	Montreal	Disqualified (Black flagged)
9 July	France	Paul Ricard	2nd
16 July	Britain	Silverstone	2nd (Fastest lap)
30 July	Germany	Hockenheim	3rd
13 August	Hungary	Hungaroring	1st (Fastest lap)
27 August	Belgium	Spa	3rd
10 September	Italy	Monza	Retired (Gearbox)
24 September	Portugal	Estoril	Disqualified (Black Flagged)
1 October	Spain	Jerez	Didn't start (Suspended)
22 October	Japan	Suzuka	Retired (Engine)
5 November	Australia	Adelaide	Retired (Accident)

WORLD CHAMPIONSHIP STANDINGS
1. Alain Prost (McLaren)   76 points
2. Ayrton Senna (McLaren)   60
3. Riccardo Patrese (Williams)   40
4. Nigel Mansell (Ferrari)   38

1990 Formula 1 (Ferrari 641/2)

11 March	United States	Phoenix	Retired (Engine)
25 March	Brazil	Interlagos	4th
13 May	San Marino	Imola	Retired (Engine)
27 May	Monaco	Monte Carlo	Retired (Battery)
10 June	Canada	Montreal	3rd
24 June	Mexico	Mexico City	2nd
8 July	France	Paul Ricard	18th (Pole position; fastest lap)
15 July	Britain	Silverstone	Retired (Gearbox)
29 July	Germany	Hockenheim	Retired (Loose undertray)
12 August	Hungary	Hungaroring	17th
25 August	Belgium	Spa	Retired (Handling)
9 September	Italy	Monza	4th
23 September	Portugal	Estoril	1st (Pole position)
30 September	Spain	Jerez	2nd
21 October	Japan	Suzuka	Retired (Transmission)
4 November	Australia	Adelaide	2nd (Fastest lap)

WORLD CHAMPIONSHIP STANDINGS
1. Ayrton Senna (McLaren)   78 points
2. Alain Prost (Ferrari)   71
3. Gerhard Berger (McLaren)   43
    Nelson Piquet (Benetton)   43
5. Nigel Mansell (Ferrari)   37

1991 Formula 1 (Williams–Renault FW14)

10 March	United States	Phoenix	Retired (Gearbox)
24 March	Brazil	Interlagos	Retired (Gearbox)
28 April	San Marino	Imola	Retired (Accident)
12 May	Monaco	Monte Carlo	2nd
2 June	Canada	Montreal	6th (Front-row start)
16 June	Mexico	Mexico City	2nd (Front-row start)
7 July	France	Magny Cours	1st (Fastest lap)
14 July	Britain	Silverstone	1st (Pole position; fastest lap)
28 July	Germany	Hockenheim	1st (Pole position)
11 August	Hungary	Hungaroring	2nd
25 August	Belgium	Spa	Retired (Electrics)
8 September	Italy	Monza	1st (Front-row start)
27 September	Portugal	Estoril	Disqualified (Black flagged)
29 September	Spain	Catalunya	1st (Front row start)
20 October	Japan	Suzuka	Retired (Accident)
3 November	Australia	Adelaide	2nd

WORLD CHAMPIONSHIP STANDINGS

1.	Ayrton Senna (McLaren)	96 points
2.	Nigel Mansell (Williams)	72
3.	Riccardo Patrese (Williams)	53

1992 Formula 1 (Williams–Renault FW14B)

1 March	South Africa	Kyalami	1st (Pole position; fastest lap)
22 March	Mexico	Mexico City	1st (Pole position)
5 April	Brazil	Interlagos	1st (Pole position)
3 May	Spain	Catalunya	1st(Pole position; fastest lap)
17 May	San Marino	Imola	1st (Pole position)
31 May	Monaco	Monte Carlo	2nd (Pole position; fastest lap)
14 June	Canada	Montreal	Retired (Accident)
5 July	France	Magny Cours	1st (Pole position; fastest lap)
12 July	Britain	Silverstone	1st (Pole position; fastest lap)
26 July	Germany	Hockenheim	1st (Pole position)
16 August	Hungary	Hungaroring	2nd (Front-row start; fastest lap)
30 August	Belgium	Spa	2nd (Pole position)
13 September	Italy	Monza	Retired (Hydraulics; fastest lap)
27 September	Portugal	Estoril	1st (Pole position)
25 October	Japan	Suzuka	Retired (Engine)
8 November	Australia	Adelaide	Retired (Accident)

WORLD CHAMPIONSHIP STANDINGS

1.	Nigel Mansell (Williams)	108 points
2.	Riccardo Patrese (Williams)	56
3.	Michael Schumacher (Benetton)	53

1993 PPG IndyCar World Series (Newman-Haas Lola T93–Ford)

21 March	Australia	Surfers Paradise	1st (Pole position)
4 April	United States	Phoenix	Practice accident
18 April	United States	Long Beach	3rd (Pole position)
30 May	United States	Indianapolis 500	3rd
6 June	United States	Milwaukee	1st
13 June	United States	Detroit	15th (Pole position)
27 June	United States	Portland	2nd (Pole position)
11 July	United States	Cleveland	3rd
18 July	Canada	Toronto	Retired (Wastegate)

1 August	United States	Michigan	1st
8 August	United States	New Hampshire	1st (Pole position)
22 August	United States	Elkhart Lake	2nd
29 August	Canada	Vancouver	6th
12 September	United States	Mid-Ohio	12th (Pole position)
19 September	United States	Nazareth	1st (Pole position)
3 October	United States	Laguna Seca	Retired (Accident)

CHAMPIONSHIP STANDINGS
1. Nigel Mansell (Lola)   191 points
2. Emerson Fittipaldi (Penske)   183
3. Paul Tracy (Penske)   157

1993 TOCA Shootout (Ford Mondeo Saloon)

31 October	Donington	Retired (Accident – Hit bridge)

1994 PPG IndyCar World Series (Newman-Haas Lola–Ford)

20 March	Australia	Surfers Paradise	9th (Pole position)
10 April	United States	Phoenix	3rd
17 April	United States	Long Beach	2nd
29 May	United Staes	Indianapolis 500	Retired (Accident)
5 June	United States	Milwaukee	4th
12 June	United States	Detroit	Retired (Throttle; pole position)
26 June	United States	Portland	5th (Front-row start)
10 July	United States	Cleveland	2nd
17 July	Canada	Toronto	Retired (Handling)
31 July	United States	Michigan	Retired (Throttle)
14 August	United States	Mid-Ohio	7th
21 August	United States	New Hampshire	Retired (Accident)
4 September	Canada	Vancouver	9th
11 September	United States	Elkhart Lake	13th
18 September	United States	Nazareth	Retired (Handling)
10 October	United States	Laguna Seca	8th

CHAMPIONSHIP STANDINGS
1. Al Unser Jr (Penske)   225 points
2. Emerson Fittipaldi (Penske)   178
3. Paul Tracy (Penske)   152
8. Nigel Mansell (Lola)   88

1994 Formula 1 (Williams–Renault FW16B)

2 July	France	Magny Cours	Retired (Engine; front row start)
16 October	Europe	Jerez	Retired (Accident)
6 November	Japan	Suzuka	4th
13 November	Australia	Adelaide	1st (Pole position)

WORLD CHAMPIONSHIP STANDINGS
1. Michael Schumacher (Benetton)   92 points
2. Damon Hill (Williams)   91
3. Gerhard Berger (Ferrari)   41
9. Nigel Mansell (Williams)   13

1995 Formula 1 (McLaren MP4/10)

30 April	San Marino	Imola	10th
14 May	Spain	Barcelona	Retired (Handling)

Summary of Nigel Mansell's Grand Prix Career

No of Grands Prix   187
Wins   31
Pole Positions   32
Fastest Laps   30
Points Total   482
GP Laps Led   2099 (5992 miles)

Records Held by Nigel

- Most Grand Prix wins in a single season (9 in 1992)
- Most Grand Prix poles in a single season (14 in 1992)
- Most World Championship points in a season (108 in 1992)
- Most poles in IndyCar rookie season (7 in 1993)
- Only person to win consecutive Formula 1 and IndyCar titles
- First person to win IndyCar title in first season
- Fastest lap of a racing circuit (235.5 mph at Michigan in 1994)
- Closest finish in Grand Prix history (93 centimetres, with Ayrton Senna, Spain 1986)

1. All-time Grand Prix winners

Alain Prost	51 wins
Ayrton Senna	41
Nigel Mansell	31
Jackie Stewart	27
Jim Clark	25
Niki Lauda	25
Juan Manuel Fangio	24
Nelson Piquet	23
Stirling Moss	16
Michael Schumacher	15 *
Damon Hill	12 *

2. Most wins in one season

Nigel Mansell	9 (1992)
Michael Schumacher	8 (1994)
Ayrton Senna	8 (1988)
Alain Prost	7 (1984, 1988, 1993)
Jim Clark	7 (1963)

3. British winners

Nigel Mansell	31 wins
Jackie Stewart	27
Jim Clark	25
Stirling Moss	16
Damon Hill	12 *
James Hunt	10
Tony Brooks	6
John Watson	5
Peter Collins	3
Mike Hawthorn	3

4. Pole positions by driver

Ayrton Senna	65 poles
Jim Clark	33
Alain Prost	33
Nigel Mansell	32
Juan Manuel Fangio	28
Niki Lauda	24
Nelson Piquet	24
Mario Andretti	18
Rene Arnoux	18
Jackie Stewart	17
Stirling Moss	16

5. Pole positions in one season

Nigel Mansell	14 (1992)
Alain Prost	13 (1993)
Ayrton Senna	13 (1988, 1989)
Niki Lauda	9 (1974, 1975)
Ronnie Peterson	9 (1973)
Nelson Piquet	9 (1984)

6. Wins from pole position

Ayrton Senna	29 wins
Alain Prost	18
Nigel Mansell	17
Juan Manuel Fangio	15
Jim Clark	15
Alberto Ascari	9
Niki Lauda	9
Stirling Moss	8
Jackie Stewart	8
Mario Andretti	8

* At time of going to press

GLOSSARY

Active Suspension
A computer controlled system for the suspension that uses four hydraulic cylinders that act as rams to raise and lower the car. The aim of the system is to maintain a level ride height under braking, under acceleration and in corners, allowing more efficient use of the aerodynamics. Active suspension was pioneered by Lotus during Nigel's time with the team and was a contributing factor to his Championship season at Williams.

Armco
The collapsible metal barriers that surround a racing circuit.

Black Flag
A black flag is shown to a driver who has breached the rules and is being ordered into the pits. Nigel's most infamous black flag incidents both occurred in Portugal at the 1989 and 1991 Grands Prix.

Boost Button/Control
A control in the cockpit of a turbo-charged car that is used to regulate the pressure of the fuel-air mixture being fed into the engine from the turbo. The higher the boost, the more power and the greater the amount of fuel used. Racing a turbo car was a management exercise in balancing power and fuel. Nigel's controlled use of the boost control enabled him to win the 1986 Canadian Grand Prix.

Carbon Brakes
Brakes made of carbon composites can operate at higher temperatures than traditional steel brakes and require less distance to slow a car down. Banned in Indycars, allowed in Formula 1.

Carbon Composite
A space age material designed for the NASA space program and pioneered in Formula 1 by McLaren in 1981. This bonded material is stronger, more rigid and lighter than traditional metals. It is arguably the greatest enhancement in car safety yet made in Formula 1.

Chutes
An American term for a short straight linking two corners.

CV Joint
The Constant Velocity Joint is located between the driveshaft from the gearbox and

the rear wheel. It is designed to compensate for any difference in velocity of the two components. Due to the constant strain it is placed under, it is often a source of mechanical failure.

Diffuser Panel
An aerodynamic panel that fits at the back of the car under the engine and gearbox. It is curved upwards to diffuse the airflow and create downforce.

Downforce
Unlike the wings of an aircraft which produce lift, the wings of a racing car create downforce which pushes a car down onto the track. Shaping the underside of the car like a wing produces further downforce and the car is 'sucked' onto the track. The downforce produced at around 150mph would be sufficient to hold Nigel's car in place if he drove it upside down across a ceiling!

Drag
Drag is the resistance to the motion of a body moving through the air; the lower the drag, the greater the straight-line speed. The greater the downforce a car produces, the greater its drag. Achieving a good set-up is a compromise between downforce and drag.

Fly-by-Wire
A development from the aerospace industry where control cables and pulleys are replaced by electronic signals sent by wire between the control and the point of operation. This saves weight and lessens the opportunities for mechanical breakage.

Fuel Mixture Switch
A switch in the cockpit that allows the driver to alter the ratio of fuel to air being fed into the engine. A lean mixture (more air than fuel) gives more power but can make an engine seize; while a rich mixture (more fuel than air) is safer but gives less power and uses more fuel.

G-Forces
A measure of the number of times the force of gravity is exerted on an object. During cornering a driver's head can be exposed to between 4 and 5 g. This means his head will feel four times heavier. This is why racing drivers develop strong neck muscles.

Ground Effect
The basic concept of ground effect is to make the whole car a wing by shaping the underside of the car to generate downforce. Sealing off the side of the car with moveable skirts creates more downforce and the car is sucked onto the road surface. Ground effect was the dominant technology in Formula 1 until rule changes in 1983 effectively outlawed it.

Gurney Flap
A small flap attached to the trailing edge of a wing. It is designed to increase downforce and reduce drag. Nigel used a small Gurney Flap to good effect in the 1989 Hungarian GP.

Monocoque
A one-piece load-bearing construction. The typical racing car monocoque comprises the driver's cockpit, or tub, and has the suspension units and engine attached to it.

Oversteer
The condition where the rear of the car slides toward the outside of a corner quicker than expected.

Qualifying Tyres
Special soft compound tyres designed to provide extra grip but lasting only a few laps. Especially for use in qualifying. Phased out by 1992 due to cost and worries about excessive speeds they generated.

Set-Up
The tuning of a car to a particular circuit and set of circumstances (such as weather). It requires balancing the aerodynamics, checking suspension settings, and choosing tyre compounds.

Slipstream
A car moving at speed creates a 'hole' in the air behind it. A following car can sit in this and be towed along at the same speed as the car in front using less fuel and without being flat on the throttle.

Telemetry
A system using radio waves to transmit information from recording devices in the car to a computer monitor in the pits.

Traction Control
A system designed to limit wheel spin during heavy acceleration or in corners. Used on Nigel's 1992 Championship winning Williams.

Turbo
Exhaust gas driven turbo-chargers use the exhaust from the engine to drive a small turbine that compresses the fuel/air mixture fed into the engine thereby increasing power. Power output is increased to the extent that 1500cc turbo engines were able to compete with, and beat, standard 3000cc engines. Turbos entered Formula 1 in 1977 and won their first Grand Prix in 1979. Thereafter they dominated Formula 1 until being banned in 1989. All Indycars are still turbo-charged. Nigel drove turbo cars at Lotus, Williams, and Newman-Haas.

Tyre Compound
Tyres can be made up from different mixtures of rubber to give a particular compound. Tyres with a soft compound give high levels of grip but wear out quickly while hard compound tyres are long lasting but give less grip. Selection of the right tyre compound to use is a vital part of set-up.

Understeer
The condition where the front of the car slides toward the inside of a corner quicker than expected.

Wastegate
The wastegate is a valve which controls the amount of exhaust gas flowing through a turbocharger. A malfunctioning wastegate has the effect of turning the turbo off, thereby reducing the power output by as much as 50%.

INDEX

We would like to thank the following for permission to reproduce
photographs for this book: Allsport, Formula One Pictures,
LAT Photographic, John Townsend, Rosanne Mansell and
Sporting Pictures.

Thanks also to Alan Porter, Alan Thatcher and Sue Robertson
for their work on this project.